Making Music Indigenous

Chicago Studies in Ethnomusicology
A series edited by Philip V. Bohlman, Ronald Radano, and Timothy Rommen

Editorial Board
Margaret J. Kartomi
Bruno Nettl
Anthony Seeger
Kay Kaufman Shelemay
Martin H. Stokes
Bonnie C. Wade

Making Music Indigenous

Popular Music in the Peruvian Andes

JOSHUA TUCKER

The University of Chicago Press
Chicago and London

The University of Chicago Press, Chicago 60637
The University of Chicago Press, Ltd., London
© 2019 by The University of Chicago
All rights reserved. No part of this book may be used or reproduced in any manner
whatsoever without written permission, except in the case of brief quotations in
critical articles and reviews. For more information, contact the University of Chicago
Press, 1427 E. 60th St., Chicago, IL 60637.
Published 2019
Printed in the United States of America

28 27 26 25 24 23 22 21 20 19   1 2 3 4 5

ISBN-13: 978-0-226-60716-0 (cloth)
ISBN-13: 978-0-226-60733-7 (paper)
ISBN-13: 978-0-226-60747-4 (e-book)
DOI: https://doi.org/10.7208/chicago/9780226607474.001.0001

Library of Congress Cataloging-in-Publication Data

Names: Tucker, Joshua, author.
Title: Making music indigenous : popular music in the Peruvian Andes /
    Joshua Tucker.
Other titles: Chicago studies in ethnomusicology.
Description: Chicago ; London : The University of Chicago Press, 2019. |
    Series: Chicago studies in ethnomusicology | Includes bibliographical references
    and index.
Identifiers: LCCN 2018054098 | ISBN 9780226607160 (cloth : alk. paper) |
    ISBN 9780226607337 (pbk. : alk. paper) | ISBN 9780226607474 (e-book)
Subjects: LCSH: Popular music—Peru—Cangallo (Province)—History and criticism. |
    Songs, Quechua—Peru—Cangallo (Province)—History and criticism. | Indians
    of South America—Peru—Cangallo (Province)—Music—History and criticism. |
    Indians of South America—Peru—Cangallo (Province)—Social life and customs.
Classification: LCC ML3487.P47 C366 2019 | DDC 781.62/9832308529—dc23
LC record available at https://lccn.loc.gov/2018054098

♾ This paper meets the requirements of ANSI/NISO Z39.48–1992
(Permanence of Paper).

Contents

Prologue vii

Introduction: Making Music Indigenous 1

1 **Setting a Scene** 31

2 **Landscape, Performance, and Social Structure** 48

3 **Song and Sound** 72

4 **Tradition and Folklore** 102

5 **Broadcasting and Building Publics** 128

6 **Success and Sentiment** 155

7 **Wood and Work** 183

Epilogue 209
Acknowledgments 221
Online Resources 223
Glossary 225
Notes 229
References 249
Index 271

Prologue

In 2008 several videos appeared on YouTube featuring Los Chikitukus de Chuschi, a group of indigenous musicians from the Southern Andes of Peru.[1] Shot in and around their hometown of Chuschi, the videos featured the group's members performing the town's *chimaycha* music and demonstrating its distinctive customs. Male musicians sported wool ponchos while lead singer Carmen Rosa Minas Quispe wore fancy festival attire, including colorful blouses and *pollera* skirts. All wore Chuschi's distinctive embroidered hats, an emblem of indigeneity throughout the Department of Ayacucho, where Chuschi is located. The Quechua-language songs they sang were accompanied by nylon-stringed guitar and by *chinlili*, a small guitar played only in and near Chuschi. They dealt with thwarted love, erotic sentiment, and outmigration, perennial themes in Andean song. However, they also spoke of injustice, decrying centuries of colonial domination that have left Peru's indigenous majority poor and marginalized. A few were more specific, denouncing the violence that engulfed Ayacucho between 1980 and the mid-1990s, when it became the central theater of conflict between Shining Path guerrillas and the Peruvian state. Despite such content, the videos looked like nothing so much as the spots that tourist boards in Peru, as elsewhere, devise to promote local attractions. Over several clips the musicians sang and danced their way through plunging valleys, grassy plains, cornfields, waterfalls, and finally the paved plazas and adobe walls of Chuschi's small-town streetscape, presenting all the human and environmental diversity of their district.

Videos like these were the preferred medium for promoting and distributing Andean popular music in early twenty-first-century Peru and in neighboring Bolivia (Stobart 2010 and 2011). Some of them were indeed meant to lure outsiders via artful presentation of village attractions. However, Los

Chikitukus' videos were not, and they presented some elements that may have confused viewers seeking vacation destinations. The youthful vigor of the singing voices, for instance, did not quite square with the images of lip-synching middle-aged performers. Several of the featured landscapes were not especially remarkable, and some of the scenes were frankly odd. A clip of the instrumentalists performing beneath a waterfall could surely not be faithful to any local tradition. And what to make of the tussle that almost erupts in the course of another video, wherein one man playfully seizes another as if to throw him to the ground?

These things are saturated with meaning for *chuschinos* (people from Chuschi) old enough to recognize their importance. For such viewers the filmic locations show mountains that are also tutelary deities, rivers that serve as weighty symbols in old songs, and waterfalls that house *sirenas*, beings with the power to make instruments sing. Several scenes take place in pastures where young people once practiced the *vida michiy*, a nocturnal courting custom that was also chimaycha's major performing context. And the intended audience for these videos is not the potential tourist. Rather it is chuschinos, especially nostalgic elders who have moved away, and younger people who have never had a close relationship with the things they feature—but who might be persuaded to develop one. The videos are meant, ideally, to be consumed in a setting like the one I witnessed in October 2013, a birthday party where older guests murmured about the images as they waited for food. They named the places they saw, discussed the things they had done there, and lamented the changes that have taken place since. They commented on clothing, attributing different outfits to the neighborhoods they typified, and mourned the disappearance of the vida michiy, replaced by house parties where their children and grandchildren played mass-popular music on USB sticks and smartphones, rather than chimaycha songs on village chinlilis. Mostly they reminisced about a time when their lives were different: when they lived and farmed according to indigenous customs, amid forces of nature that they treated as fellow beings, and made music by recycling the words and melodies of their ancestors.

Such explicit commentary would have pleased the man behind the videos, for he meant them precisely as an injunction to remember and preserve past practices. Arturo Chiclla is a chuschino and the director of a Lima-based record label called Dolly JR. By the late 2000s he was distressed by recent changes in chimaycha performance, changes introduced by younger artists who had grown up in Lima or Ayacucho City, capital of Ayacucho Department. This younger generation had, predictably, blended Chuschi's hometown style with the commercial popular music favored among Andean migrants.

PROLOGUE   ix

From Peruvian *huayno* they had borrowed themes of alcohol use and abuse and urban anomie, while their melodies and electric instruments reflected the influence of the *cumbia* music that is popular across Latin America. The shrill music-box tinkling of the chinlili, chimaycha's defining sound, was increasingly muted beneath the drum machines, electric bass, and *requinto* guitars that typified urban pop. Incensed, Chiclla had asked Los Chikitukus—long since retired—to help him arrest these ongoing musical developments. His label held the rights to their seminal 1992 recording *Vida Michiy*. Why not, then, simply relaunch those twenty-year-old sound recordings with videos in the style of more recent Andean productions, in an effort to remind audiences of the treasure that was being buried under the sonorous emblems of modern musical commerce?[2]

Chiclla was not the only media worker pursuing a project of musical purification in the late 2000s and early 2010s. Radio Quispillaccta, a station run by indigenous activists from Chuschi's neighboring town of Quispillaccta, had been broadcasting in Quechua since the year 2000. Based in Ayacucho rather than Quispillaccta, due to the city's superior infrastructural advantages, its broadcasts often foregrounded a rhetoric of indigenous affirmation that had been brought to Ayacucho not long before by the station's parent NGO. Such rhetoric remained suspect for many observers, in a region that has long been famous for its dearth of indigenous politics, but it identified the station with a mode of identity politics that was otherwise muted in the local mediasphere. Quispillacctinos (people from Quispillaccta) played chimaycha music too, and the style took a central place in Radio Quispillaccta's broadcasts, where it became linked to the station's emergent project of Andean cultural affirmation. Hoping, like Chiclla, to counteract the hybrid stylings of younger musicians, its directors favored old field recordings and new work by quispillacctino traditionalists like Óscar Conde, whose group was pointedly named Los Auténticos de Patario (The Authentics of Patario), and whose recordings the station actually commissioned to support their effort.

When I surveyed these efforts in the early 2010s, it seemed that people like Chiclla and Conde were fighting a rearguard action. The hybrid chimaycha of younger musicians was soaring in popularity among Ayacucho's Quechua-speaking majority, and not only among migrants from Chuschi and Quispillaccta. Even members of Los Chikitukus conceded its legitimacy—above all Marco Tucno, the group's musical director and the leading instrument maker to Ayacucho's indigenous communities. As a scholar with some experience researching Ayacucho's musical life, I found myself asking a number of questions about the evolving relationship between chimaycha music and indigeneity. Why were all of these actors invested in such different definitions of indigenous musical legitimacy? Where had competing conceptions of indigeneity come from? What might be lost when one definition displaced another? What might be gained? What does it mean for a musical instrument to be understood as a bearer of indigeneity, and what happens when its sonority is transformed? How might the new experiences of urban indigenous peoples be transforming the very definition of indigeneity? And finally, how do the twin forces of global indigenous politics and mass popular culture inflect those experiences?

INTRODUCTION

Making Music Indigenous

This book is about the many things that it means to be indigenous in the contemporary Peruvian Andes, as viewed from the perspective of chuschino and quispillacctino music workers. More specifically, it is about the way different sonorous practices became articulated to different lived experiences among Ayacucho's Quechua-speaking people, and the way musical activity has become a means for listeners to negotiate their commitments to different varieties of indigeneity. For there is more than one variety of indigenous experience (Clifford 2007), and while they are related, particularly insofar as they place indigenous people in a position of social inequity, they are not quite commensurate. They have radically different sources, and sometimes they are rooted in different epistemes. In the Andes, some arise from immersion in the lifeways of Quechua-speaking communities, which partially predate the full integration of those communities with Peru's dominant, nonindigenous social order. Others owe their parameters to the work of social scientists, and especially to the performance conventions that folklorists have used to stage indigenous culture for outsiders since the early twentieth century. Still others come from the global indigenous movement, which relies on presumptions about indigenous peoples that translate poorly into the Andean context. In short, many varieties of indigeneity compete for the allegiance of the people who are potential claimants of an indigenous subject position, and contemporary Quechua speakers may participate simultaneously in several distinct "communities of [indigenous] practice" (Van Vleet 2003:357). My approach does not aim to legitimate one over the others. Instead it is processual, aimed at illuminating the shaping mechanisms of indigenous experience today (de la Cadena and Starn 2007). It shows how networks of people, objects, ideas, and technologies interact to harden certain diacritics of lived experience into distinctive ideologies of indigeneity, ideologies that dissolve and reconfigure themselves when new elements become entangled with those networks.

Most especially, the book is centered on chimaycha music. In fact chimaycha is a type of huayno music, despite the distinction made above between the two genres. Huayno has been the dominant music of Andean Peru for over a century, and it is as beloved in indigenous as in nonindigenous communities. It sometimes takes different names in local contexts, and performance practice varies by community, but everywhere its basic traits are the same: strophic songs in binary meter, with largely pentatonic melodies that fluctuate between major and minor modes, with verses that may be in Spanish or local indigenous languages. Older songs tend to thematize love, loss, and social angst, often in figurative language that draws symbols from the natural world. Chimaycha fits this definition perfectly and might best be described as the huayno variant of Chuschi, Quispillaccta, and the neighboring district of Sarhua. It is distinguished mainly by some local melodic tendencies and the use of the chinlili as the accompanying instrument. However, since the early 1990s musicians and activists in those towns have chosen to call their music chimaycha, and in deference to their usage I call it that too, reserving the term *huayno* for the cognate music produced elsewhere.[1]

This act of musical self-differentiation is tied to the contemporaneous appearance of self-identifying terms like *indigenous* in Ayacucho's public discourse. The appearance of this language marks a striking change from the situation I found among Quechua-speaking peasants and migrants during fieldwork I conducted there between 2000 and 2003. My observations then matched those of anthropologist Frank Salomon: "far from connoting healthy pluralism, as they do in international academic discourse, terms such as 'indigenous' seem to peasant ears . . . to be freighted with unacceptable racial connotations and unpleasant memories" (2002:475)—especially memories of *indigenismo*, a nationalist movement in which nonindigenous intellectuals presumed to valorize indigenous culture by appropriating its expressive practices, reworking them, and presenting their own products as improvements.[2]

The Quechua-speaking people I knew in Ayacucho similarly refused the stigmatizing label, despite the stubborn insistence of commentators who described them as "indigenous people" or "Indians." The recent choice to claim it is a strategic one, promoted by local activists. They have seen other colonized people achieve some autonomy after assuming the identity, and then leveraging it to access the rights and recognitions of international treaties that specify indigenous peoples as beneficiaries. Their efforts have led some Peruvian commentators, invested in the continued exspoliation of indigenous communities, to level charges of falsification, undermining the newly claimed identities of people whom they cannot see as "indigenous" following nearly five hundred years of exchange with Euro-descendant neighbors.[3] Even scholars have described them with a skeptical tone, attributing the trend to a specious "Indian demand" in the Global North, where "there are increasing numbers of people inclined to give money to [Indians] who NGOs present as . . . peoples with ancient, exotic habits and customs; stewards of the environments and bearers of wisdom that lets them live in harmony with nature" (Favre 2009:36–37).[4] Those who take indigenous movements seriously, or lament the forces that impede their development, are liable to be accused of "veiled nostalgia" (Cavero Cornejo 2011:193), for despite a well-documented surge in indigenous activism, such phenomena are ostensibly "not at all the result of a movement or social activism on the part of 'indigenous' sectors . . . because in the [Peruvian Andes] those movements simply don't exist" (Azevedo 2009:73).

In this book I take a less dismissive stance, without abandoning the critical tools needed to parse the emergent meanings of Andean indigeneity and indigenous activism. It is indeed the case that Quechua-speaking activists, like others who wield emergent tools of indigenous lawfare, frequently find themselves "constructing idealized notions of self and culture that do not fit their own complexly layered experience" (Gustafson 2009:130). But this is hardly the same as saying that their move is a ruse. It is, rather, to say that the rhetoric of indigenous politics is the latest weapon that they have seized in a long-running effort to defend themselves from the genocidal forces in Peruvian society.[5] Protestations to the contrary seem to rely upon the presumption that there is a version of indigenous experience that lies outside of encounter with outsiders, processes of cultural exchange, and the subsequent work of boundary definition. However, scholars of ethnicity have long shown that identities are defined when neighboring social groups, who share many cultural traits but not full intersubjectivity, try to distinguish themselves from one another, typically through the selection and amplification of those traits that do serve as effective markers of distinction (Barth 1970). Indigeneity is a complex social identity of this kind. It is produced in an ongoing encounter between a colonizing power and colonized peoples who negotiate the terms of their survival with that power, even as they adopt elements of the colonizers' culture. Its content is always emergent and contested, because such cultural sharing leads to disagreements over the proper markers of insider and outsider status. Here tradition is a perennial resource, evidence for distinctiveness and hence the right to self-determination. To insist upon treating chimaycha as its own object supports precisely such a notion of indigenous difference—a notion that is otherwise fragile in the Peruvian Andes.

Indigenous Fragility and Andean Coloniality

This notion of indigenous fragility demands some explanation. The colonial era produced a society in the Andes unlike those that exist in many of the places where indigenous politics has found the firmest footing. Unlike the Anglophone colonies in particular, it saw relatively free fraternization between a permanent indigenous majority and a smaller group of colonizers. After invading the territory that became the Viceroyalty of Peru in 1532, the Spanish settled only thinly in the Andean mountains, where populous indigenous communities had flourished under Inca rule, or in the Amazon jungle. They concentrated instead in scattered outposts of colonial rule, including small Andean cities like Ayacucho, and especially the viceregal capital of Lima. Physically and socially isolated from indigenous civilization, coastal cities like Lima developed a distinctive and thoroughly Eurocentric *criollo* culture, even despite some accretions from indigenous subjects and especially African slaves. Andean cities developed differently.[6] Populated by growing numbers of mixed-race people and acculturated Indians, they became defined instead by a cultural formation dubbed *mestizo* (mixed), in recognition of its blended quality.

Originally used to denote the child of a Spanish settler and an indigenous person, the term *mestizo* later came to designate anyone who claimed any degree of mixed European and indigenous ancestry. After several generations of colonization they made up a huge percentage of the Andean cities, and they occupied an interstitial social stratum. Mestizos shared much of their cuisine, attire, music, and spoken language with the people of neighboring indigenous communities, and like Indians they were barred from the highest ranks of colonial society. However, they tended to live in cities or larger towns, speak Spanish, work as petty merchants or bureaucrats, and participate in the sociopolitical life of the colonial state. They did not suffer the same burdens of taxation, forced servitude, and cultural denigration as their indigenous fellows. Their culture and ancestry may have been "mixed," but mestizos lay closer to whiteness than to indigeneity, and Quechua speakers came to name criollo and mestizo outsiders alike with the term *misti* (see Weismantel 2001). Indeed, in a perpetual effort to escape the stigma of indigenous inferiority, mestizo cultural discourse has always shored up lines of distinction between the two social groups, even as mestizo cultural chauvinism continued to rely upon affectations of pride in indigenous heritage.[7] This boundary work means that Andean indigeneity remained stuck fast to connotations of rural residence, Quechua or Aymara linguistic competence, subsistence agriculture, participation in communal obligations, and powerlessness—as well as the many cultural practices that do in fact distinguish indigenous from mestizo communities.

Peruvian independence in 1824 did not change these basic social relations, for the elites that championed it had economic interests that were tied to the exploitation of indigenous labor. Furthemore, the wars of independence and the later nineteenth century left the Andes in wretched economic conditions. Residents fled to Lima in massive numbers, and amid the chaos unscrupulous mestizos dispossessed remote, subliterate indigenous communities nearly at will. These patterns continued into the twentieth century and intensified after World War II as the Peruvian state concentrated industrialization efforts in Lima while abandoning the development of the Andes, further centralizing an already centralized society in the national capital.

What did change over the late nineteenth and early twentieth centuries was Peru's public conversation about race and national identity, in tandem with trends elsewhere. In an age of ascendant nationalism, Latin American intellectuals distinguished their countries from the societies of Europe, and from a United States that many considered imperialist and irredeemably racist. They reframed *mestizaje* (mixture) as a benefit rather than a liability, celebrating the contributions of indigenous and African peoples to national cultures they interpreted as hybrid, stronger because of that hybridity and fairer because they eschewed legal segregation. This ideology of mestizaje rested upon a positive vision of generative cultural fluidity. It promoted interaction, exchange, and tolerance as the engines of an inclusive national culture. However, it remained largely blind to power relations and to their implications for colonized and enslaved peoples. The acts of cultural exchange that nationalist theories extolled were executed on unequal terms, and many of them would more properly be described as rape, theft, and forced assimilation. It is clear that indigenous and African peoples often wished to preserve their own societies rather than contributing by fiat to a "mixture" whose terms were set by the powerful. To the extent that mestizaje became naturalized as a virtuous ideology of national identity formation, however, such claims came to be regarded as treasonous.[8]

Indigenismo was a theory and practice of mestizaje, despite its title, and indigenista elites spoke for rather than with, or as, indigenous subjects. They praised the achievements of the long-dead Inca but treated the expressions of living indigenous communities as inferior, bastardized practices that could be redeemed only through their own guidance. They based artworks on practices of the indigenous peoples they claimed to respect, but they rarely asked them to collaborate. Their plans for redressing indigenous marginalization assumed indigenous peoples' adoption of Western education, Spanish literacy, and the manners that connoted urbanity. Indigenous uplift meant assimilation into their own metropolitan mestizo identity, and it was impossible for an individual to achieve personal advancement while remaining suspended within indigenous cultural norms. In short, indigenismo raised many citizens' awareness of their country's indigenous heritage, but it failed to respect the living culture of indigenous communities or to recognize their cultural dynamism. Instead it erased "contemporary indigenous identity from the public sphere as meaningfully relevant to the national project . . . rendering invisible an indigenous politics potentially autonomous from state authority" (Albro 2010:152).[9]

The influences of colonialism, theories of mestizaje, and indigenista activity never really ebbed, and by the twentieth century they had saddled Peruvians with the catch-22 that Povinelli has glossed as "the cunning of recognition" (2002). Indigenous communities were still viewed by power holders as vestigial remnants of the past, incapable of becoming conversant with the modern life of the city, and hence destined for extinction. Any indigenous person capable of engaging with metropolitan norms was, by definition, likely to be considered a nonindigenous person. The dissociation was so complete that the masses of Indians who migrated to the city and adopted some of its cultural norms were deemed to have abandoned Indian status. They were instead given the name *cholo*, a term that was widely taken to denote imperfectly assimilated Indians, in transition to mestizo status.

In truth, these conditions typified most of Latin America, which nevertheless saw the rise of powerful indigenous movements over the 1960s and 1970s.[10] The exception of Andean Peru is explained by political factors. Peru was ruled in the late 1960s and 1970s by leftist dictators who sought to consummate the failed promises of the earlier indigenista President Augusto B. Leguía (1908–12; 1919–30). Leguía's regime had mapped out mechanisms for the legal recognition of indigenous communities, and towns all over the Andes registered in hope of gaining the promised control over communal landholdings and the right to juridical representation.[11] The program was implemented weakly, however, leading the later Velasco and Morales Bermúdez regimes (1968–80) to implement one that was framed instead in terms of Marxist dogma. Disavowing ethnicity in favor of a rigid class-based framework, the regime reconceived Andean communities as labor cooperatives and restored land lost to nonindigenous families and businesses, under the assumption "that once peasants had control over their land and labor, they would regain their dignity and . . . cease to be 'Indians'" (Seligmann 1995:3; see also Mayer 2009). The regime went so far as to mandate the replacement of terms like *indigenous* and *Indian*, converting registered indigenous communities into *comunidades campesinas* (peasant communities; see Bourque and Palmer 1975:232).[12]

These events moved the politics of Andean Peru firmly into the register of class conflict just as movements elsewhere in Latin America set about destigmatizing indigenous identity, laying a foundation for political projects that came to fruition over the 1980s and 1990s. That moment was even less propitious in Peru, however, for the Marxist regimes of the 1970s were followed immediately by the 1980 revolt of the Shining Path guerrillas, who staged their uprising from within indigenous Andean communities. Rigidly communist in their ideology, Shining Path leaders viciously persecuted alternative political movements. Their enemies in the Peruvian government, meanwhile, were perversely likely to misinterpret all social activists as rebel allies. These severe barriers to alternative forms of political organization were then replaced in the 1990s by the soft authoritarianism of the Fujimori regime, which continued to repress attempts at political organizing, and then in the 2000s by the government of Alejandro Toledo. Toledo, who was billed as Peru's first modern leader of indigenous descent, was elected in part on his promises to promote indigenous rights, and he even established a National Commission of Indigenous, Amazonian, and Afro-Peruvian Peoples (CONAPA) to advance the cause— only to see its members disaffiliate in August 2003 over mismanagement and corruption at the toothless agency (see Pajuelo Torres 2007).[13]

Never effectively destigmatized, indigenous identity remained so closely associated with abjection in Andean Peru that people were loath to assume it in the years around the millennium.[14] Peru's default discourse of uplift remained premised on passage from indigenous to cholo or mestizo identity. The very idea of an indigenous politics remained oxymoronic, for anyone versed enough to mount such a campaign was, by local definition, no longer a proper Indian. It is little wonder, then, that indigenous movements failed to emerge in Andean Peru—or more precisely, to be recognized as such, for a number of recent studies have argued that indigenous politics was present but misrecognized in the Andes (de la Cadena 2015; García 2005).

Transnational rhetorics of indigenous rights found ready reception after 2000, suggesting that well-prepared ground awaited their arrival (Apfel-Marglin 1998; Oliart 2008). As Peru rebuilt its economy and communications infrastructure and reestablished political freedoms, small-scale indigenous movements emerged across the Andes, characterized everywhere by the factors that are "characteristic of indigenous mobilizing in general: self-determination and autonomy, with an emphasis on cultural distinctiveness; political reforms that involve a restructuring of the state; territorial rights and access to natural resources, including control over economic development; and reforms of military and police powers over indigenous peoples" (Warren and Jackson 2002:7). Within the Andes these activities became bound up especially with environmentalist organizations, which have long made common cause with indigenous movements worldwide (Conklin 2006; Conklin and Graham 1995). NGOs in Peru had been agitating against unregulated extractive industry since the 1990s, and they were ready allies for inexperienced Andean activists seeking connection with the funding agencies and political levers that might be used against a disattentive Peruvian state. This is why "NGOs have been described as instigators of [indigenous social unrest] by many businesses . . . they are largely responsible for the ethnicization of mining-related social conflicts" (Salazar-Soler 2009:203)—a statement that rings true enough, but that slights the agency of the indigenous actors who eagerly sought out NGO assistance in framing their struggle (see also Hogue and Rau 2008).

The local exemplar of this alignment between indigenous politics and environmental protest is CONACAMI (National Confederation of Communities Affected by Mining). Founded in 1999 to combat mining contamination, CONACAMI entered a new stage in 2003, one "characterized by the construction of an international network of relationships with indigenous organizations in neighboring countries" (Salazar-Soler 2014:94). Through such networks CONACAMI affiliates learned to wield the legal instruments and orders of discourse that such organizations had developed in their own struggles for rights and protections.[15] Its delegates "voted to reconstitute CONACAMI as an indigenous confederation that would center its demands on defending indigenous rights, promoting indigenous political participation, and refounding the nation-state" (Poole 2010:30), and its program became thoroughly infused by the ecological discourses that partner organizations had wielded against extractive industry in their own countries. By 2005 this convergence was so complete that in a statement before the World Forum in Caracas, then vice president Mario Palacios declared that the organization's goals were "to organize and to defend our identity. We no longer speak of defending the environment but rather Pachamama [Quechua: Mother Earth], because historically our peasant and indigenous communities considered themselves children of the earth and lived in harmony with it" (cited in Salazar-Soler 2014:91).

CONACAMI was, furthermore, a bellwether for parallel developments. Allied actors like the powerful NGO Chirapaq had been working since the mid-1990s in sites across the Andes, including Ayacucho, to foster "a network of indigenous leaders, increasingly familiar with . . . indigenous rights discourse" (Oliart 2008:292). Now a larger coalition of fellow travelers dubbed COPPIP (Coordinadora Permanente de Pueblos Indígenas del Perú) emerged to promote a "process of articulation, aimed at forming an indigenous political movement in Peru" (Pajuelo Torres 2007:122), convening a 2004 meeting of delegates from some seven hundred different organizations located in all twenty-five of Peru's departments as well as Ecuador, Bolivia, Colombia, and Brazil. Held in the Andean city of Huancavelica and dubbed the First Summit of Indigenous Peoples, it focused in particular on mining, water rights, and free trade agreements. However, "it was clear that many of the Andean leaders were looking to promote a return to self-identification as 'indigenous' among their community members, so as to access the protection of [international treaties]. . . . A future objective of COPPIP is to incentivize indigenous valorization of their own customs" (Alfaro Rotondo 2005:8). Finally, from this meeting emerged yet another organization, the CAOI (Andean Union of Indigenous Organizations), which described itself as the "representative of the Originary Indigenous Peoples of the Andes *in the process of consolidation* [and] which proposes alternatives for good living" (CAOI n.d.:6; emphasis added). Especially telling here is the invocation of "good living" or *allin kawsay* in Quechua, a key term that names the instrumentalized vision of indigenous ecological harmony that is wielded by Bolivia's indigenous movement—or, from another perspective, "the practices of living in harmony with nature, with other communities, and within families and communities" (Poole 2010:32).

Taken together, these events demonstrated the "construction of a modern and strongly instrumentalized [notion of] ethnicity" (Huber 2008:260). And indeed, the notion was promptly instrumentalized in a variety of contexts as "peasant communities" defended their lands from mining companies, accessing the protections that were afforded to "indigenous communities" alone under Peruvian and international law.[16] Still, notions of indigenous rights and autonomy remain fragile propositions in contemporary Peru, for older ideologies of mestizaje survive beneath surface-level changes in terminology. They lie, for instance, at the heart of an alternative nationalist project centered on the cholo culture of Lima, a project that has attracted enthusiastic support from much of Peru's academic and popular commentariat.

Lo Cholo and the Persistence of Assimilationist Mestizaje

Over the twentieth century the Eurocentric self-conception of Lima, Peru's social, economic, and political center, was challenged as wave after wave of provincial migrants moved to and remade the city. By the late twentieth century they were Lima's overwhelming majority and, despite long exclusion, they had gained a firm hold over the city's public culture. New generations of intellectual and cultural mediators have, since the year 2000, claimed Lima's hybrid culture as the basis of a renewed Peruvian nationalism, largely under the banner of *lo cholo* (roughly, "cholo culture"). No longer dismissed as the shabby detritus of an unlettered migrant community, cholo music, attire, and especially cuisine have all been promoted to leading national symbols.[17] Sincerely inclusive in its intent, this movement nevertheless insists upon the same vision of cultural hybridity that was promoted by earlier mestizo ideologies. As "furiously assimilationist" as indigenismo, it too demands that Indians remain "excluded from this new national imaginary until they [become] deracinated and [adopt] mestizo ways" (Canessa 2012:8). Devoted to the disintegration of cultural barriers, it remains dismissive of indigenous difference and self-determination, attacking them as either the deluded romanticism of indigenista holdouts or the treasonous impositions of alien NGOs. Most perniciously, it relies on the dubious conviction that the inventive practices of cholos themselves are evidence of a desire for assimilation rather than a testament to indigenous cultural creativity.[18]

There is another way to characterize lo cholo. It might be seen as a thriving urban indigenous culture that remains unrecognizable as such under the dominant terms of Peruvian discourse. For indigenous communities have, since the very moment of colonization, absorbed the habits of their colonizers and redefined cultural patterns as they saw fit, without abandoning their claims to distinctiveness (cf. Arguedas 1966:22). A "kaleidoscopic simultaneity of similarity and difference," Andean indigeneity defeats analyses that "demand simply either difference or sameness from indigeneity, and thus manifest the negation of its historical condition" (de la Cadena 2015:33). This dynamic, vigorously incorporative form of indigeneity is oxymoronic only from the perspective of a mestizo ideology that fails to contemplate the possibility of urban indigenous survival. And this is precisely why transnational discourses of indigeneity have become critical tools, and tools of critique, for certain indigenous activists: rhetorics of indigenous difference and persistence that are also resolutely oriented toward the future, they show that Peru's dominant vision of indigenous etiolation is but a provisional construct. If the lettered intellectuals who define Peruvian social discourse have misrecognized urban Indians and their indigenous politics, then the use of new labels by educated and newly empowered Indians is a means to audibilize claims to identity and autonomy that have remained largely unheard.

Cholo culture dominates the city of Ayacucho too, and I take it seriously as one variety of Andean indigeneity, rather than a series of habits that distance their bearers from their indigenous roots. It is, like all manifestations of "indigeneity," nothing but the discursive epiphenomenon of a power-laden dialogue between different Peruvian communities, a contested space of identification that appears when Andean peoples hold a line against the assimilationist norms of a mestizo society. The performance scholar Diana Taylor has made the related claim that "the very categories—criollo and Indian—are a product of [interethnic] conflict, not its reason for being" (2003:195). Taylor's object is theatrical performance, through which actors and playwrights can lead their audiences to reimagine the boundaries and the content of categories like these. Mine is mass popular and folkloric music, a more mundane practice that saturates the lives of humble citizens via mediated dissemination and weekly concert events, and that thereby plays a more everyday role in naturalizing different versions of indigeneity. However, the musical elements of Andean indigeneity cannot be understood via analysis of music alone. They are tied up with the history of interactions between indigenous musicians and nature, university education, new technologies, foreign NGOs, materials, alcohol, national ideologies, and transnational political rhetoric, among other things. And so this is not simply a story about indigenous music: it provides a window onto the networks through which indigeneity itself is made.

This story can be told in many different ways. As I tell it here, it centers on two men, the chuschino Marco Tucno and quispillacctino Óscar Conde, longtime performers and key figures in the chimaycha scene (see figures 1 and 2). Many others appear in supporting roles, and some of them are critically important for the narrative, but these two men have guided my understanding of chimaycha music, and the interpretation I present here is a particular one, bound to their generation. In their lifetimes they have witnessed tremendous musical and sociopolitical transformations, changes in which they were centrally involved, meaning that their experiences are illuminating lenses through which to refract the story of Andean music and indigeneity. Both learned to perform chimaycha as young men in their hometowns, where the genre was a key vehicle for courtship, and one vehicle for elaborating an ecocentric worldview particular to the indigenous Andes. Tied to annual cycles of pastoralism and agriculture, themselves determined by seasonal change and the physical landscape, and to the social and physical reproduction of human beings, chimaycha underlined the interwoven nature of human and nonhuman, sexual and agricultural reproduction—domains that are never entirely separate in Andean thought (Mannheim 1998).[19]

Later both men helped to transform the style between the 1970s and 1990s, a period when NGOs, scholars, and Ayacucho's university all invested in indigenous music. Radio programs, informal cassette recordings, competitions, and festivals of staged folklore all became showcases where Marco, Óscar, and their peers developed new performing techniques and new lyrical sensibilities, and where they found outlets for a surging pride in stigmatized cultural manifestations. Perhaps more important, development projects and new educational opportunities gave people like Marco the opportunity to attend university, and new kinds of economic power to indigent Quechua-speaking communities like Óscar's hometown, laying foundations for their influence later on. This era also saw the violence of the Shining Path conflict, which drove many traditional performance contexts into extinction and indirectly fostered substitute performances in new sorts of spaces. Marco's group Los

FIGURE 1. Marco Tucno Rocha, posing with guitar molds received from Abrahám Falcón. Photograph by author.

FIGURE 2. Óscar Conde, posing with his grandfather's armadillo-shell chinlili. Photograph by author.

Chikitukus de Chuschi, a group composed of indigenous university students, made a name for themselves by singing about the conflict, and their rise is inconceivable without the disparate engines of education and violence.

Finally, in the most recent moment, Óscar and Marco saw the traditional music of their hometowns become a leading style in Ayacucho and bifurcate predictably into two streams. On one hand was the traditionalist version, promoted by Radio Quispillaccta since its founding in 2000. Echoing tactics deployed in other movements for cultural affirmation, they decried the threat of assimilation and instead supported the traditional agrocentric culture of their hometown. On the other hand was a pop version, saturated with sonic and lyrical references to commercial music, urban life, and the indigenous experience of the city. In this guise, chimaycha was but one in a long line of musical media through which cholo migrants developed a collective conversation about their emergent subject position—a topic that has regularly occupied theorists of Andean music and society.[20] Indeed, in every age Andean migrant music has been transected by concerns that are unique to those who live it, and the post-2000 practice of urban chimaycha became defined by an affective hexis and a neoliberal ideology that guided much of Peruvian discourse more generally.

Although I figure this study via the stories of two exceptional musicians, its concerns are hardly parochial. Their experiences relate to durable concerns in indigenous scholarship, which have received new attention in the present moment of unprecedented indigenous activism, including indigenous relations to place and environment (Gordillo 2004; Sawyer 2004); the role of aesthetics in carrying unique ways of being in the world (Magowan 2007; Simonett 2014); the folklorization and commercialization of indigenous culture (Brown 2003; Comaroff and Comaroff 2009); and the impact of the global indigenous movement on local indigenous communities (Merlan 2009). In short, this is a story of how large-scale forces became embedded in the sonorous materials of one highly local musical scene. It holds lessons for scholars of indigeneity, about the understudied role of commercial and noncommercial sounds in structuring that identity (see also Ochoa Gautier 2014; Seeger 2004), and lessons for music scholars about the heteronymous networks of ideas, objects, and actions that give shape to sonorous experience (Bates 2012; Roda 2015). For like many recent studies my account is underpinned by a processual understanding of the things it describes. It takes for granted the notion that the things that matter are objects and experiences of contingent importance, their influence granted to them by human and nonhuman actants who dialogue in unexpected ways. In this sense "the primary ontological unit is not independent objects with inherent boundaries and properties but rather phenomena" (Barad 2007:139), which is to say, the series of forces and relationships that determine which things become perceptible as things of importance. The forces that raised chimaycha to prominence within Ayacucho's soundscape in the early twenty-first century ranged from transnational development work to scholarly folklore, and its meanings for individual musicians are inseparable from such arcane matters as rural topophilia and craft knowledge. Those issues are central to the account that follows, but what they support is a meditation on the many contemporary meanings of indigeneity.

Indgeneity in Theory

In recent decades indigenous peoples have seized opportunities for cultural survival, self-representation, and limited self-governance that seemed impossible only a generation ago. Their efforts have generated a parallel scholarly literature devoted to understanding the ramifications of these changes, and there are two strong threads within it that inform my approach here.[21] One is devoted to indigenous conceptions of being, which are contrasted with a modern Western ontology that is pitched as radically distinct from it.[22] Authors in this area have explored diverse belief systems, but all are seen to share an ecological rationality that treats human and nonhuman things as commensurate beings, entities with similar forms of consciousness, and which are made mutually unintelligible only by virtue of their incarnation in different kinds of bodies. This does not only mean that indigenous peoples take the animals, plants, landforms, and nonordinary beings that surround them to be agentive manifestations of the same animating principle that gives rise to humans. The flourishing of human life also depends on cultivating proper relations with them, relations that may take forms ranging from mutual predation (Viveiros de Castro 1992) to reciprocal care (Nadasdy 2007). This demand gives rise to practices like ritual (Lima 1999), storytelling (Blaser 2010), and playing music (Bastos 2013; Brabec de Mori 2013; Hill 2009 and 2013; Piedade 2013), which are not well described by labels like "expressive culture," since they are world-creating means of maintaining existence for those whose practice them.

It is hardly surprising that scholars have found such systems, which foster nonutilitarian and antiextractive relationships between humans and nonhumans, to be worthy of new attention in an age of environmental crisis. Such studies also engage concerns for political justice, for they help explain aspects of conduct that have long baffled outsiders, discrepant assumptions that impede the development of respectful relationships between indigenous and settler societies. However, they have also been criticized (see Ramos 2012; Turner 2009; Cepek 2016): for reading observations made among Amazonian peoples onto a diverse hemispheric group of societies; for overstating the coherence and the sheer difference of the systems they describe; and most trenchantly, for making their own theory of radical indigenous alterity into a benchmark of indigenous legitimacy (Bessire 2014), with possibly disastrous consequences for others who deserve the rights and benefits of indigenous identity. All of these are serious concerns for scholars of the Central Andes, where Quechua- and Aymara-speaking peoples have spent half a millennium absorbing Western practices and beliefs, view themselves to be distinct peoples despite their clear ability to move amid overlapping cultural systems, and continue to suffer the slings and arrows of that difference. Still, studies of ontology have prepared outsiders to respect indigenous natural philosophies that had been dismissed as the romantic inventions of sympathetic but deluded outsiders (Krech 1999) or simply as New Age nonsense. My account touches upon some of these themes without adopting the view that indigenous and Western experiences are radically incommensurable—an interpretation that is badly out of place in the Peruvian Andes.

Contemporary indigenous studies have also been concerned with the legal and political mechanisms through which indigenous peoples are attaining power and the ways those mechanisms affect the self-identities and social boundaries of the communities that rally to the cause.[23] Many of the tools that indigenous peoples wield in these efforts have been developed in transnational forums, including United Nations meetings and those of other international treaty organizations. The final report of the 1992 UN Conference on Environment and Development in Rio de Janeiro (commonly referred to as the Rio Declaration) and the Indigenous and Tribal Peoples Convention of the International Labour Organization (commonly dubbed ILO 169) loom especially large for the powerful recognitions they grant indigenous communities.[24] Even activists working at national or subnational levels tend to take their cues from the language of these and related instruments, hoping to leverage them against government signatories that have failed to honor their commitments. However, this is not always easy to do, for such documents tend to be driven by the interests, self-conceptions, and political realities of the particular groups that worked for their creation—groups like the Maori, the Northern Cree, Scandinavian Sámi, and Australian Aboriginal peoples, all of whom have played leading roles in the consolidation of global indigenous politics (Niezen 2003). Indigenous peoples in other national contexts often manage different notions of identity, face different relationships with the societies around them, and do not quite fit the portrait of "indigenous peoples" that such documents seem to envision. A central issue in the transnational study of indigeneity, then, has been how the tools of the political process incite new performances of indigeneity. Such enactments must match the expectations built into the forums where indigenous people go to seek redress, and they may fail to respect distinctive local conceptions of belonging—leading to potential crises of identity and exclusion within the very communities that are targets of political aid (see Kauanui 2008; Sturm 2002; Tallbear 2013).[25]

Politics is, furthermore, only one arena that refracts the new identitarian pressures and possibilities facing indigenous peoples. Most people remain uninvolved in direct political action, and are more likely to engage this sort of identity work in realms like popular culture (Jacobsen 2017; Samuels 2004; Tucker 2011) or erudite culture (P. C. Smith 2009; Taylor 2003). Expressive culture is, indeed, a fruitful arena in which to examine the way that everyday people negotiate tensions between "global and local" indigenous identities (Merlan 2009). Scholars of indigenous music in places like Australia (Fisher 2016; Magowan 2007; Neuenfeldt 1997), Northern Europe (Diamond 2017; Hilder 2015), and especially North America have routinely touted musical performance as a medium for shaping such changing notions of indigenous community. Attending to the adoption, spread, and evolution of practices as diverse as powwow (Browner 2009; Ellis, Lassiter, and Dunham 2005; Goertzen 2001; Scales 2012), Christian song (Lassiter 1998; McNally 2000), Native American fiddling (Dueck 2013), or First Nations hip-hop (Berglund, Johnson, and Lee 2016), these studies show how often indigenous culture involves the repurposing of borrowed elements. The era has long passed, in short, when indigenous authenticity was tied to pre-Columbian inheritance rather than ongoing cultural creativity. For this reason ethnomusicologist Beverley Diamond has pointedly called for scholars to use the language of "vitalization" rather than revitalization (2012), a term that implies illness and mistakes the vibrancy of indigenous culture.

Despite these precedents, scholarly work on the social politics of indigeneity has remained mostly delinked from work on expressive culture within Latin America. Part of this disconnect can be traced to indigenismo's failed promise to deliver progress through "de haut en bas" forms of cultural production (Salomon 2002). Another influential strand of thinking has even dismissed cultural matters as a direct threat to the serious work of indigenous affirmation. After all, nonindigenous power holders readily make concessions in the realm of culture, allowing indigenous people to dress, cook, make music, and worship where and as they wish. Writing about such multiculturalist tokenism, Hale has cautioned that it allows settler elites to claim tolerance without addressing basic structures of inequality, and it is rarely accompanied by more substantive concessions in the realms of land rights or juridical independence (2002; see also Hale 2006). Such concerns are real enough, but "there are no criteria for properly politicizing art [and] it is generally the 'state of politics' that decides if a work of art is interpreted as harboring a political critique or encouraging an apolitical outlook" (Rockhill 2009:206). Indeed, in a related article Hale and Millamán (2006) have made the somewhat different point that the ramifications of cultural activity must be examined on a case-by-case basis. Understanding the difference between a cultural development that is mere multiculturalist window dressing and one that grants indigenous people "wiggle room" (Sommer 2006) for greater self-determination requires the groundwork of primary research. The few studies that do treat expressive culture as a channel for indigenous sociopolitical affirmation in Latin America tend to support this thesis, showing how indigenous performance can become linked to matters as substantive as language revitalization (Faudree 2013; Minks 2013) and land rights (Seeger 2004 and 2013).

Of course, mobilizing these kinds of claims involves the prior creation of a discourse community that conceives of itself as indigenous and deserving of redress and recognition in the first place. Like philosopher Jacques Rancière (see Rockhill and Watts 2009), I take the creation of such a public to be not only a sociopolitical act but the foundational act of any politics (see also Dewey 1946). Such foundational acts often seem difficult to achieve, because they bring different individuals' priorities and conceptions into conflict with one another. However, Habermas's seminal account of public formation

(1989), like the theories that descend from it (see especially Calhoun 1992; Fraser 1990; Warner 2002), takes such debates to be the very arena in which members of a public become aware that there are controversies, convictions, and mutual investments that unite them as a community. Tracking the different visions of self and community that compete for indigenous loyalty, then, and teasing out the developing relationships between them, is anything but a distraction: it is tantamount to tracking the most fundamental of political activities.

In this book, then, I document various versions of sonorous indigeneity that enrich the lives of Quechua speakers in contemporary Ayacucho. Few are meant overtly to be political, but all are effective in capturing the attention of the subjects who might claim that position. In fact music, cheap to produce, perpetually in circulation, undemanding since it can be consumed with little conscious attention, and indifferent to the literacy of its target audience, is so effective a vehicle for this kind of parapolitical activity that it is routine to claim as much.[26] Scholars of the Central Andean countries have made such claims, and I build on their work with its attention to musical processes of boundary definition and social difference (Bigenho 2002, 2007, and 2012; Hornberger and Swinehart 2012; Ríos 2008; Solomon 2000; Stobart 2006 and 2008; Turino 1984, 1988, and 1993; Wong 2012). Within Peru, this work has tended to center on either mestizo music or indigenista folklore (Mendívil 2002; Mendoza 2000 and 2008; Romero 2001 and 2002; Tucker 2013b; Turino 1988). Most accounts that do approach music from the point of view of indigenous peoples either date from a period before the impact of global politics and popular cultural circulation remade the conditions under which indigenous identity is imagined (Arce Sotelo and Vivanco 2015; Holzmann 1986; Ráez Retamozo 2002 and 2005; Romero 1988; Ulfe 2004) or concede to the dominant notion of indigeneity as a subject position that lies outside the modern nation (Bellenger 2007).

Ethnomusicologists Thomas Turino and Jonathan Ritter and anthropologist Gisela Cánepa Koch have, however, provided accounts that prefigure mine in key respects. Besides showing how indigenous aesthetics differ from those of mestizo communities, Turino's account showed how indigenista policies affected practice within indigenous communities. It thereby demonstrated how thoroughly indigenous music might be mediated by histories of interaction with mestizo intellectuals, bearers of their own unique ideologies of indigenous difference (1993; see also Mendoza 2008). Similar dynamics occupy me in chapters 3 through 5 below, though it is remarkable how thoroughly the political movements, social changes, and technological developments of the quarter century between Turino's text and mine inflect the possible relationships between the parties involved. Ritter's work, meanwhile, deals with a situation where nearly all of the social, historical, and geographic factors are shared with the one that I describe (2002 and 2006). It focuses on the same era and the community of Colca, only a few miles downstream from Chuschi and Quispillaccta—and yet the two areas have taken very distinct musical and political trajectories. These differences arise from the decisions of key agents, working with the affordances of hyperlocal socioeconomic and political developments, and it is instructive to note how the actions of a few well-placed actors can create such starkly different results. Finally, Cánepa Koch's work (2002 and 2010) has long focused on the ways that indigenous musical and festival practices change in the process of urban migration, serving as a resource for urban Indians to reimagine the meanings of indigeneity.

My account has also benefited from wider readings on the culture and society of the Peruvian Andes, where scholars have routinely described the persistence of distinctively indigenous ideas and behaviors, denounced unequal power relations, and documented indigenous resistance.[27] Unique ecological concepts and notions of nonhuman animacy, debates over change and cultural survival, complicated relationships with mestizo neighbors, the savvy manipulation of legal regimes—all of these issues are perennial themes of Andean ethnology, and recent work has woven them seamlessly into the newer languages of ontology (see especially de la Cadena 2015; Dean 2010; Mannheim and Salas Carreño 2015) and indigenous activism (Alfaro 2005; Cavero Cornejo 2011; Li 2015; Paredes 2016; Salas Carreño 2008; Salazar-Soler 2014).

All of this literature informs my understanding of events in Chuschi, Quispillaccta, and Ayacucho City, and it is liberally referenced in the text below. However, I am especially inspired by two recent texts on the Andean region. One is anthropologist Marisol de la Cadena's study of indigenous politics over the longue durèe of the twentieth century, told from the point of view of two Quechua-speaking "shamans" from Peru's Cusco region (2015). This work shows how early movements for justice were rooted in a distinctive indigenous ontology, one that recruited as participants the tutelary "earth beings" that are also Andean mountains, and thus remained unrecognizable as politics to a modern liberal state that conceives of human beings alone as rights-bearing citizens. However it also shows how such ancient conceptions have been rerouted through the recent growth of New Age tourism. Here the new and specious figure of the "Andean shaman," invented to commoditize Andean spirituality for credulous and wealthy outsiders, nevertheless became a ground for a new and generative conversation about indigenous identity—a conversation whose terms are neither wholly "Andean" nor "global," and which is capable of articulating several different sorts of indigenous projects.

The distinction between "old" and "new" indigeneity also animates a second and more cautious text, by anthropologist Andrew Canessa (2012). Describing the conduct of indigenous community life in neighboring Bolivia, Canessa contrasts the distinctive habitus that governed everyday action in the 1980s with the performative model of indigeneity that came to dominate his host community after the rise of indigenous President Evo Morales and his triumphant MAS party.[28] Noting that MAS's globalized mode of indigenous activism has ensured the social uplift of indigenous communities and can hardly be protested on grounds of political representation or economic progress, Canessa notes that it may still "deny a voice to those people who are unable or unwilling to articulate their identities in the public domain, whose identities and allegiances, moreover, are often taken for granted by indigenous politicians and scholars of indigenous movements" (2012:4–5). These people and their interests, difficult to represent in terms intelligible to modern politics, are often sacrificed when indigenous actors are forced to make their claims in the idioms recognizable to the liberal state, meaning that indigenous liberation may entail the terminal loss of certain lifeways. It remains, then, worthwhile to ask "what it means to be indigenous to indigenous people themselves, not only when they are running for office or marching in protest but especially when they are in the small spaces of their lives" (Canessa 2012:2).[29]

My account builds on these, in its emphasis on constitutive musical dialogue between individuals and groups with different sorts of investments—in my proposal that the subject position we gloss as Andean indigeneity is best conceived as the precipitate of a debate between actors with disparate interests in the future of Quechua-speaking communities. I focus on "the authenticators—on the authorities in indigenous communities and the experts beyond who determine what is deemed authentic at any one time [and on] the choices that people in different settings make in the ongoing process of their own identity formation" (Warren and Jackson 2002:10–11), and I remained "less concerned to identify particular traits [as markers of a particular social position] than to describe the . . . dynamics in which attributions are made" (Herzfeld 2004:30). In the service of this effort I draw insights from contemporary literatures on ecology, folklore, public formation, emotion, neoliberalism, craftsmanship, and embodiment, as appropriate, leaving discussions of the relevant concepts for the moments in which they are most germane. Throughout, however, I keep foremost the activities, ideas, and emotional investments that constitute musical indigeneity.

Some of these investments arise from what many contemporary scholars would call a distinctive ontology of indigeneity, and after a first short chapter surveying essential elements of this book's ethnographic settings, I spend chapters 2–3 describing the web of relations between people, animals, land, and sound that framed chimaycha practice before the advent of mass communication, outmigration, and economic development thoroughly remade the conditions of community life in the 1960s and 1970s. Doubtless these practices always varied by era and according to the preferences of individuals and communities, but a set of general norms is nevertheless traceable in the accounts of people who experienced the moment of transition. Thus I recount their perspectives, in full recognition that it is likely to be an idealized and abstracted portrait of chimaycha practice, while registering what variation and contingency they are able to offer, in the absence of written or recorded sources that might offer other kinds of evidence.

In chapter 4 I focus on the role of academic folklore and university-based activism, showing how applied scholars and new educational opportunities rerouted chimaycha through staged performance idioms over the 1970s and 1980s, with significant effects for performance practice and community self-conception. Chapter 5 moves to the role of radio and the impact of the global indigenous movement, showing how the actions of one local broadcaster and its parent NGO reframed chimaycha once more over the 2000s and 2010s by placing it into mediated contact with new indigenous ideologies gleaned from their transnational dialogues. Chapter 6 describes the counterreaction that emerged after this exceptional station's success, as urban indigenous entrepreneurs blended the highly "folkloric" style patronized by that radio station with elements of mainstream national pop music, setting up an urban chimaycha scene that reflected with greater fidelity the evolving lifeways of its migrant audience.

Finally, in chapter 7 I refocus on the evolution and the construction of the chinlili, chimaycha's outstanding marker of musical distinction and a fruitful carrier of embodied versions of indigeneity that otherwise remain unmarked in everyday debates over the genre's meaning and direction. Here I am particularly interested in the way that people come to dwell in the world and in their selves by literally incorporating tools, by extending bodies to include them (Polanyi 1966:15–16). This chapter also provides a wider overview of Marco Tucno's influence on Ayacucho's chimaycha scene, situating him within the changes that have remade Ayacucho's city-space, rendering it a prime site for the refashioning of indigenous experience. Readers who are familiar with the characteristics of everyday life and social relations in Andean Peru may even wish to begin here, given the extent to which the chapter touches on the rest of this book's themes.

On Interpretations, Methods, and Responsibilities

In mid-2014, toward the end of a sabbatical-year fieldwork trip to Ayacucho, I realized how central Marco Tucno would have to be in my account of chimaycha music, so I asked if I still had permission to cite the ideas and experiences that he had shared with me. "Of course," he told me, spreading his hands in a gesture of magnanimity, "but only what's relevant." This astute response speaks volumes about ethnography, for any ethnographic text is partial and selective. Drawing upon a tiny set of the actual observations made during fieldwork, it is a provisional theory about "what happened" or "what happens," and the success of that theory rests upon an ethnographer's careful arrangement of the details deemed relevant. Marco's response to my question demonstrated considerable trust, for he was leaving in my hands the responsibility to determine which among our many exchanges might be germane to my interpretation of his music culture. By the same token, however, his response points to a mass of words and acts that, however freely shared, and however important for my own sense of *ayacuchano* life, might not be germane, and that should therefore not appear in these pages.

Such are the hazards of writing ethnography. Fictive in the sense that they are constructed objects, ethnographies are shaped by the skills, biases, and intentions of their authors, and they tell "partial truths" (Clifford 1986). The selection of an interpretive frame that is adequate to any topic means leaving out things that from another analytical perspective might seem terribly relevant. This is particularly risky in a place like Ayacucho, which has experienced human tragedy on a scale that might seem to overdetermine all possible interpretations. Recent scholarship on Ayacucho has in fact focused almost completely on the Shining Path conflict and its effects, and I am often asked why I do not similarly place the violence at the center of my own analyses. The reasons are several. First, the choice reflects the self-conception that is held by most of the people that I work with. They lived through the conflict or its aftermath, acknowledge the devastation that it wrought, and are usually forthcoming about the topic. However, they do not often think of themselves or their society as, first and foremost, products of that violence.[30] Many specifically resist such a characterization, tired of Ayacucho's image as either villain or victim, and focus instead on the strides made since or even during the war, a time when many activities besides murderous terror proceeded apace. They are eager to move past flattened stereotypes toward a future in which they might appear with a full measure of humanity. Such a future, in which conversations about Ayacucho do not ineluctably lead toward Shining Path, would closely resemble their experiential present. It is that experience of past, present, and future that I mean to respect.

Second, to write about the violence might be to put some people at risk. This is the case even when the activities of particular individuals are well known, for speaking specifically about them can be deeply taboo. In an extraordinary book about such "public secrets," anthropologist Olga González has shown how perpetrators of conflict-era crimes might continue to live in the towns where they committed them, long after the end of the war (2011). Their identities might be known, and their actions referenced obliquely in everyday discourse, without being named explicitly—an act that might threaten the fragile balance of reconciliation that many communities achieved in the postviolence period. I have heard many such public secrets and have received unverifiable hints about much more. In most cases I have been asked not to speak of them, or have elected not to, to spare undeserving people undeserved grief, to protect them from social and legal reprisal, or because they are not relevant.

Finally, I do not dwell unduly on these events because I believe that commentary on them often appears merely prurient rather than constructive, the rubbernecking of observers with obscure motives for scrutinizing human depravity. I have no interest in aiding such a spectacle. None of this means that I minimize the effects of the conflict or that it is absent from the analysis that follows. Rather, the violence exerted upon indigenous peoples and its remediation is as central to my account as it is to Peruvian history—a conviction that appears in the report of Peru's postviolence Truth and Reconciliation Committee, which concluded that the Shining Path war stemmed ultimately from the profound abuse of Andean communities (CVR 2003). The war was shocking in its extremity and distressing in its implications for human dignity. This book, however, focuses per Marco's request on what is relevant for interpreting chimaycha music and indigeneity in Ayacucho, rather than on theories of violence, reconciliation, or other urgent themes that are covered in the reams of text that have been produced on the region.

Of course, the violence is not the only area in which this text is constructed around choices that others may not have made. My interest in ideas of indigeneity, for example, was not shared by all of my interlocutors. In speaking with some people I felt much as Salomon did in speaking with his research partners about practices that they viewed from a different perspective from his: "No other ethnographic moment gave me such a clear feeling of 'pulling teeth.' . . . I thought they were mistakenly hearing my question as a challenge to their expertise . . . it later turned out the difficulty was more intellectual and more fundamental" (2002:91). My interlocutors did not always value or understand the political rhetoric of indigenous difference, despite their clear sense of ethnic distinction and their interest in traditional Andean lifeways. Rather like Canessa's Aymara-speaking research partners in Bolivia, who "positively reject the term" despite being "the same people whom other Bolivians or anthropologists might describe as indigenous or indian" (2012:5), my interlocutors often "don't want to be [Indians], but they are perfectly aware that they are so" (2012:9) from the perspective of others. Many of those others now include fellow Quechua speakers who advocate the framework of indigeneity as a useful idiom for achieving sociopolitical progress. Insofar as my interest lay in exploring the importation of this framework and its relation to other understandings of Andean experience, my interpretation is my own, and there are many lenses through which others might read the social politics of contemporary Ayacucho. Indeed, many of the statements I cite regarding music and indigeneity would not have been spoken without my presence. They are not, however, inventions. They are truthful claims that my interlocutors and I could agree upon as reasonable descriptions of their reality, even when we approached the matter from different perspectives. Titon has described such coproduced knowledge as the basis of all ethnographic work, and in my case too "there was no original outside of our conversations: their texts and mine were coconstituted in practice, and though they were 'only' partially connected, they were also inseparable" (1988:xxvii).

In this sense this text is a window onto Andean music and indigenous experience in contemporary Ayacucho, a sound interpretation based on real dialogue, but it is nothing like the definitive statement on the topic. It is not an account of "indigenous peoples," "Andean society," or "highland music." It does not claim to tell the musical story of Chuschi, Quispillaccta, Ayacucho, or Peru. It is, rather, an account of indigeneity's changing meanings, told from the point of view of a handful of people, above all the two men who were my main guides through this milieu. It focuses on the ideologies, technologies, sociopolitical developments, and popular cultural forms that shape their lives, determining their sense of what it is to be and to sound indigenous. Biased by their ideas and experiences, and more importantly by my own, it bears significant blind spots. Two of them deserve special comment: gender norms and the cocaine trade.

Given the dominant mores of Andean communities, it was difficult for me to converse freely with older women about chimaycha music. Traditionally it was an erotic idiom, one that seemed inappropriate for a woman to discuss with a man who is not her husband—especially a white male foreigner. I spoke with some middle-aged female friends about the topic, in the company of their husbands, but found those conversations to be so heavily mediated by the male partner as to cast doubt upon the frankness with which they were conducted. However, previous ethnographers have attended to the musical ideas and responsibilities of indigenous Andean women (Arnold 1992; Harris 1978; Isbell 1997; Stobart 2008), and I draw on that secondary literature where possible to complement the perspectives I gleaned from my interlocutors. Furthermore, taboos have become attenuated among younger generations, partly because the tenor of chimaycha performance has shifted away from sex and romance. Given the largely chronological ordering of this text, readers will therefore notice an increasing representation of female voices, as it approaches the present day.

In fact this tendency indexes a broader generational shift, one that is especially pronounced in urban areas. Here opportunities to amass cultural and economic capital, and to spend it in pursuit of greater voice and representation, easily outweigh those available to women who remain suspended within patriarchal structures of village custom (Babb 1989; Seligmann 1995).[31] Certainly some long-standing gender norms have changed in the last two decades in both urban and rural milieus, not least the principle by which Quechua-speaking women were barred from public sites of political action (Bourque and Warren 1981; Harris 1978). National and transnational NGOs have played key roles as both promoters of gender parity and vehicles for female political agency (Arnold 1997; Oliart 2008; Rousseau 2011), while ethnic tourism and demand for indigenous craft production have allowed women, unparalleled symbols and stewards of Andean tradition (de la Cadena 1995), to become occasional protagonists in the economic life of their communities (Babb 2012; Femenías 2005; Ypiej 2012; Zorn 2005). Popular music, too, has been a notable vehicle for the public exploration of women's lived experience, with Lima's commercial huayno scene utterly dominated by female performers, all presenting songs and public narratives that are understood as partly autobiographical (Butterworth 2014).

Chimaycha's contemporary situation in Ayacucho evidences most of these shifts. It is unimaginable without the mediation of the extraordinary Machaca sisters, agronomists and cultural activists whose NGO work and parapolitical labor has transformed their home community of Quispillaccta. Ayacucho's outstanding chimaycha singers are overwhelmingly women, and several key radio DJs are too. In a sense, then, the increasing centrality of women in directing the public life of Andean society might reasonably be taken as a subtext of this book's later chapters. Still, caution should be exercised in interpreting these matters as signs of radical transformation, because in most ways the chimaycha scene continues to obey age-old Andean gender norms. It is premised on a rigid differentiation between male and female musical roles, one that is premised in turn on the notion of a gendered distribution of capacities. Its lyrics and its modes of performance take for granted the idea of gender as a firmly binary system, offering no real room for alternative gender expression.[32] These naturalized gender ideologies are the inheritance of an earlier era, when chimaycha was a vehicle for enacting and claiming gender identities during adolescence. Given this, I mainly treat the theme of gendered performance in chapter 3, a historical chapter that describes the musical activities that Marco, Óscar, and their peers cherished in their younger days. Other chapters make glancing reference to the persistence of the habits detailed there, but it should be remembered that to the extent that it accounts for the way that Andean norms of masculinity and femininity are enacted and inhabited musically, this text remains largely an account of men's perspectives on the matter.

A second aspect of contemporary Ayacuchano life that must remain opaque involves the city's illicit economy. Over the 2000s the jungle lowlands east of Ayacucho became one of the world's leading sites for growing coca and converting it into cocaine paste, a key step in the leaf's transformation into street cocaine. Many residents of the city and its rural hinterland, an officially impoverished region with little waged employment, responded to the industry's demand for *burriers*, smugglers who carry the raw product out of the region to be processed and sold abroad. Ayacucho became a key transshipment point and a site to invest the proceeds of the business, though not a significant point for the sale of cocaine. The resulting economic boost was tangible, as the city experienced a boom in housing, luxury automobiles, and leisure services that seemed incommensurable with its formal economy. Its prison population changed in composition as smugglers fell to police patrols, and it often seemed like everyone I knew in Ayacucho had a cousin, nephew, aunt, or uncle in jail. It was, however, hard to tell exactly how the cocaine industry related to mundane business and social life, and how many people were involved directly as opposed to being indirect beneficiaries of its economic dynamism. Rumors of cocaine's influence thickened everyday conversation about nearly every subject, but as is typical in the case of organized crime, most of them were hard to verify, and asking truly knowledgeable people was a risky proposition.[33]

Music did not stand outside these trends, but it had not developed the symbiotic links to the industry that characterize other Latin American centers of the drug trade. Unlike performers of Mexican *narcocorrido* (Wald 2001), Brazilian *funk* (Sneed 2007), or Colombian *vallenato* (Marre 1990 [1983]), Ayacucho's artists did not sing in praise of cocaine bosses or their organizations. They nevertheless benefited significantly as cash flowed from the hands of low-level employees into the local economy, supporting a concert life that had been much more attenuated in previous years. Many artists, in many different genres, told me that they had been approached about smuggling cocaine paste during their travels to and from gigs across provincial lines. Stories circulated about major Lima-based artists being flown into tiny, remote jungle communities for concert events on a budget that only a titan of the industry could meet. And I heard repeatedly that large concert events in Ayacucho featuring national cumbia and huayno stars were fronts behind which the financial managers of the cocaine trade laundered its proceeds.[34]

However, it seemed clear that chimaycha performance remained aloof from these developments. While the genre had become quite popular, most concerts remained below the threshold where they might serve as effective fronts for laundering money. Artists sought out "godparents" to support their gigs, a custom that had already been in force for a generation, and while some supporters may have been tied to the trade, their role as financial patrons was not different from the role adopted by other successful businesspeople. Audiences doubtless included people tied to the business as well, but they came to hear music that obeyed patterns of production and consumption that had evolved outside its influence. In oher words, the sustainability of a chimaycha scene featuring regular performances by major local artists was almost certainly secured by the petty cash that the industry put into the local economy. However, this cash was no more and no less influential than that which might derive from a more licit industry, and the social, financial, and aesthetic principles that organized chimaycha performance were in no sense direct products of a cocaine economy.

Other blind spots must remain, including many of which I am not even aware. This being the case, I have tried to present, to the best of my ability and within the limitations of the narrative form, the sources of the knowledge that underpins this text. Throughout I try to show how facts were learned, either naming the people who gave them to me and presenting their words when possible or showing how they emerged in the course of conversation or observation. Indeed most of what I learned came not in formal interviews but in the chatter and activity that is the infrastructure of everyday life.[35] What this means is that many of the statements I cite are drawn from fieldnotes and informal interaction rather than formal interviews. They are, however, quoted verbatim where possible, so that my authorial voice can be leavened by those of other people. Statements that appear in quotation marks are citations from fieldnotes, unless an interview is indicated in the text; block quotes are excerpts from interviews unless an article citation is provided; and statements without quotation marks are my paraphrases of other people's words. In most cases the timing should be clear from context, but I have not put in a specific date for each quotation, due to the tedious detail it would add to the text. Unless otherwise noted, all translations from Spanish are my own, as are those from the spoken Quechua of radio broadcasts. Marco and Óscar aided my interpretation of Quechua-language song texts, which are often more arcane in their phrasing and meaning than everyday speech.

Finally, an informed reading of this text requires some knowledge of my methods and the way that the project developed. It draws upon material gathered during fieldwork on another topic, between 2001 and 2003; during a second fieldwork period, focused centrally on chimaycha music, that I conducted over a 2013–14 sabbatical year; and over the course of several shorter visits in 2012, 2015, and 2017. I first became interested in chimaycha music during dissertation research I conducted in Ayacucho between 2001 and 2003. At that time explicit discourses of indigeneity were almost entirely absent in Ayacucho, and my project focused on the music of the city's mestizo elite. In the course of that research I happened to meet Marco Tucno, who demonstrated unparalleled insight into the music of indigenous communities due to his long performing experience and his status as a leading instrument maker. Over several hours of visits and formal interviews at his workshop, he introduced me to the music of his hometown, which I instantly loved. I also visited and interviewed at Radio Quispillaccta, then a fledgling community station, because radio was a part of my project and the station's Quechua-language broadcasts were unique in Ayacucho. Neither topic had a real place in my first research project. Many years later, however, after reviewing my earlier notes and recordings, I decided to revisit them. I returned to Ayacucho in January 2012 to do so and was surprised to discover that chimaycha had become one of city's most dynamic styles, that Radio Quispillacta had expanded its influence considerably, that languages of indigenous affirmation were circulating in the public sphere, and that all of these things were linked. I conducted new interviews with Marco, people at Radio Quispillaccta, and people they recommended, including Óscar Conde, who was described to me as the foremost expert on Quispillacta's chimaycha style. I bought all the new recordings that I could find and listened to Radio Quispillaccta's broadcasts to see how they had changed. Finally, I returned in 2013–14 seeking to understand how chimaycha had become so popular, what its relation was to indigenous politics, and how the two factors were changing ethnic discourse in Ayacucho.

With the knowledge that Marco's workshop was a central node in the city's indigenous music scene, I proposed to apprentice with him, learning to make the chinlilis that he provided to chimaycha musicians. I was interested in the way that ideologies of indigenous sound are built into the instrument, but also in regular access to Marco's thoughts on other matters and in observing the daily interactions that enlivened his shop, a space that he had already billed to me as a center for the circulation of musical knowledge. I also resumed contact with Óscar Conde, who similarly spent many hours conversing with me, accompanied me on trips to Chuschi and Quispillaccta, and invited me to his group's rehearsals. Both men accompanied me to performances, and they put me in contact with other musicians, often attending interviews, where their reminiscences aided greatly in fostering conversation. I spent a great deal of time at Radio Quispillaccta, chimaycha's major organizing institution, where I had ample opportunity to watch broadcasts, converse with DJs and engineers, observe artists and fans who came by and the way that their interactions unfolded, and otherwise glean data about the way that the chimaycha scene was organized. Finally, I made a few short visits to Chuschi and Quispillaccta in the company of Marco or Óscar, in 2003 and during my 2013–14 fieldwork period, to speak with performers residing there. However, such visits were only days long, and my main research site site was the city of Ayacucho: data regarding practices in the rural towns is based on the memories of performers who lived there between the middle of the twentieth century and the present day. And while I interviewed dozens of artists, conversed informally with many more people who were not, and conducted hundreds of hours of participant observation, I returned again and again to Marco, Óscar, and Radio Quispillaccta.

This heavy reliance on a small number of interlocutors raises legitimate questions about the comprehensiveness of the claims that I make about the chimaycha scene. In truth "privileged informants," intimates who facilitate a researcher's knowledge production at the expense of others, have always weighed heavily in ethnographic work, though ethnomusicologists (and anthropologists) have rarely named them and even more rarely made them central foci in their texts. The reasons for this obfuscation are clear: as long as ethnographers believed themselves bound to "concentrate on what is 'typical' of a music culture without addressing . . . 'the personal, the idiosyncratic, [or] the exceptional'" (Stock 2001:7), their reliance on a few people could be taken only as a threat to the goal of cultural representativity. However, with culture itself having long been reconceptualized as an emergent, heterogeneous "mosaic of individual decisions, evaluations, actions and interactions" (Stock 2001:10), it no longer makes any sense to write as if individual experiences can stand in for a putative cultural type. Indeed it is dishonest to misstate the real scope of one's ethnographic experiences and the ways they have conditioned the ideas that a text holds up for a reader's consideration. It is even self-defeating, for a tight focus on a few individuals in fact presents a considerable analytic advantage. If the individuals are well placed in relation to the topic at hand, then a close working relationship allows a researcher an extraordinary opportunity to consult, debate, follow up, develop ideas across months and years of acquaintance—to engage, in short, in the coproduction of knowledge, which is the only morally sound way to conduct ethnographic work (Levin and Süzükei 2006).

Finally, this kind of focused attention hardly means that significant issues touching entire communities become deemphasized in favor of mere biography, for such significant issues register in any case only as repercussions in the lives of real people. Anthropologist Michael Herzfeld has made a similar point in justifying his decision to study the world-system of commodity production from the vantage point of a Cretan shoe workshop: there, he notes, "we will be hearing echoes of sources of authority that lie beyond the immediate confines of the workshop, but we will be hearing them with the ears of those who work there" (2004:26). Just so, my account registers Andean indigeneity and popular cultural development through a focus on two mentors and friends, claiming only to provide a window onto that topic through the experiences of them and their peers.[36]

None of the preceding paragraphs should be taken to mean that those interlocutors bear any blame for this text's failings. I, of course, assume the responsibility for all mistakes and interpretations that are presented herein. This caveat is essayed in full recognition that the text is not likely to please some of those invested in chimaycha music, indigenous discourse, and Ayacuchano society writ large. My position is like that of González, whose study was "not the romanticized representation of Sarhua for which some villagers and migrants have praised the Ayacuchan anthropologist Salvador Palomino [and which] contributed to an essentialized view of a harmonious Sarhua that since has fueled the identity politics of Sarhuino artists" (2011:18). Rather than simply repeat the similarly (strategic) essentialist claims that are essayed by many people involved with chimaycha, I have tried to represent the voices of those who believe in various conceptions of indigenous authenticity. Some conceptions, however, are in conflict with one another, and my presentation of different experiences as equally legitimate may be seen as pandering rather than evenhanded treatment. These claims are furthermore time-bound: given the rapidity with which popular culture moves, I doubt that the conditions described here will remain stable, and it will soon be possible to protest that they have changed. I do believe, however, that the processes described, whereby indigeneity is experienced as an evolving construct tacking between different social, political, and environmental realms, are permanent features of that identity and that any future analyses will profit from portraits of the past.

1

Setting a Scene

Most of the account that I develop over the course of this text pertains to the city of Ayacucho. However, some of it pertains instead to customs and practices that developed before the late twentieth century—the era of mass migration to that city—in Chuschi and Quispillaccta. Later musical events continue to respond to the social distinctions, political boundaries, and geophysical particularities that organized life in those communities. Thus this chapter provides a historical and geographic overview of the communities, of Chuschi District's relationship to the city of Ayacucho, and of certain events that undergird the developments traced in later chapters. Above all, perhaps, it underlines a key dynamic of Andean life, a contrast between the persistent disprivilege that indigenous communities have suffered and the vibrant sociopolitical dynamism that they have maintained in its face.

Chuschi and Quispillaccta: Geophysical and Social Topography

The southern part of Chuschi District is located within the valley of the Pampas River, while the northern section lies behind a mountain ridge, around the upper drainage of the Cachi River. The entire surrounding area, typically dubbed the Pampas Valley region, is renowned for the strength of indigenous custom and the Quechua language. That reputation led several scholars of the 1960s and 1970s to choose Pampas Valley communities for a pioneering series of anthropological and ethnohistorical investigations (Palomino 1971 and 1984; Quispe 1969; Zuidema 1966; Zuidema and Quispe 1968; see also Isbell and Barrios Micuylla 2016). Written at a time when Peruvian elites still viewed indigenous communities mainly as barriers to national development, these influential studies instead depicted Andean culture as a complex system worthy of respect. They are invaluable documents, and I quote frequently from those penned by anthropologist Billie Jean Isbell, who worked in Chuschi at that time and has worked with chuschinos ever since (1985; 1997; 1998; 2009; Isbell and Barrios Micuylla 2016).[1] However, by seeming to overstate the persistence of traits that dated back to pre-Columbian times (see especially Isbell 1985; Zuidema and Quispe 1968), these studies sometimes mischaracterized the region's cultural conservatism.[2] The towns of the Pampas region have never been isolated from outside forces. For centuries their residents have interacted with outsiders, adapting new practices that were thrust upon them, including Spanish political systems and the Catholic religion, as well as things that suited their needs like the stringed instruments, clothes, and crops of Iberian invaders. The region's vaunted traditionalism, then, should be seen as a practice of actively controlling the pace and direction of cultural change, rather than a protective isolationism.

This kind of traditionalism is a strong force in Chuschi District, but its indigenous communities are otherwise much like the others of the Peruvian Andes. They span an enormous altitudinal range, from the warm bottom of the Pampas River valley at about 8000 feet, where locals raise tender fruit trees, to freezing *puna* (high grasslands) between 12,000 and 14,000 feet, where they graze camelid herds beneath snowy peaks. Of course residents of these different zones do not inhabit a single conurbation. Rather, "indigenous communities" like Chuschi and Quispillaccta include many dispersed settlements situated at different altitudes and occupying distinct ecological niches. Called *barrios*, *pagos*, or *anexos*, these settlements are all governed from a *centro poblado* (populated center), the name of which serves as a synechdoche for the entire community.[3] Chuschi and Quispillaccta, situated at the middling altitude of about 10,000 feet, are examples of such community seats (see figures 3 and 4; for a map see figure 5 below). They house important businesses, political offices, religious sites, and transportation hubs, so members of all barrios make frequent trips there in order to conduct business. Much of the time, however, barrios function independently, under the guidance of local subofficials. Such quasi-independence is a necessity given the sheer distance and difficulty involved in travel. Some of Chuschi's barrios, for instance, are separated from its centro poblado by a journey of almost forty miles over steep, heavily broken terrain.

This dispersed settlement pattern is part of an old strategy dubbed "vertical ecology" by Andeanist scholar John Murra (1972). It ensures access to a diverse set of crops and animals, all suited to different climactic niches, which together provide a sustainable base for community subsistence. Here the seasons play a key role as well, because they drive the annual cycles of crop production

FIGURE 3. View across the Pampas Valley from within the community of Quispillaccta. Photograph by author.

FIGURE 4. José Tomaylla (left) and Óscar Conde (right) in the main plaza of Chuschi. The peak of Comañawi (also called Wamankiklla) is in the background. Photograph by author.

and herding. In the rainy season (roughly October–April), a fertile mosaic of greens replaces the drab browns and yellows of the dry-season landscape, and herd animals thrive amid new growth in the high puna. Until the 1980s and 1990s, when the communities' economic bases were altered by development work, herders spent those wet months in the district's high barrios, moving animals from site to site as they exhausted local fodder. Around the turn to the dry season, cows and sheep were driven to low areas, and eventually to the district's lowest corn-growing reaches after July, when the harvest was complete and animals feasted on leftover stalks. There they remained until after the plowing period in September and October, at which point the animals were once more driven to the puna to await the rains. This process has been rendered obsolete by new agropastoral techniques as well as land enclosure in the puna, and no more than a few families still practice it. However, it was once central to social life, for it helped to structure the annual cycle of vida michiy celebrations, and it therefore lives in the memory of older chuschinos and quispillacctinos as a central factor in musical production.

This verticality is also conjoined with various kinds of social relationships, two of which feature in this book. First, it is very common for a resident of one barrio to contract marriage with a partner from another. Such alliances give families access to plots of land in different niches, with all the increased productivity that results from it. They are also expedient since a typical barrio, housing only a few hundred residents at most, may contain no marriageable age-mates outside one's own family circle. Historically, much of teen life was devoted to the search for a partner in another barrio—and chimaycha played a central role in that search.

A second important relationship that is conjoined with Andean verticality is an opposition between high-altitude herders and low-altitude farmers. This binary is widely reported in studies of Andean society, and it bears strong characterological associations. Valley dwellers typically regard the pastoral people of the high, cold puna as wild and primitive and their own temperate agricultural settlements by contrast as local centers of civilization.[4] Binary oppositions like these are omnipresent in indigenous Andean communities, but quispillacctinos described theirs in especially strong terms. The community functioned as a political unit and presented a united face toward the outside world, but internally there was a recognized division between, on one hand, the barrios of Cerce, Huerta Huasi, Llaccta Urán, Pirhuamarca, Socubamba, Tuco, Yurac Cruz, and the centro poblado of Quispillaccta, all situated on the jagged slope that rises from the Pampas River; and on the other, the higher, colder barrios of Unión Potrero, Puncupata, Catalinayocc, Pampamarca, and Cuchoquesera, all of which lay beyond the peak of that slope, strewn among the grasslands of the Cachi basin. The rivalry between the two factions came alive in musical competition, and it became especially marked during dry-season festivities, when adolescent quispillacctinos departed for the vida michiy from named base camps associated with different factions—a site called Amayni, in the case of the Pampas-side barrios, and one called Pukawasi, in the case of the Cachi-side barrios.[5] However, the rivalry was more than a musical matter. Sometimes fierce and deeply felt, it could erupt into violence, and it had even given rise to a sort of ethnic slur used by the residents of the Pampas side to name those of the Cachi basin: they called them *qipakuna* (the ones behind [the mountain peak]), as if to underscore their geophysical separation from the community's dominant centro poblado.[6]

Between 2013 and 2017 Quispillaccta was stretched to the breaking point as the increasingly powerful Cachi-side moiety sought to secede, a move that Peruvian law had recently made possible. I return to that project in chapter 5 because it is related to chimaycha's transformation into an emblem of indigenous politics. I raise it here because it demonstrates how indigenous peoples have always accommodated emergent political systems, bending them to their advantage when possible. After the European invasion of the sixteenth century, for instance, Andean communities were placed under the tutelary vassalage of Spanish settlers, who typically lived nearby in planned communities.[7] The colonial state created a bipartite structure of governance through which settlers and indigenous subjects chose different slates of community authorities, each responsible for overseeing their respective peoples. The duties of indigenous officials, called *varayuqs* (staff-bearers) after the ceremonial staffs that marked their office, revolved around the orderly functioning of the indigenous community, and they remained subject to Spanish and mestizo administrators. However, the system allowed them a measure of representation, and as Andean customs and mores changed the varayuqs enforced adherence to evolving community norms. By the twenty-first century, this indigenous authority system was viewed as anything but a Spanish imposition. Rather, in those rare cases where it had been maintained it was viewed as an index of indigenous traditionalism—nowhere more so than in Chuschi and Quispillaccta.[8]

This is not to minimize the severity of colonial domination. Indigenous peoples owed ruinous taxes to the Spanish crown. Delinquent communities were penalized, partly though the forfeiture of land, and community holdings steadily passed into nonindigenous hands. Spanish administrators, blessed with literacy and versed in administrative chicanery, also used their power to procure territory, wealth, and sex. They consolidated *hacienda* estates staffed by dispossessed Indian peons, created commercial dynasties, and founded

36   CHAPTER ONE

family lines of mestizo descendants. After Peruvian independence, mestizo landlords and politicians used the bureaucratic chaos of the nineteenth century to snatch ever-greater swaths of indigenous territory. Governorships, prefectures, judgeships, mayoralties, and other state positions that came with significant power continued to be filled by well-connected mestizos rather than disenfranchised Indians, largely excluded from access to education and hence lacking the means to assert their rights. By the twentieth century indigenous communities lived in a shocking state of indigence and subjection.

The impact of these events was not homogeneous across the Andean region. Rugged and steep, most of the terrain in the Department of Ayacucho was capable of supporting only small agricultural plots.[9] Large-scale haciendas were therefore few in number. The Pampas Valley was furthermore far from Ayacucho City, the local center of cosmopolitan society. The centros poblados of Chuschi and Quispillaccta, for example, lie some sixty winding miles from the city—a journey of three hours or more on today's mix of paved and gravel roads, and much more in the years before a road connected them to the departmental capital in 1961 or 1962. Somewhat isolated and land-poor, places like Chuschi District saw little Spanish settlement, and they maintained relative territorial and cultural integrity over the long term. Even so, the preceding sketch of interethnic dynamics fits Chuschi District up to the moment that Isbell and her colleagues arrived to do research in the 1960s—the period from which this book departs, and which is therefore useful to summarize.

Quispillaccta had been officially recognized as an indigenous community on August 24, 1935, and Chuschi on May 27, 1941, but conditions remained neocolonial in both communities. Chuschi was a district capital dating from early colonial days. It housed a tiny mestizo population who rotated key governmental positions among themselves, and they had the power to abuse indigenous subalterns with impunity. They secured consent by occasionally defending the interests of the indigenous majority, but all were regarded as perennial outsiders, settlers who defined themselves as mestizos first and only secondarily as chuschinos.[10] Writing in the 1970s, Isbell captured the difference from the perspective of the 85–90 percent of chuschinos who called themselves *comuneros*, holders of title to Chuschi's collective goods and rights by virtue of membership in the indigenous community: "The comuneros . . . participate in the [varayuq system], wear traditional dress, and speak Quechua; versus the *vecinos* [Sp. neighbors"], or *qalas* (literally, peeled or naked ones), who are Spanish speaking, western dressed, foreign nonparticipants in communal life" (1985:67).[11] Strangely attired and antisocial people, qala shopkeepers, health workers, agronomists, schoolteachers, priests, and their kin mostly

SETTING A SCENE

declined to participate in the customary rites, collective labors, and reciprocal obligations that defined the lives of indigenous peasants.[12]

The comuneros of Quispillaccta viewed Chuschi's qalas even more negatively, a view that was colored by community rivalry.[13] A poorer and more homogeneously indigenous community for most of its history, Quispillaccta is next to Chuschi. Their centros poblados are on opposite banks of the tiny Chuschi River, their main plazas are only a few hundred feet apart, and residents of the two communities have intermarried since time immemorial. Nevertheless, due in part to long-standing boundary disputes and in part to an imbalance between the shrinking district capital and the growing community of Quispillaccta, the two have long had a tense relationship. A recent history of Quispillaccta penned by indigenous comuneros even attributes the conflict's roots to pre-Columbian times, noting that the two communities descend from rival ethnic groups settled in the Pampas basin by earlier Inca rulers. Possibly spurious, the attribution nevertheless underlines the popular understanding of the community rivalry as ancient, intractable, and quasi-ethnic in nature.[14]

Statistics gathered in 1961, just as a gravel road to Ayacucho was being completed, testify to the district's grinding poverty. It was overwhelmingly young, with almost half of residents under the age of seventeen. Educational attainment was extremely low: under 10 percent of Chuschi's residents were literate, only 26 percent had received any schooling, and fewer than 50 percent spoke Spanish. Quispillaccta's numbers were far lower. These statistics in turn explain the high contemporaneous levels of outmigration. Chuschi's centro poblado had shrunk from 1,310 to 1,099 residents between 1940 and 1961, a period when the overall population of Ayacucho Department had grown by 15 percent. Chuschinos and quispillacctinos were already heading in large numbers to Ayacucho and Lima, seeking jobs for themselves and schooling for their children.

Brute statistics and ethnic generalizations hide the variation that existed within these communities. Certain indigenous households, for example, were regarded as prosperous, their wealth measured by ownership of agricultural plots and herds, which grazed in the communal pastures of the puna (Isbell 1985:200). Several comuneros had become merchants, and by 1967 eighty-one district residents supplemented subsistence farming by carrying on a specialized trade (La Serna 2012a:4). Another kind of prominence came from service in the indigenous authority system. Offices rotated, such that every male adult might act as a varayuq at some point in his life, but some men took on more offices than others, moving farther up the hierarchy and accruing greater respect for doing so.

In the end, however, power and progress depended upon access to literacy and education. In 1959 the Peruvian government reopened the Universidad Nacional San Cristóbal de Huamanga (UNSCH), a university in Ayacucho City that had been closed for nearly eighty years, during which the department had lacked any institution of higher education. The reopening was intended to stimulate prosperity in Peru's poorest region, and its centerpiece was a teaching college, charged with sending grade-school instructors across the department, where they would provide social uplift in new rural schools. Nine years later Chuschi District hosted nine primary schools and one secondary school. Enrollments were very low, especially for girls, but in 1970 Isbell recorded forty-nine students in Chuschi's secondary school. Remarkably, 40 percent of them were between the ages of 24 and 40, while another 50 percent were between 15 and 23—testament to a fierce adult-level thirst for the tools that might ensure social advantage in a lettered society (Isbell 1985:68–69).

The reopening of the UNSCH brought other kinds of progressive interventions as well. Some of its offices partnered with foreign universities or NGOs to pursue development projects, one of which had transformative effects in Quispillaccta. It was a partnership between a Swiss agronomic organization called COTESU and the UNSCH's Centro de Capacitación Campesina (Center for Peasant Development, or CCC), devoted to developing livestock management practices in Ayacucho's puna (Múñoz Ruiz and Núñez Espinoza 2006:77). Aimed at improving husbandry, stock, feed, forage, and irrigation, the project had already targeted several different communities by the time it reached Quispillaccta in 1982, where it focused on managing the town's communal herds (Múñoz Ruiz and Núñez Espinoza 2006:46). When it withdrew in 1986, it left behind new canals, prized Brown Swiss cattle, improved pastures, and the knowledge required to augment the precious animal resources of one of the region's poorest communities.

This was in fact a development of major consequence for Chuschi District and for chimaycha music. As will be detailed in chapter 4, the CCC's work extended beyond agronomy to support for Quechua-language radio and the promotion of cultural traditions, and musicians from Chuschi and Quispillacta were key beneficiaries. Perhaps more important, the project focused on the high, Cachi-side barrios where Quispillaccta's livestock was pastured, empowering them at the expense of the other, historically dominant side of the community and of Chuschi itself. No barrio benefited more than Unión Potrero, from which a new group of indigenous leaders would emerge in the 1990s, armed with university education and the desire to change Ayacucho's politics of indigeneity. When they founded Radio Quispillaccta to further their cause (see chapter 5), they transformed chimaycha music, remade indig-

SETTING A SCENE

enous discourse, and brought the two together. Indeed, much as Ayacucho's indigenous communities adapted new political tools in order to defend their collectively determined interests, they took up new technologies in order to support traditions they deemed worthy of "defending"—a word cited in the title of Isbell's 1985 book and one that I too have heard countless times from the lips of chuschinos and quispillacctinos.

This is not to say that such promotion was painless or uncontested, for it might involve significant adaptation and cultural change. A generational conflict, spurred in part by hopes for the social advancement linked to metropolitan education, and a consequent turn away from indigenous systems of authority, may have helped pave the way for Shining Path's recruitment of indigenous comuneros over the 1960s and 1970s (La Serna 2012a).[15] Here the District of Chuschi was especially central, for it was not only at the center of the conflict: it was the site of its first formal action.

The Impact of the Shining Path

The Shining Path guerrillas came together at the UNSCH. The group's leaders were professors there, and its initial cadre was drawn from the student body. Over the 1960s and 1970s, they created a program of theory and action by combining elements from Marxism-Leninism, Maoism, and the writings of José Carlos Mariátegui, founder of the Peruvian Communist Party. Stated very briefly, Shining Path doctrine characterized Peruvian society as feudal and advocated the creation of an egalitarian state inspired by the putative communism of pre-Columbian peoples. It taught that a revolution could be achieved by leading Andean peasants into frightening and bloody action against the state, coercing a panicked government into violent overreaction against indigenous communities, and thereby driving more villagers to join Shining Path ranks in search of protection. Officially the group dismissed ethnicity and cultural difference as bourgeois tools for mystifying exploitative labor relations, and despite initial reports it was no "indigenous movement."[16] Its leaders did, however, believe that oppressed Indians possessed a prerevolutionary consciousness, and they planned to stage their uprising from Quechua-speaking communities. Seizing control of the UNSCH's teaching college, its leaders indoctrinated budding schoolteachers and scattered them across the countryside, where they taught revolutionary doctrine to talented indigenous youths.

Shining Path-affiliated teachers began arriving in Chuschi by the late 1960s, increasing in number over the 1970s as the school system expanded (Gorriti Ellenbogen 1999). This happened in other communities too, but it was Chuschi that the party chose as the site of its first military action, meaning that the community has become indelibly associated with the conflict that followed. On May 17, 1980, on the eve of the country's first democratic elections in seventeen years, guerrillas destroyed Chuschi's ballot boxes. The act seemed puzzling and eccentric, since few observers had yet taken seriously the harangues of communist intellectuals in faraway Andean villages. It was followed, however, by increasingly sophisticated attacks on state installations, the seizure of rural towns, and the torture or murder of individuals deemed enemies of the people—businessmen, bureaucrats, and mestizo elites, who were often punished in an effort to gain the goodwill of the indigenous comuneros that guerrillas meant to recruit. After years of perplexed half-measures, the state finally responded in force in 1983, sending military units and paramilitary forces into rural Andean communities, where, as predicted, they trained their fire on innocent villagers and guerrillas alike, massacring indigenous peoples and students in the mistaken belief that they faced a mass indigenous uprising rather than a limited revolt sponsored by white intellectuals.

The conflict expanded rapidly across the Andes, encompassing half of the national territory. By the time it subsided in the mid-1990s, an estimated 70,000 Peruvians had been killed or disappeared, most of them Quechua-speaking peasants. In Chuschi and Quispillaccta, the conflict's early years were the most severe.[17] On July 1, 1982, after years of sporadic recruitment and some executions of cattle rustlers, a Shining Path column invaded Chuschi, summoned residents to the central plaza, and declared the community to be a liberated zone under their control. They proceeded to show trials, punishing but not killing the district governor Bernardo Chipana, vice mayor Francisco Vilca, and local authority Ranulfo Infanzón, a mestizo teacher who played a key role in chimaycha's development (Sánchez Villagómez 2009:89).[18] The next year the Peruvian military established a base in Chuschi, and the violence escalated considerably. The soldiers demanded the names of Shining Path sympathizers and other information about the guerrillas, leading to denunciations and to the routine disappearance of comuneros innocent and guilty alike. Quispillacta became especially stigmatized as a collaborationist community, and by 1985, 141 villagers had been seized, with 23 killed and 50 disappeared. Chuschi, by contrast, saw 46 villagers arrested, with 9 killed and 6 disappeared over the same period.

The district remained under military occupation for a decade, and the violence never abated entirely during that period. People were disappeared as late as the early 1990s, while surivivors lived in an atmosphere of dread, their movements and freedoms severely curtailed. Nocturnal travel, for instance, posed the risk of an encounter with military patrols or Shining Path columns, both inclined to disappear anyone who appeared to be an enemy collabora-

SETTING A SCENE   41

tor. Even so, after an initial period of intensified outmigration as villagers fled
the countryside for the relative safety of Lima and Ayacucho, populations
stabilized. Those who stayed led diminished lives, their everyday routines and
festive customs attenuated by the inability to socialize freely. Still, they farmed
fields and raised children under the cloud of war, keeping communities alive
and establishing a foundation for postwar recovery. Returnees began to swell
Quispillaccta's population as early as 1986 (Flórez Salcedo 2012:234), presag-
ing the official resettlement projects that would bring other peasants back
once the violence ended in the 1990s, as well as other developments that would
spur the community's protagonism in years to come.

The Growing Power of Quispillaccta

One striking effect of the violence was to spur indigenous communities to
greater political engagement, as they sought internal means to defend against
malevolent state and guerrilla forces. Quispillaccta, historic underdog to
neighboring Chuschi, emerged from the violence as a leading political actor,
a development that was partly related to demographics. As Chuschi shrank
over the twentieth century, Quispillaccta grew, becoming the most populous
community in Chuschi District by 1940 (Múñoz Ruiz and Núñez Espinoza
2006:88–89). In 2001 the district's strategic plan, developed by its elected leaders, reported that Quispillaccta had 3,975 residents to Chuschi's 1,656, with a
total district population of 8,281 (the balance resided in the district's remaining communities of Uchuyri, Cancha Cancha, and Chacolla; Flórez Salcedo
2012:241). A second reason has to do with a "rural urbanization" process that
Quispillaccta experienced over the late twentieth century, and increasingly
after the arrival of CCC projects in the 1980s. Barrios in the high Cachi basin actually became more prosperous during the violence. They were already
somewhat wealthy in local terms, due to their proximity to pasturelands for
the herd animals that function as investment assets in Andean communities.
Now, however, they acquired services and amenities formerly reserved for the
larger towns where their residents might otherwise have moved, including
health posts, schools, and improved fields. They even acquired a municipal
building like the one in Quispillaccta's official centro poblado—a sign of quasi-
independence that might have augured the Cachi-side barrios' later drive for
secession.[19]

A third factor and the most important of all was university education,
which gave quispillacctinos tools that they turned to brilliant advantage over
the 1990s and 2000s. By the 1980s, after a generation of improvements in rural
education, indigenous students began to enter the UNSCH. Unusually, in a

region where a university education was usually followed by a permanent move to the city, some quispillacctino graduates brought their new talents and ideas back to their community. They executed agronomic projects and repopulation initiatives, consolidating the community's economic base. They also started cultural projects, drawing on indigenous rights discourse gleaned through their schooling to vindicate customs and practices that had been threatened by the violence and by metropolitan prejudice. Above all, they created a powerful NGO to channel such efforts, an institution that acted as an interlocutor with state and nonstate agencies and that also provided various kinds of training for community residents. Dubbed the Asociación Bartolomé Aripaylla, or ABA, after a colonial-era leader, it was founded and staffed by Cachi-side comuneros, and its activities are discussed extensively in chapter 5, since its role in popularizing and resignifying chimaycha music can hardly be overstated.

By 1998 Quispillaccta's communal assembly was working to throw the community's votes behind quispillacctino candidates for mayor of Chuschi District, a position that had always rotated among Chuschi's mestizos, and quispillacctino Teófilo Achallma was elected to that office in 2010 (Flórez Salcedo 2012). ABA played a significant role, coordinating community efforts in tandem with Quispillaccta's varayuqs—that is, with officers of the newly revived indigenous authority system, which had been lost and then reconstituted in the postviolence period, with ABA's aid and urging. Over this same era Quispillaccta saw an increase in such acts of cultural affirmation, typically sponsored by community authorities in conjunction with ABA, an institution that in turn worked increasingly closely with the funders and political entities that guided international indigenous politics. By 2012 quispillacctinos routinely occupied important political offices, and with ABA's guidance they had even initiated a process of secession, aiming to carve out a new and unprecedented sort of district, one to be governed by strict indigenous custom. They had, in short, remade the district's politics, its ethnic discourses, and the local meanings of indigeneity itself, largely by drawing principles and methods from the global indigenous movement.

These developments paralleled things that were happening across Andean Peru in the wake of the violence. The Peruvian government decentralized governance while communities rebuilt themselves, and local actors often channeled long-standing demands for respect and self-determination via new languages culled from global indigenous politics, often with the mediation of local authorities and NGOs. Describing an artisans' collective-cum-NGO in Sarhua, across the Pampas River from Chuschi, González states that their "concerns about an increasingly deritualized Sarhua had given them the impetus to embody in their earlier artwork the traditions that they claimed were

SETTING A SCENE   43

threatened by oblivion and essential to Sarhuino identity" (2011:7). Elsewhere, Salomon notes that peasants in the Andean community of Tupicocha were researching elements of their history and culture, creating new interpretations of what it meant to be an indigenous tupicochano to counter ideas from outside the community. Insofar as this newly "entrepreneurial" approach to indigenous cultural experience arose from dialogue with outside agencies, it bore "a marked 'local/global' publicity dimension, as NGOs become interlocutors in the spectacle of legitimation" (Salomon 2002:52–53).

ABA's efforts to restore the primacy of Quispillaccta's varayuq authorities, promote rituals, recover lost Andean agronomic techniques, and, critically for my purposes, support traditional music, all amounted to similarly effective forms of "vernacular statecraft" (Colloredo-Mansfeld 2009)—politics carried out in parapolitical arenas. Tellingly, however, the agency was not headquartered in Quispillaccta but in the city of Ayacucho, the department's hub for communications, commerce, and political activity—and so too was Radio Quispillaccta, the station that had been established under its auspices. After all, despite postviolence recovery and economic progress in communities like Quispillaccta, the Department of Ayacucho remained highly underdeveloped. In 2008, 64.8 percent of the population lived beneath Peru's official poverty threshold, with 30.7 percent in conditions of extreme poverty. Forty-two percent of the population lived in rural areas; 85 percent of that group was composed of Quechua-speaking peasants, and although most were bilingual, only 73 percent were literate (Crisóstomo Meza 2012:7). In the District of Chuschi levels of Quechua monolingualism were higher, and despite development its power grid remained unreliable, its telecommunications feeble. It could hardly serve as a hub for the kind of work that is involved in running a transnational NGO or dealing with state administrators. The city of Ayacucho, in short, was a significant locus of community development and community life for Quispillaccta and Chuschi alike. In fact, this had long been the case.

The Country and the City: Lines of Indistinction

A full generation ago, it was already possible for an Andean ethnographer to note that "it has become increasingly difficult to apply the terms peasant, proletarian, migrant, or cash-cropping small farmer to rural dwellers. A single individual may occupy all of these roles in the course of a lifetime" (Collins 1986:655). Indeed rural outmigrants, organized into official community associations, have been involved with the business of their Andean home communities since the 1940s. Many make regular, often season-long visits to their home communities, and their urban associations have always provided material aid, support for administrative business, and other services that are hard to access from remote, impoverished Andean towns. Chuschinos in Lima established their first migrants' association, the Progressive Society of Santa Rosa of Lima, in 1941. Designed "to promote and safeguard the welfare of the village" (Isbell 1985:181), it immediately oversaw the process of getting Chuschi designated an official indigenous community. It later continued to monitor the community's legal and economic interests and to raise funds for village amenities, and by the 1970s some migrants even served as community authorities, performing their duties from afar.[20] Other chuschinos founded a comparable association much later in Ayacucho, reflecting the fact that Lima was at first the preferred destination for migrants. Quispillaccta underwent a similar process, and by the turn of the millennium its Ayacucho-based association, founded in 1970 and named the Centro Progreso, worked closely with ABA in the development of their home community. Such fluidity challenges the image of rural isolation that can easily accrue to descriptions of the Peruvian Andes. With their residents in regular motion, circulating between rural-indigenous and urban-mestizo milieus, transacting different kinds of business with village authorities and state interlocutors, farming when required and working in the city during agricultural downtime, indigenous communities like Chuschi and Quispillaccta have been translocal organizations for many decades.

Such dynamism hardly means that migrants themselves were well received in urban areas or that their omnicultural status led Peruvian power holders to treat them as equals. For most of the twentieth century, Andean migrants were socially excluded in metropolitan centers of mestizo power like Lima and Ayacucho, even as their numbers swelled. Demeaned due to their indigenous heritage, they were mostly limited to menial jobs or to work in Peru's vast gray marketplace. Usually incapable of purchasing adequate housing, and unwanted in the respectable precincts of mestizo society, they were pushed to the literal margins, living on the ever-expanding edges of Peru's cities, where access to water, sewage, power, and transportation was precarious. They brought their cultural traditions to the cities with them and found means to carry them on, sites and media through which to communicate with one another about their homes and about the changes they were experiencing over generations. However, the dominant channels of Peruvian society remained closed to them, focused instead on Peru's criollo elite or on the Euro-American cultural manifestations that criollos consumed with equal avidity. This situation began to change only toward the end of the twentieth century, once Lima's migrant community had become too numerous and powerful to marginalize and its culture moved to the center of an emergent cholo national imaginary.

Most accounts of this national project have focused understandably on

SETTING A SCENE 45

Lima. The city holds a full third of Peru's population, and it has historically been the driver of economic development and social discourse in this heavily centralized society. The events that I relate in this book, however, are centered in Ayacucho, a regional capital and a very different place, even if the fundamentals of its power relations are largely commensurate with those of Lima. Founded in 1540 as Huamanga, a name that is still used by locals to denote the city, Ayacucho was given its current name after Peruvian independence in 1824. It served as a provincial administrative center under Spanish colonialism and as the capital of the Department of Ayacucho afterward. Indigenous peoples resided in its outlying neighborhoods for centuries, acting as maids and laborers in the houses of its elite. Nevertheless, the barrier between urban mestizo and rural indigenous societies was strong, and Ayacucho's dominant community maintained an unusually fervent sense of identification with Spanish roots and Peruvian criollo society.

So strong was this self-image that intellectuals writing in Ayacucho during the heyday of indigenismo specifically disavowed the focus on rural indigeneity that animated the movement. Instead they carried out projects centered on the mestizo identity of their urban area and prioritized the city in their plans for the region's development. Members of this intellectual community agitated for the reopening of the UNSCH between the 1930s and the 1950s, pitching the idea as a means to revitalize the blasted regional economy, which had last thrived in the eighteenth century. It is therefore no surprise that the university's initial years saw little material change in intercommunity power dynamics between urban mestizo and rural indigenous societies. The institution had an electric effect on the city, prompting an influx of hip intellectuals whose social mores and sartorial habits challenged the ingrained conservatism of what had been for centuries an isolated and insular city of landowners, artisans, and petty merchants. However, despite the focus on rural development that drove faculty initiatives in education, anthropology, agronomy, and allied departments, social legitimacy within the city for rural residents continued to depend on the abandonment of indigenous customs and habits. Rural students were expected to adopt urban norms and promote them among their fellows.

The result is that rural migrants, who began to arrive in significant numbers over the 1960s and 1970s, still experienced the city as a deeply hostile territory. Forced to live on its outskirts, excluded from polite society, and demeaned for maintaining customs from their home communities, they faced daily prejudice in a city that fought to maintain its mestizo character. Their position worsened over the 1980s and 1990s, when indigenous communities became stigmatized as guerrillas as well as primitives. Those same decades, however, saw both the first inklings of indigenous political advocacy and a demographic turning point like the one that was reached in Lima. Ayacucho had been a mestizo-run midsized regional capital of 72,000 in 1972 (Caballero Martín 1995), but by 2014 it held 177,000 residents, most of whom traced their roots to rural-indigenous communities. Over that period, the urban migrant population became too large, too economically important, and too rich in educational and political resources to fully exclude. As in the national capital, the 2000s and 2010s saw indigenous cultural traditions, as well as new manifestations created among migrant communities, emerge from the marginal places where their adepts had been forced to practice them. They took over large swaths of the city's public sphere, making clear that it was no longer a staid bastion of its mestizo elite. Most important, by making the city safe for new expressions of indigenous culture and new discourses of indigenous politics, they created new channels for indigenous peoples to converse about the changing parameters of indigenous experience.

It was in this environment that chimaycha became an emblem of indigenous affirmation, and its scene a crucible for forging new discourses and experiences of indigeneity. Musicians and mediators from the Pampas Valley grew up in an age when the boundaries between city and countryside, mestizo and indigenous cultural realms, were more permeable than ever. Improvements in the road connecting Ayacucho to Chuschi District meant that travel was easier, and chuschinos and quispillacctinos grew up moving easily between the two contexts. This was a fertile environment for the emergence of an urban indigenous cultural formation that drew upon but did not precisely resemble that of their forebears, and for its contemporaneous adoption in the rural area. Meanwhile the mood of political affirmation that was promoted by organizations like ABA made conformity to rural-indigenous rather than urban-mestizo standards into a marker of savvy, overturning a half millennium of metropolitan cultural pressure.

Finally, as noted in the introduction, the city's changing economy provided another element that supported the growth of a new music scene. The postviolence period saw little serious investment in remedying Ayacucho's poverty, despite state rhetoric to the contrary. However, as often happens in the postguerrilla regions of Latin America, Ayacucho became a major center of cocaine production, with erstwhile Shining Path soldiers serving as enforcers or captains within a new trade centered in the department's jungle region. As the city of Ayacucho became a major transshipment point and home to many of those who ran the trade, petty cash flowed into the pockets of the peasants and migrants who worked at the industry's lowest levels. That money was often spent on weekend entertainment, and chimaycha musicians were among the beneficiaries. Most of those musicians relied, in turn, on instruments built by Marco Tucno, instruments whose design grew from his deep roots in Chuschi's music and in the vida michiy. It is with those experiences that I begin my account of chimaycha and its relation to changing varieties of Andean indigeneity.

2

Landscape, Performance, and Social Structure

> Ordinary talk . . . is usually just a beginning. . . . Represented and enacted—daily, monthly, seasonally, annually—places and their meanings are continually woven into the fabric of social life, anchoring it to features of the landscape and blanketing it with layers of significance.
>
> TUAN 1974:56–57

For generations chimaycha has been the all-purpose music of Chuschi district, as likely to enliven the communal *yarqa aspiy* (annual canal-cleaning ceremony) as a chance meeting between teenage pastoralists following their herds. People who grew up in an era before chimaycha's commodification, however, associate it mainly with the vida michiy. Celebrated in semi-clandestine fashion, safe from the ostensible disapproval of parents, the vida michiy was a sort of nocturnal party. It brought young men and women together to drink, dance, fight, make music, and above all court members of the opposite sex, mainly through musical, physical, and verbal competition. Many middle-aged chuschinos remember the adolescent years when they practiced the vida michiy as the best of their lives, a time when a relative lack of responsibility gave them leeway to pursue its pleasures. However, the vida michiy should be regarded as more than a party and its songs as more than vehicles for romance. They drew meaning from and gave sense to the landscape, environmental cycles, and natural elements with which participants were entangled. Courtship was a key element of this web: stable marriages were, after all, the vehicle for the community's social and physical continuity. However, human reproduction was only one thread in the ecological tapestry that governed village life. Indeed, although *vida michiy* can be translated literally from Quechua as "the pasturing of life," it has typically been glossed to me (in Spanish) as either "to enjoy life" (*gozar la vida*) or "to make/do life" (*hacer la vida*)— translations that gesture toward hedonism but also toward the conduct of a proper existence.

My thin familiarity with the district's geography, and with the conditions of Andean transhumance, meant that my understanding of the vida michiy came in fits and starts (see figure 5). Most flashes of insight came while working alongside Marco Tucno in his instrument workshop and listening to reminiscences about his youth, but one interaction stands out for its particular clarity. As we sat on stools just outside the shop in late 2013, he told me how he and his peers helped girls steal away from their homes in the night some thirty years before, befriending the family dog so that their arrival raised no alarm. This left them free to head for one of the many sites where Marco customarily met his companions, round patches of trampled grass called *lazas*, which were scattered throughout the district's high reaches.[1] Imagining the rough terrain and the sheer distance that separated Chuschi's temperate town core from the barren heights, I asked if it wasn't a long and tiring journey. Marco frowned in puzzlement and then said, "No no, I'm not talking at all about the main town." Picking a wooden shiv from the scraps at hand, he began to scratch in the dirt, incorporating the yard's bumps and hollows into a relief map of Chuschi proper and its outlying settlements.

"Look," he said, "here's the main town," tracing a circle and then a line northward, toward the crest of the mountain slope that rises from the Pampas River. "That's the path that leads up toward the puna. Over here is Sullkaray-pata," he continued, naming a propitious vida michiy site near the town of Chuschi and drawing a side trail to end in a tiny circle. He then extended the main path farther north, curving around a lump of earth to show how the real route skirted a small peak, going over the ridgetop to the puna beyond. Here behind the watershed that divides the district, waters flowed north toward the Cachi River, not south toward the Pampas, through a region of rolling puna called Chicllarasu. Making a westerly depression into Lake Yanaccocha, one source of the Cachi itself, he added several lines radiating outward from the main branch, indicating that they led to Chuschi's high puna barrios. One of them was Pucruhuasi, where his family kept their large bovine and camelid herds during the rainy months, when Chicllarasu's grasses turned green and provided rich fodder for grazing.

What he wanted me to understand was that it was here, in the community's high reaches, that conditions were most propitious for the vida michiy. Back then places like Pucruhuasi were not "town-shaped towns, with blocks and such," but scattered compounds of houses, animal pens, and *chuqllas*, small outbuildings near the corrals. Young people often slept in those chuqllas during the rainy season, when they were charged with pasturing livestock—especially girls, who were more typically kept from school for the purpose.[2] In the puna, then, parents were physically separated from their daughters, who might more easily sneak away to dance and sing—the only catch being that they had to return by four in the morning, when they would surely be required to cook breakfast and start the workday.

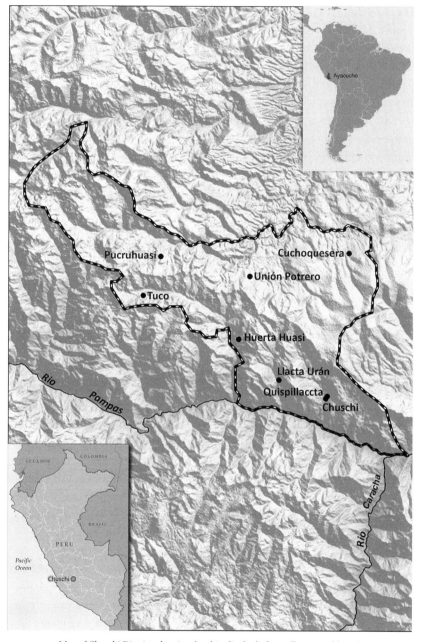

FIGURE 5. Map of Chuschi District, showing the altitudinal relief as well as several key sites.

Sentient Ecology, Social Structure, and Environmental Registers of Indigeneity

At the time I barely grasped the significance of Marco's map, but our conversation showed me how thoroughly his experience of chimaycha had been tied to seasonal change, climatic stratification by altitude, and the needs of the animals upon which villagers depended.[3] It has been noted elsewhere that Andean music and storytelling are means through which performers ground aspects of human history and organization in community lands.[4] However, if Andean ritual performance is "a practice for embodying community identity, inscribing it on earthly landscapes as well as in the landscapes of the mind" (Solomon 2000:258), then Marco's words suggested that landscapes themselves are made and partitioned in and through musical performances and parallel acts.[5] Moving along and between ecological boundaries, performers organize environmental perception, giving cultural and political significance to major geophysical distinctions and weaving them into the social.[6] Marco and his fellows retraced those paths in their musical narratives, intertwining ecology, affect, and sociopolitical topography in order to fill the district's places with sonorous significance. Stories of musical activity helped to reify various kinds of nonmusical distinctions, such that social, natural, and sonorous processes came to stand as cognate expressions of the same underlying relationships. Understanding the chimaycha of their era, then, means teasing out a distinctive acoustemology linking sound and youth, landscape and livestock, human life cycles and annual seasonal cycles. The existence of this distinctive acoustemology, in turn, lends weight to the notion that sound can be meaningfully linked to a variety of indigeneity that does not escape but holds at a distance the expectations which govern nonindigenous life and musical practice.

Leaving the sonorous and lyrical aesthetics of this system for the following chapter, which focuses on chimaycha music, here I describe instead the parameters of the vida michiy as it was practiced in the late 1970s and 1980s, focusing especially on two key features that organized Marco's map. The first is the way that performance occasions were determined by cycles of transhumance. The second relates to social oppositions between settlements within the District of Chuschi. Intercommunity animosity between Chuschi and Quispillaccta sometimes affected events at the vida michiy, as it did other elements of the district's daily life. Intracommunity distinctions, between Pampas basin barrios and Cachi basin barrios, appear by contrast to have been a central facet of Quispillaccta's vida michiy. They were viscerally manifested when quispillacctino youths from the Cachi side dueled with those from the

Pampas side, seeking to best their rivals with lutes, fists, and words of warning. However, even in Chuschi a basic distinction was recognized between the high, "wild" region of the puna on the Cachi side of the district and the low, civilized zone on the Pampas side, where Chuschi proper was located. In short, the vida michiy mapped and helped to make tangible the intertwined social, geophysical, and ecological relationships that organized the lives of Chuschi District's indigenous peoples.

Over the late 1980s and 1990s, delicate dairy and wool-bearing breeds replaced hardy transhumant herds, Chicllarasu's hamlets grew into proper towns, and their residents enclosed communal grazing lands with electric fences. And so the account I present here captures the texture of musical life in an earlier age, one governed by an ecological rationality that has withered for most contemporary listeners. I draw heavily on the memories of Marco Tucno and Óscar Conde, and not only because they are widely admired as performers. Both men described the vida michiy to me in ways that were bound to season and to animal husbandry, and both emphasized its ties to intercommunity and intracommunity rivalry. Furthermore, their experiences are almost perfectly complementary, together spanning the district's musical life over a period extending from the late 1960s to the mid-1990s. For roughly the first half of this period, Marco lived in the town of Chuschi. His move to Ayacucho in 1982 or 1983 coincided almost precisely with Óscar's arrival in Quispillaccta, where the young return migrant became one of the community's dominant musicians despite having passed his early childhood in Lima.

It is, of course, risky to generalize from their observations to characterize Chuschi District en masse, and I do not mean to do so—though it should be noted that the earliest available field recordings, broadcast regularly on Radio Quispillaccta and dating to the 1980s era of their youth, show a remarkable uniformity of practice and considerable continuity with practices that remained current in the 2000s. Nor do I mean to suggest that chimaycha was a static musical genre, for it clearly changed over time in accordance with local fashions and changing tastes within indigenous communities—trends that I specify where possible. Still, performers agreed widely on a fundamental, underlying sameness underlying what they deemed to be surface-level changes in instrumentation or singing style.

What I mean to show, then, is how musical experiences like those of these men helped them to develop and enact an awareness of what it meant to live as a member of their indigenous communities. For the stories of Marco, Óscar, and their peers are not simply data of historical or biographical interest. They clarify the ways in which Andean indigeneity might be understood as a function of a distinctive socionatural orientation rather than simply a collection of linguistic and material cultural habits or a category inherited from the era of Spanish rule, reserved for descendants of those who predated the European invasion. Scholars of indigenous Amazonia, where the binary between "nature" and "culture" is construed differently, have argued forcefully for just such an approach to indigeneity, in a series of works centered on the idea of indigenous perspectivism (see especially Kohn 2013; Viveiros de Castro 1992). Recent studies have focused similarly on the distinctive, remarkably durable ways that indigenous Andean people interact with the tangible and intangible objects and beings that populate their milieu and the modes of thought and action that guide those relationships. Construing Andean communities as "socionatural collectives," which include not only humans but also the sentient earth-beings that share their territory (de la Cadena 2015) or animate stones that are "both nature and culture, both part of the earth and part of human society" (Dean 2010:14), these studies add depth to clichéd observations about the centrality of nature in Andean art and culture.[7]

Such clichés frequently animate studies of Andean music, which often note composers' reliance on nature metaphors. Many have taken those compositional devices as evidence of "respect for nature [and] a wise politics of ecological respect" (Montoya Rojas et al. 1997 [1987]: 44). Here, however, I argue that the ecological qualities of Andean musicmaking amount to something other than environmentalist bromides. For what is verifiably distinctive about most indigenous ontologies is not a disposition toward stewardship but rather a vision of "the human" as coextensive with "the natural." Whether relationships are based on reciprocation, kinship, mutual predation, or some other principle (Descola 2013), the conviction that nonhuman others are animate, and potential interlocutors, entails a particular orientation toward the nonhuman world. It is different than the one entailed in the Western division between "the natural" and "the cultural" that Latour describes as the "modern constitution" (1993)—a constitution that has never fully encompassed people who move on modernity's periphery in any case.[8]

Just so, my account is framed by the assumption that indigenous Andeans have long conducted their lives as dialogues with nonhuman beings and processes that demand attention, care, and reciprocation. However, rather than questions of ontology or animacy, I explore something rather simpler: the kind of environmental attentiveness that arises from such a belief system, expressed as a familiarity with the constituents and processes of the nonhuman world. This intuitive awareness, akin to what Anderson has called "sentient ecology" (2000), is made manifest when people like Marco and Óscar narrate their musical experiences in terms of environmental determinants or sing songs that rely upon listeners' ecological knowledge of particular spaces for their symbolic resonance.[9] In this sense my interest lies in the idioms through which "nature is imbued with meaning by, and for, social praxis and identity" (Impey 2002:15).[10] It lies in the way that inert terrain becomes saturated with indigenous memory and affect, and in the spoken performances through which such maps of sentiment are narrativized for uptake by interlocutors.[11] Scholars elsewhere have described comparable performances, organized around such concerns as myth (Lima 1999), royal kinship (Impey 2006), or property (Roseman 1998). Chuschinos' tropologies of places are instead entwined with courtship, combat, and intracommunity rivalry, but they function similarly to "map and mediate their relationships with the land and each other" (Roseman 1998:111).

Finally, although my emphasis on ecology distinguishes my account from previous ones, I am not the first to highlight the vida michiy's importance in the life of Pampas Valley towns like Chuschi and Quispillaccta (see González 2011; Isbell 1985, 1997, and 2009; Isbell and Barrios Micuylla 2016; La Serna 2012b; Palomino 1971).[12] Other writings similarly describe it as a pivotal stage in the life cycle of local Quechua speakers. However, they tend to center on coitus, and to a lesser extent on gender identity, a matter I defer to the next chapter. In Isbell's detailed report (1997), the vida michiy appears as a formalized ritual centered on public sex with multiple partners and as a rare forum for the exercise of female dominance.[13] Subsequent scholarly references have followed Isbell, but I do not characterize the vida michiy this way because my interlocutors rejected her account as an exaggeration of the things that they had experienced. It overstated both the formality of their vida michiy and the libidinous energies it unleashed, making a ceremonial orgy of a practice that was more loosely structured and, typically, much less hedonistic than what they found in her description. Certainly, they said, people behaved excessively. The vida michiy drew adolescents together to drink, flirt, and sing amorous songs, and it would be truly difficult to believe that sex was far behind. Couples also eloped directly from the event, providing fuel for prurient rumors. However, such couplings typically happened after a period of previous courtship, during prior vida michiys and other social occasions.[14] In this light, it is telling that a counterweight to Isbell's depiction appears in the earlier work of Ayacuchano anthropologist Salvador Palomino Flores, who insisted that the vida michiy did not involve "what is termed 'sexual liberty.' Although collective at times, but always in couples, by mutual consent, it is simply a propitious ritual of fertility" (1971:84).

The stories that I present here, then, suggest that the vida michiy was both tamer and more variable than earlier writings imply, at least for many people who participated in the custom after the mid-1970s. Still, it should

LANDSCAPE, PERFORMANCE, AND SOCIAL STRUCTURE 55

be recognized that for reasons detailed below, my rendering is as necessarily secondhand as those earlier writings. Isbell credits her data to indigenous informants, including a research assistant from faraway Andahuaylas who participated in sexual competitions. I credit mine largely to Marco, Óscar, and other men of their generation. Each account is liable to distortions and elisions that serve the interests of the tellers, and to the sociopolitical moment of the telling. Here it is worth considering historian Miguel La Serna's insights into the era of Isbell's research, which his consultants remembered as a time of social crisis. Elder chuschinos described the late 1960s and the 1970s as an age of "generational conflict in which an increasing proportion of local youths were engaging in criminal activity, shunning traditional values and practices, and challenging local leaders" (La Serna 2012a:35–36). It is possible, then, that Isbell's writings chronicle episodes that many chuschinos would now describe as historically and socially contingent.[15]

Just so, my own research took place in an environment of indigenous sociopolitical affirmation. Comuneros from Quispillaccta and Chuschi were working against dominant, demeaning stereotypes of Indians as brutal primitives, and Isbell's account resonates uncomfortably with those stereotypes. Indeed, it is worth noting that I gleaned stories like hers only from a chuschino mestizo, a former teacher and politician who is also remembered as a symbol of abusive qala authority. La Serna reported a similar conversation with the same man, arguing cogently that his description of the vida michiy was tailored to justify his own aggressive behavior, which garnered him repeated denunciations for rape and assault from indigenous comuneros over the 1970s (2012a:112–13). It is little wonder that my interlocutors reject descriptions of the vida michiy that resemble his: quite possibly they would do so even if they contained some truth. What cannot be doubted is the tie that binds the vida michiy to social and physical reproduction, which is lost on no comunero. Palomino's characterization of the event as a "ritual of fertility" may overstate the matter, but the songs and the joking behavior that attend the vida michiy regularly thematize sex, and they celebrate its pleasures unfettered by the inheritance of shame that attends sexual conversation in much of the Judeo-Christian West.

The Vida Michiy: An Outline

My understanding of the vida michiy is secondhand, for two reasons. First, it appears to have died out, much to the dismay of older musicians, who blame its disappearance on two different developments. One is the rapid growth of Protestant fundamentalism since its arrival in the late 1960s. Today around half the residents of Chuschi district are followers of conservative North

56   CHAPTER TWO

American sects, and whether they are Pentecostals, Mormons, or Jehovah's
Witnesses, all of them discourage non-Christian music and customs. A second
factor relates to technologies and infrastructures that have facilitated the circulation of people and objects, tying village life ever more closely with urban
Peru over the last half century. Traveling easily to and from Ayacucho or Lima
on newly paved highways, young people increasingly favor the commercial
cumbia and huayno styles that dominate Peru's cities, while USB drives and
smartphones obviate any need to make their own music. The result is that every young person I met from the district of Chuschi—that is, everyone under
thirty—told me that they had never participated in the vida michiy, nor knew
of its recent practice, and that they too understood it to have disappeared.

This means that they grew up in a very different musical world than elders
who came of age before the millennium, when chimaycha performance and
pursuit of the vida michiy were almost obligatory—the principal vehicle for
courtship, for finding a life partner, and hence for attaining full adulthood.[16]
Back then young women cultivated strong, high voices and developed a deft
lyrical sensibility, seeking to impress their peers with their stamina and their
intelligence. Young men learned the chinlili, on pain of failing ever to attract
feminine attention.[17] The notion that good playing was an erogenous skill was
treated as settled fact, at least among male performers. Quispillacctino Miguel
Espinoza only echoed others when, drawing on the lewd humor that enlivens
much Quechua-language social discourse, he told me that for a young man
who played well, "legs would spread all by themselves."

All of this suggests another reason that I could never provide a firsthand
description of the vida michiy. It was restricted to unmarried youths, due to its
role in pursuing sex and marriage. I heard tales of nostalgic elders disguising
themselves to participate surreptitiously, but attendance by married adults was
discouraged, evidence of both immaturity and adulterous yearnings. José Tomaylla, widely regarded as Quispillaccta's foremost chinlili player over the past
three decades, gestured toward the consequent social sanctions in describing
his continuing love for chimaycha. He confined his playing to relatively prim
occasions, like folkloric competitions or informal house parties, but he told
me that some fellow quispillacctinos would nevertheless "Mormon" him (*me
mormonan*) for his activities—a striking neologism that captures both the
moralizing tone of his critics and the local rise of conservative Christianity.

In fact, injunctions against the vida michiy predate the arrival of Prot-
estantism. Many musicians told me of parental admonitions against it and
occasionally of being punished when their participation was found out. It is
likely that such admonitions were spoken in part with an eye toward curb-
ing an excessive love for the musical hobby and the dissolute bohemianism

LANDSCAPE, PERFORMANCE, AND SOCIAL STRUCTURE

that was held to accompany it. They were also meant to forestall the very real threat of losing daughters to other families or, conversely, of gaining unwanted daughters-in-law. This was, after all, the logical conclusion of a successful romantic encounter at the vida michiy, and although it was not as common as is sometimes made out, it is easy to collect stories of girls who disappeared after a night at the vida michiy, only to be found living in the parental household of a new husband.[18]

Such admonitions probably ring familiar to musicians around the world. The pattern of discouraging in children those excesses that parents held dear in their own youth, while fully anticipating the uselessness of such a proscription, may be as old as the idea of generational difference and as widespread as music itself. In the Pampas region, the culture of admonition meant that both the vida michiy and preparations for it took place far from prying parental eyes, generating a long-standing series of techniques for evading detection. Speaking in 2014, the septuagenarian luthier Jacinto Tucno told me of tales that he heard from his own ancestors of an older instrument called the *bonsés*. A small guitar with a collapsible neck, it could be folded up and hidden among other items without attracting attention. In the olden days, Jacinto told me, anyone returning from the lands outside town would routinely bring back sticks to feed the village's daily cooking fires. By folding up a bonsés and squirreling it away in a bundle of firewood, a reveler returning from the vida michiy at dawn could avoid the notice of elders, who might otherwise upbraid him upon spying the evidence of a dissolute night in the puna.

Since I'm a married and middle-aged man, then, and a foreigner to boot, my appearance at a vida michiy would have violated an important moral code. Fortunately, congruent accounts that I heard from dozens of people who did participate gave me a portrait of its general parameters. Young people began to prepare for the vida michiy long before they attended it, by learning to perform the songs that were its centerpiece. This meant something slightly different for young men than for young women, since musical practice in the Pampas region is divided by gender, as elsewhere in the Andes, up to the present day. Except for the *tinya* drum used in some festive contexts, women do not play instruments. Instead they sing, and while men sing too, female voices are preferred over male voices. In the era when the vida michiy was still a vigorous custom, women were expected to be able to sing well, and to excel in composing songs, in a way that was never quite as true of their male counterparts. Therefore children and young teens sought out opportunities to learn songs, and in the case of boys, to develop chinlili skills as well. Even in the era before recordings, many such occasions presented themselves. Marco spoke, for instance, of the *pasllas* that he witnessed over the 1970s, two consecutive nighttime sessions of house-to-house singing visits, much like Euro-American caroling practices, that coincided with the annual yarqa aspiy. Visiting the houses of the communal authorities in each neighborhood, composers debuted their finest songs, making the pasllas key occasions for learning powerful new works and the elements of compositional craft. Other sacred and secular occasions, including town anniversaries, saints' days, and Easter, featured chimaycha performance as an adjunct to the main activity, and once song competitions emerged in the 1970s, these too provided further models. Many people were also exposed to chimaycha performance in the home via unmarried siblings, cousins, uncles, and aunts who had already begun to attend the vida michiy. For young men, it was not terribly difficult to teach oneself chinlili skills, given the uniformity of chimaycha performance. A player had only to develop the chugging arpeggiated accompaniment that is played with the thumb on the instrument's open bass strings, to begin picking out pentatonic melodies on the treble strings, and then to cultivate sufficient manual dexterity to put the two activities together.

Young performers with burgeoning expertise needed peers with whom to make music, and here pastoral activities were invaluable. Herding provided an apt set of circumstances for developing one's skills, playing with others, and arranging to hold a vida michiy. Trailing animals in lonesome plains far from home, with little to occupy the hands and mind, boys and girls might play or sing to their hearts' content without fear of interference. Moreover, the common lands of the high puna were used by young pastoralists from all over the district and provided ample opportunity to meet and develop intimacy with youths from other communities—a matter of some urgency for people who might be related to almost everyone in their home barrio. Meetings in the puna became chances to play and sing together, to flirt, tease, and gradually deepen and communicate one's affections for a member of the opposite sex— leading logically to courtship in the vida michiy, the ultimate target of such romantic feints and hints.

The vida michiy proper was arranged in an ad hoc fashion and could happen at any time, though it was more commonly celebrated during the months between May and July, the most mobile months of the herding cycle. Typically, someone with a romantic interest in another young person arranged a nighttime session and secured the attendance of a few friends or relatives of the principals, ideally with even numbers of young men and women. Arrangements might be transacted directly or through intermediaries: in one classic method, a young man contrived to steal an article of clothing—an earring or a sash—from a young woman he meant to court, telling her that she could recover it by joining him at a vida michiy.[19] Or a young man might ask

LANDSCAPE, PERFORMANCE, AND SOCIAL STRUCTURE

a female acquaintance to hold a vida michiy and bring a friend he had had little chance to meet, promising in exchange to rope in a likely male partner for his coconspirator.

After agreeing to meet at a site accessible to all relevant parties, word was spread to invitees, who set out within a few hours of sunset—late enough for family members to have fallen asleep but early enough to make a journey over rough terrain that might take some two hours, with time left for singing and dancing. The group made its way to an open space in the mountainous landscape, preferably one that lay behind a ridge or peak, an effective barrier between the noise of their music and nearby settlements. There they typically found a round patch averaging less than six feet in diameter where grass had already been flattened by dancing feet. After instruments were tuned, one of the young men would call a tune, and the music would begin: men playing and women singing, with the men perhaps joining in as they saw fit. They danced too, following a standard formation wherein women stood at the center while men stomped in circles around them, but also interspersing evocatively named dance moves and formations—*wayta pallay* (flower-gather), *maswa qatay* (follow the *maswa*, a sweet tuber), *muyu-muyuchiy* (spinner), or *cruzcha* (little cross)—that waxed and waned in fashion over the years. Events typically wrapped up early enough for the youths to return home in time to commence the chores of the agricultural day, which began at 3:00 or 4:00 a.m.

The vida michiy was also enlivened by physical combat, a matter that is often spoken of with nostalgic glee by those who participated. Such contests typically occurred when more than one group found itself at the same site, practicing their separate vida michiys within earshot of one another. Especially if the two groups were from rival communities, the situation provided ample opportunity for bravado as they sought to outplay one another and to provoke ire with shouted taunts. Once the accrued tension demanded release, a referee was designated, and individuals came to square off under his eye. The contest pitted young men and women of comparable size from each group against one another, in a series of one-on-one battles using a techniques dubbed *lapyay*. Combatants took turns striking each other on the chest with one hand, and the goal was simply to knock down the opponent. Though they sometimes devolved into general melees, ideally these battles were rule-governed tests of strength rather than free-for-alls. Even when they proceeded in genteel fashion the results could be painful; Óscar Conde told me laughingly of the green bruises that would spread across the chest of a combatant for days afterward, testifying to youthful ardor.

This highly schematic portrait of the vida michiy hardly accounts for the substantial variation that emerged in practice. Neither the custom nor its arrangements, for instance, were transacted exclusively in the high grasslands. Marco told me that people in Chuschi proper often visited the nearby sites of Sullkaraypata and Wayunka to hold their vida michiys; mestizo teacher and musician Ranulfo Infanzón told me that during his youth in the 1960s, young men loitered near the communal pump in the main square, waiting to arrange things with daughters who came alone to fetch water for their households; and Isbell reported the cemetery site of Qonopa, just below town, as another familiar location for the practice (1985). Still, the principle of avoiding parental interference made the puna into an ideal site for practicing the vida michiy, linking it to that climatic zone and to the season in which it was a lived environment for young comuneros. In order to present a more fully fleshed-out account of the vida michiy as lived by indigenous youths, I turn now to the experiences of my primary interlocutors, Marco and Óscar.

Marco Tucno Rocha's Vida Michiy

Born in 1966 to a relatively prosperous family of comuneros, Marco Tucno Rocha spent most of his youth in Chuschi. His father was serious about education as a means of self-advancement, so he lived mainly at his grandmother's house in Chuschi proper, where he attended elementary and secondary schools. However, he made regular trips to the high barrio of Pucruhuasi, where his family kept large herds of alpacas, llamas, sheep, cattle, and horses in ancestral corrals amid the community's shared grazing lands. To aid the relatives who cared for the herds, he was sent there on weekends, during school vacations, and sometimes even overnight toward the end of the rainy season, when the animals were driven closer and closer to the town of Chuschi. This meant, in his own words, that he "grew up on horseback," since the rugged trip between Chuschi and the grazing zones in the communal territory of Chicllarasu might take up to twelve hours.

Though he was a serious student, Marco was also a precocious musician, taking up the chinlili at the tender age of seven. The Tucno family had produced the region's foremost luthiers since at least the late nineteenth century, and by the time of Marco's birth his great-uncle Jacinto Tucno was the district's dominant guitar maker. Removing a willow trunk from the central patio of his father's house in Chuschi, Marco surreptitiously brought the wood to his great-uncle and asked him to make from it two chinlilis. Once they were ready, he kept them hidden inside a flour sack, itself buried amid stored wheat in his residence, removing them only to tease out clandestine melodies and rhythms far from prying eyes and listening ears.

By the late 1970s Marco was also taking his instruments along on trips

LANDSCAPE, PERFORMANCE, AND SOCIAL STRUCTURE   61

to Pucruhuasi, where he helped keep watch over animals that might otherwise fall victim to rustlers or (more likely) foxes, or mix with other herds, or
stray into neighboring communities and hacienda lands, where they might
be seized. In and around Chicllarasu's grasslands, he routinely encountered
people from communities that he had never visited, striking up otherwise unlikely friendships and flirting with youths of the opposite sex. He met chinlili
players from the quispillacctino settlement of Tuco and girls from neighboring Paras District, who were "tall, white, and spoke Spanish correctly" due
to its denser pattern of European settlement. Such intercommunity interactions maximized the chance of meeting partners from outside one's family
and minimized the risks of discovery, and pursuing them meant that Marco's
vida michiys often occured in sites near community boundaries. In this era,
for instance, he often attended vida michiys at one of three sites that lay near
Tuco and Pucruhuasi, named Dandanchayuq, Yanaqaqa, and Antaqaqa. Encounters with musicians from the neighboring community of Cancha Cancha
were likely to happen at Intiwatana, a site within its territory, while between
the districts of Chuschi and Paras lay Putunku.

Sites like these were used mainly during the rainy season and according to
the circulation of livestock. Like their fellows in the nearby Chuschi barrios
of Chaquiccocha, Huaracco, Waqraccocha, Lerqona, Yupana, Yanaccocha,
Qullpa, and Pampahuasi, Marco's relatives drove sheep from their high puna
residences beginning in April, leaving camelids and caretakers behind. They
moved them to the still-fertile grasslands around the communities of Niño-
bamba and Rumichaca, sometimes clustering in family groups so as to minimize the threat from rustlers attached to local haciendas. During this time the
mostly adolescent caretakers lived in chuqllas, small round structures made
of stones that stood empty and roofless most the year but could be thatched
with ichu grass and made habitable in a day. The vida michiy, meanwhile,
moved to nearby sites like those around the lake called Saqsalqucha, at least
temporarily—for once the animals had browsed this area the families continued moving in stages, grazing patches of grassland according to successively
lower limits set by Chuschi's varayuqs. They eventually stopped at Totora, an
area just outside Chuschi proper, from which the animals were released on
the festive date of July 28, free to feed on postharvest vegetation within the
town boundaries—at least that which lay outside the lands of Chuschi's qalas.

It was over this period between May and July that the vida michiy became especially frequent, taking place in sites that marked stages on the route
from high puna to the town limits. Anticipating the season, young men approached Jacinto Tucno to request new chinlilis, instruments made on the
cheap in anticipation of heavy use and breakage. Sound travels far in steep

Andean valleys, and Marco told of hearing strong female voices reverberate from peak to peak as youths celebrated with increasing frequency in places like Milluyaku and eventually Sullkaraypata, just above the town of Chuschi itself. The vida michiy was also more intense at this time, and young people would redouble their efforts at courtship, romancing potential partners whom they had heretofore been eyeing more circumspectly. Even after the animals reached Totora, the vida michiy continued. With adults wrapped up in the annual festival season, revels continued in the *lazas* near Chuschi proper. Things only began to wind down following the animal-marking ceremonies that began on August 15, after which animals and herders headed back to the puna.

Marco did not begin attending the vida michiy until the age of twelve, several years after he began to play and soon after he had gained a local reputation as a fine performer. It began when a distant cousin from Quispillaccta returned from military service bearing a tape recorder. Hoping to make recordings of local music for home use, he asked Marco to arrange a vida michiy where he might do so. The group that Marco put together included a much older twenty-seven-year-old guitarist as well as a female cousin, who in turn brought two female friends. The night was a success, because the same man asked Marco to arrange another meeting and to include the same female cousin. At this point in his narrative, Marco paused to say that the vida michiy was mostly about this: meeting potential mates, courting them over successive events, and gradually getting to know one another. On a May night shortly thereafter, then, they met at Sullkaraypata, but things took a slight turn. Focused on courting the young women that had come along with them, he and a classmate realized that they had lost track of Marco's two cousins. Finding them asleep together inside a nearby hut, the two preteens began to berate their senior relative for his immorality, insisting that he marry the young woman in question. When I asked Marco if this wasn't somewhat absurd, given that they had been engaged in precisely the same activity, he ruefully noted that it was something of an obligation for them, as her relatives, to watch out for the young woman's interests. The older cousin not only gave assurances but also took the relationship to a new stage, appearing with his partner at future vida michiys, thereby signaling the seriousness of his intentions.

Marco's budding reputation came with a certain amount of risk, since outstanding musicians were also outstanding targets, especially when they dared to cross into rival territory. With one paternal branch in Quispillaccta, Marco was sometimes invited to perform in Patario, the most hallowed site for the festivity in that community—a situation rare enough that he could not recall encountering another chuschino there. He did recall one session in which a member of a quispillacctino group marched over and smashed his chinlili. In general, though, Marco experienced the vida michiy as a tamer event than was suggested by his older relatives. He participated in intergroup musical competitions but he never saw the lapyay or other forms of physical combat. Nor did he personally witness an occasion on which two people eloped directly from the vida michiy, and he was incredulous about the possibility: how, he asked, could one ever have known that one was leaving with a reasonable life partner, based only on such a chance meeting? Indeed, his suggestion that the vida michiy was a space for ratifying relations developed elsewhere is borne out by Óscar Conde, who experienced the vida michiy in a somewhat different fashion in neighboring Quispillaccta.

Óscar Conde's Vida Michiy

Marco maintained that Quispillaccta was much less of a herding community than Chuschi: at one point he asked, rhetorically, whether Quispillaccta had even had a proper vida michiy, underlining the extent to which he perceived the custom as a function of Chuschi's herding cycle. However, Quispillaccta's musical practices were fundamentally similar, and the annual cycle of transhumance brought people and sound into motion in the same fashion. The primary differences lay in the matter of intracommunity rivalry, which lives in memory as a far more serious matter in Quispillaccta, and in the selection of a single site as the definitive place for staging such rivalries. It was called Patario, and while it was one of many places where people made chimaycha music, it surpassed the rest as a place to show one's worth.

Óscar described this to me one day in 2014, after we ran into each another near a construction site in Ayacucho. Sitting on a bench before the massive empty lot, we discussed another quispillacctino who, Óscar told me, had "only played for one year." After I protested that I had heard a recording of the man playing at a recent house party, Óscar clarified that the man had played a single year *in Patario*, the standard by which performing skills were ultimately judged. He pointed to the space before us and said, "Think about it this way. It's like playing on neighborhood soccer fields, a place that looks like that, as compared to playing in the national stadium in Lima. It's in Patario where you prove yourself and make your name by competing with other people, and if you return year after year, three, four years, then you really become something to talk about." He spoke from experience, as a musician who had played in Patario for six consecutive years between 1984 and 1989. However, Óscar's path to musical success was more unconventional than that of his chuschino peer.

His parents were comuneros from Huerta Huasi, a settlement on the Pampas side of Quispillaccta, but he himself was born in the city of Ayacucho, in

64 CHAPTER TWO

1969, and taken to Lima as a newborn. In 1980 his parents returned to Quispillaccta, bringing with them a cosmopolitan son who could not yet speak proper Quechua and whose musical tastes inclined toward salsa, rock, cumbia, and especially the hit soundtrack to *Saturday Night Fever*. Within two years, however, he had learned the local language and mastered the town's musical style. He was aided by José Tomaylla, whom Óscar described as the greatest chinlilista of his generation, while characterizing himself as Tomaylla's "disciple." Speaking in 2012, Óscar eloquently described the sense of culture shock that he experienced upon arrival, as well as his success in overcoming it:

> I arrived in 1980 and saw the way guys played. They thought they were the greatest things ever, with their [sheep's wool] *bayeta* pants, ponchos, and homespun scarves. . . . I was the only one in trousers, and they made fun of me, I felt marginalized. Because I also wore a different hat, a bigger one from the city, like John Wayne's. But they put a local hat on me, and I watched how they played, and I liked it. . . . I borrowed a chinlili from some uncles, but my father didn't want me to play. I had to practice in secret, because they said it was perdition, that I was forgetting my studies in favor of customs, and they were right, I forgot all about school. Behind the house, in a rocky area full of little corrals, I played at night, quietly. I pressured my cousins to teach me, and little by little the art seized hold of me. And I came to surpass the guys who were born there.

At this point Óscar's wife Máxima murmured an interjection, and he continued: "My wife reminds me, there was also a discrimination, let's say, the girls would go with the best guitarists. That also drove me to get better, to become the best."

In its emphasis on music and courtship, this passage echoes Marco Tucno's experiences. However, it also gestures toward the force of traditional custom in Quispillaccta, the everyday social pressure to conform to community standards of behavior. Despite centuries of disdain from their mestizo neighbors, indigenous comuneros had no doubts about their sociocultural values. They ridiculed people who inclined toward the strange practices of Peru's dominant classes, and Marco too remembered how young peers had made fun of Óscar's poor Quechua when he showed up at the local secondary school. Indeed, this traditionalist attitude was also strong in Chuschi, where clothing featured with equal prominence in evaluations of commitment. Marco would sometimes deploy a phrase that I heard from others, recounting how nobody dared to dress like Chuschi's qalas for fear of "looking like someone from another planet"—like someone disavowing comunero lifeways.

By adopting their customs Óscar moved past the incredulity of his fellows, becoming a respected community member and part of a group that

LANDSCAPE, PERFORMANCE, AND SOCIAL STRUCTURE   65

dominated Patario over the late 1980s. Just as the puna appears in Marco's memories as a keystone space co-ordering social, ecological, and musical categories, Óscar described Patario in ways that tied it to Quispillaccta's social organization and its mode of subsistence. As in Chuschi, Quispillaccta's herds were brought to the low part of the community around the midpoint of the dry season, a process called the *vaca yaykuy* (cattle entry), and the flat plain of Patario was located at the route's end. In contrast to Chuschi's practice, Óscar told me, the transfer of the herds took place entirely on June 24 each year. On that day, herders drove their animals to an area called Huayllapucro, which sits just above Patario, itself situated outside and above Quispillaccta proper. There they would graze for three weeks before being admitted to Patario on July 14. Meanwhile, the youths who tended the animals made temporary homes in two nearby sites, dividing themselves such that people from the Cachi side stayed in an encampment called Pukawasi and those from the Pampas side in one called Amayni—place-names that Óscar and his peers often used, in synechdochic fashion, to refer to the communities and residents of the community's two distinct geophysical sections.

As in Chuschi, this period provided the most propitious annual conditions for holding the vida michiy, with youths from Amayni and Pukawasi holding frequent, intense meetups in the lazas associated with their respective encampments—reminiscing in 2017, Óscar told me that one was lucky to get two nights of sleep in a week and to avoid falling asleep during the agricultural tasks that continued during daytime hours. Still, the biggest burst of celebration was reserved for after July 14, when the herds entered Patario. During the 1980s music might be heard there every single night in late July, with multiple groups from different parts of the district playing simultaneously and trying to outdo one another in a spirit of intracommunity competition that sometimes turned ugly. The groups that played there were not exactly "music groups" in the sense of formal entities with a rehearsed membership. Since married adults were expected to stop attending Patario altogether, long-term stability was impossible. Rather, they were somewhat ad hoc affairs made up of friends who played regularly with one another, and although they might adopt temporary names, they were recomposed each year. Still, some members might play together for several successive years, especially if they were highly skilled musicians who could be counted upon to defeat rival groups. And such outstanding performers might also become music directors of an informal sort, organizing a group each year after carefully observing the up-and-coming youths who showed musical promise.

Óscar became such a leader, recruiting to his Amayni group well-known players like José Tomaylla and Saturnino Ccallocunto, who would later go on participate in Waylla Ichu de Llacctahurán, one of the first formalized music groups in Quispillaccta. His repeated participation and influence in Patario gave him ample firsthand knowledge of the vida michiy's competition and courtship practices. He had not only witnessed the orderly lapyay but also participated in the more unruly skirmishes that tended to break out between groups from different towns. Sitting one day in the patio of his house in Ayacucho, I asked him to explain to me exactly how and why these fights developed, upon which he stood to physically demonstrate the course of events. First, he said, one group would arrive and begin playing at one of the many lazas scattered around the plain, most likely the one that contained a moss-covered rock where young women might sit while accompanists tromped round them in a tight circle. If another group arrived, they might set up in the same formation no more than two or three meters away and commence playing as loud as possible in order to drown out their rivals. What followed was a competition of escalating musical intensity and verbal provocation, for it never failed to pass that group members began to hurl verbal insults to one other. In the best of cases, group leaders halted things and arranged a lapyay session to settle the tension, but often tempers would flare.

By way of illustration he recounted a still-famous dustup from 1985, in which his Amayni group faced rivals from the Cachi-side settlement of Unión Potrero, composed largely of people from the Machaca family. In his view, his own group was clearly outdoing the Machacas, leading someone from the latter to launch an insult his way. Provoked, his colleague Domingo Flores strode over and struck two of the Machacas, leading to a brawl involving young men and women alike. The unfortunate Flores ended up with a series of bloody gouges across his chest, courtesy of a brave Machaca teen who scratched him furiously with her nails; at the time he told me the story, he said that he and Flores had only recently been reminiscing fondly about the event and lamenting the disappearance of the customs that had so engaged them in their youth.

This story is especially notable because the valiant young woman in question was Máxima Machaca Ccallocunto, who went on to marry Óscar after a long period of acquaintance and courtship, perfectly illustrating the way that performance in the vida michiy engaged with the broader business of making a life. According to Óscar's statement in our initial interview, the two "had already known each other by sight, but we fell in love as she sang and I played. Little by little we fell in love, like a lot of people, 90 percent of them met playing and singing." There were ample musical reasons for mutual admiration, since Óscar was recognized as a great chinlilista and Maxi as one of the community's great singers—in fact, this distinction tracked a broader trend of the era, according to which people from the Cachi side were recognized as great vocalists while those from the Pampas side were famous instrumentalists. The young musicians spent a few years admiring one another's abilities in Patario but didn't begin formally courting until 1988, when Óscar was obliged to participate in a community work project to widen the road near her home community of Unión Potrero. That was when they came to know one another socially, to begin seeing each other publicly, and to become recognized as a couple. In the following year Maxi sang in Patario not with the young men of her home community but rather with Óscar's group and, again in his words, "adopted his style" rather than the style of Unión Potrero. Finally, after 1989 both stopped participating altogether, because they got married and moved to a different life stage, one that was supposed to lie beyond such musical behavior. By the time I met them, Óscar and Máxima lived with their grown son and young daughter on the northern outskirts of the city of Ayacucho, maintaining themselves through Máxima's labor as a food vendor at the city's central market and proceeds from Óscar's agricultural activities. They were active in the city's quispillacctino residents' association, and Óscar returned regularly to the community to work his land in the barrio of Huerta Huasi or for communal labors and social visits. They continued to perform chimaycha together on social occasions, such as urban house parties, where such activities were no longer seen as licentious or out of place but as harmless nostalgic entertainment. However, they returned to serious performing only when invited to do so, as Los Auténticos de Patario, by the director of Radio Quispillaccta (see chapter 5).

Musical and Cultural Change through Patario's Lens

Patario, then, held a central place in the musical and social life of Quispillaccta that had no exact parallel in Chuschi. Moreover, it clearly had for at least two full generations prior to Óscar's. When in 2014 we visited Marcelino Tomaylla, the eighty-five-year-old father of José Tomaylla, he painted a scene from the 1940s or 1950s that hardly differed from Óscar's own memories. Recalling that the district's two sides had always been "confronted against one another," he told how he and his fellows from Amayni—that is, the Pampas side—would deliberately head out with their guitars when they heard that the *qipakuna*— that is, youths from the Cachi side—were celebrating their vida michiys, looking to "bury" them with their superior playing. This long-standing link between the site and its musical activities led Óscar to tell me, in our first interview in 2012, that Patario was not only his community's "discotheque" but "the birthplace of our music, our style, our attire, our autochthonous musical instrument, invented by our grandparents, with five notes, a very rustic guitar with a special sound."

Such institutional longevity hardly entailed immunity to fashion, and in the same interview Óscar noted that "1980 to 1990, those were the boom years of chimaycha in Patario. In 1980, it all changed." In that decade, Óscar's generation helped develop changes in music, dance, and attire that they understood to mark a break between their generation and that of their parents—as their parents may well have viewed their own practice as a departure from the practices of their own parents. The most notorious of the changes observed by Óscar's generation was an increase in drinking, which grew apace as local comuneros gained new access to cheap hard liquor and new sources of income with which to buy it. Elsewhere, Óscar and his friends put an end to the custom of decorating women's hats with large *caucho* flowers, teasing them with the label *waytasapakuna* (very roughly, "too-big-flowers"), telling them they looked like flowerpots, and thereby driving a trend toward the use of smaller flowers instead.[20] Attire changed too, and while this was driven by other factors, the trend was reinforced when people from the Amayni side ridiculed high puna residents who dared to arrive at Patario without new clothing each year. Young people adopted increasingly steep-sided hats decorated with colorful needlepoint designs, marking a stark contrast with the somber hats of generations prior, and the designs eventually spread to black bayeta pants as well, with needlework flowers and birds appearing around cuffs, pockets, and crotch. Other changes were strictly musical: if young women had once begun their performances using vocables to outline melodies before proceeding to sing lyrics, then this generation's men stopped the practice by making relentless fun of anyone who dared to appear so old-fashioned. The chinlili playing too changed in this generation, becoming much more intense and virtuosic. Even here, however, there is reason to believe that the change marked not so much a disruption with a deeply rooted custom as a stage in an ongoing process of musical variation, for the chinlili itself was adopted in its contemporary form only in the 1970s. Even the expectation that all young men would play the instrument, universally attested by people of Óscar's generation, seems to have been based on relatively recent practice. Both the octogenarian Marcelino Tomaylla and the septuagenarian Jacinto Tucno told me that this was not true in times past, when playing was limited to those who were inclined and talented enough to do so.

In light of such historical dynamism it is perhaps unsurprising that the vida michiy and the Patario custom have faded in Quispillaccta. Extrinsic factors are blamed by many artists, including Óscar, who initially told me in our 2012 interview that "it ended in 1993 or 1994 because the famous stereo systems came out, the woofers, with all that music, and the kids started listening to it in their houses. Now most of them don't even know how to play, and if they play, they play modern electric instruments." José Tomaylla pointed to something else, noting how development agencies had improved pasture in the high parts of the district and replaced the tough native cattle of earlier times with delicate Brown Swiss, which were incapable of making the journey from puna to Patario without injury. Today's cattle live out their lives in high enclosures of recent vintage, feasting on quality feed, and transhumance has gone by the wayside along with its attendant customs. Further contributing factors emerged in conversations with others. Alejandro Núñez, Óscar's brother-in-law, told me that authorities had become increasingly concerned about the liquor being consumed at the vida michiy and tried to discourage it out of concern for the well-being of the town's citizenry. These concerns only intensified during the violence of the 1980s, when young people caught at night in the community outskirts might risk their lives at the hands of murderous Shining Path or government forces.

Despite such etiolation, experience at Patario continues to stand as a marker of artistic legitimacy among contemporary quispillacctinos. This is surely a transitional stage, as future generations will know the old customs as rumor alone, but the most influential contemporary chimaycha artists point universally to their experiences there and at the vida michiy more generally as the root of their credibility. David Galindo, founder of the group Los Legales de Cuchoquesera and a chinlilista who accompanied most of Ayacucho's chimaycha singers in the early 2010s, was one of many prominent musicians to tell me of growing up musically in Patario. So too did Lucio "Pachi" Ccallocunto, director of Los Amaynis de Llacctuahurán, a group through which many important vocalists had passed while developing their careers. When I asked him and his wife Sabina if they had ever attended the vida michiy, they burst out laughing and responded with "*How* many times have we been to the vida michiy!" Pachi went on to describe in detail how his own community of Llacta Urán and the higher settlement of Tuco had dominated Patario during his youth, with musicians from other towns fearing to even approach them for fear of embarrassment.

Such statements testify to the enduring symbolic importance of Patario and the vida michiy even after their disappearance. Much of the competitive spirit that animated them lived on at other events where chimaycha was heard, including annual festivals like Easter and the Virgin of Carmen. Pachi Ccallocunto and José Tomaylla each reminisced about the community's anniversary celebration, describing it as another occasion for demonstrating talent and working out intracommunity rivalry. Dating at least to the 1970s, each of the community's thirteen barrios was obliged to send a group to compete in the centro poblado's main plaza. Quispillaccta's authorities offered an animal from the communal herds as a prize to the winners, and judgments were ratified with respect to criteria that Tomaylla summarized in a single (though complicated) word: "authenticity." In such places Ccallocunto and Tomaylla expended considerable energies in defeating their musical rivals, playing all night in the service of personal and barrio pride.

By the time I was conducting research on chimaycha, this too had faded. In 2013 a student organization in Ayacucho attempted to resurrect Quispillaccta's anniversary competition, only to be done in by community disinterest, compounded by a power failure that rendered their amplifiers inoperable. Easter had long dwindled as a serious performance opportunity within the community, since every available artist performed instead in Ayacucho at the anniversary of Radio Quispillaccta, celebrated on the same date. And the patron saint's festival in July 2014 featured only professional artists from the city in place of the competitions from years past. Indeed Jorge Núñez, director of the Ayacucho-based group Cuerdas Andinas, discouraged me from wasting time on a festival that had begun to lose its luster around the turn of the millennium. He remembered that in the 1990s, groups would still gather in the central plaza of Quispillaccta, in new skirts and hats ordered months beforehand. The plaza would be full of listeners, including high barrio residents who had descended to harvest corn. Today, with corn growing even in the formerly barren high areas, their houses stood abandoned. Meanwhile the quispillacctino residents in Lima and Ayacucho, once reliable organizers of such festivities, had shown themselves increasingly less inclined to patronize the festival. With the community itself dominated by evangelical Protestant authorities and with young people turning away from traditional performance, the energy required to sustain the event was simply gone.

Conclusion

My early conversations with Marco about the vida michiy often revolved around the parallels between his adolescence and my own. Gathering at night in uninhabited spaces with other youths to sing and drink; hoping to impress members of the opposite sex through musical skill; looking for fights with rivals from the other side of town, and proudly displaying the resulting bruises—all of these activities seemed strikingly similar to my own youthful experiences in a working-class neighborhood peripheral to North America's putative mainstream. Over time, however, opacities in our interactions suggested that Marco routinely omitted a world of detail that made the vida michiy meaningful—and different from anything in my own experience. These omissions were hardly intentional: much of his relevant knowledge was implicit, and by that token difficult to elicit. Not until the moment of miscommunication described at the beginning of this chapter did it become clear that his musical life was grounded in mutually implicated senses of time, space, and social structure that were specific to Chuschi District; and it was only after subsequent explorations of geography, seasonal change, and sociopolitical structure that I was able to solicit his commentary on chuschino acoustemology that I draw out here and in chapter 3.

Those later conversations confirmed my growing sense that Chuschi's geophysical and sociopolitical landscapes were coinscribed through sound and intimately tied to calendrical time. Different places became musical in particular seasons, and the ecological and cultural partitions that sonic practice made year after year created a chronotopic form of musical memory that continues to organize the narratives of people long removed from the days of their youth. This lived fusion of calendar, environment, place, memory, and culture amounts to the acoustemology of what I am calling one variety of indigeneity, and it leads conversations about musical performance to veer as easily into ecology or geography as aesthetics. This is not to argue that indigenous peoples are ineluctably tied to the land—a tired argument that has often been used to delegitimize the claims of displaced, landless, or urban Indians. It is, however, to argue that experiences of "nature" marked a real distinction between the indigenous people of Chuschi and Quispillaccta and the nonindigenous peoples who shared their space, in the era prior to mass urban migration. Without this detailed knowledge of local ecology, their musical system was unimaginable as such, and their musical system became in turn a tool for sustaining consciousness of that ecology. In this chapter, I have explored that in relation to personal narratives of musical experience: in the next, I show how it affected musical aesthetics in ways that continue to resound today.

3

Song and Sound

Tools and weapons are specialized extrapolations of man's own organs for pushing, pounding, crunching, cutting, stabbing—all basic motor activities.
MUMFORD 1966:306

In March 2014, Óscar Conde took me to visit Don Marcelino Tomaylla, the eighty-five-year-old comunero whom he credited with much of his musical success. Father of Óscar's bandmate José (see figure 4 in chapter 1), the elder Sr. Tomaylla had been a stalwart performer in his own youth. Many of the songs that Óscar and José had brought to their teenage performances at Patario were based on tunes and lyrics they had solicited from Don Marcelino, and he dated them to the 1940s and 1950s, if not before. Several of those songs also appeared on recordings by their group Los Auténticos de Patario, and they supported the group's reputation as a bearer of tradition. Notwithstanding his own expertise, Óscar was convinced that I needed to hear the songs and their stories from the source, so he offered to accompany me on a trip to Chuschi and to mediate a conversation with the aged comunero.

We came to Chuschi's brick-and-concrete tourist hotel early on a rainy-season morning to converse with Don Marcelino about his memories and his musical opinions. Advised of my interests, Sr. Tomaylla initially stated that he had "forgotten" all he knew—a token demurral that Óscar and José had anticipated and to which they responded with a memory-jogging offer of cane liquor. Admitting that he would probably be able to sing once fortified, the older man accepted the offer and sat chewing coca and gathering himself while José fetched a bottle of alcohol and Óscar lectured me about the stamina that campesinos like themselves derived from coca, cigarettes, and cane liquor—stamina enough to work fields for hours without a meal or to perform entire nights without a break. Returning with a small bottle, José offered a plastic glassful to his father, who stood to open the window. Whis-

SONG AND SOUND

pering upward to the mountain peaks, he dipped a finger into the glass and flicked drops of liquor in three directions, aiming, so Óscar explained, toward peaks like Comañawi (also known as Wamankiklla; see figure 4)—the region's principal *wamanis*, or mountain beings.

Having discharged his obligations of courtesy to the wamanis, don Marcelino sat and sang several tunes to his son's chinlili accompaniment. Following suggestions from Óscar and José, he chose songs that were already well known in his own adolescence, telling me that they were "from our grandparents." Several matched the model that I had been led to expect by traditionalist friends, people who reminisced wistfully about chimaycha's nature metaphors and the artful way that composers used them to express the sentimental life of their indigenous communities. One song told, for instance, of birds that stood on the plain of Patario beating one another with their wings and pecking each other with their beaks; another adopted the voice of a lonely, loveless soul who saw himself in wild grasses, wilting in the rain and sleet.[1]

DON MARCELINO'S SONGS OF LOVE AND CONTEST

Urqupi qasapi wayllacha ichucha	*High Mountain Grass*
Urqupi qasapi wayllacha ichucha (bis)	Wild grass in the mountains and the passes (bis)
Parallay chayllaptin kurkuyllay kachanki	When the rain falls, you huddle in on yourself
Lastallay chayllaptin kumuyllay kachanki	When the snow falls, you turn in on yourself
Kurkuyllay kurkunki	You huddle in on yourself
Chayñama ñuqalla kurkuyllay kachkani	Just the same, I turn in on myself
Chayñama ñuqalla kumuyllay kachkani	Just the same, I hide myself
Runalla pasaptin, kurkuyllay kachani	When people pass by, I hide away
Runalla puriptin, kumuyllay kachanki	When people walk by, I hide away
Kurkuyllay kachani	I hide away
Patario pampachallapisi	*There on Patario Plain*
Patario pampachallapisi	There on Patario Plain,
Liwlichallay waqachkan (bis)	They say the gulls are crying (bis)
Waqinsi, waqinsi alanwan	Some of them, some of them
waqtanachakusqan,	are beating their wings against each other
Waqinsi, waqinsi piconwan	Others, others
chuspanachakuchkan	are pecking at one another
Alanwan waqtanachakuchkan	Beating their wings against each other

As with all chimaycha songs, such selections assume that a listener familiar with standard lyrical tropes will grasp contextual information that is not stated clearly. The image of high mountain grass, for instance, immediately keys memories of the lonely and barren puna and the passes through which people travel when forced to journey away from town—a frightening and uncertain prospect that may follow romantic disappointment or familial abandonment, and that stands as a general metaphor for the loss of love. Against this background it is clear that the speaker's withdrawn affect is tied to unlucky love. The second song instead assumes both a listener's knowledge of the fighting that sometimes animated events at Patario and of the behavior of flocking mountain birds, whose flapping wings resemble the wheeling arms of fighting youths.

Together, then, these songs captured the elements of romance and contest that people expected from the vida michiy. Other songs presented instead a facet of the chimaycha tradition that was addressed more infrequently by my interlocutors. Ribald and brash, they spoke without metaphor, in swaggering terms, about amorous conquest. They advertised the speaker's talent for finding his way into the beds of sleeping girls or bragged about consummating liaisons during pastoral labors in the high puna:

DON MARCELINO'S BAWDY SONGS

Maypitaq warma puñun	*Where the Girls Sleep*
Maypitaq warma puñun	Here where the girls sleep,
chaypitaq warma puñun (bis)	There where the girls sleep (bis)
Nuqama yachakuni	I know how
imaynam yaykuychata	To get inside
Nuqama yachakuni	I know how
pantalón suchuykuta	To get the pants off
Warata chustuychata	To get the trousers off
Urqupim michiniy michiniy	*While Pasturing on the Mountain*
Urqupim michiniy michiniy,	While pasturing on the mountain
cabrata michiniy michiniy (bis)	While pasturing goats (bis)
Runanta saqtaniy saqtaniy,	I take her down
niñucha kuraycha nichkaptin (bis)	While she says honey, don't! (bis)
Niñucha kuraycha nichkaptin	While she says honey, don't!

A different sort of bravado emerged in other parts of our conversation. During a break Óscar and José drew my attention to Sr. Tomaylla's faded physical prowess, pointing out his still-strong hands and encouraging me to imagine their might in his younger days, when he was not only a talented musician but also a legendary brawler. They pointed out that the link between chimaycha

SONG AND SOUND   75

performance and combat was inscribed on the man's very body, in the form of a deeply scarred ear. Chuckling as he recalled the circumstances some six or seven decades later, Sr. Tomaylla described a particularly contentious season of chimaycha performance in which he came to blows with three Machaca brothers—members of the same Cachi-side family that Óscar had battled in the 1980s. According to Sr. Tomaylla's version of events, the Machacas, perennially frustrated with his superior musicianship, resolved to tame him physically and ambushed him in the streets of Quispillaccta. He managed to break the teeth of one brother and punch another in the throat, but a third bit into the upper portion of his ear, tearing it half off and leaving the disfigured organ to stand afterward as evidence of his grit.

Though gruesome in its details, this story was presented in a tone of quiet pride, leavened with hilarity. Don Marcelino smiled faintly as he reminisced, while Óscar and José shook their heads and chuckled, wondering at the fortitude of generations past. Perhaps picking up on my own difficulty in reconciling the delicate-voiced man I had just met with the image of the bruiser he had apparently been, they returned to music and to his body, reminding me to consider how hands capable of physical defense were equally suited to sonic domination. Indeed, when Óscar asked Don Marcelino to speak about the instruments of his youth, his phrasing drifted into metaphors of competition. Describing the larger guitars that he and his fellows played before the invention of the chinlili, he characterized their efficacy in terms of their capacity to defeat rival players. He spoke of the roles that virtuosity and sheer volume played in the vida michiy's musical contests. Sometimes, he said, he and his fellows from Amayni triumphed with their showmanship, but just as frequently the men from Pukawasi and their large, long-necked guitars carried the day, "burying" rivals beneath a wall of sonic force.

Such stories of physical and musical prowess are probably tinged with exaggeration or idealization.[2] Even so, by using similar tropes of power to describe musical and extramusical elements of the vida michiy, they richly illustrate how chimaycha performance sustained norms of behavior that transcended the musical realm. They also suggest how those norms guided aesthetics, which turned in part on a sustained production of vocal and instrumental energy.

Energetic musicianship was indeed one of chimaycha's core principles. However, the lyrics of Don Marcelino's songs, filled with references to nonhuman beings and things and to landscapes of personal or communal significance, also suggest a pervasive environmental attunement that underlay chimaycha lyrics and comunero life more generally. This was hardly a point of focal awareness for the musicians I consulted, and in the absence of my prompting, songs were never discussed in terms of ecological insight. They were treated as vehicles for romance, even—or especially—when that romance took a turn into combative braggadocio. Still, if love and sex were marked aspects of song, then successful composition rested upon the savvy use of ecologically resonant symbols, meaning that environmental awareness was the unmarked infrastructure of lyrical craft. In this sense, the songs of the vida michiy are one effective means to approach a worldview in which humans habitually orient their actions and their sense of self by reference to the nonhuman realm—the kind of worldview that leads every social occasion to be conducted as if the mountains themselves are valued invitees.

In the previous chapter I described how memories of the vida michiy were structured by resonances between courtship, landscape, animal husbandry, and social organization. Here I explore the related domains of romance, sonic aesthetics, and natural metaphor. Few demonstrated the links between them as well as don Marcelino Tomaylla, but conversations with other musicians usually invoked the same points of reference that guided his reminiscences. I use what I learned from them to draw a portrait of the way that chimaycha sounded, its saturation with environmental semiotics, and its use as a vehicle for inhabiting local norms of desirability, at a life stage when this became a matter of real importance.

These norms meant showing determination in besting rivals, in musical as in physical combat. The ability to do so was a means to consolidate one's own sense of a worthwhile self and ratify it before others, but also a means of making clear one's fitness as a life partner. Marco gestured toward this matter when in 2017 he told me that the vida michiy's lapyay contests allowed young people to show that they were "ready to defend themselves." His statement should be interpreted both in a literal sense, as a matter of physical toughness, and in the figurative sense of standing on one's own, of having the inner resources required to succeed in life. For despite its associations with adolescent hedonism, the vida michiy was simultaneously a site for establishing certain diacritics of maturity. This is why Marco elsewhere described chimaycha as something that could make a performer feel "manly," and Óscar and Máxima's account of chinlili skills highlighted the way that superior chinlili playing helped win a wife's affections. As the tenor of these statements suggests, preparation for adulthood entailed the ability to perform the gender identity expected of an adult in a Quechua-speaking community—places where gender differentiation and the pressure to organize a household around a male-female dyad are both strong indeed.

SONG AND SOUND

Gender played such a clear role in organizing chimaycha performance at the vida michiy that a chapter on the subject merits some consideration of the category, its place in Andean life, and its relation to music. Like anthropologist Krista Van Vleet, I understand gender as "an analytic category in which the differences, and the power asymmetries, between men and women are denaturalized—located in particular historical moments, social institutions, cultural meanings, and political economies" (2008:7). I believe that describing how the institution of chimaycha performance fostered the enactment of gender ideologies helps to clarify the ongoing naturalization of such persistent asymmetries. Andean ethnographers, however, have staged an often-fraught debate about gendered difference and hierarchy over the last half century, and not every writer is likely to agree about the local applicability of Van Vleet's statement, or mine. Many have interpreted indigenous communities as sites of nonhierarchical complementarity, wherein the public power of men is offset by women's control over the home and the family, providing a strict form of gender equity that shames the enduring patriarchal structures of Western societies (Arnold 1997; Bolin 2006; Flores Ochoa 1988). Others see them instead as "fraught with imbalances and inequalities. Many women in the countryside are subjected to double or triple days of labor, physical abuse, and subordination, despite the respect their impressive skills in domains such as curing, herding, cooking, and weaving and their knowledge of seeds command" (Seligmann 2004:4). These scholars point to indisputably elevated levels of male literacy, social mobility, labor flexibility, and political tenure, as well as the widespread normalization of spousal abuse, as evidence that indigenous Andean life is firmly patriarchal in tone (Babb 1989; Bant and Girard 2008; Bourque and Warren 1981; de la Cadena 1995; Harvey 1993:129–32).[3]

What remains undisputed is the notion that gender roles are strongly differentiated and heavily enforced in daily life, through a thousand mechanisms that obscure their contingency. Even scholars tend to assume the transparency of "man" and "woman" as personal identities and social slots.[4] Nor does the rote observation that the Andean gender system is performative mitigate the hegemonic force of its binary logic (Canessa 2005; Van Vleet 2003:256). It may be true that differences are conceptualized in terms of the things that men and women do, rather than what they are, but mainly what they do is to model their performances on inherited norms, and little margin is made for nonconforming gender identity.[5] Whether differences are assigned or achieved, failure to fully inhabit one's role invites ridicule, and as Van Vleet has noted, "neither gender nor ethnicity is simply chosen outside of a system of constraints, or put on or taken off like polleras or pants" (2003:357).

78   CHAPTER THREE

This choice of simile is significant, for no domain of gender expression is as marked and mundane as attire. Similarly, no domain of gender expression demonstrates so clearly how unequally indigenous women bear the responsibility and suffer the limitations of ethnic identity (de la Cadena 1995). Femenías notes that "women's bodies are the focus of ethnic differentiation through dress, while men's bodies rarely are. . . . Layers of clothes envelop them from neck to ankle. Their long full skirts blaze with hummingbirds and fuchsia blossoms. But the men . . . look drab in monochrome jeans and shirts" (2005:21). Here "wearing garments produces persons" (Femenías 2005:19), but no matter how fictive the produced identities may be, "idealized norms of gender do exist, and they are policed" (Femenías 2005:28). Furthermore attire is hardly the only realm in which everyday performance seems to ratify gendered difference. Inside and out women tend to sit on the ground, while men use chairs; when food and drink are had at public occasions, men are served first; men are expected to expend heavy effort on the companionable public consumption of liquor, while women may suffer social sanction for indulging to a similar degree. Other axes of differentiation are task related. Men, for example, serve in political office and speak in public meetings, perform most heavy agricultural work, and participate more commonly in waged migrant labor, save for marketing. Women, by contrast, manage households and family finances, care for children, and aid men in their public duties, for instance by serving food and drink at ritual or political events.[6]

This differentiation might be attenuated in childhood and early adolescence, when children of both sexes remain tied to the home and often perform similar kinds of labor. However, in indigenous communities "the couple is highly valued because it insures productivity, familial subsistence, and communal order" (Bueno-Hansen 2015:119), and the attainment of adulthood demands the establishment of a proper household, headed by a properly gendered duo. Indigenous youths were therefore strongly motivated to establish their bona fides as men and women of proper character, people desirable to members of the opposite sex. Certainly, men who remain unmarried do not suffer the same levels of disempowerment as women who do so, but they do face social sanction and limited opportunities.[7] More broadly, teenage boys face the same framework of gendered expectation as teenage girls, bound to demonstrate their value as men before male and female peers alike. The stakes of claiming a normative gender identity and, partly by doing so, winning a spouse were therefore high for boys and girls alike.

Isbell has suggested that in Chuschi District "the performative aspects of gender identity were principal foci during adolescence" (1997:281).[8] As the

SONG AND SOUND 79

principal adolescent rite of passage, the vida michiy might be expected to have been a place for such virtuosic performance of gender, and so it was. In this sense it resembles the practices described in most studies of indigenous Andean performance, especially adolescent performance, for music is a key practice through which the binarized traits of gendered identity are inhabited and naturalized. It is often suggested, for instance, that "the public discursive power of men can be set alongside the power of women's song as 'complementary forms of power'" (Arnold 1997:45; see also Harris 1980), making competence in vocal performance and composition a means of both inhabiting proper femininity and securing the influence that went along with it. This is why "displays of fashion and ritual prowess (including singing and dancing) are significant facets of what cholitas (unmarried teenage girls) do" (Van Vleet 2003:355) on festive occasions. The productive labor of teenage boys' musical performance is equally urgent. Focused attention to marked masculinity lags behind that devoted to femininity in the Andes, but music studies have nevertheless shown how central instrumental performance, musical competition, and cognate forms of combat are in ratifying male identity (see especially Sikkink 1997; Stobart 2006; Turino 1984).

Physical fortitude, however, was itself not a quality that distinguished male from female performance. The opposition between brute strength and delicate beauty that characterizes many Western contexts hardly operated in the indigenous communities of Chuschi District (see also Bolin 2006:17). As noted in chapter 2, women were not exempt from the kinds of physical contest that happened at certain vida michiys. Just so, much of the language that was used to evaluate men's instrumental and women's vocal performances was commensurate. My interlocutors focused insistently on performative female strength, and especially on strong singing, as evidence of the steely character that was desirable in a life partner. This was a quality that women sought from men in equal measure, but in service of its demonstration men were expected to use their proper resources—chinlilis, which thereby exemplified the implemental extension of human capacities for battle which Mumford saw in tools more generally (1966).

Finally, gendered musical distinction and the performance of desirability also turned on chimaycha's other outstanding element: intelligent wordplay. Thus Isbell, who characterized verbal riddles and songs as central facets of the vida michiy, could claim that "one who could win the day in the riddle competitions was, presumably, a good lover" (1997:281). Indeed, Óscar attributed his nascent affections for his future wife to the cleverness of her lyrics, and a keen mind was a privileged domain of attractiveness for young women. All in

80   CHAPTER THREE

all, the custom's effectiveness in securing the community's social and physical reproduction—as a ritual of fertility—cannot be understood without considering chimaycha's musical and lyrical aesthetics. In the rest of this chapter I outline those aesthetics from the point of view of the men who were, in the main, my interlocutors. This account, in other words, is a partial one, constituted from men's views about properly masculine and feminine musicmaking and the influence that these evaluations have had in chimaycha aesthetics.

Andean Song: Sentient Ecology and Romantic Competition

Everywhere in the Peruvian Andes, traditional songs use plants, animals, geophysical features such as rivers and mountains, and meteorological phenomena like rain and wind as figures for human experiences—paradigmatically, love and abandonment: "among indigenous people, love is lived by way of nature . . . and special attention is paid to the thing that lies within the words, the thing that is implicitly understood" (Montoya et al. 1997 [1987]: 55). As I spoke with musicians from Chuschi and Quispillaccta, it became clear that the power of these metaphors, and hence the excellence of a given song, turned on their success in tying them to places and things that had been experienced personally by listeners. My interlocutors paused again and again to explain geographic and climatological features of the district so as to clarify the impact that a particularly effective song might have for a native listener. These songs, then, resemble all Andean songs in their attention to emotion and metaphor, but they are also means through which performers sustained a shared and highly localized sense of resonance between music, people, and nature.

This intense evocation of meaning-laden places has received little attention in writing on Andean song. Isbell has touched on the matter, though she writes of a radically different context. Speaking of songs composed during the violence era, she notes that "one of the most important vehicles for constructing memories of the events is the invocation of geographic locations. . . . Localities such as Infiernillo [Little Hell] encapsulate horrific experiences and become emblematic in the process of re-creating and remembering the events. The audience must know and imagine why a place is significant. This becomes especially important if we recall that the earth is a living being for Andean people and that localities such as Little Hell are animated" (1998:286).

These words echo Basso's insights about landscape and storytelling in Apacheria, where named places condense wisdom about proper personhood, in the form of myths and tales that recount what has happened in them and therefore how to behave. In somewhat similar fashion, Andean places and talk about them "possess a marked capacity for triggering acts of self-reflection,

SONG AND SOUND   81

inspiring thoughts about who one presently is, or memories of who one used
to be, or musings on who one might become" (Basso 1996:55). However, here
the relevant places are only sometimes particular sites such as Infiernillo or
(more likely) named passes, ledges, and towns in the rural landscape. More
frequent is the invocation of generalized spaces like "the puna" or "the pass,"
which serve as placeholders for archetypal experiences that are widely understood to happen in such environments. It is not uncommon for a song to make
both kinds of topographic moves, bringing each to bear upon the other—to
speak, for instance, of the puna in order to claim its metaphorical power as a
space of despair, and then to name in a separate verse a *particular* place in the
local puna, thereby setting such archetypal emotion in a familiar landscape.

These evocations of nature and place mean that lyrics are rarely transparent enough for a novice to parse entirely, especially since the songs are
highly allusive rather than narrative in form. In this sense chimaycha resembles several song traditions from other world contexts, such as Polish Górale
songs that "express a complete, synoptic thought or idea in a haikulike fashion that may juxtapose a potentially revelatory personal expression with a
reference to the surrounding landscape" (Wrazen 2013:133), or the songs of
Australian Dhalwangu performers, which are "often no more than a juxtaposition of names (of places, people, and ancestors) [and] require a theory
of poetics that goes beyond taken-for-granted notions of metaphor" (Toner
2005:7). Above all, perhaps, they recall the songs of early blues performers,
not only in that they are elliptical and tropic but also in that they are widely
understood as autobiographical ruminations about love, especially frustrated
love and its consequences. Such specifics are never stated overtly; rather, chimaycha aesthetics uncannily echo Gioia's description of Delta blues performances, where "the psychological aspects . . . almost always overwhelmed the
incidents related. Indeed, these songs almost never told a complete story, but
merely sketched enough detail to communicate a charged and turbulent state
of mind" (2008:6).

Of course, not all Andean songs are dour in tone. As don Marcelino made
clear, the vida michiy also featured picaresque songs thematizing the pleasures of sex and romance. Previous commentators have often remarked on
the frank treatment of this subject in Andean life, where adolescent desire
is not stigmatized for either sex and women are not expected to be passive
actors in romance. Despite the patriarchal gender stereotypes that seem to
permeate songs like those of don Marcelino, Andean adolescence has typically been described as remarkably egalitarian with respect to sexual mores
(see Arnold 1997; Bolin 2006). Isbell goes so far as to claim that women were
dominant at this stage of life, characterizing male musical performances in

Chuschi as "public compensatory displays" (1997:282) aimed at remediating a sense of inadequacy before female disdain for their inadequate sexual prowess. Indeed it cannot be stressed enough that despite the tone of songs like those of don Marcelino, which outside hearers might easily hear as references to sexual assault, they are understood by their performers and listeners to be tall tales—statements so exaggeratedly bold that they are clearly contrived and therefore pathetically humorous. Much of the pleasure involved in performing them lies, in fact, in the attempt to top or outdo rivals of the opposite sex, a game that women and men can play with equal facility (see Solomon 1994).[9]

Against this background, it seems most likely that sexual boasting provided yet another realm in which men and women competed, seeking as elsewhere to prove their worth by humiliating rivals. For indeed, the drive to demonstrate competitive fire was the central organizing principle of the vida michiy, and it united every one of the custom's modalities, including music, dance, riddling, physical combat—and probably sexual prowess. In the last chapter I noted how easily Isbell's account of the vida michiy might be taken to echo long-standing discourses of indigenous primitivity for those so uncharitably disposed as to do so. My words on physical and rhetorical violence in the vida michiy may be liable to the same critique; however, each of my interlocutors spoke of those contests in such glowing and wistful terms that I do not believe it possible to do justice to their experience without registering them here. To elide these qualities of experience is only to reproduce the very structure of thought that deems some experiences to be valuable and worthy while relegating others to the scrapheap of history. I proceed, then, on the premise that a viable understanding of the expressive forms that animated a sense of indigeneity for people like Óscar, José, don Marcelino, Marco, and their peers can be appreciated only by honestly engaging with the things that they loved. In this context it is worth recalling Mosely's insights into the links between violence, play, and music that animate musical history in the heart of the West, where "play was often as brutal as it was divine: from the [Greek] pankration . . . to the Roman ludi" (2015:161), and where such play has routinely devolved onto metaphors of musical weaponization—as when accordionists, guitarists, or rappers "duel" and "battle" one another or dancehall performers "murder" their rivals.

Finally, since the timbral elements of vocal and instrumental production received the most attention in my conversations about indigenous aesthetics, and since they continue to animate contemporary chimaycha, I devote considerable attention to them here. In this instance chimaycha echoes the music of Stobart's Bolivian interlocutors, which foregrounds "young women's voices, their highly distinctive timbre and gestures seemingly almost impossible for non-rural singers to adequately reproduce" (2008:219). Here too there is a clear connection between the terms used in evaluating women's voices and men's instruments. Chinlili construction and vocal technique alike are designed to foster complex, strident sounds that bear sonorous witness to youthful fortitude, a quality that in turn is the basis for the performance of romantic desirability that lay at the heart of the vida michiy.

The Sound of Chimaycha: Strength, Timbre, and Tessitura

Chimaycha is but a variant of the huayno genre favored in Quechua-speaking communities across the Andes, and as if to underline its commensurability with other styles, Óscar told me of consulting sources well beyond don Marcelino in his youthful performing days. He and his friends, he said, tuned in radio broadcasts from faraway Cusco in search of fresh melodic material over the 1980s: "We also based our songs on music of Cusco; they sing more or less like us.... We copied the notes, and sometimes, because their music was huayno, we converted it to chimaycha. We just adjusted the notes or added instrumental runs."

Differentiated mainly by its instrumentation and by the constant recycling of tunes particular to its home region, chimaycha otherwise shares rhythmic, melodic, and lyrical traits with the huayno music of communities as far away as Ecuador and Bolivia. Its lightly syncopated melodies emphasize the notes of the Western pentatonic scale, though they may incorporate passing tones and ornaments that lie outside that pitch series (see figure 6 for an illustrative transcription of don Marcelino's song "Urqupi qasapi wayllacha ichucha"). Performed in duple meter, sometimes emphasizing off-beats through instrumental accents or clapping, songs are organized into binary strophes without refrains. Like most huayno tunes, chimaycha strophes follow an AABB pattern of repetition in lyrics and melody, but they typically end with a shorter fifth line, usually an abbreviated or altered version of a line found earlier in the strophe—a distinguishing trait that can be seen in all four of don Marcelino's

FIGURE 6. "Urqupi qasapi wayllacha ichucha," as sung by Don Marcelino Tomaylla. Transcribed by author.

FIGURE 7. Traditional chinlili, probably dating to the 1980s. Photograph by author.

FIGURE 8. Standard "comuncha" tuning for chinlili. Transcribed by author.

songs presented above. Finally, verses always cadence in the same way, with a penultimate phrase coming to rest on a major chord, and the last phrase finishing on the relative minor chord. Outsiders often hear this modal alternation as melancholy or bittersweet, but the notion is irrelevant in Andean communities, where mode carries no emotional connotations.

When musicians spoke with me about chimaycha's distinctive qualities, they pointed to the chinlili, the physical structure of which plays a vital role in shaping chimaycha's unique sound (see figure 7). Predictably enough, luthier Marco Tucno spoke most precisely about this point, beginning with our very first interview in 2003. Asked to distinguish the two genres, he acknowledged that chimaycha is a variant of huayno but went on to insist that his hometown music was differentiated by instrumental timbre: "Instruments, of course, there everything is different, because [the chinlili] has its own tuning and a particular set of strings.... The fourth string has a [double], a smaller string that sounds an octave higher [than its mate], and that makes it completely different. It harmonizes and gives the music a different flavor."

The chinlili's doubled fourth string, in tandem with the instrument's mode of execution, does indeed produce a distinctive sonorous effect. Like the guitar, the chinlili is strung in six courses, but the fourth is doubled at the octave and the first at the unison. From lowest to highest pitch, the standard tuning, dubbed *comuncha*, is GBDgbe (see figure 8), meaning that the three open bass strings form a major triad. Using the thumb of the right hand, performers chug out a rhythmic accompaniment using those open bass strings, leaving the left hand free to move up and down the neck and fret melodies as needed.[10] As in many styles of huayno performance, the rhythmic accompaniment consists of an ascending arpeggiated major chord. In Chuschi the pattern takes the form of an eighth note and two sixteenths, while in Quispillaccta it consist of an eighth rest followed by two sixteenths (see figure 9).[11] In either case, the two sixteenth notes are played on the fifth and fourth courses. Good performers damp the bass notes, resting the flesh of the thumb's knuckle on the string it has just crossed and producing a punchy effect that adds considerably to chimaycha's rhythmic drive. However, this cannot happen with the higher string in the doubled fourth course, since it is positioned on the wrong side of the pairing. The back of the thumb mutes the bass string but leaves the other sounding, and each beat ends with it ringing out strongly in the treble range,

FIGURE 9. Standard chinlili accompaniment pattern, as rendered by quispillacctino and chuschino performers. Transcribed by author.

FIGURE 10. "Bleeping" effect in chinlili accompaniment. Transcribed by author.

creating a persistent upbeat bleep on the pitch of D that is part of what Marco describes as chimaycha's "flavor" (see figure 10).

This is not the only way that chinlili performers have brought sonorous density to chimaycha performance. In the 1980s young Óscar Conde, José Tomaylla, and their quispillacctino peers borrowed a technique from guitarists in the downriver Pampas Valley province of Víctor Fajardo, in order to compensate for the instrument's short sustain. It consisted in using a "brushing" stroke to perform melodies with the index finger of the right hand. Moving the finger back and forth across the instrument's treble strings, striking them with both the top and the bottom of the fingernail, they produced a tremolo effect much like the one that mandolin players use to sustain tones on their similarly disadvantaged instruments. Though it was adopted in the 1980s, by the turn of the millennium the mastery of this technique had become regarded as a minimum qualification for serious playing—at least according to Marco and Óscar. Marco told me that players who failed to master the back-and-forth brushing were simply not as pleasing to hear, while Óscar lamented in our 2012 interview the abilities of a fellow quispillacctino who "despite being born there doesn't play our style; he's still a little behind . . . needs to focus on the tremolo, which I learned from [José Tomaylla]."

This tremolo technique added "horizontal" body to chimaycha performance by filling space between notes. The last half of the twentieth century also appears to have witnessed a "vertical" expansion as performers began playing chinlilis in consort, featuring instruments of different sizes, playing the same thing in parallel harmony at different pitch levels (see figure 11). In this format chinlilis received standardized numbers, using the even integers between 4 and 12, with the #4 chinlili being the smallest and the #12 the largest. Such consorts are familiar from other Andean contexts, especially where flute ensembles are central to musical life (see Stobart 2006; Turino 1993), but the configuration appears to be rare and recent in the Pampas Valley. The exact timing of its development is unclear, since guitar makers in Chuschi District have long worked with a casual notion of standard sizing.[12] However, don Marcelino and other performers of his generation insisted that they performed on guitars of a single size, and the consort configuration appears to have been quasi-institutionalized by a later generation, probably sometime between the 1960s and 1980s. Certainly Óscar, José, and Marco all insisted that the most pleasing chimaycha performances were animated by large, harmonized groups, and on the day that Marco brought out the series of instruments illustrated in figure 11 he wistfully asked whether he would ever again hear such a "full" chinlili consort in performance. It is rare to hear large chinlili consorts today, even in traditionalist performance, where most artists use a single #4 chinlili tuned in E minor / G major and sounding an octave above a companion nylon-stringed guitar. Sometimes performers add a #6 chinlili, which sounds a perfect fourth below the #4, but only Óscar Conde's group Los Auténticos de Patario performs consistently with what he deemed to be a full consort of three chinlilis. This format consists of a #4 and a #6 as well as a #8, which sounds an octave below the #4—thereby creating a harmonization that resembles certain pan flute styles of southern Peru and Bolivia (see figure 12).[13]

The chinlili also bears a timbral quality that can be understood as yet

FIGURE 11. Chinlili consort. Photograph by author.

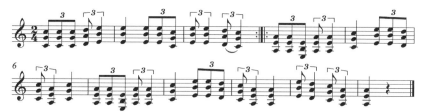

FIGURE 12. Harmonized chinlili consort of the kind played by Los Auténticos de Patario. Transcribed by author.

another vector for sonorous plenitude, a quality that is highlighted in everyday speech and in technical conversation alike. The layperson's appreciation appears in the use of the slang term *chivear*, "to sound like a goat." Chinlili players routinely appeared in Marco's shop to ask for speedy instrument repairs so that they might chivear—that is, play the chinlili—in an upcoming show. This perhaps unappealing gloss is in fact an effective metaphor for the shrill, penetrating sound that chimaycha performers cherish—a type of timbral complexity that has been described elsewhere as a key element of Andean aesthetics.[14] Indigenous music tends to stand apart from that of mestizo communities by virtue of its stridency. Bright, harmonically rich sounds like those produced by instruments played at high volume and slightly out of tune are favored over the clean delivery that governs, for instance, the huayno music of mestizo elites. In the case of the chinlili, the requisite out-of-tune quality and the consequent production of complex overtones are inscribed in the instrument's very form, with an intentionality that can be traced by comparing it with the Spanish guitar played by the mestizos of the surrounding region.

In the first place, the version of the chinlili that became preferred in the 1970s was built to be small, facilitating portability in an environment where the journey to sites of performance may involve many hours of walking over vertiginous terrain. Small size is strongly correlated with high pitch, meaning that this functional adaptation was also aesthetically adaptive. At some point music in Chuschi District also became shriller than it had been formerly, as gut strings were replaced with steel and the chinlili acquired the brighter, louder tone that come from steel strings. Meanwhile, the doubled fourth and first strings introduced the microdissonant shimmering effect that comes with the inevitable harmonic misalignment between strings of microscopically different thicknesses and pitted frets that distend stopped strings to different tensions. Finally, though it was originally built with twelve frets, the chinlili lost most of them by the 1980s, leaving only those necessary for chimaycha's pentatonic melodies. This seemingly trivial change might be understood as a result of convenience: after all, who needs frets that serve only to articulate notes that are never played? However, it has significant sonorous ramifications. The variable gaps between the remaining frets mean that the string can be pulled more or less taut depending on the point of finger pressure. The same note, then, is articulated with varying degrees of tension, according to factors like preferred left-hand position, hand size and strength, and individual energy level. Since pitch is a function of tension, such variability creates yet another source of microtonal dissonance.

As the luthier charged with reproducing this sound, Marco was well aware of the physical properties that produced it, and he built them into the instruments he created. In our 2003 interview he touched briefly on this point by lamenting the then-recent move toward playing chinlilis with twelve frets once again. This change facilitated performances with factory-produced, equal-tempered instruments like the electric keyboard and the guitar, a change that Marco supported. Still, he construed the move as a loss, saying that such instruments had "another flavor. It's not the same—when you make it with lots of frets it doesn't have that zing." When I raised the issue again ten years later he amplified his comments, catering to my increased familiarity with his work. "You're a musician," he said; "you know that when you have all those frets the pressure is different." He then moved on to discuss the similar harmonic interference that is produced by salsa trombonists playing in pairs—a sound that Marco likened to the sound of a good chinlili.

All of these traits supported the goal that don Marcelino ascribed to chimaycha performance: producing a barrage of sound, efficacious in moving dancers and drowning out rivals. Nor was he the only performer to make the association. Whether thematizing events of the past or casually evaluating a contemporary artist in passing fashion, conversations about chimaycha practice and aesthetics came again and again to weave together contest, force, and sonic plenitude. In our 2003 interview Marco described how agonistic principles crossed all the modalities of the vida michiy, interrupting himself repeatedly in his eagerness to convey the scene:

> Sometimes groups from two, three places met, and then it became competitive, and man, it was fierce. It was chinlili against chinlili, song against song, and within that there were contests that—*caramba*, there was the lapyay, where you had to strike the chest, right? See who could stand up to that, it was a custom, and while wearing ojotas [sandals] too. Those things happened. And see who was the best dancer, who played the best . . . who had a rhythm that was more, that was faster, more energetic, almost like the *huaylas*, get it? And it was tough, you get tired, you're exhausted . . . the contests were fierce because [they were] groups like the street gangs that exist today in [Ayacucho], something like that, they formed music groups. Right? And they went

to make war on the other group, using rhythm, dance, song, *toque* [roughly, playing style or accompaniment figure]. The war was in [the lazas of] Patario, in Sayapucro, in Sullkaraypata, and it was a tough contest, so that's where you developed your skills the most.

Other commenters tended to describe the same dynamics in the parsimonious fashion of elder Alejandro Núñez, who told me that the vida michiy's competitions aimed "basically to see who could play the noisiest or dance the hardest." Without exception, however, they treated the production of sonorous plenitude and the demonstration of physical strength as two means to the same end.

It was not the instrument that chimaycha fans and musicians typically placed at the center of chimaycha aesthetics, however, but the female voice. Vocal aesthetics parallel chinlili aesthetics in striking fashion, given the radically different capacities of the instrument and the human vocal apparatus. High, pinched, loud voices were favored over chest voice or bass tessitura, and the same principles of grit, vigor, and strength that animate discussions of chinlili playing weighed in the appreciation of vocalists. Figured through references to volume and pitch—facets of vocal production that are difficult to sustain over a long period and that index stamina—evaluations of female singing were deployed much more commonly than evaluations of chinlili playing when the worth of a particular group or recording was being assessed. Marco himself insisted that the evolution of chimaycha's instrumentarium responded to a vocalist's rule of thumb, which he expressed as "the higher the better, the louder the better, to show how strong the singer is." Reporting on the development of ever-smaller chinlilis during his youth in Chuschi, he noted that the drive toward ever-higher singing necessitated their creation. Larger versions were simply unable to withstand the stress produced when strings were tuned to ever-higher tension in efforts to bring instruments up in pitch—to say nothing of the dexterous difficulty involved in playing instruments with such stiff strings. He also interpreted the expansion of the chinlili consort as a function of the growing intensity of female vocal delivery—a force that could be balanced only by a larger instrumental group. After telling me that a diminutive #4 chinlili was adequate for accompanying an eight- or ten-year old girl, or even a fourteen- or fifteen-year-old, he went on to note that "there are girls that have a voice, a high, sharp sound, and who sing, and do they ever shout loud. So it has to be with two or three [instruments]."

Other musicians too noted that audiences preferred high, energetic voices that recalled the sounds of young competitors at the vida michiy. The value of sounding young and strong is so prevalent that artistic evaluations are frequently phrased in terms of childlike vocal production—that is to say, a woman's ability to retain into adulthood the vocal qualities that she possessed as an adolescent. Marco's admiration for the voice of Zenaida Paredes was phrased in just those terms: commenting one day on a song that came onto the radio as we worked in the shop, he noted approvingly that her voice had not changed at all since her girlhood. Elsewhere, Jorge Núñez told me that his wife, artist Ninay Urucha, was lured back into artistic life after many years due to repeated requests from fans for a recording that dated to 1989. That recording featured the high, strong voice of the *chibolita* (small girl) that she had been at the time, and indeed, when she returned to artistic life she maintained it, recognizing her strikingly high, loud voice as the key to her success.

Chimaycha aesthetics, then, might be understood in part as a sonorous cognate of the other means through which young comuneros performed their desirability in the vida michiy. The stamina and stoicism that animated physical contests, for men and women alike, became rendered in musical terms. Stated succinctly, it is difficult to sing or to play at high pitch and high volume for very long, so pitch and volume became weapons to use against rivals and—to the extent that they stood for youthful vigor and desirability—became cherished musical aesthetics. Marco's understanding of the custom's evolution over the 1970s and 1980s was explicitly informed by this notion of aesthetic translation across domains. During his youth, he said, Chuschi's authorities became worried about increasing levels of physical violence, going so far as to prohibit the lapyay. In its absence, competitive verve and demonstrations of physical prowess devolved upon the musical aspect of the vida michiy.

Of course certain chimaycha performers dissented from dominant aesthetic principles. Alberto Infanzón, director of chimaycha group Los Aires Chuschinos and a man well known for contracting especially good singers, lamented in a 2013 interview that "chimaycha musicians sometimes sing at a really high pitch, and in doing so they, how can I say it, they strain too hard for a higher note." In fact, his complaint was not aimed at high pitch per se but rather at performers who so strain themselves that they complicate a listener's ability to interpret the sung word. He is far from alone in this evaluation. The ability to enunciate clearly tends to provide an upper limit on the range employed by a particular singer, and clarity of diction matters in what is, after all, a genre of sung poetry.[15] Indeed if chimaycha's sonorous properties gesture toward values of youthful potency, then the genre cannot be understood without appreciating the countervailing strands of romance, personal experience, and ecological knowledge that animate its poetics.

Romance, Experience, and a Sense of Place:
Chimaycha Lyrics as Sentient Ecology

Chimaycha songs overwhelmingly treat of romance and love impeded, and Marco's feeling was that love was so dominant a theme that "you'd have a hard time finding another." In fact I did find one song, on an old cassette housed in the collection of the UNSCH's Centro de Capacitación Campesina, speaking with invidious humor about the superiority of chuschinos over their quispillacctino neighbors. Marco dismissed it as unnaturally "topical," clearly written on the spur of the moment for a CCC-sponsored competition. However, his dismissal ended by pointing to a second quality that is central to successful chimaycha songs: probably, he said, the composer responded to criteria presented by the competition organizers, drawing on the first personal experience that came to mind.

Such truth to experience—the sense that a song draws on something lived by the composer—and the lyrical construction of verisimilitude, by which a universal experience is placed into a familiar landscape shared by composer and hearers, together make up another central feature of chimaycha aesthetics. Marco lent this quality of experience a special sort of clarity by telling me about something he had witnessed as a six-year-old boy. He recalled being left alone one night with a female cousin when both were caring for animals in the puna. A young man showed up with a chinlili, serenading the cousin and bringing her to tears. When Marco remonstrated, the tearful girl told him to let the youth be, and he drifted off only to wake in the night and find them singing and crying together. Later he would discover that the girl was meant to be married to another man that week, but her young suitor's sung pleas to explain her looming departure had the desired effect—the couple fled to Lima, where they married and lived out the remainder of their lives.

Chimaycha's romantic stories and dilemmas, then, were not necessarily fictive, nor metaphors for some other experience. However, in all cases successful songs demonstrated a composer's facility with using, adapting, and renewing fictive elements, stock tropes drawn from the natural world and the geography of community life. Elliptical and allusive, never fully narrative in form, chimaycha songs tended to gesture in a brief word or phrase toward the experience that lay behind them, expending lyrical energy instead on communicating the emotional charge of that experience through appropriate figures and places that symbolized the speaker's state of mind. This presupposes a deep knowledge of a sentient ecology shared by composer and audience.

Savvy deployment of ecological knowledge, then, is another key element of chimaycha lyrics, but it tends to operate in a register that is less explicit than strength, romance, or experiential fidelity. It is not that practitioners overlook the centrality of nature to their songs: queries about chimaycha lyrics typically elicit responses like that of José Tomaylla, who told me that they spoke of "nature, lived experience, [and] love."[16] However, musicians rarely dwell on nature as a theme in its own right, emphasizing instead the genre's role in structuring affective communication and treating the natural world as a resource for the metaphorical play on which such affective communication depends. Nature, in other words, is typically treated as a mere vehicle for chimaycha's poetics of love and loss—and yet the very metaphors through which experiences of love and loss are translated into art remain inert unless they are grounded in a rather sophisticated knowledge of village ecology.

When performers did make explicit connections between chimaycha and the natural world, they tended to emerge via stories about the local belief system that organizes relations between human and other-than-human beings. Both Marco and his great-uncle Jacinto had watched chinlilistas leave new instruments at waterfalls or springs inhabited by *sirenas*, aquatic entities that are linked throughout the Andes to musical power.[17] After a night or a week, performers would return to collect instruments that played as if a competent musician had broken them in and were filled with new melodies, tunes that emerged effortlessly under the fingers of those who had hazarded a trip to the sirena's haunt. And this was not the only way to fill a chinlili with power. Marco spoke of seeing men at the vida michiy lay instruments on the ground, where young women stepped over them in pollera skirts, thereby exposing the instruments at once to the earth and to the female genitalia, twinned symbols of fecundity.

By contrast the presence of nature in chimaycha lyrics tended to be figured as secondary to matters of love and romance. Most often musicians introduced the matter by drawing a contrast between older songs and the somewhat more direct, prosaic lyrics of more recent times. When, for instance, I first asked Óscar Conde to teach me old chimaycha songs and to tell me what they were like, he said that they "were all about love, but they used animals as figures— vicuñas, *chiwakus*, which are thrushes, *qintis* [Q: hummingbirds], and so on." The songs that he went on to discuss with me in that session featured as their central figures glowworms, partridge, gulls, sparrows, and wild grasses, in addition to the occasional human being. Given the same request, Marco presented me with songs that leaned more heavily on other beings that populate the Andean landscape: geological or hydrological features such as rivers or mountains, nonordinary entities like the enchanted sirena that fills the chinlili with its power, and several plants that he described as having medicinal properties, like the *wamanripa* and *anquripa*. Each man's songs, moreover,

94   CHAPTER THREE

set these elements along familiar pathways that cross the district or placed them near particular peaks, passes, and rocks, thereby situating them not only within their proper climatic and topographical context but also within a lived geography recognizable to composer, performer, and hearers.

Marco's choice of "Chikllarasu mayu" (Chikllarasu River) neatly illustrates the way these various elements hang together. He raised this song after I asked him directly about the apparent—to me—centrality of nature to songs that he insistently tied instead to romance and lived experience. Taking this disjuncture in stride, he referred to an earlier conversation in which he had lamented the employment of outside judges for contemporary song competitions. How, he now asked, were such people to evaluate the songs that they heard without an intimate knowledge of the local landscape? How could they evaluate the fit between their natural metaphors and their sentimental purposes? He went on to describe both how such an intimate knowledge of the natural world was inculcated and how it came to fit with the task of affective expression: "You know how this comes about? Look, you're walking around with your parents, as a kid, and they point at plants, animals, and so on, and say, 'You have to care for this, it's like a relative.' And you feel a sort of tenderness toward it, so when you want to court someone, find a way to express [your feelings], of course you draw upon what you know of tenderness to do so."

"Chikllarasu mayu" illustrated the connections between what we had now agreed to be three central pillars of chimaycha lyrical style—love, nature, and personal experience. Marco had often mentioned the song as an especially good example of chimaycha tradition, but he now fleshed out its significance, attributing its authorship to a woman with whom he had consorted during his early days in Ayacucho. Her lover, he said, had fallen into the song's eponymous waterway and drowned, and this personal tragedy gave the song its weight. It did not, however, gain such power from any direct statement about the event itself; rather, in a sterling illustration of the way that chimaycha lyrics work through implication, it conjured a highly specific landscape through geographic references and description of things and activities that pertain to that landscape. Then, through judicious use of conventionalized references that index accidental death and personal abandonment, it invited listeners not only to identify the location but also to divine its significance for the speaker.

These words place the speaker in the fields below Antaqaqa Mountain and near the river's banks, gathering high-puna plants that grow there. Such ecological verisimilitude allows listeners to imagine themselves within a scene that is as familiar to hearers as to the singer. However, other lines use old familiar tropes, such as the mother-father pairing and the figure of high and

Chikllarasu mayu
Chikllarasu mayu, ackha yaku mayu (bis)
Tayta mamallaypa sunquchallampi kach-
    kaniraqchu icha manañachu (bis)
Kachkaniraqchu icha manañachu

Antaqaqa urqu yana puyuchallay (bis)

Amaraq tutallaykamullayraqchu
Anquripatam maskamullachkani
Amaraq tutallaykamullayraqchu
    wamanripatam maskamullachkani

Mayupi sirena qaqapi encanto
    clarochallayta willachaykullaway
Mayupi sirena qaqapi encanto
    ciertochallata willachaykullaway
Yanachallay kuyawachkanraqchu icha
    manañachu
Sunquchallampi kachkaniraqchu icha
    manañachu

Fuga
Sichu mana chaypi kaptiyqa
    willachaykumallaqay
Hatun ñan camino hanaypas uraypas
    pasakunaypaq
Hatun ñan camino hanaypas uraypas
    ripukunaypaq

Chikllarasu River
Chikllarasu River, full, high river (bis)
Am I still within my mother's and father's
    heart, or not? (bis)
Am I, or not?

Antaqaqa mountain, with your little black
    cloud (bis)
Don't let night fall on me yet
I'm searching for anquripa
Don't let night fall on me yet
I'm searching for wamanripa

River siren on your enchanted rock, speak
    clearly to me
River siren on your enchanted rock,
    speak truly to me
Does my lover still love me or not?

Does my dear heart still love me or not?

Fuga
If [he's] not there
tell me so
Then I will travel by the high and the
    low roads
Then I will return by the high and the
    low roads

low roads, to suggest the universality of the speaker's emotional concerns—worries about one's standing with one's family, about a lover's commitment, and about the value of staying in place or journeying elsewhere. It is, in fact, the very tacking between such general concerns and a sense of specificity—the realization that the speaker asks this *particular* siren in this *particular* river because this place holds a personal significance—that lifts the song into a realm of chimaycha artistry. By using stock tropes to indicate that the song's subject is of general interest, but also by using figures that are specific enough to imply a real actor behind the text, the song elicits both empathy and identification. It makes clear that the composer's concerns are neither abstract nor metaphorical: they could occupy the mind of anybody, they *have* occupied the mind of someone much like those who hear it, and they *may* soon occupy the hearer as well.

It is, however, the song that has become Quispillaccta's "anthem" that most

96   CHAPTER THREE

masterfully ties together landscape, nature, human experience, and courtship. First recorded in 1983 and composed slightly earlier, "Yutuchay" is familiar to any devoted follower of Radio Quispillaccta, because it opens the morning program of station director Graciano Machaca. However, it is beloved not only because of that institutional sanction but also for its rich content. Like "Chicllarasu mayu" it proceeds telegraphically, presenting "a rich body of narrative detail through the allusions it makes to a shared repertoire" (Reily 2001:19), rather than detailed narrative:

Yutuchay	*Little Partridge*
Yutuchay yutuchay	Little partridge, little partridge
Kimsa cruzllapi tuparqanchik	We met at Three Crosses
Yutuchay yutuchay	Little partridge, little partridge
Puka kunkapi tuparqanchik	We met at Red Throat
Enemigoyman hamuniptiy	I came for my enemy
Ama willaychu nillarqayki	And said not to tell
Ama willaykuy nillasqakuy	Though I said not to
Enemigoyman willaykunki	You told them anyway
Contraparteman willaykunki	You told my enemies anyway
Yutuchallay, yutuchallay	Little partridge, little partridge
Fuga	*Fuga*
Yutuchallay yutuchallay	Partridge, little partridge
pankusiki yutu	Big-rumped partridge
Patario pampapim	At Patario
kunkaykita qiwisaq	I'll wring your neck
Wayrapunku pampapim	At Wayrapunku
kunkaykita tipisaq	I'll snap your neck

When the song's cues are fully understood, it becomes clear why it resonates powerfully for people like Graciano Machaca with a vested interest in defending a distinctive indigenous ontology. Here the speaker, understood to be a young indigenous woman, begins by addressing another young woman as a little partridge, taking advantage of the Andean custom whereby women are metaphorized as birds in song. When I discussed the song with Óscar, however, he was careful to underline the special, original nature of this particular bird choice. One reason becomes clear in the song's concluding verse, which takes the form of a *fuga*—an appended section, often based on a different song, and which often includes a clue reframing the lyrics that come before it. Here the reference to a large rump evokes the meaty haunch of the wild bird. However, it also evokes the female body type that is prized in the indigenous Andes, where body fat, not blood or muscle, is considered to be the vital human substance. Anthropologists have long noted that women are admired for a stout, low-centered body and often emphasize those qualities by wearing multiple pollera skirts (Femenías 2005; Weismantel 2001). The bird's shape, in other words, is wonderfully iconic of female desirability.

The song's ecological resonance does not end there, though a full grasp means parsing the song's apparently violent message and its geographic references. For listeners attuned to traditional lifeways, references to combat between young women can only evoke the vida michiy, and the geographic references place the scene even more specifically. "Kimsa cruz" (Three crosses), in the Cachi-side barrio of Catalinayocc, and "Puka kunka" (Red throat) place the scene en route to Patario, the vida michiy's central arena. Finally, the element that ties the song together is the residential pattern of the partridge itself. Patario happens to be well populated by these birds, meaning that it not only stands as a metaphor for standards of female beauty but also evokes the very context in which young men and women staged their desirability for one another—the maximal site of romance, according to traditional custom.

Few chimaycha songs condense sentient ecology, social and physical geography, and youthful bravado in such a pleasing fashion. This song, like "Chicllarasu mayu," is more tightly plotted than songs are likely to have been in traditional performance and may betray what Rothenbuhler has called a "phonographic consciousness" (2007), a postcommodification imperative to think in terms of compositional design, making it different from songs deployed in the emergent musical circumstances of the vida michiy.[18] Whatever its genesis, however, the perfect balance of chimaycha's relevant poetic resources in "Yutuchay" is the reason that the song is highly regarded by traditionalists.

Sex, Humor, and Competitive Boasting

Finally, however, the vida michiy involved another, entirely different sort of song as well—crowing songs of sexual innuendo, like those of don Marcelino. Strikingly, conversations with casual acquaintances did not yield references to such songs, and most writings on the vida michiy do not either. This may suggest a personal bias on the part of the elderly campesino; however, in separate conversations, closer friends like Marco and Óscar also spoke of these songs as a part of the custom. There are two complementary ways to understand this discrepancy. On one hand, many chimaycha traditionalists in the present day lament the way that contemporary artists mimic the lyrical style of commercial huayno, singing songs of sexual and alcoholic dissolution in language that is entirely devoid of poetic metaphor—a stark contrast to the ecocentric poeticism of songs like "Chicllarasu mayu" and "Yutuchay." In this context, recognizing older chimaycha songs that are similarly frank may undercut the contrast between cherished tradition and a corrupted modern style. Even more likely is the possibility that songs of ribaldry have come to seem embarrassing for people all too used to demeaning stereotypes of indigenous sexual primitivism. In a moment of indigenous resistance to such images, discussions of matters that could reinforce the stereotype may well have seemed inappropriate.

In any case there is ample reason to believe that songs like those of don Marcelino were central to the vida michiy. First, it should be understood that in Andean communities sexual activity bears little stigma. Unmarried young people are expected to be interested in and experimenting with sexual relations, and even after marriage open conversation about the topic is not deemed scandalous. Like many ethnographers in the region, I have often been confronted with open questions about my sexual history and procreative abilities, particularly given the fact that I remained childless until my mid-thirties—extremely late by Andean standards. I have also been present for innumerable all-male conversations, often with mere acquaintances, where issues like impotence, prostitution, masturbation, and adultery are discussed with an openness that I have rarely encountered in North America.

Second, it should be recognized that sharp, humorous badinage is a key modality of Quechua conversation. Billie Jean Isbell has noted that "humor and irony are probably the dominant tropes of Andean discourse" (1997:286; see also Allen 2002 [1988]; Harvey 1991), and in this light such songs are easily recognizable as humorous exaggeration or perhaps bluffs, a quality that Lott has tied to the similar sexual boasts of blues artists like Howlin' Wolf (2011).[19] Hearers are expected to respond to them with skepticism or with an even more exaggerated claim. These songs acted, then, as vehicles for the posturing and flirting that the vida michiy was supposed to channel, and as further vehicles for the competitive display of prowess—in this instance setting men against women, for women too were expected to maintain a repertoire of bawdy, bragging songs. In this sense they should be regarded as a cognate of the vida michiy's physical and musical contests, in which displays of power applied as centrally to female as male attractiveness. Isbell has made such a claim, going so far as to single out verbal combat over sexual prowess as *the* central act of the vida michiy: "There is a positive link between sex and language. . . . Conceptual frontiers [about sex] were explored in a warlike atmosphere of competition against a musical backdrop, with dancing and verbal duels as principal weapons" (1997:281). However, Isbell's argument turns on the notion that Andean adolescence is a time of female dominance, wherein young women wield sexual superiority over supplicating men, who are reduced to compensatory boastfulness in a vain effort to cover the shame of their sexual inadequacy. Perhaps unsurprisingly, the men with whom I worked did not understand these songs in this way. Rather, they described ribald songs like those of don Marcelino as means by which women and men alike flirted and celebrated the joys of sexual gratification. They echoed more precisely the words of Peruvian anthropologist Rodrigo Montoya and his coauthors, who have noted that when it comes to sex "[young] men and women are equal in to one another; unlike everything that happens in the feudal, Catholic notion of love, women take the initiative, and are not just passive actors" (Montoya et al. 1997 [1987]: 48).[20]

In the end, songs of sexual braggadocio might be taken as a practice that ties together all of the vida michiy's other aspects. For if the ceremony's timing is determined by seasonal change and the work of animal husbandry, and if the lyrics combine amorous intent with ecological wisdom, then the element at the nexus between these activities is reproduction. Writing of practices and belief systems in nearby Cusco, Mannheim has noted similarly that "domains of sexual, agricultural, animal, and social reproduction ... are, in fact, a single conceptual domain for Quechua speakers" (1998:264). The vida michiy is, after all, a ritual of fertility, per Palomino (1971); that its great themes should be romance and sex ought to come as no surprise.

Conclusion

For men like Óscar, Marco, Graciano, José, their peers, and elders like don Marcelino, the songs I have discussed here recall an age in which music was highly attuned to agronomic cycles and village customs. These have waned before modern demands and devices that obviate the kinds of delicate ecological figuration they treasure. Tellingly, Óscar dated the fundamental change in chimaycha music to the appearance of "modern" elements in their lyrics, such as the title appliance in "Radiocha" (Little radio), and Marco echoed him at length in a separate interview: "[Ranulfo] Infanzón recorded 'Centro Andino,' right? So imagine, it's about a bus that's taking you away, away from a normal life. . . . [Before that] it was Andean things, things from the heartland, things that happened every day, that were sung. Really every song told of everyday life, a normal life, what happens in the world around, but only in the immediate surroundings."

The irruption of new technologies into song texts was retrospectively heard as the beginning of an era's end—the moment at which indirect metaphor, indigenous traditionalism, and long-standing relations between people and nonhumans all began to wither before new influences. This notion of an epochal shift, however, should be regarded with some circumspection, for as the stories told in this chapter and the previous have made clear, chimaycha was always evolving in response to outside forces. Performers favored larger or smaller instruments in different eras, and they apparently used different strings at different times. Such changes might owe to fluctuations in available technology, but performers also favored voices at different pitch levels, a matter that is harder to link with anything but generational fashion. In this sense the portrait of chimaycha that I have painted here is best regarded as the experience of a generation—a generation that was and remains influential, but one whose influence is no less provisional than any other.

Of course chimaycha did not die out: it incorporated new influences, retaining some of its older aesthetic principles while adjusting others to new modes of performance and performing contexts. In chapters 4 and 5 I move on to discuss those contexts and the changes that they drove. Before I move on, though, it is worth devoting some final words to the relationship between chimaycha and gender identity—a matter that has changed but little in recent times. The situation that I have traced in this chapter has tended to emphasize gendered complementarity in chimaycha performance, for much like Stobart's charango-playing interlocutors in Bolivia, mine treated music as a practice in which roles were equitable rather than hierarchical. The chinlili players of Chuschi District, too, understood their performances as "provoking women to sing [and] there is a strong sense that [the instrument] ultimately serves, accompanies and creates a public performance context for young women's voices" (Stobart 2008:74). Nor should the absence of female instrumentalists be construed necessarily as an instance of patriarchal control over women's musical opportunities, for again, as in Bolivia, "there is little sense that women's role as singers is seen as subordinate to men's role as instrumentalists. Rather, it is the intellectual capacities necessary for singing and for the creation and remembering of song poetry which are stressed" (Stobart 2008:88) and treated as the foreground element that men's playing complements.

As noted above, such ideas of complementarity have been challenged by many scholars as a thin discursive veneer over the deeply patriatrchal power relations that characterize Andean communities. It is true that chimaycha performance, collaborative as it may have been, relied upon unstated, highly binarized, rather rigid norms of gendered musical expression. I have not sought here to challenge the normativity of that vision, because the musical narratives that I heard presented little evidence of nonnormative musical interpretation. This does not mean, of course, that such performances are inexistent: it does mean that they will have to await another scholar's attention. In lieu of such a portrait, I have sought instead to show how people inhabited the norms they inherited and how those norms gave rise to aesthetic principles that continue to inform chimaycha aesthetics today. Chimaycha is indeed one among many social institutions through which gender ideologies were and are naturalized; calling attention to that fact is one first step in denaturalizing relationships that may be less symmetrical than commonly believed.[21]

4

Tradition and Folklore

So far I have described chimaycha music and the socionatural order of Chuschi District as if they formed a closed and stable system, but neither was ever static. They refracted the social and ideological currents that moved the district's residents, and they were always liable to change under the influence of determined actors. By the 1970s and 1980s, when Marco and Óscar were beginning their careers as chimaycha musicians, many of the more influential actors were not indigenous comuneros. Others were indigenous comuneros who chose to follow ideas from outside the community as readily as they did the mores of local elders. By the 1990s they had brought chimaycha into new spaces, working largely through Ayacucho's university, local NGOs, and media institutions that broadcast indigenous sounds. The genre's sonorous, lyrical, and performative parameters changed, laying the foundations for a very different scene to emerge after the millennium. Thus when I first spoke with Marco about chimaycha in 2002, he spoke of the genre's topical transformation: "[Before] in chimaycha you sang about love. About love and life. You sang about little animals, comparing [other things] with animals, or about images, landscapes, happiness, all that, you sang about all that. For example you might say, 'You're like this, I'm like that, let's go make a nest,' like that, no? It was an idyll. . . . Nobody ever sang about a *sinchi* [counterterrorism officer], a judge, or about injustice. Who talked about injustice, the military, about laws?"

Here Marco's final words allude to songs by the group he cofounded in the late 1980s, Los Chikitukus de Chuschi. The second professional chimaycha group, Los Chikitukus was the first to be composed of comuneros. Its membership was drawn from the first generation of indigenous chuschinos to study at the UNSCH, and their work responded in part to the violence that afflicted their home community after the 1980 Shining Path uprising. Debates

TRADITION AND FOLKLORE

over social justice and ethnic inequality raged at the UNSCH in the 1980s and 1990s, and Los Chikitukus coalesced in that intellectual climate. However, the group's work was also shaped by the activities of earlier figures: teachers and intellectuals who had organized the staging of Andean music over the 1970s, an era of increased attention to indigenous communities and their cultural practices. In this sense the chimaycha of Los Chikitukus moved within a very different sphere from the musical activities of their ancestors: a sphere where indigeneity is less a lived quality of experience than a staged performance, one in which sonorous, sartorial, and gestural tokens are used to "explain" the content of indigenous identity. In the Andes this register of objectification is readily recognizable as the realm of folklore—"a Peruvian term for portions of culture immobilized and separated for display as fetishes of localism" (Salomon 2002:490).[1]

Andean Folklore, Presentational Music, and the Staged Variety of Indigeneity

It has been widely noted that folkloric activity—that is, the staging of culturally distinctive practices for didactic or preservationist ends—emerges in contexts of social change as unsettled people attempt to figure out what their community is becoming.[2] Just so Los Chikitukus de Chuschi might be seen as a musical instance of social transformations that transected all of Peru in the late twentieth century: the growth of indigenous migrant populations in urban centers; their creeping empowerment as they gained new levels of educational and social capital; and nascent social commitments to assuaging the exclusion of Indians.[3] In this climate government functionaries and thinkers came to treat indigenous cultural practices more as national heritage than as evidence of retardation, and to grant them limited economic and infrastructural support.

Of course this move had ample precedent in the indigenista movement of the early twentieth century, a movement that nevertheless promoted a lamentable diagnosis of indigenous Peru's cultural life. Deeply invested in preserving the cultural hierarchies that they ostensibly challenged in their work, indigenistas inveighed against the modern "corruption" of indigenous culture, insisting upon the glories of the indigenous past at the expense of a debased present, while nevertheless drawing freely upon elements of that present in their own elitist artworks. At the century's end Ayacucho's culture workers adopted a different approach, one that sprang from a different intellectual lineage even if it shared some goals and rhetorical gestures with indigenismo. Instead of proposing to honor indigenous culture via stereotyped romantic imageries and performances of their own creation, these later activists, scholars, and businesspeople tended to move within a milieu that might be called applied anthropology, and they provided space for indigenous performers to develop their own views.[4] In this sense, the contrast between the two moments helps to shed light on perennial debates about cultural agency and social power in research on the Andes and elsewhere: when disenfranchised culture bearers become empowered to present their work in spaces formerly reserved for elites, can they do so on their own terms, or must they mold their activities to the expectations of others? Is it ever wise for marginalized peoples to make much of their traditions, or per Fanon (2001 [1959]: 265) does the demonstration of cultural riches suggest a stagnant traditionalism, leading to paternalistic treatment?[5] The questions of hegemony and cross-cultural dialogue that lie behind these concerns can be extended beyond the realm of staged folklore to the conditions of indigenous life more generally, since indigenous practices often bear traces of earlier mediation by nonindigenous elites. Might indigenous peoples, long used to processes of cultural dialogue and appropriation, routinely manage such interactions to their advantage? Finally, when (if ever) do changes in expressive culture augur deeper changes in the cultural system that they support—when do they signal the withering of behaviors and dispositions that are constitutive of indigenous difference?

Ethnomusicologist Thomas Turino has investigated all of these questions, but he has been especially trenchant on the last one. Posing a comprehensive system for analyzing musical activity and its social effects, he has proposed a key functional distinction between the music that typifies small-scale, relatively egalitarian, precapitalist societies and the music that typifies large-scale, cosmopolitan, postindustrial societies (2008). In the former, "participatory" forms bring musicians to collaborate in relatively horizontal fashion, cultivating intersubjectivity through music that emphasizes deep mutual attention and cooperation. In the latter, "presentational" musicians develop more complex, audience-directed forms in order to further causes for which they stand, such as aesthetic vanguardism, political protagonism, and especially cultural vindication. A change in emphasis, from participatory to presentational musicmaking, is more than a change in aesthetics: it marks a change in habitus, a move toward a worldview wherein social identities are experienced more like commodities to be managed than as frameworks for apprehending the world.

The processes through which participatory musics are rendered presentational, however, are not uniform. In Bigenho's work on "folklorization," or "the multilayered process whereby groups consciously choreograph, compose, and perform for themselves and others, what they want to represent as distinct about their identity," she has advocated specifying the agents involved and compromises made, noting that the "middle ground in folklorization of indigeneity is between performers' desires, audiences' expectations, and the different meanings that folklore performances acquire as they move between . . . contexts" (2007:249). Folklorization, in other words, is a process through which performers negotiate ways to speak about who they are and who they want to be. It presents considerable room for maneuvering, and outcomes depend heavily on the character and the programs of those involved.[6]

This, indeed, is why the stakes of folklorization are perennially interesting in the Peruvian Andes: they unfold against a brutal but unstable background of ethnic conflict, where actors shift positions and allegiances in unpredictable fashion. Demeaned, despised, and exiled from power by members of a dominant mestizo class, who nevertheless felt invested in Andean cultural forms that they shared with their Indian neighbors, indigenous musicians have often conducted their careers in an atmosphere of uneasy, ever-provisional alliance with their enemies. Hardly limited to music, this state of affairs animates much of the best writing on the Andean society (see, for example, Arguedas 1985 [1941]), and Chuschi District is no exception. La Serna's (2012b) study of ethnic relations in the decades prior to the violence, for example, describes a "power pact" that united some actors across the town's ethnic divide, as well as the disagreements that festered within its distinct communities. Detailing the logics by which participants made their alliances, his work provides a portrait of Andean life that is much more realistic than studies that treat the region's ethnic communities as two solitudes (MacLennan 1945), mutually alienated and opposed. However, such pacts are fragile, and La Serna's study also argues that its breakdown is the very thing that led the Shining Path to identify the Pampas Valley as a site to foment insurrection against the social order (see also Díaz Martínez 1969; Heilman 2010; Isbell 1985; Theidon 2013).

Folkloric musical activities may seem far removed from such weighty events, but they are not entirely irrelevant. In a series of works focused on the province of Víctor Fajardo, downstream from the district of Chuschi, Ritter has shown how performers adapted folkloric modes of performance introduced by mestizo intellectuals over the 1960s and 1970s, using them to disseminate Marxist and other kinds of counterhegemonic concepts (2002 and 2006). The 1970s had indeed been an extraordinarily dynamic age for folkloric activity, an age when the era's leftist governments promoted culturalist rhetorics of social inclusion and invested resources to support Andean art forms (see Turino 1993). Chimaycha too benefited from this environment, and while it rarely became as politically strident as the music of Víctor Fajardo, it did change as local teachers, intellectuals, and their charges implemented the principles of folkloric work.

However, if musical folklorization involves deep cultural change, then it is also a means for subaltern performers to communicate with their associates about the way that social transformation should be negotiated. Chimaycha musicians found space for such conversations over the 1980s, through agencies centered at the UNSCH and related institutions. These channels were mainly run by mestizo scholars and activists, but, invested in indigenous social justice, they tended to respond to the priorities of indigenous musicians rather than presuming to speak for them.[7] Their broadcasts and concert promotion helped indigenous musicians boost their artistic prestige, personal autonomy, and self-esteem, and laid a foundation for later culture workers to establish an entirely self-organized scene. Although the term is anachronistic in this context, such people might best be described as advocates for cultural sustainability, insofar as this "refers to a music culture's capacity to maintain and develop its music now and in the foreseeable future" (Titon 2015:157).

Finally, it would be impossible to overstate the role of education in chimaycha's transformation. Long viewed as a lodestar of social advancement by Andean citizens (see de la Cadena 2000; Degregori 1997; García 2005), university studies were held in high esteem, and good teachers were treated with reverence. The UNSCH, reopened in 1959 in an explicit effort to "deal with 'the region's utter poverty'" (Castillo Melgar and Cueto Cárdenas 2010:11), was meant to mitigate that poverty by training teachers and sending them to rural communities.[8] The new forums for chimaycha performance that emerged after the 1960s were engineered by these very schoolteachers, or by UNSCH-affiliated scholars, and came with their imprimatur. Only a few were locals, but all had passed through a training program that placed an increasing emphasis on social justice and cultural valorization. It should, then, come as no surprise that this piece of chimaycha's story begins with a teacher.

Ranulfo Infanzón and Los Aires Chuschinos

In the 1970s a man named Ranulfo Infanzón became pivotal in the development of chimaycha in Chuschi. A mestizo born in Chuschi in 1934, he taught at Quispillaccta's elementary school for more than a decade, and he made three key musical interventions. First, by recording and hosting performances in his home, he encouraged local musicians to cultivate their art. Second, he made the first commercial chimaycha recording with a group called Los Aires Chuschinos, which he had created to promote the district's music. Finally, he intervened in the manufacture of the small guitar that would become chimaycha's signature instrument, the chinlili, and may have even commissioned the first of the model that became the standard over the late twentieth century.

TRADITION AND FOLKLORE

Infanzon's role in shaping Chuschi's emblematic musical style exemplifies an irony typical of musical development in Andean Peru (see Turino 1993). As detailed extensively in La Serna's study (2012a), the district's mestizos, and especially men, had long abused indigenous chuschinos and quispillacctinos with the terrible impunity of the well connected. Ayacucho's judicial archives contain a litany of lawsuits, dating from colonial times to the late twentieth century, charging theft, extortion, land usurpation, assault, rape, and even one 1970s-era petition from comuneros for the government to expel a particularly noxious man from Chuschi—all dismissed by administrative bodies staffed by fellow mestizos. Many of the people named explicitly and without pseudonym in La Serna's study are Infanzón's relatives by marriage, members of the prominent Azcarza family. Infanzón was never, to my knowledge, convicted of any crime, but many indigenous chuschinos and quispillacctinos spoke of him in the wary terms that they reserved for the district's mestizos more generally. In his case, their reticence extended into the comparatively banal realm of chimaycha terminology, for Infanzón insisted on calling his hometown's music by a different name from that used by his indigenous compatriots. Defending the word *qisarita*, a term that does not seem to be used outside his own family, he went so far as to issue public statements devoted to the theme of proper terminology after the word *chimaycha* became current in the 1990s. Many contemporary musicians dismiss such efforts at asserting authority, but the genre's development cannot be understood without him, and his musical contributions underline the extent to which Andean cultural change is transacted across lines of race, class, and power.

Infanzón identified himself as a chuschino, but he was also a qala. Speaking with me about his career and his family in 2013, he told how his father, a muleteer from Ayacucho who plied the routes of the south Andes, had bought land in Chuschi due to its size and strategic location, probably in the 1920s or 1930s. He married a local mestiza, and Ranufo Infanzón himself grew up spending much of his time in the rural town, especially during breaks from schooling in the city of Ayacucho. He, too, grew up to marry a mestiza from Chuschi's landowning Ascarza family and soon settled into a house near the town's main plaza. Over the 1960s and 1970s, as he taught school in nearby Quispillaccta and conducted a parallel career as an elected authority, he became one of the district's more prominent citizens.

Neither an outsider to Chuschi nor a member of its indigenous community, Infanzón had a position that was typical of the Andean misti elite. His family background and his Spanish mastery made him far more powerful than his indigenous neighbors, who did not consider him one of their own. He did not participate in the communal labors or the relations of reciprocity that marked membership in the indigenous community, and still less did he take up any positions in its hierarchy of authorities, instead occupying the political offices identified with the state and, in practice, limited to and well-connected literate mestizos. Even his son Alberto, a chimaycha musician who was widely respected by indigenous musicians of the 2000s and 2010s, characterized the Infanzón family as "foreigners" in Chuschi, and he spoke in 2013, some seven decades after the first Infanzón settled there.

Despite their difference in station, Ranulfo Infanzón did not shrink from interactions with his indigenous peers or from practicing some of their customs. Like most mistis he grew up speaking fluent Quechua. In adolescence he socialized with indigenous agemates who would become his students, and in adulthood he became godfather to their children, arranging the jobs, loans, and other favors that come with such a bond. Finally, throughout his life he participated avidly in musical performance. Rumors circulated claiming that he had been a devotee of the vida michiy, routinely accompanying his quispil-lacctino students on their nocturnal excursions. For a nonindigenous person to attend a vida michiy was extraordinary, but it is reported to have happened. La Serna, for instance, reports references to one abusive mestizo who treated the vida michiy as "his discotheque" (2012a:14)—words that the scholar heard from the man's own daughter.[9] I never spoke with anyone who actually saw Infanzón at a vida michiy, so such statements should be treated with skepticism: as testament to reputation, and not matters of fact. However, many people did reminisce about playing by invitation at his house in Chuschi, home to the town's first and most energetically used tape recorder.

According to Infanzón, the house parties and the other musical activities of his adulthood were part of an effort to safeguard chuschino musical difference, which was threatened by new forms of popular culture. In his telling, the arrival of the highway in 1961 brought merchants selling cassette recordings of music from Ayacucho and Huancayo, with the result that "foreign" music began to replace the "autochthonous" music and dance of Chuschi. After speaking with fellow teachers, then, Infanzón and his colleagues formed a group aimed at performing and preserving customs they viewed as threatened, singing with young women from around the district. Somewhat later he formalized these activities with the creation of Los Aires Chuschinos.

Formed in the mid-1970s, Los Aires Chuschinos appears to have been the first music group in Chuschi to designate itself as such. It was not unique for very long, since Infanzón and his colleagues sponsored local competitions, attracting new groups from Chuschi's various barrios. Los Aires Chuschinos also traveled farther afield, playing at competitions in Ayacucho in 1976 and

1979, and at the studios of Lima's Radio Unión, then Peru's leading Andean music broadcaster. The group sometimes included Infanzón's own children, including sons Wílber and Alberto as well as daughter Erli. The patriarch himself withdrew from performing activities in 1979, but not before overseeing the group's most tangible legacy: a 45 rpm single, released the same year by a Lima-based record company, featuring vocals by Wílber and Erli, Ranulfo and Alberto on guitar, and a fellow chuschino nicknamed Pichinkucha on a chinlili-like instrument the group was using at the time. One side bore a song titled "Relojito de oro" (Little golden watch), and the other a song called "Ay destino" (Oh destiny). Each was labeled "huayno," the catchall term that has historically been used for Andean song by Peru's record industry. Nevertheless, each was composed of old, familiar, but lightly reworked textual tropes and melodies, and the 45 stands today as the first commercial chimaycha record.[10]

This record was a benchmark in Chuschi's musical development, but more than a decade would pass before the appearance of Los Chikitukus de Chuschi, the next chuschino group to make a professional recording. In this sense Infanzón's more substantive contribution may lie with the informal cassettes that he made in his house, using Chuschi's first tape recorder. He made them at parties where he hosted the district's best singers and instrumentalists, and he became the steward of a unique bank of relatively high-quality recordings. Other chimaycha performers remembered those cassettes as both infrastructure and inspiration—new means to circulate songs and build one's repertoire, but also a new source of pride. The chance to hear one's voice on a recorded medium was unprecedented, since the national record industry preferred to market the work of less humble performers—star celebrities, or mestizos like Infanzón who financed their own recordings. In one interview Marco Tucno remembered his first experience hearing Infanzón's chimaycha recordings, incredulity giving way to interest, and went on to characterize his response as

Relojito de oro	*Little Golden Watch*
Relojito de oro, dueño de la hora (bis)	Little golden watch, master of the hours (bis)
Tócame la hora para despedirme	Strike the hour for me to take my leave
Tócame la hora para despedirme	Strike the hour for me to take my leave
Para retirarme	For me to depart
Ñachu hora tocaña, ñachu hora marcaña (bis)	Has the hour yet sounded, has it yet struck,
Ñuqa puruchayllay ripukullanaypaq	The time for me to travel alone
Ñuqa sapachayllay pasakuyanaypaq	The time for me to walk alone
Ripukullanaypaq	To travel alone

part of a trend among his generation: "All the songs of the community, not just his group but also other aficionados—he recorded all of it. Not just one girl but many. Imagine a girl who's dying to record, just like now [2003]: many want to, but they don't have the means. That's how it was then. Imagine I record you here and now, and later you hear your own music somewhere else: back then it was a new thing and nobody wanted to miss out."

It was not long before Marco's father bought a tape recorder, and others with the means did so too. Infanzón, then, was an intermediary through which chuschinos came to develop a cassette-based economy of musical circulation like those emerging in contemporaneous communities worldwide (see Manuel 1993), with all its power to bypass hegemonic media actors and expand the narrow range of profit-laden wares they offered, and also the "recording consciousness" alluded to in chapter 3, which leads performers to come to treat their traditions as reified commodities rather than processes of communication, lending more attention to principles of compositional design, coherence, and aesthetic contrast than may have guided earlier modes of chimaycha performance.[11]

Less clear is the contentious question of whether, and how, Infanzón's own stylistic preferences might have influenced the era's chimaycha performances. Comments by his son and successor Alberto Infanzón seemed to be a preemptive effort to forestall criticisms about stylistic meddling. In a 2012 interview he characterized the family's work with other singers as minimally invasive: "What we did was evaluate, not educate. We could ensure that the notes were in tune, maybe give things more emotion, more heart to the performance, to the words, take care to ensure good audio quality." He was, he said later, especially proud of their work with pronunciation, noting how his father insisted that singers remove their hands from over their mouths, a common practice that naturally impeded lyrical comprehension.

Marco Tucno was more explicit about three innovations of Los Aires Chuschinos that pointed toward chimaycha's later development. The first was lyrics featuring conspicuously modern elements, such as the golden watch of "Relojito de oro" and the transport agency that appeared in "Ay destino." The themes of travel, apprehension, and loneliness that animated these songs were familiar enough, but where, he asked, had anyone ever heard those themes figured via metropolitan technologies, rather than the natural symbols that typically filled chimaycha lyrics? In fact, Marco might have further underlined the transition by calling attention to Los Aires Chuschinos' language choices. They tended to alternate verses in Quechua and Spanish, a common practice in the era's commercial huayno recordings, but one that was rare in a community still characterized by high rates of Quechua monolingualism.

A second element of change was the three-note arpeggiated bass figure that provided the rhythmic drive of Los Aires Chuschinos' recordings. Tucno was unsure whether the responsible party was Infanzón or instrumentalist Pichinkucha. He was, however, sure that nobody in Chuschi had played that way in previous times. Instead, chuschinos originally performed using the same two-note bass figure that was later identified as distinctive to Quispillaccta. The key rhythmic distinction separating the two rival towns, in other words, was produced through the recordings of Los Aires Chuschinos.

A lack of preexisting recordings makes it difficult to evaluate these claims. However, a third element of the group's recordings incontrovertibly marked an epochal change. "Ay destino" and "Relojito de oro" feature the high, shimmering instrumental sound that has come to be the keynote of chimaycha music. In fact the instrument heard on the record is not exactly a chinlili: Pichinkucha instead played a mandolinlike instrument built for the group by a quispillacctino named Pacotaype, a small guitar with doubled strings and frets outlining the chromatic scale. However, this instrument was meant to stand as an approximation, a "refined" version, of the chinlili—which Infanzón claimed to have invented by proxy in the first place as he sought to adapt the metropolitan sound of Ayacucho's mestizo music.

It had long been common for mestizo performers in the city of Ayacucho to pair mandolin and guitar, a timbral duo that presented an attractive mix of high, bright melody and low, rich accompaniment. In Infanzón's recounting, he and his mestizo peers wanted to bring that sound to their chimaycha performances in the early 1970s but found local instrumentalists, used to plucking strings with their fingers, unable to master the plectrum-based technique of the mandolin. Since they were unable to use a mandolin as such, the idea emerged to commission something else, an instrument with the size and tone of a mandolin that might be played finger-style. In 1972 they approached quispillacctino luthier and carpenter Jacinto Tucno with the request, and after some experimentation he came up with a prototype. It gained the onomatopoeic name chinlili in recognition of its eccentrically bright timbre and was quickly incorporated into Infanzón's group, where a trio of guitar, "semi-guitar," and chinlili displaced the earlier guitar-based sound of chimaycha performance.

Given the centrality of the chinlili to contemporary chimaycha performance, it is perhaps unsurprising that Infanzón's claims are disputed. Jacinto Tucno himself was glad to credit Infanzón with the invention of the word *chinlili*, since he believed that the older term *vigoyla* was the only proper name for the stringed instruments that accompanied chimaycha performance.[12] However, he took sole credit for inventing the small #4 vigoyla, which he took to be the only instrument that should bear the name *chinlili*. Speaking as a member of the same luthier family, Marco Tucno provided a third perspective on the subject. In Jacinto's day, he said, luthiers in and near the district of Chuschi were always making guitars of highly variable size and shape. Given the constant experimentation that characterized the trade, it was suspect to claim sole credit for any one innovation: the chinlili was, from this perspective, an emergent, collaborative invention of many hands.

It seems most likely that all three versions are true, in their own way. Despite idealized claims of customary uniformity, performance practice appears to have varied quite a lot before the 1970s. Thus Jacinto Tucno spoke of goat gut strings as the sound of yesteryear's vigoyla, while his agemate Marcelino Tomaylla remembered playing steel. Musicians who remember chimaycha performance before the 1970s universally agree that the genre's preferred instrumental medium was large, guitar-sized vigoylas, and some existing photos from those years support such claims.[13] By contrast, Isbell's pictures from the 1960s and 1970s clearly show small chinlilis in the hands of performing schoolchildren, making it clear that by that era, at least, vigoylas varied widely in their size and morphology. Perhaps these are not quite "chinlilis," however: in examining those pictures in 2017, Marco Tucno pointed to several aspects of sizing and design that make them different from the model that became dominant during and after the 1970s. Constant experimentation seems to have been the norm, in other words, but the precise configuration of the instrument now dubbed chinlili was consolidated in the 1970s. Clearly Infanzón had either commissioned such a variant or taken advantage of one that Jacinto essayed, and it became a defining part of his group's sound over the 1970s. What is safe to say is that the instrument was new in the 1970s, and that instead of fading away it lingered to become thoroughly indigenized. It is further safe to say that its appearance on Chuschi's first commercial recording consolidated the association between the district's music and the distinctive instrument.[14]

Infanzón's influence began to wane after the Shining Path seized control of Chuschi in 1980. Attending to complaints long unaddressed by the Peruvian state, the guerrillas tried and convicted local figures they considered threats to the community, subjecting some to lashes and public humiliation. Infanzón was one of those arrested (Sánchez Villagómez 2009:89), and the experience surely influenced his subsequent move to Ayacucho City, where he still lived when we spoke in 2013. Meanwhile, a somewhat different community of mestizos became central agents in objectifying and transforming chimaycha over the 1980s: folklorists and scholars tied to Ayacucho's national university.

Uriel Salcedo and the Centro de Capacitación Campesina

Infanzón was hardly the only mestizo to become involved with chimaycha music after the 1960s. Comuneros who attended school in that era recall concerts commemorating Independence Day and Mother's Day—itself a custom brought by the mestizo teachers—where schoolchildren were encouraged to display their command of the local musical style.[15] "Foreign" teacher Bernardo Asurza Paucar, a Shining Path militant who achieved infamy after coordinating the burning of Chuschi's ballot boxes on May 17, 1980, sought out local children away from the schoolyard, motivating them in both their studies and their cultural pursuits. According to Marco, he intervened one day after overhearing some of the younger students discuss the moral restrictions that prevented them from playing their chinlilis. At first he only admonished that they should be proud to display their talents, but he took things a step further shortly thereafter, when he placed Marco onstage at a school talent show. He and other Shining Path militants may even have taken a short-lived interest in sponsoring revolutionary music. In her study of violence-era Chuschi, Sánchez Villagómez cites a pseudonymous informant to the effect that "in 1978 they formed groups of young musicians with Mariátegui thought [i.e., communist ideology], in popular art everything was linked to politics, they always said 'us poor people have to revolt, the armed struggle is the path'" (2009:69). Such direct ideologization does not, however, live in local memory as a durable contribution to chimaycha's development. When I asked about the matter, I heard no stories about the kind of politicized folklore that Ritter describes for nearby Víctor Fajardo; rather, students like Óscar and Marco were taught Marxist anthems like the Internationale, a common practice of cultivating revolutionary consciousness among Shining Path cadre. More significant was Azurza Paucar's sincere interest in folkloric music, which seems to have ranged well beyond political ideology. Sánchez's study notes that he "established close ties of friendship with the comuneros" and also cites a pseudonymous informant who details the revolutionary's avid participation in community musicmaking: "My dad played mandolin, it was carnival time, we went out in a group with my uncles, and the guy joined up. There were several friends of other kids too. 'That's it, *chino* [Azurza Paucar's nickname], let's sing! Teach us a song from your town!'" (2009:72–73).

Such activities spilled beyond the patronage of mestizo teachers in the 1970s, affecting the everyday work of the district's musicians as well. Comunero Mauro Huaycha organized a formal music group in the quispillacctino barrio of Llacta Urán, a cognate to Infanzón's Aires Chuschinos. Meanwhile the district's anniversary celebration came to include a music competition organized along the same lines as metropolitan folkloric competitions—and here events in Chuschi do parallel those in Víctor Fajardo, where local intellectual leaders similarly adopted the competitive framework as a means of "modernizing" musical life (Ritter 2002). In Chuschi each barrio was responsible for sending a representative group of musicians, and they were judged in part on what Marco Tucno called "la autoctonía": fidelity to traditions of their home barrio as displayed in attire, instrumentation, performing styles, and lyrics. Substantive prizes were at stake, such as bulls from the communal herds, but competitions were informal and largely in good fun, roping in people who hailed from outside the district, including teachers and staff from the medical post, as impartial judges.

All of these efforts were eclipsed by developments in the 1980s, when scholars directly tied to the UNSCH worked through university offices to foster a flourishing Quechua-language music scene. Uriel Salcedo, an anthropologist and broadcaster from the distant city of Andahuaylas, stands out above his peers. Several influential artists urged me to consult him, and when I met him at the UNSCH in 2014, he evaluated his own reputation with modest confidence. He had, he said, provided channels for indigenous music to claim a public space in Ayacucho, and while he credited the sonorous evolution of Ayacucho to the talents of the musicians, he was glad to recognize his role in facilitating it. It began after Salcedo's 1979 graduation from the UNSCH, when he began working for an agronomic program in Ayacucho's countryside and developed a keen interest in the music around him. It was topical and continually fresh, a far cry from the unchanging themes of romance and heartbreak that guided pop cultural production. "They're well informed," he told me. "For instance, if there's a new president in your country—Clinton, Obama—a song will appear about it right away." Intrigued, he began to make field recordings and quickly gained a reputation as an expert on the topic.

His activities intersected felicitously with a project housed by the UNSCH's Centro de Capacitación Campesina (Center for Peasant Training, or CCC). Shortly after its 1959 reopening, the UNSCH had partnered with foreign NGOs to execute development projects in the poorest communities of Ayacucho's hinterland. The CCC became a key office for channeling such activities, working over the 1970s with the Dutch agency COTESU to improve irrigation and livestock management in places like Quispillaccta. Ayacucho's indigenous musicians, however, remember the CCC most fondly for *Allpanchik* (Our soil), the radio program that it aired in the early 1980s via La Voz de Huamanga, a radio station in Ayacucho City with the signal capacity to cover the indigenous countryside.

Broadcast in Quechua, *Allpanchik* aimed at rural communities and worked along collaborative lines. The CCC made community-based associates into citizen reporters by lending them tape recorders and encouraging them to capture sounds and stories from their milieus. These citizen reporters sent their recordings to the CCC offices in Ayacucho, where *Allpanchik*'s producers stitched together a mix of current events, advice, "sociodrama," and music for daily broadcast.[16] This model quickly became imperative due to the eruption of the internal conflict. As the countryside plunged into bloody violence, citizen reporters became more crucial than ever, since it was risky for CCC workers themselves to travel within the conflict zone. In fact, the institution scaled back efforts to focus on communities relatively close to the city, such as Quispillaccta's high barrio of Unión Potrero. However, from the relative safety of the city it continued to broadcast sounds of affected communities to the countryside, copied from the tapes sent in by the associates who remained in those villages.

While the violence certainly affected the stories that *Allpanchik* ran, it did not significantly affect the featured music. Songs of political protest or support for the Shining Path received little airplay: it was unwise to broadcast them given the state's interest in repressing followers of the guerrillas. Chimaycha, meanwhile, avoided explicit politics before the emergence of Los Chikitukus de Chuschi late in the 1980s. This is not to say that the violence had no effect on chimaycha, but the influence was indirect, tangible in three primary ways. First, it drove migrants to the cities of Ayacucho and Lima, where performers re-created practices from home in their kitchens, bedrooms, and courtyards, establishing the bases of an urban chimaycha scene. Second, it aggravated the dwindling character of the vida michiy, already threatened by Christian fundamentalist zeal and the increasing concentration of young chuschinos in the district capital, where they were schooled far away from the puna and its ready opportunities for performance. Military curfews and Shining Path patrols added an element of danger to nighttime celebrations in outlying areas. Finally, by driving CCC staff out of the countryside, it inadvertently thrust much of the responsibility for curating broadcasts into the hands of community members.

The net result was to make *Allpanchik* into a kind of entrepôt for circulating chimaycha, especially new songs that were otherwise unknown to musicians who had abandoned the countryside for work or studies in Ayacucho. Soon indigenous students with musical skills made the CCC's offices into something of a clubhouse. Hanging around and connecting with the show's staff, learning from the cassettes that arrived from the countryside, making themselves available to produce quick recordings for impending broadcasts, forming relatively stable groups that might generate the reliably high-quality performances that come with regular rehearsal—all of these activities, which amount to the infrastructure of musical professionalization, were channeled through the CCC. Furthermore, as rural dwellers became aware of the program's promotional qualities, they too began to form groups in their hometowns, sending in tapes to promote their skills or coming to the city to record in CCC offices. In this way the CCC became a launching pad for formal chimaycha bands based in Quispillaccta and neighboring towns, like Los Kulikulichas de Tomanga, Las Once Estrellas de Quispillaccta, or Huaylla Ichu de Llacctahurán.

Allpanchik's importance for Ayacucho's nascent indigenous music scene only grew after the departure of host Félix Gavilán.[17] This provided a space for Uriel Salcedo to deploy his expertise and his impressive collection of field recordings. He became admired not only for his knowledge but also for visiting afflicted communities at personal risk, pursuing music and unheard stories. *Allpanchik*'s broadcast hours grew apace, but the program soon yielded influence for two reasons. First, the CCC lost the support of its international partners by the mid-1980s, forcing the program to wander unstably among other funding agencies and peripheral media organs before petering out in the late 1990s. Second, Salcedo decided to establish his own program, one entirely under his own charismatic guidance. In 1983, with the experience of *Allpanchik* under his belt, he created *Takiyninchik* (Our songs), the program with which his name is associated.

Takiyninchik's influence grew in tandem with competitions and festival performances, that Salcedo began to sponsor in the city. Folkloric competitions had long been a staple of musical life in highland Peru: the CCC had already run music contests in the towns where they operated, awarding communal prizes and inviting participants to the UNSCH's annual anniversary parade in Ayacucho. Salcedo himself minimized the importance of such events when I spoke with him, preferring to extol the organic context of community-based performance. His own shows, he said, were mechanisms to raise money for materials and thereby to support the continued dissemination of that music. Nevertheless, his competition-cum-concerts, advertised via his radio program, fostered a dynamic indigenous music scene in Ayacucho. Other local institutions copied the model, but years later musicians singled out Salcedo's events and the CCC-sponsored parades as early, rare instances of legitimation in an urban context that remained hostile to indigenous culture.

Óscar Conde, who remained in Quispillaccta during the 1980s, was especially clear about the solidarity and support lent by *Allpanchik*, *Takiyninchik*, and the CCC in our 2012 interview. After detailing how *Allpanchik* aired chimaycha recordings made by community members during Quispillaccta's annual festive season, and showing me pictures of himself and his wife at CCC-sponsored events in town and in Ayacucho's plaza, he went on to characterize the work of the CCC in terms of cultural confidence: "They worked directly with the communities; for the university's anniversary they brought the best groups to compete in [Ayacucho's] main plaza. You went there to show off your customs, your music, your attire, so little by little we were losing that fear. Or let's say, little by little, we conquered the city, something like that. Yes, the 1980s, that was the boom era."

Óscar estimated that the number of groups that formed to play in Quispillaccta during the festive season increased by half and that these groups grew three- or fourfold in size. Furthermore, as he put it, "the music developed more," since publicity and competition drove compelling changes in vocal technique, instrumental dexterity, and lyrical composition. "That's where the improvements in vocals began," he said, noting the same qualities of standard pitch intontation and clear pronunciation cited by Alberto Infanzón. Most important for Óscar, however, was the right-hand technique used by chinlili players (see chapter 3). He conceded that quispillacctino musicians had copied it from the *pumpin* musicians of Víctor Fajardo in the 1980s, after a series of interprovincial folkloric competitions organized by a promoter called Raymi Llaqta. The representatives from Chuschi District, outdone by flashier pumpin musicians, resolved to improve their presentation, leading José Tomaylla to diligently master their rivals' tremolo technique. All in all, Óscar suggested, today's chimaycha musicians are only repeating and modifying the innovations that animated his own "golden age," one that resulted from a confluence between talented indigenous musicians and new institutional channels of support.

Marco Tucno and Los Chikitukus de Chuschi

Marco Tucno and Los Chikitukus de Chuschi provide the clearest windows into the social systems that reframed indigenous music between the 1970s and the 1990s. Marco moved to the outskirts of Ayacucho City in the early 1980s, when the effects of the violence led to the cancellation of classes at Chuschi's high school. He brought a chinlili but soon set it aside, drawn instead toward the pop chicha music preferred by his urban classmates. That situation was reversed with the arrival of Teodulfo Carhuapoma, a cousin who pushed Marco back into playing chimaycha with him after school hours and on weekends. This was a means of amusement but also of courting the many young women that Carhuapoma knew in the city. Reminiscing, Marco described how Ayacucho's maids strolled on Sundays in the central plaza, attracting young men like themselves who would invite them home to "do a vida michiy." Out of such sessions coalesced a trio composed of the two men and another relative, vocalist Emilia Tucno, and soon migrant families throughout Ayacucho were inviting them to enliven house parties and community celebrations.

The young chuschinos developed aspirations beyond these informal opportunities after attending folkloric competitions like those organized by Salcedo or the CCC. Inspired by the quasi-professional tone and the avid followings of the groups they saw, they raised funds from family members—Marco's own relatives sold an alpaca, and three armadillo shells they had been reserving to make instruments—and commissioned outfits and instruments from compatriots in Chuschi. They began to play their own songs as well as old favorites and to follow opportunities for performance at festivals and competitions in Ayacucho.

Marco and his companions, in other words, followed a path typical of migrant musicians, wherein urbanizing populations manage dislocation by re-creating experiences from home in altered conditions as best they can. However, it was the atmosphere and opportunities they found later at the UNSCH that decisively shaped their group's identity. Marco and Teodulfo began studying there in 1990, the former as a student of social sciences and the latter in the department of literature. Faculty and students were committed to competing agendas, ranging from hardline Maoism to the conservative principles of agronomic development or the culturalist legacies of indigenismo. Most movements, however, were devoted to social justice for the peasantry—a community that had become heavily represented among the student body over the 1970s and 1980s.[18] Faculty members like Salcedo and Ranulfo Fuentes, a literature professor of rural-indigenous origin and a composer of huayno music, encouraged their students to promote native traditions. Equally important were peer models, fellow students from Víctor Fajardo, Puquio, and other places in rural Ayacucho who were already dominating university competitions and concerts. According to Marco, the catalytic event for the group's professionalization was one such competition:

> One day we went to an event, a contest. We watched: "Just look how they're playing. What about us?" It was a contest of folkloric sketches, not at the university itself but organized by the university, in the municipal theater. There was mostly stuff from the south, some stuff from Vinchos, and scissors dance too. And that made us more eager. We asked ourselves, "How come they play and we don't?" So we presented ourselves at the university's anniversary in 1988 and we won—we won the competition, we got a diploma and a prize.

It was around this time that the group took on the name Los Chikitukus de Chuschi.[19] The qalas who directed the chuschino student association may have been embarrassed to see Marco, Teodulfo, and their bandmates represent Chuschi onstage in the distinctive hats and sandals of its comuneros. However, indigenous colleagues became their ardent fans.

The group's prizewinning performance attracted the attention of people who managed Ayacucho's folkloric venues. The CCC was already well known to Marco, who had listened diligently to *Allpanchik* since moving to Ayacucho, but now the group became program regulars. Marco remembered the CCC as an engine of indigenous musical performance more generally: "They sponsored recordings for the radio, publicized artists. . . . They also held competitions, they had a meeting of indigenous communities almost every year. And there were other events, too: other university departments had symposiums, and the CCC coordinated with them." He singled out Carlos Condori, a university colleague who ran *Allpanchik*, as especially instrumental:

> He helped arrange opportunities for us, but more than that, he encouraged us. He'd say, "Why don't you record this song for us, or that one," and he had a habit of picking songs from all over, unknown songs, that came from new groups. I don't know how he got them. He probably had contacts. It was a university office, so professors, or sociologists who traveled, probably brought things back to the CCC. Anyway, he had them there and would say "Hey, listen to this song, it's a nice one." He made us listen, and we'd laugh and talk about it.

Other opportunities came from outside the UNSCH. Ernesto Medina, owner of Ollanta Records, an Ayacucho-based cassette recording company, approached the group immediately following their triumph at the UNSCH competition. He offered no royalties or fees, but Los Chikitukus were anxious to get their songs into circulation, and they took advantage. Against the group's judgment, Medina recorded them unrehearsed, "as is," aiming for the lively feel of a house party. They need not have worried, for shortly after the release songs like "Peruanachallay bandera" (My little Peruvian flag) and "Altar mayuscha" (Altar river) became smash hits, or *golazos*, sounding from radio stations and cassette players all over the city and the countryside. A second recording followed, and then a pair for the Dolby JR. label, founded by fellow UNSCH student Julián Fernández in partnership with chuschinos Rosa, Salvador, and Arturo Chiclla (Tucker 2013b). Marco described these Dolby recordings as somewhat stiff: unlike Medina, engineer Salvador Chiclla had insisted on multiple takes and clean execution, leaching the performances of spontaneity. Nevertheless, these cassettes and particularly the second, titled

Vida michiy, featured daring compositions that made Los Chikitukus into trendsetting performers.

The group continued to perform, benefiting from the support of a Tucno cousin who was also a beer distributor and who covered expenses like regional attire and instruments. No longer confined to houses and open lots on the city's periphery, Los Chikitukus increasingly played at venues like the municipal theater on Ayacucho's central plaza, the Cine Cavero movie theater a block away, or the nearby stadium of the Luis Carranza school. Salcedo organized many of these concerts, and his show *Takiyninchik* was a key venue for popularizing the group's songs alongside other indigenous music dear to the anthropologist. However, Los Chikitukus also played with Ayacucho's elite mestizo musicians at promotional concerts run by Fernández, the Dolby JR. producer. Competitions tended instead to be sponsored by educational institutions, NGOs, and governmental organizations such as the local office of Peru's National Institute of Culture or the tourism organization DIRECTUR, each of which hosted a contest featuring Marco's composition "Aymara lliqllacha" (Aymara shawl). The reuse of a song in this way was against the rules and resulted in an embarrassing disqualification, but Los Chikitukus won many such competitions, further consolidating their reputation. Few of these events were paying gigs, functioning instead as means to advertise the group's skills toward the goal of receiving contracts for house parties. Demand for home performances remained high, and Marco recalled their appearances at professors' homes as a particular point of pride. Some nonlocal professors even learned to play along, and the experience set those professors in stark relief against "others, who still discriminated sometimes, saying 'those Indians, those people from the fields.'"

Members of Los Chikitukus never became full-time musicians, pursuing their performing careers alongside their studies or, later, their jobs. Its personnel also fluctuated constantly in its early years, testimony to the widespread facility that indigenous chuschinos had with their town's music (see figures 13 and 14). Marco and Teodulfo were able to rope in a revolving group of instrumentalists and vocalists as needed, including Eusebio Carhuapoma, Segundino Dueñas, Julio Jorahua Dueñas, Juan Huaycha Rocha, Lucio Tucno, Teodosio Tucno, Luisa Bautista, Celia Tucno, Emilia and Juana Allcca Tucno, and two sisters surnamed Rodríguez from the town of Waripirqa in neighboring Vinchos, many of whom went on to establish artistic careers of their own. They even had the support of Alberto Infanzón, another fellow UNSCH student, whose experience with Los Aires Chuschinos lent him an expertise rarely acquired by other scions of Chuschi's qala community.

By the time the group recorded *Vida michiy* it included Guillermo Allcca

FIGURE 13. Los Chikitukus de Chuschi, pictured in the early 1990s. From left to right: [first name unknown] Carhuapoma, Marco Tucno Rocha, Luisa Bautisa, Julio Jorahua, and Alberto Infanzón. Photograph from the private collection of Marco Tucno. Used by permission.

FIGURE 14. Los Chikitukus de Chuschi with their larger carnival group, pictured in the early 1990s. Back row, from left to right: Juana Allca Tucno, Emilia Allca Tucno, Marcelina Huaman, Modesta Quispe, Rosa María Huaycha, Isabel Rocha, Fernandina Tucno. Front row, from left to right: Haydé Huaycha, Julio Jorahua, Segundino Dueñas, Teodosio Tucno, Juan Huaycha, Teodulfo Pacotaype, Marco Tucno Rocha, Reny Tucno. Photograph from the private collection of Marco Tucno. Used by permission.

and Carmen Rosa Minas Quispe, students in the UNSCH's highly activist education department. Marco described them as "people who were already way ahead in bettering themselves, not only with respect to caring for their customs but also intellectually," and together they ensured that *Vida Michiy* showed a noticeable departure from traditional chimaycha standards. It featured several chimaycha warhorses and "potpourris" of short traditional tunes, but it also featured topical songs that addressed listeners in new ways. Songs like "Sulkaray," named after one of Chuschi's sites for practicing the vida michiy, thematized customary practices so as to educate listeners about them. Others were songs of social commentary, arguing for justice and empowerment. Allca's songs, for instance, wove contemporary events together with symbols of resistance from the past, suggesting the long-standing disenfranchisement and the potential energies of rebellion that characterized the Pampas region. Reminiscing about one of them in a 2003 interview, Marco noted that "there was another protest song [on *Vida Michiy*], one by Guillermo, I think it's 'María Parado de Bellido'? About Micaela Bastidas, I think, and Qala Maki, a kind of protest thing . . . and we had another one about Mariscal [Cáceres]"—all famous Ayacuchanos who fought Spanish colonial authorities or invading Chileans in the War of the Pacific (1879–83), and all but one hailing from the Pampas Valley.

Didactic songs like this marked a substantial departure from the intimate tenor of indigenous Andean song.[20] However, *Vida Michiy's* topical songs were not unprecedented within the Ayacucho region (see Ritter 2002 and 2006; Tucker 2013b), and they were not even new for Los Chikitukus. The group had already circulated politically potent songs informally, via cassettes that were traded from hand to hand over the late 1980s. Some of those songs reached anthropologist Billie Jean Isbell, who in a 1998 article discussed "Democraciaña libertadllaña" (Democracy and liberty), a savage critique of a murderous government's platitudinous discourse, and "Chinkaqkuna" (The disappeared), a song she characterized as an early 1990s hit among displaced chuschinos in Lima. Amid tamer numbers about local history and peasant custom, *Vida Michiy* contained similarly frank songs of political protest, including "Campesino," which alluded to the victims of the violence before calling out members of the government's *sinchi* counterterrorism forces:

Campesino	Peasant
Urqupi qasapi pukupuku waqan	In mountains and passes the *pukupuku* cries
Urqupi qasapi kulikuli llakin	In mountains and passes the *kulikuli* weeps
Parapa lastapa ukuchallapinña	Amid the rain and snow
Chiripa wayrapa chawpichallampiña	Right at the center of the wind and cold
Chawpichallampiña	There at the center

CHAPTER FOUR

Así lo mismo campesino waqan	Just so the peasants weep,
Así lo mismo llaqta runa llakin	Just so the townspeople weep,
Llaqtallan ukupi yawar mayu kaptin	While blood runs in the town,
Ayacuchopi yarqay muchuy kaptin	While Ayacucho feels hunger and misery,
Yarqay muchuy kaptin	Hunger and misery
Chuschi llaqtapi pares palomitay	The two doves in Chuschi,
Chuschi llaqtapi turi-ñañaykuna	Brothers and sisters in Chuschi,
Maytaq kunanqa rikuriyllañachu	Where are they now?
Chaytaq kunanqa kutimullañachu	They're not coming back
Vueltamullañachu	Not coming back
Wakincha carcelpi, wakincha allpapi (bis)	Some are in jail, some beneath earth (bis)
Kaychun democracia, lleno de injusticia (bis)	This is no democracy, it's full of injustice (bis)
Lleno de injusticia	Full of injustice

Hablado	*Spoken*
Democraciaña nispa niwachkanchik	"Democracy," they say to us
Sumaq democraciaqa runa wañuyllawantaq	If democracy is beautiful, why do they kill us?
Por ello marchemos todos unidos	That's why we march united
Con la justicia y la libertad	For justice and liberty
Yawllay sinchichayllay moro pachachay sinchichay (bis)	Hey sinchi, sinchi in your dark clothes (bis)
Haykataq balayki valan, takayman igualanmanchu	What are your bullets worth? Let's see if they equal my fist
Haykataq balayki valan, takayman igualanmanchu	What are your bullets worth? Let's see if they equal my fist
Chaqayman igualanmanchu	If they equal that

Such songs were new and exciting for the listeners whom Los Chikitukus attracted in the early 1990s, but they show a notable continuity with previous modes of composition. The use of linguistic parallelism, the tropic invocation of landscapes and beings familiar across the Andean highlands, and the setting of those elements within a local geography all make "Campesino" structurally similar to its antecedents and powerful for those who knew the sites named. In fact throughout this heavily politicized period Los Chikitukus never abandoned their commitment to more traditional songs, gathering, recombining, and recording material from their compatriots as a means to present and preserve the best that Chuschi had to offer. This meant that several songs by other emergent composers became registered to their authorship. The group made those songs their own, however, by adjusting to their standards lines they found deficient and by interpolating new verses of their own composition.

The group also tinkered with instrumental performance, introducing elements of sophistication while remaining largely faithful to traditional standards. Here Marco was key, having studied at Ayacucho's Condorcunca music conservatory between 1990 and 1992, in tandem with his university studies. Named the group's musical director because of this background, he instructed cousins Teodulfo Carhuapoma and Juan Huaycha Rocha, elevating their chinlili technique to improve the group's intonation and rhythmic precision. He took up the task of constructing new, technically accomplished chinlilis, launching himself toward his later career as a luthier. Finally, he drew upon the huayno music of Ayacucho's elite to develop a characteristic style of accompaniment. Since the 1960s Ayacucho's elite huayno musicians had been renowned for two related attributes: their guitar skills and the sophistication of their performances (Tucker 2013b). The instrument was tied to Spanish rather than indigenous heritage, redolent of European prestige, and guitarists built on that baseline by adopting a virtuosic style. They included fast instrumental runs between verses, developed an ornamented melodic style that echoed the figurations of baroque music, and played syncopated bass-string countermelodies that gave their performances rhythmic élan. Without adopting that style wholesale, Marco incorporated new instrumental runs between sung chimaycha verses, rather than sticking with a single figure as had long been typical. He also kept the nylon-stringed Spanish instruments that Los Aires Chuschinos had added to the chimaycha ensemble, balancing tinny chinlilis with a registral and timbral complement of warm, bassy guitars.

These innovations were partly a matter of commercial distinction, according to Marco. Los Chikitukus tried to stand out in a developing musical marketplace—and, in particular, to stake their distance from Los Aires Chuschinos:

> When Los Chikitukus recorded, we did it differently, with other instrumental runs, some ornaments, guitar combinations. . . . In that sense we tried to stylize our own, and why? So that there wasn't a monotony. For example, if we had recorded just like Los Aires Chuschinos there wouldn't have been a difference. Whoever heard our music or the melody would say, "No, it's them [Los Aires Chuschinos] playing" . . . so it was in order to differentiate ourselves that we put in those instrumental runs and ornaments.

Marco went on to clarify that the intention was to reach "the market beyond our own zone." Los Chikitukus never really gained a listenership beyond Ayacucho Department, but they were successful within it. Chimaycha connoisseurs routinely single them out as pioneers, the most important and memorable group of the era. Such testimonials came from leading mediators like Salcedo, CCC employee Carlos Condori, and current Dolby (now Dolly)

JR. director Arturo Chiclla, and from artists working in Ayacucho's concert venues over the 2000s and 2010s—people like singer Élida Núñez, whose face lit up as she said, "I was their biggest fan," and influential chinlilista David Galindo, who gave a two-word response when I asked what groups he listened to in his youth: "Los Chikitukus." Both artists were youths during the band's heyday, but its listenership certainly was not limited to young people from Chuschi District. As noted above, the group appeared alongside elite huayno artists on Ayacucho's concert stages, artists who were mining a similar vein of political protest in the years of the violence, and Marco characterized audiences at those events tellingly, as "petit bourgeois and above."

However, after the era of violence, interest in explicit musical politics waned, and the group's most tangible influence lay in the vigorous neotraditional chimaycha scene that sprang up over the 1990s. A welter of groups emerged from Chuschi District and nearby Sarhua, recording and releasing cassettes that circulated alongside those of Los Chikitukus in the Ayacuchano marketplace. They were often likewise composed of university students, and sometimes they actually predated Los Chikitukus, though they had never before participated in commercial ventures. In either case, their recorded output rarely imitated the frank political lyrics of Los Chikitukus, instead adopting elements of the group's instrumental practice. They often approached Marco or his fellows for advice in the matter of developing a unique sound. In the process groups and entire towns came to be identified with particular instrumental runs and accompanimental figures.[21] Groups from Chuschi, for instance, adopted the three-note bass pattern introduced by Los Aires Chuschinos and continued by Los Chikitukus—but they also developed between-verse cadential figures, using them as hooks to distinguish themselves from others. Meanwhile, groups from Quispillaccta continued to use the two-note pattern heard on "Yutuchay," meaning that each town's mode of instrumental accompaniment came to be defined by its first commercial recording.

Los Chikitukus themselves ceased most performance activities by the mid-1990s as core members graduated from university, began their professional lives, and found themselves short on time. A second factor was a change to the tax regime introduced by the Fujimori administration, which forced Marco's cousin to curtail his beer company's sponsorship. A final blow came after a farcical-sounding incident that nevertheless continued to reverberate in the city of Ayacucho a half decade afterward, when I first arrived in 2000. Between 1993 and 1995 Walter Ascarza, a member of a chuschino qala family, acted as mayor of Ayacucho, in which capacity he managed to outrage its citizenry. In what was widely described as an effort to "modernize" the city's central plaza, he had its towering palm trees chopped down late at night, thereby evad-

126   CHAPTER FOUR

ing opposition from the city's populace. Subsequent weeks and months were difficult for chuschinos, who faced the considerable and often racist vitriol of Ayacucho's old guard. Parading with a group of chuschinos during carnival, Marco heard shouted insults and threats of violence, as residents vented their frustration with the mayor, and perhaps with the city's demographic transition—knowing full well that rural migrants might wrest further social, political, and economic control from the hands of Ayacucho's established power brokers. Amid these circumstances Los Chikitukus largely retired.

Conclusion

Scholar-activists of the 1970s and 1980s ushered in an era that Marco, Óscar, and their peers describe as a high-water mark for indigenous performance. Their memories are perhaps filtered through generational nostalgia, but their reminiscences point to a key, often underspecified aspect of such institutional efforts—the emotional charge of tangible respect. For in evaluating this era they emphasized support, appreciation, and solidarity over opportunities for paid performance, which were infrequent in any case. The *communitas* and the emotional infrastructure that the CCC offered to young musicians are one noteworthy element of this structure of feeling: Marco judged the CCC recordings of Los Chikitukus as superior to later efforts, more emotionally authentic and hence more "natural." Salcedo too was instrumental, regularly inviting musicians to play for birthday parties and other celebrations at his apartment in the respectable neighborhood of Pío Max. Marco insisted that this patronage foreshadowed a looming challenge to the marginalization of indigenous music, and of indigenous people generally, in Ayacucho City. Critically, he and his peers transmitted that feeling to their followers via acts of comfort that were especially welcomed amid the violence:

> We were giving support. That is, listening, or dancing, enjoying yourself for a while and forgetting your pains, that's how I took things in those days. We would play a contest or an event, and our *paisanos* would follow us around after. Hearing us play they would cheer up, shake our hands, invite us to a pop or a little liquor in the neighborhood. . . . It was the only thing we could do as students, we were poor, we couldn't really do anything else, support people [financially] or say "Know what? You don't have to suffer," but through music we could do *something*.

Allpanchik, Takiyninchik, music competitions, and intellectual support all had an electrifying effect on indigenous performance. Without exception, chimaycha musicians of the same generation confirm the outlines of Marco's and Óscar's experiences. Ninay Urucha, who enjoyed renewed success in the early 2010s, owed that opportunity to recordings aired by *Allpanchik* in the 1980s, recordings of her girlhood self that were remembered two decades later by fans who encouraged her to record again. José Tomaylla launched the long career of his group Waylla Ichu de Llacctahurán by recording the first of seven cassettes at the CCC. There was, in short, a dynamic scene that would hardly have existed if not for the mediation of dedicated professionals located within academic and nongovernmental institutions. This scene was not organized along the narrowly nationalist lines of indigenismo, nor primarily for commercial profit, and it was insulated from the representational challenges that cling to those kinds of efforts. Rather than speaking for indigenous artists, these institutions let indigenous artists speak through them.

This is not to say, of course, that their interventions were free from unexpected consequences. The CCC, for example, had focused on Quispillaccta's high barrio of Unión Potrero and nearby neighborhoods, at the expense of other barrios. The main legacy of its investment may be Radio Quispillaccta, which I turn to next: the institution that mediated the next generation's chimaycha scene, and that is staffed almost entirely by people from that very barrio.

5

Broadcasting and Building Publics

On October 12, 2013, I sat near Radio Quispillaccta's DJ booth, listening as station manager Graciano Machaca wrapped up his morning show. His 6:00 a.m. program typically featured news and announcements from Ayacucho's rural-indigenous hinterland, leavened with chimaycha music. Sometimes it also included commentary, and on this day Graciano spoke about the politics of indigeneity. His words followed the announcement of a festival in nearby Chupas, marking the twenty-fifth anniversary of the town's official designation as an indigenous community. International treaties offer key protections to such settlements, including the inalienability of communal lands, and control over resource extraction. The Peruvian state often fails to respect such agreements, but Graciano didn't speak of governmental bad faith. Instead he spoke of the listening public's duty to claim the identity bound to those rights. Speaking in Quechua, he used the first-person inclusive pronoun that marks speaker and addressees as members of a shared community: "we," he said—meaning "I who speak and you who listen"—need to "recognize and remember that we are members of *indigenous* communities," with all the entitlements enumerated in international law.[1]

Such politicized invocations of indigeneity remain rare in Ayacucho, but Radio Quispillaccta is not a typical organization. Staffed by people from its eponymous town, it was the only entity in the city of Ayacucho that broadcast entirely in Quechua, and the only one that followed a program of service to the indigenous majority of the surrounding region. It provided a public voice for silenced citizens and acted as a vehicle for vitalizing indigenous practices. For indigenous activists in a place hostile toward their interests, and lacking the support of the ethnic parties that operate elsewhere, its cultural vitalization efforts might reasonably be described as a way to broker indigenous politics by other means.[2]

After Graciano's program I asked him about his comments, pointing out that ten years prior, hardly anyone in Ayacucho had so openly embraced labels like *indigenous* and its cognates. In response he spoke of the Asociación Bartolomé Aripaylla (ABA), the Ayacucho-based NGO, also staffed by quispillacctinos, that created Radio Quispillaccta in the late 1990s. "ABA has been like a school for us," he said, "and its staff are university educated, they're always reading over the treaties." They had explained, for instance, the global indigenous movement's key legal instruments, including ILO 169 and the Rio Declaration. These documents specified indigenous communities as beneficiaries, but Quispillaccta had been forcibly redesignated as a peasant community under the Velasco government. Making quispillacctinos into rights-bearing indigenous people meant fostering the renewal of the earlier label.

Graciano and his peers knew, of course, that terminological change was insufficient to sustain a claim to indigeneity. Success also meant vitalizing practices like chimaycha, which made quispillacctinos legible as culturally distinctive. His cousin Marcela Machaca, cofounder and codirector of ABA, dwelled upon this conviction when I interviewed her two years later.[3] "Music in peasant life is more than a question of artistry, " she said. "Many of our cultural lifeways are expressed in music. It's a sign of our cultural strength. . . . Without music, without singing about nature, feelings, we wouldn't be alive." Wrapping up moments later, she was even more explicit: "The music is in Quechua, and we Quechuas have a unique vision, of a world of beings, people. This is expressed in a particular language, and it's everywhere in the music."

By invoking nonhuman elements that are also animate interlocutors, Marcela echoed Marco Tucno's memories of being encouraged to care for such elements as "relatives" (see chapter 3).[4] However, sentiments like these never appeared unprompted in my conversations with musicians. Marco's words were prompted by questions from me, and my questions in turn grew from dialogue with people like Graciano and Marcela, activists versed in the ecocentric idioms of indigenous politics. This is not to propose that the link between music, nature, and indigeneity was a contrivance of politicized intellectuals: it was recognizable enough that performers were all able to speak about chimaycha's ecological resonance when asked. However, it does suggest that chimaycha was not habitually framed in this way and that the creation of such an ecocentric framework resignifies the genre, marking out a new way to think about musical indigeneity.

This chapter treats that variety of indigeneity, one that is slightly different from those discussed in previous chapters. Its discursive parameters come from global indigenous politics, but those parameters are also translated through local practices and customs. Most important for my purposes, Graciano, Marcela, and their peers harnessed chimaycha to projects of indigenous vitalization and community empowerment, encouraging the genre to be interpreted as one key component of a distinctive identity and worldview. Their actions meant that chimaycha became instrumental in consolidating a new Quechua-speaking public in Ayacucho, one that was shaped as strongly by musical practice as by translocal indigenous activism. By the same token, the developments they fostered demonstrate a great deal about the possibilities and limitations of such activist efforts.

Indigenous Activism in the Peruvian Andes

In one sense the Machacas might be regarded as outliers. As they themselves recognized, few residents of the Department of Ayacucho were so eager to take up stigmatized labels like *indigenous* as terms of self-identity. Nevertheless, their words echo those found in other recent studies of politics in the Peruvian Andes. Such accounts are, like mine, couched in careful terms of exceptional cases rather than mass movements. However, insofar as they document instances wherein people defend inherited lifeways and land rights by instrumentalizing "an emergent, specifically indigenous, ethnic identity which is novel in the ethnohistory of contemporary highland Peru" (Hogue and Rau 2008:293), they point to an inchoate movement that may yet yield a broad-based indigenous coalition like those at work in neighboring Bolivia, Ecuador, and the Peruvian Amazon. In this sense the Machacas should be regarded as part of a wider trend.

South American indigenous movements have often emerged in the wake of neoliberal reforms, such as the privatization of land and natural resources, which deny people inherited rights that are critical for their survival (Postero 2005; Turner 1993). Typically those people learn strategies from political agents that are versed in resisting similar pressures; sometimes those agents and their organizations are even sanctioned, at least initially, by neoliberal states themselves as they offload responsibility for vulnerable populations onto development agencies and other private actors. At the intersection of neoliberal policies and transnational aid, then, has grown "a sort of professionalized activism with a clear political stance, but not necessarily affiliated with any political party" (Oliart 2008:295). In Peru indigenous politics has coalesced at this intersection, with water rights playing a central role in the Andes, where the substance is central to cultural and political life as well as basic survival (see Gelles 2000; Alberti and Mayer 1974).[5] Similarly, it is usually a local consortium of teachers, community leaders, and university graduates that has overseen the development of political tactics and rhetorics effective in crafting resistance, after contact with outside organizations whose scope ranges from UN offices (Oliart 2008) to the indigenous political parties of Bolivia (Hogue and Rau 2008) to Lima-based NGOs (Alfaro 2005; Pajuelo Torres 2007).

ABA's development fits this pattern neatly. Already in 1998, a volume on the politics of development work highlighted the Machacas' links to PRATEC (Proyecto Andino de Tecnologias Campesinas, or Andean Project of Rural Technologies; see Apfel-Marglin 1998), a translocal consortium of agronomic NGOs. Around the same time the activist organization Chirapaq began to foster an Andean network of leaders conversant with transnational indigenous rights discourse over the 1990s, making Ayacucho one center of activity (see Oliart 2008:292). Like these and other nascent indigenous organizations with which they are allied, ABA's directors "elaborate three aspects of local identity to legitimize and solidify a politicized indigenous ethnic identity and a framework for resistance: their role as agrarians, unifying cultural practices, and their relationship to the land and the natural world" (Hogue and Rau 2008:300). With respect to agrarian activity, they promoted the same principles of "ethnodevelopment" (Partridge and Uquilla 1996:5)—that is, the promotion of agronomic practices that grow from community custom rather than Western technologies—as Hogue and Rau's Cusco-based interlocutors. With respect to cultural practices and ecocentric discourse, the Machacas and their peers stressed respect for ancestral customs in all of their work. In other words, they adopted traditionalist forms of strategic essentialism that have been described throughout the Andean region, where cultural heterogeneity, intracommunity conflict, and indigenous modernities are often sidelined in public discourse, as means to secure the rights and respect that accrue to millennial, communitarian forms of ethnic distinctiveness (Swinehart 2012; Rousseau 2011). Here their links to PRATEC are especially telling, since that organization gained fame for its attacks on Western principles of development, and for promoting "an essentialist and romanticized view of indigenous cultures, because they were generally reluctant to acknowledge that cultural transformations occurred in indigenous communities" (Oliart 2008:296).

Organizations like PRATEC and ABA, then, promote hypermodern, globalized forms of indigenous action via rhetorics of traditionalism and custom. This can make for an awkward clash of discursive registers, and their work sometimes involves the management of such disjunctures. It is noteworthy, for example, that ABA was founded and led by two indigenous women, since it follows NGOs like PRATEC in emphasizing "complementarity between genders as well as between human beings and nature" (Hernández Castillo 2010:540). This ideology of complementarity has historically discouraged female political leadership in Quechua-speaking communities, and the Machacas might therefore be seen as radically nontraditional, emblems of the transnational forces that increasingly allow indigenous women to occupy new arenas of empowerment (see, for example Ypiej 2012; Zorn 2005). In practice, this contradiction is assuaged via a rhetorical device whereby ABA characterizes itself as "accompanying" rather than directing local political projects (see also Rousseau 2011:17)—even if most local actors readily single out the NGO as the engine of politics in Chuschi District.

Such acts of accommodation saturate indigenous activism in the Andes as communities find ways to make their existing goals and principles chime with new political and cultural norms. ABA's workers, too, tack between different political and cultural registers as they draw actors to their cause, and their heterogeneous modes of discourse as thought leaders help to shape the collective sense of self that their community bears. Of course, as with any discourse community, their influence is susceptible to pressures from the people that they gather and address. This indigenous public has grown dialogically, and nothing is more emblematic of this negotiation than the changing forms of patronage that ABA and Radio Quispillaccta extended to chimaycha music. The genre was central in their effort to attract radio listeners, and broadcasts initially featured chimaycha recordings of a predictably traditionalist bent. That impulse toward traditionalism, however, soon suffered a challenge from the very public that their broadcasts gathered, suggesting a need to revise the organization's vision of indigenous community more broadly. This chapter and the next trace the role of sound and music in these two moments of that public's development: this one shows how Radio Quispilaccta channeled activist projects of its parent NGO, while the next explores the expansive responses of listeners and musicians.

A Sonorous Indigenous Public

In previous writings I have relied upon the idea of the public as a framing device to understand sound and society in Peru (Tucker 2013a; 2013b), and I continue to believe that it provides the best analytic purchase on the relationship between music, community, and social identity.[6] I understand the term to name a grouping of people linked by common involvement with things that draw their attention. As an analytical category, a public is distinguished by two qualities: first, its members' awareness of other members with similar investments, and second, its tendency to change content and boundaries as members debate their shared interests. A social form of obvious importance in a world defined by protean communities of circulation and consumption, publics present daunting analytical challenges since membership may be fleeting, occasional, and traceless. Telling the story of any public means specifying not only the things that tie it together and their means of circulation but also less tangible matters like the forms of engagement that those things elicit from users.

Music sits at a particular disadvantage here, for it is not always obvious how such a nonpropositional idiom affects those who become involved with it. It is hard to specify when musical publics arise and to argue convincingly for their sociopolitical impact. My approach adapts insights from several post-Habermasian theories of public discourse. Warner (2002), for instance, makes the crucial observation that periodical publics evolve in relation to the time lag that separates published statements and counterstatements, during which readers absorb, contest, and refine written opinions while imagining others to do the same.[7] Similar observations about co-presence, self-abstraction, and communication have animated popular music studies, where "genre communities" (Frith 1996) are described as the epiphenomenon of a dialogue between musicians, mediators, and audiences that accept or reject their work, thereby forcing changes in the musical behavior of performers and producers (see also Peterson 1997). This cycle of stylistic thesis, counterthesis, and synthesis is a musical analogue for Warner's cycles of periodical readership, and attention to it may be the best way to understand a musical public's mode of operation.

There is, moreover, a great incentive to understand the role that music can play in founding such a public. Rancière has placed this act of public formation at the heart of democratic politics, dubbing it *dissensus*. By producing a public that is not yet nameable in the terms that govern its host polity, an act of dissensus troubles the existing categories that channel communications within the public sphere—its "partition of the sensible" (Rancière 1999; see also 2006 and 2010). It alters the perceptual habits of its users, as "what was formerly heard as noise by powerful persons begins to sound to them like 'argumentative utterances'" (J. Bennett 2010:105). In like fashion, emergent musical styles often render tangible unheralded communities of sentiment before they can properly be described as political actors, and genres ranging from New York disco (Lawrence 2003) to South African kwaito (Steingo 2016) or Peruvian chicha (Turino 1990a; Romero 2002) can therefore be described as politically significant, while defeating any attempt to specify their politics in propositional terms.[8]

ABA and Radio Quispillaccta initiated a cycle of dissensus by rupturing Ayacucho's partition of the sensible. Their successful attempt to gather

Quechua speakers around discourses of politicized indigeneity revealed an unheard listenership receptive to new ideas of indigenous agency. By placing traditional chimaycha at the heart of their projects, they linked it to rhetorics culled from the transnational sphere of indigenous activism. Transmitting via AM waves, the station brought this chain of signifiers into a countryside where it faced no serious rivals, due to the dearth of Quechua-language radio and the emptiness of Ayacucho's AM band.[9] Radio Quispillaccta had a captive audience, and as curious listeners well beyond the District of Chuschi became chimaycha fans, they also were drawn into a relationship with sonorities of marked indigeneity.

Explicit discourse about indigeneity was actually uncommon on air, given Quechua speakers' enduring reluctance to identify with the term. However, activists like Graciano simply voiced indigeneity in a different register, turning to cognate rhetorics of difference like shared ancestral inheritance, cosmological principles, and ecological wisdom. The figurative heart of the station's discourse was the notion of a distinctive Quechua *cosmovisión*, a term that glosses cosmology and ecology simultaneously and is widely used by indigenous activists throughout Latin America.[10] To speak of indigenous cosmovisión is to speak of belief systems about the cosmos, the beings that populate it, and their entanglement with humans, as well as the expressive culture, material practice, and modes of subsistence that respond to those beliefs. Consolidating a sense of a shared Quechua cosmovisión was pitched by Radio Quispillaccta as a means to preserve a distinctive way of being in the world and to build a strongly defined sense of indigenous corporate identity.

The space that Radio Quispillaccta opened was quickly occupied by competing varieties of indigenous musicality. New artists experimented with tropical dance rhythms, electric instruments, and lyrics of modern anomie, and by the early 2010s they took advantage of cheap, accessible video technology as well as their increasing internet access and the advent of YouTube—the dominant means for circulating the music videos that are currently Andean music's dominant media form—to bypass the efforts that Radio Quispillaccta made to marginalize their wares. The circulation of such recordings presented the station's staff with a dilemma that faces other cultural sustainability advocates: balancing a mission of preservation with service to evolving community preferences. This second moment is developed more fully in the next chapter. Briefly, however, it represented a serious challenge to the variety of indigeneity promoted initially by ABA and Radio Quispillaccta, limiting the extent to which that identity could remain identified with traditionalism. To the extent that new artists and their listeners insisted on sharing Quechua-language music that was self-consciously urban and modernist in tone, their efforts marked a crucial "counterthesis" moment for Ayacucho's musical public—a moment in which it became clear that the versions of indigeneity native to the region would be shaped dialogically, rather than promoted from above; and that they would be resolutely modern and populist, at least in part, rather than the projects of traditionalist intellectuals.

In what remains of this chapter I show how chimaycha's mediators pursued at first a project of purification that de la Cadena has identified as endemic to indigenous activism. Describing, for instance, a display about Quechua-speaking peoples created for the National Museum of the American Indian in Washington, DC, she comments insightfully on the challenges involved with making Andean experience intelligible in terms of North America's different discourses of indigeneity. Close and long-standing contact between indigenous Andeans and their nonindigenous compatriots has given rise to religious syncretisms and ideologies of nonbinary identity, such that "the history of indigeneity in the Andes is one of fusions among different collectivities" (de la Cadena 2015:226). Rendering Quechua speakers acceptably "indigenous" to North American audiences, then, requires "purification": a falsification of Andean history that suppresses forms of cultural, social, and religious fluidity which trouble the clear ethnic boundaries demanded by mainstream American discourse.[11]

Such purification is a productive strategy of ethnogenesis as well as identitarian mystification. It is a cognate of the act typically dubbed "revalorization" in the Andes, whereby fading or lost symbols of collective identity are vitalized to serve as rallying points for cultural activism. In the Pampas Valley community of Sarhua, for example, residents revived their tradition of painted *tabla* boards to further "a project of 'revalorization and preservation of Andean culture,' which they blame 'the influence of modernity and the penetration of capitalism and the Western world' for destroying" (González 2011:78). Similar principles guide the discourse of quispillacctino institutions, which borrow languages of cultural distinctiveness, political empowerment, and environmental stewardship directly from the global indigenous movement. Their "fears of cultural discontinuity," however, drive strongly against the interests of some chimaycha artists. In this sense their work treads in the hazardous terrain that Canessa has identified (2012), where indigenous politics privilege certain forms of activity, those that facilitate recognition by the liberal state and empower those capable of making themselves legible to that order. The varieties of indigeneity that become legitimated in this context are always already informed by their promoters' access to state organisms, transnational political actors, and the educational institutions that prepare activists to deal with them. This is a matter of some importance in evaluating ABA and Radio

Quispillaccta, staffed by university-educated quispillacctinos who owe their educational opportunities to the long-term economic effects of CCC projects in their home barrio of Unión Potrero. Indeed, while ABA came to reject the development model promoted by the CCC, its offshoot radio station hewed closely to the precedents set by *Allpanchik* and *Takiyninchik*, thereby combining old academic models of cultural conservation with new activist ideologies of indigeneity.

This, finally, is partly a familiar story about media tools as vehicles for indigenous cultural vitalization.[12] However, in the Andes such stories have typically ignored the radio technologies that have proved so productive in other contexts, due to the scarcity of community radio endeavors.[13] Only a few communities have taken advantage of the opportunity that Peru's radio licensing process provides for the creation of such broadcasters. Most are not even run by community members but serve instead as vehicles for outside hobbyists or entrepreneurs desirous of a broadcast license. Like Radio Quispillaccta, such stations fill their programming with the recordings of nonprofessional or local artists and "clearly assume the role of cultural reclamation" (Rivadeneyra 2009:7). Unlike them, however, Radio Quispillaccta's reach extends well beyond the boundaries of its namesake community. It spans most of northern Ayacucho and streams online. Its impact has been significant, but it cannot be assessed without a portrait of ABA, its parent organization.

The Asociación Bartolomé Aripaylla

ABA's effects on chimaycha and on local notions of indigeneity have been profound, but its activities are not limited to Radio Quispillaccta. It is formally an agronomic NGO centered on ethnodevelopment in Quispillaccta, and its agricultural projects and repopulation efforts helped regenerate lands and barrios devastated by the violence. It has also supported the recovery of abandoned customs and worked to strengthen Quispillaccta's political influence. Alongside local leaders, it helped to restore the *varayuqkuna*, the indigenous authority system that had disappeared in the 1970s. This provided a counterweight to the authority of the Peruvian state, but it also made a strong claim about Quispillaccta's claim to indigenous difference, since "the maintenance of the varayoqkuna system in any peasant community has been taken to indicate its high degree of traditionalism" (González 2011:34).

Despite its location high on the southern outskirts of Ayacucho, my first visit to ABA's headquarters suggested its centrality to quispillacctino life. Indeed, the organization's employees tended to remain in constant motion between the city and the village. That quality did not distinguish them from

BROADCASTING AND BUILDING PUBLICS

many of their fellows: it often seemed that all the quispillacctinos I knew passed freely back and forth between the two locations, taking advantage of educational and agricultural downtime to visit and accomplish tasks that needed doing in either location. Still the stucco and cement building seemed like a especially nodal point in this roundabout, something like a clubhouse where people of all ages conversed in Quechua while using the front office's computers to browse the internet. Accountant Lorenzo Núñez, a longtime staffer, received me there and explained courteously that their central goal was the vitalization of indigenous lifeways and knowledge, naming crop management, water conservation, and terracing techniques as examples. When I asked about "cultural affirmation," a goal that Radio Quispillaccta advertised and that seemed outside their agronomic focus, he objected: "In our culture, agriculture is the center of everything, and everything else grows from it." It was imbricated with expressive forms and belief systems that were rarely addressed by other agronomic agencies which were founded upon an "occidental" separation between the technical, the social, and the cosmological. Characterizing ABA's practices as "antiscience," he described their commitment to an "Andean cosmovisión" centered on managing relations with nonhumans. Offerings, he said, must be made to the earth and other persons, like mountains or lakes, before beginning any task, to ensure their blessing. He spoke about harnessing the knowledge of the community's *yachaqs* (literally "knowers"), who guided planting cycles by observing the Pleiades or determined the date to sow potatoes by watching for the September appearance of the *tankar* flower. Examining photos I showed him, taken by Isbell at a canal-cleaning ceremony in the 1970s, he called my attention to the flower tucked into a girl's hat, admonishing me that it was a sign of nature's presence in the ritual "for those who know." Such tidbits of wisdom, he said, they gathered into files, distributing them through workshops for comuneros or via radio segments entitled *Kawsayninchikmanta* (About our life).

ABA's public activities and my conversations with its directors all echoed Núñez's claims. Words that prefaced a 2014 presentation at the UNSCH noted that the NGO "was born as a family initiative, in response to the severe cultural, social, economic, and environmental effects of the Shining Path era in Quispillaccta. . . . Its founders join their Andean origins and cosmovisión with university knowledge." Those founders, sisters Marcela and Magdalena Machaca, are UNSCH-trained agronomists, and they are not precisely "antiscience." Rather, they are indigenous women who profit from their conversancy with two different bodies of insight and practice—or, in the words of Marcela, "*iskaynintin* [roughly, 'both together at once']. Both knowledges, neither one nor the other."

The sisters founded ABA in 1991 to address what they described as a crisis in indigenous knowledge, one whose roots ran deeper than the conflict. Certainly the Shining Path war had left Quispillaccta a social and infrastructural shambles. However, in promoting an alien communist system for rationalizing production, the guerrillas themselves had only advanced an agenda initiated earlier by development organizations like the CCC. Both actors worked to change agricultural traditions that inhibited yield maximization, destroying a ritual and social apparatus that organized indigenous life and leaving nothing but failed initiatives—initiatives that foundered on their promoters' ignorance of the very ecological and social wisdom that had been encoded into traditional practices. Adding insult to injury, the violence had also hastened the conversion of quispillacctinos to evangelical Christianity and Mormonism, as Protestant sects targeted communities abandoned by Catholic priests and the indigenous beliefs tolerated by the latter. Developmentalism, socialism, and evangelical Christianity were all alike, then, in their hostility to Andean cosmovisión.

The Machacas, by contrast, came to believe that Quispillaccta's economic recovery would require salvaging traditional knowledge after their postgraduation return to the community. Designed to promote large-scale, water-intensive monoculture, the principles they had learned at school were badly suited to Quispillaccta, where the rain cycle complicates water management, steep terrain impedes the creation of large mechanized plots, and altitudinal variation demands communal investment in a diversity of crops. Even worse, the Central Andes were undergoing severe dislocations from climate change, with shortened rainy seasons, abnormal temperature fluctuations, and unpredictable storms challenging the abilities of even expert farmers. Dismissing, then, what Marcela dubbed "so-called agricultural modernization," the sisters began to ask about older principles, tapping their ancestors' millennia-long experience in managing risk and uncertainty.

Beginning with the *oca* and *olluco* tubers that had been the subjects of their theses, the sisters worked with family members in Unión Potrero, using the very techniques and ritual apparatus that their education had encouraged them to set aside. They moved to crop diversity, then a battle against fertilizers and pesticides, and then to water management—a perennial concern that became acute over the 1990s, when the regional government expropriated community lands and dammed the Cachi River, creating a reservoir in Quispillaccta to serve the city of Ayacucho. By the early 2010s water was one of the NGO's central concerns, and as Magdalena looked back from that vantage point she spoke eloquently about an ideology of Andean difference that informed their work. At the UNSCH, she said, they were taught "to use steel and

BROADCASTING AND BUILDING PUBLICS

cement, and to favor the use of surface water: little streams. And it made the springs dry up. . . . It left behind enormous white elephants, like the reservoir of Puncupata, the eight-kilometer-long canal of Tuco. When that happens, since water is a person, it escapes" (Orjeda 2014:3). Rather than trapping water, they promoted a relationship of care (*crianza*), treating the element as a living thing to be raised and shepherded. "Cement," she explained, "doesn't foster growth [*no cria*], it kills. But there are materials that help water grow, help it regenerate." Using those materials takes time, and "one must have patience and tenderness to be a breeder [*criador*]": however, water responds to care by growing rather than fleeing, lending weight to her contention that "Western technology is for the desperate."

ABA's staff grew apace as the Machacas hired other quispillacctino graduates from the UNSCH. The organization rented office space in a community-owned property near Ayacucho's downtown, but employees were encouraged to return to and invest in their home community, overturning the typical trajectory of a titled professional. The scope of their operations expanded from Unión Potrero to Quispillaccta's other barrios, and they gained respect and influence by mediating relationships with outside parties, a facility that came with the territory of managing a successful NGO. A tipping point was reached when, in the late 1990s, ABA became the local executor of a government program designed to foster resettlement.

Not all of their efforts were welcomed. The Machacas' promotion of ritual practices was particularly offensive to Quispillaccta's evangelicals, who eventually placed members into political office and evicted ABA from community offices in the mid-2000s. Marcela noted that the act was "an attempt to exclude us, because we really promote rituality. Behind all of our ways of being, there is rituality. They are ways of doing, a way for us to recuperate forms of love and respect for nature." Echoing her sister, she went on to describe agriculture as the conduct of relationships between beings:

> [At first] we were [propagating plants] without feeling: feelings for that person the potato, for that person the oca, for that person the olluco. Not just a living thing, but a person . . . since they don't talk, you grab a scalpel, you manipulate it, you don't respect it! Even though your grandfather has told you that it's a mother seed. Realizing this shook us awake: we realized that we could do without those barbarities, that we had technologies of our own that would let us reproduce seeds.

And technical or cosmological concerns were not easy to separate from social relationships, since Andean agriculture relies upon mutual aid. Soon enough the sisters were also asking "how to reestablish reciprocal relations between families" and fostering ties that had been grievously weakened over the previous decades.

ABA dabbled from the beginning in expressive practices too. In 1992 the organization partnered with Ayacucho's association of quispillacctino residents to promote an intercommunity chimaycha concert in the city's Cumaná soccer stadium. Coinciding with the five-hundredth anniversary of Columbus's American landing and bearing the pointed slogan "500 years of resistance," the event attracted what Núñez estimated to be eight hundred attendees. Later, in the 1990s and 2000s, ABA also sponsored music contests in Quispillaccta, created a daytime folkloric festival at Patario, and contributed to the occasional recording project. Throughout, the organization encouraged musical traditionalism, insisting upon instrumentation, melodies, and texts that would have been recognizable to their grandparents.

ABA, then, channeled a kind of social, cultural, and political vitalization that was the envy of many neighboring communities. Publicly the organization underplays its role, insisting that it "accompanies" Quispillaccta in its projects. Nevertheless, community members and Ayacuchano professionals point to the Machacas and their coworkers as the principal force behind sweeping changes in the town. Núñez characterized these changes in rather concrete terms, noting how improvements in lands, crops, and herding practices had given women and children more time to study or to take on paying work. Marcela, by contrast, spoke to deeper attitudinal changes. She noted how strange the sisters seemed upon their postgraduation return to Quispillaccta: "We weren't normal anymore, not normal comuneros. . . . [We were] women agriculturalists and, to top it off, engineers." By 2013, however, young professionals moved freely between the urban and rural contexts. They felt little need to hide their cultural identity in the city, nor to minimize their professional accomplishments in the town: "Now you're proud, because you know your music is worthwhile, your culture is worthwhile, your way of living is worthwhile. So now people are wanting to be professionals, live here [Ayacucho], without ceasing to be from there."

Postgraduation returnees, moreover, made their lives in a community where some traditions were growing, not diminishing, in importance. Young people once again expected to become indigenous authorities, and quispillacctino professionals no longer abandoned traditional attire for the slacks, jeans, blouses, and jackets of the city. "Now," Marcela said, "everyone's saying, 'We've undressed ourselves so.' And we're undressing ourselves in another way when we do that, because our knowledge is in our clothes too."[14] According to Magdalena, community elders spoke frankly of a restoration: "The community says that we have reestablished what the community was forty years

BROADCASTING AND BUILDING PUBLICS

back. We have reestablished respect, environmental conditions, now there is water, pasture, good milk . . . we are sowing young people who are proud of what's theirs" (Orjeda 2014:3).

Finally, ABA was central in bringing contemporary indigenous politics to Ayacucho as it became ever more involved with transnational organizations ranging from NGO Terres des Hommes to UNESCO to foreign political operations.[15] In 1998, as their focus turned to climate change, they began working closely with German NGO Weltungerhilfe, an institution with an interest in food security. In tandem, ABA's goals came to be expressed in a language of proud indigeneity and environmental stewardship. Marcela made the point clear when, in 2014, I asked outright how they had come to adopt the language of indigeneity. The term *indígena*, she said, was "a very complicated word . . . a pejorative term used throughout the colonial period to destroy us and to fix us in place, to say who is an Indian and facilitate the destruction." Speaking expertly of the term's entailments in colonial law, she noted that Indians had been defined as legal minors, "people who can't think for themselves. Who wants to be in the category of a legal minor?"

This history made the term difficult to use. However, they found it necessary to do so, since the legal instruments upon which they relied invoked the rights of indigenous communities. Describing the legacy of the label "campesino community" she asked laughingly, "So why are we now indigenous? It's strategy more than anything. We are who we've always been." She went on:

> In 1993 a new Peruvian constitution left the comunidades campesinas unprotected. It favored extractive industries, private property. So we have to figure out how to protect our land. And we have no other alternative but to take up, strategically, notions that are internationally recognized. ABA was founded in 1991, and the year after that came the [Rio Declaration], in '92. That's been our means of support, that and [ILO 169]. We almost always have those laws to hand. . . . That's how it is for our community. We recognize that the laws don't favor us. But those treaties might, and Peru is a signatory to them. So somehow in that way we can defend ourselves.[16]

Of course the state might well continue ignoring indigenous claims, in frank disregard for the treaties it had signed. More important, community members themselves remained resistant, according to Marcela: "If you ask someone 'Are you indigenous?' they'll say no. No one will say so." Indeed, although ABA challenged received terms of indigenous discourse, for non-quispillacctinos its most perceptible influence came via Radio Quispillaccta. By the early 2010s the station was formally an independent organization, but it remained linked to ABA, and staff at both institutions characterized it as the NGO's main channel for cultural promotion.

Radio Quispillaccta

Radio Quispillaccta was organized over the late 1990s in response to two challenges. The first was the discriminatory coverage that permeated Ayacucho's airwaves following Mayor Ascarza's cutting of the city's palm trees. Often framed in bigoted terms, this new coverage reminded community leaders of the unchallenged role that mestizo-owned media had in conducting Ayacucho's sociopolitical debates. A similar reminder followed the Cachi River dam project, as quispillacctinos protested the regional government's failure to compensate them for lost lands. Letters to news outlets in Ayacucho were futile, according to Graciano Machaca: radio stations "didn't even air them, because they were from mere peasants." Clearly Quechua-speaking activists were hobbled by their lack of access to channels for communicating about their problems.

The idea for the radio station was born after a pilot study, conducted by ABA, suggested the efficacy of an AM station, its offices to be located at Quispillaccta's building in Ayacucho and its antenna mounted on community-owned land in the city's high district of Carmen Alto. Marcela proposed that they solicit contacts in the world of transnational funding to cover startup costs, connecting eventually with Swiss NGO Traditions for Tomorrow. Radio Quispillaccta began transmitting in January 2000, directed by a board containing Quispillaccta's community president, ABA representatives, and members of Ayacucho's quispillacctino migrant organization—all of whom delegated control over programming to Graciano Machaca.

Graciano assumed the directorship with some reluctance. He had interned as an accountant at Ayacucho station Radio Jesús Nazareno while studying at the UNSCH—hardly strong qualifications, but they sufficed for Marcela, who believed that the directorship should remain in quispillacctino hands. This, at least, was how Graciano glossed her interests in a 2012 interview: "[She said,] 'We have to do radio ourselves, we have to be the DJs, the administrators, because we're not going to do radio like others. Our station will have programming aimed at Andean cultural affirmation, about our own customs, with our own music, and we have to talk about Andean knowledge, all of that. We have to talk about freezes, hail, livestock rustling, and we don't need a costly experienced electronics administrator.'" Initially programs were often chaotic, with DJs improvising haphazardly while engineers fumbled cassette cues. However, the directorship sought help from quispillacctinos with radio experience like former *Allpanchik* employee Edilberto Núñez Mejía, who created smoother broadcasts packed with information that spoke to comunero interests otherwise unaired in Ayacucho's mediasphere. Quispillaccta remained foregrounded, but the station attracted and relied financially upon listeners from outside the town, so programming was correspondingly diverse. In addition to music and the chatty, off-the-cuff conversation of people like Graciano and Núñez Mejía, it filled airtime with a mix of news, educational programming, and paid messages from people in Ayacucho to relatives at home or vice versa. It sold broadcast slots to allied NGOs as well as community organizations, concert event promoters, and regional or municipal governmental entities that the directorship deemed compatible with its mission.

The station aimed at musical diversity as well. It committed itself to indigenous sounds that otherwise went unplayed on Ayacucho's airwaves, like the harp and violin duos or the pumpin bands beloved in neighboring communities. Still, it had a special responsibility toward chimaycha music, and speaking in 2012 Graciano placed it at the heart of the station's purpose, saying that "its principal objective is to [serve as] a radio institution for Andean cultural affirmation. That's its slogan, and we play chimaycha music . . . it's there in almost every program." Indeed, Núñez Mejía had convinced the CCC to lend the fledgling station its 1980s-era field recordings, and they were integral to the station's early success. Not only did they enable nostalgic listeners to tune in for music that was rarely heard elsewhere—they listened, in many cases, to hear recordings of their younger selves.

I first visited the station in July 2002, shortly after it had become economically self-sufficient. It employed only four staff members, broadcast only between 4:30 and 9:00 a.m. and 4:00 and 8:00 p.m.—farmers' hours—and it still had the air of a grassroots project. Graciano received me in a cramped, dark office off the concrete courtyard of Quispillaccta's Ayacucho premises. Sitting before his file-strewn desk, he and Núñez Mejía characterized their operations as an act of defense against the "internationalized" Andean music that had "taken over" Ayacucho's airwaves (Tucker 2013b). Ninety-five percent of their music, Graciano said, came from the countryside; he played me selections from cassettes that performers sent in to promote their art. Alongside musical fare they ran programs by institutions like the NGO Chirapaq as well as APRODEH, an organization that advocated for victims of the violence. Soon a messenger came in bearing APRODEH's weekly program and asked for a signed receipt. This was only one of the tasks that called away Graciano's attention, for he spent much of the hour copying cassettes and running them upstairs to the broadcast booth. Meanwhile, paying customers came in to press their requests, driving Graciano to switch from Spanish to Quechua. One client arranged to advertise some furniture for sale, while another requested a birthday message and song for a relative in Putaqa, paying the rate of one sol (ca. $0.30) per on-air delivery. More distressingly, an older couple came in to ask that the station cover the plight of their son, an army recruit who had been sexually assaulted at the city's barracks.

On later visits I accompanied Núñez Mejía in the DJ booth amid a similar atmosphere of busy improvisation. Its two compartments were set among private rooms that the municipality of Quispillaccta let to young quispillacctinos studying in the city. One housed the engineer's booth, a cubby furnished with a desk, chair, mixer, dual tape deck, microphone, and cassette rack, all hidden behind a plywood partition separating the engineer from visitors, who in turn waited in the midst of chairs, boxes, stray newspapers, a pair of chinlilis, and a quispillacctino hat. Behind glass, the DJ booth housed a table, some chairs, and a pair of microphones. Both were plastered with colorful posters promoting community festivals, but the DJ area also contained a page diagramming the Quechua-language kin terms for brother and sister, which change depending on the gender of the speaker. I spoke with Núñez Mejía during songs while his engineer received visitors, took phone requests, and managed cassettes, laboriously hunting songs down and cueing them up, pressing cases to the glass and turning on the DJ mic as each selection ended. Núñez Mejía then announced the group name and, if he was so inclined, spoke about the song, the group, or the recording occasion.

DJs were also responsible for reading paid advertisements and covering the emergent circumstances that arose from phone calls, sudden visits, and other day-to-day business. In the aggregate, Radio Quispillaccta provided an ear on the daily business of Ayacucho's indigenous community, filtered through a quispillacctino perspective. A typical hour in 2002 might yield an announcement for a patron saint festival in the town of Pampa Cangallo and a message asking a man in the Chuschi barrio of Waripirqa to call relatives in Ayacucho. Ads might include an appeal by political party Renacimiento Andino (Andean rebirth), admonishing listeners from "Deep Peru" (i.e., indigenous Peru) to vote in upcoming elections, or a message from the National Bank. In that era they would usually include a communiqué from Peru's Truth and Reconciliation Commission exhorting victims to come forth with testimony, as well as one of ABA's spots discouraging the use of pesticides. The hour would certainly include chimaycha music if it were run by quispillacctino staffers, but if it were a rented slot occupied by a different program then it would include music and commentary from the host's community. There were news programs, didactic soap operas like one developed by women's rights NGO Manuela Ramos, and a live music show on Sundays. All of them tended to follow the loose, self-directed model that I saw in visiting Núñez Mejía's program. Insisting that "there [was] no guidebook," Graciano explained to me that DJs were free to speak and select music as they saw fit, as long as their work was in line with the station's mission—a determination that was up to Graciano himself, who emerged from his office to holler upstairs if he heard something he didn't like, such as a surfeit of Spanish-language conversation.

Radio Quispillaccta's Musical and Social Effects

However precariously professionalized, Radio Quispillaccta had a profound impact on young quispillacctinos, who began asking to work as DJs or engineers while studying in Ayacucho. They were paid a pittance, but they gained an opportunity for professionalization, making the station "a kind of school," in Graciano's terms. Marcela noted how working at the station required a re-dedication to traditional knowledge: "The radio's purpose is to share our way of life via music, our everyday tasks, [and] sometimes there are young people who have forgotten in the course of their schooling. And the radio obliges them to return. 'What am I going to disseminate, if I don't know?' It obliges them to ask their grandparents." She went further, crediting the station for a newfound self-esteem: "Before you had to disguise [your identity] to avoid being demeaned, discriminated against. Now it's always 'I'm from Quispillaccta, we have a radio station.' It's elevated their cultural pride."

Uttering these words in 2014, Marcela spoke after a sea change. The station aired the same Quechua-language mix of music and information and rented slots to the same sorts of organizations. However, its fortunes had improved dramatically. The DJ booth held an impressive desktop computer and stacks of commercial VCDs, which had long replaced cassettes. Engineers managed everything via a desktop broadcasting program, dragging and dropping sound files pulled from VCDs, mixed with rarities transferred from old cassettes by DJ Miguel Núñez, son of ABA's Lorenzo Núñez. Broadcasts were also saturated with lively sound effects designed to create a fun atmosphere, and even the advertisements were noticeably slicker, promoting major players in the local economy like Sombreros Wanchester and Sombreros El Caballero, rival hatmaking companies that sponsored concerts by national artists.

Nothing, however, had changed as thoroughly as chimaycha music, which had become one of Ayacucho's most popular genres. Local and Lima-based artists held concerts every week, and most were publicized via the station that was regarded as the genre's proper home. When I visited in 2012, after an interval of almost a decade, an older Graciano Machaca greeted my renewed interest by saying "Whoo, right now there's a chimaycha boom," echoing Óscar Conde's contention that "today's youth, let's say 40–50 percent of them, are once again accepting what's ours." Other long-standing performers, like José Tomaylla and Pachi Ccallocunto, evaluated the situation with bemusement, while the younger chinlilista David Galindo spoke about the disappearance of the "shame" that once clung to chimaycha as it had to most indigenous manifestations within the city's boundaries. All laid responsibility with the station that some Quechua-speakers called "Radioninchik" (Our radio)—the title of a song penned for the station, which regularly appeared on the air.

The reasons for chimaycha's newfound appeal are not easy to specify, but three factors suggest Radio Quispillaccta's central role. First is the matter of sheer exposure. As rural listeners came to rely upon the station as a source of news, insight, and communication, they were also inundated with the chimaycha that the station preferentially broadcast. It is likely that, as typically happens when new media create new markets, a listenership was simply habituated to and came to love the sound of Quispillaccta's music—music that is, after all, overwhelmingly similar to other traditions in Ayacucho. The geographic expansion of chimaycha's fan base was readily perceptible. People came to the station from the communities of Socos, Ticllas, and Vinchos, or the provinces of La Mar and Huanta—to cite some of the places that Graciano listed—and while they might request music from their hometowns, they also asked for the quispillacctino groups that the station promoted. Chimaycha artists began to receive solicitations from as far away as neighboring Cusco and Arequipa Departments, and Marco Tucno spoke to me of his surprise at being confronted with requests for chimaycha tunes on a 2011 visit to Santillán, in faraway northern Ayacucho.

The growth in listenership was most apparent at the station's anniversary concert, celebrated each year on Easter Sunday. At first it had been small and parochial, mainly bringing people from Chuschi District to hear established and emerging artists, many of whom practiced by performing on the station's Sunday-evening live program. By the mid-2000s it featured up to eighty groups in a concert that lasted from dusk to dawn, drawing a huge audience from across northern Ayacucho. This annual event showed the potential profits to be had from chimaycha, particularly in a city where the cocaine industry was placing spending money into the pockets of formerly impoverished people. The simultaneous rise of cheap independent recording studios allowed artists to finance decent recordings, and chimaycha videos begin to circulate in the markets and on YouTube. By 2012 promoters began to organize shows on holidays and major anniversaries, leading to a more or less fixed annual cycle of chimaycha performance that challenged the centrality of Radio Quispillaccta's own anniversary show.

Radio Quispillaccta, then, placed chimaycha in the public ear just as economic and technical changes enabled independent artists to strike after success on their own. More important, the station's work lent chimaycha an aura

BROADCASTING AND BUILDING PUBLICS

of dignity. Certainly Graciano spoke in our 2012 interview of the respect with which he and his peers treated their fellows and their traditions as key factors in the genre's popularity:

> Before 2000 hardly anyone allowed chimaycha to be broadcast . . . and peasants from the countryside were hardly allowed in the broadcast booth. Nobody wanted them to speak Quechua, everything was Spanish, Spanish, Spanish . . . but then Radio Quispillaccta was born, and when they come here the first thing we say is "Sir, madam, come into the booth, you should speak yourself" . . . and they feel as if they were at home.

Such feelings of ownership and confidence stood in stark contrast to the situation prevailing a decade earlier, when Graciano's own brother had upbraided him for listening to a chimaycha cassette, saying. "What are you doing listening to that? You're in the city."

Finally, if exposure and respect were two factors in chimaycha's rise to prominence, then stylistic change was an unmistakable element of the process. The "chimaycha boom" created predictable problems for the station that had produced it. Young quispillacctinos in the city, first- or second-generation migrants accustomed to the "commercial," "internationalized" sounds that Graciano had lamented in our first interview, began to leaven chimaycha with riffs and rhythms cribbed from mass-popular cumbia. These musical developments soon ran up against the station's traditionalist mission, and by the mid-2000s they forced a reaction from Graciano. He spoke of the issue in our 2012 interview: "It almost doesn't seem like chimaycha anymore. It's a mix, a little chimaycha and a little [huayno], and like I say it twists things. That's what I think, and as the director of this medium of communication, Radio Quispillaccta, for now I am content and proud to carry the name of my community and my chimaycha music."

The indirect quality of these words may have been a means of softpedaling a campaign that the station had waged over the late 2000s. David Galindo, Pachi Ccallocunto, Julia Barrios, and other artists all told me of being admonished on air, or of being relegated to the worst slots at the station's anniversary concert, acts they interpreted as ways of combating chimaycha's stylistic drift. And such efforts were not merely defensive in nature. Graciano took a positive approach by sponsoring recordings by Óscar Conde's group Los Auténticos de Patario, ensuring that they received heavy on-air rotation, and popularizing the notion that their traditionalist format was a benchmark of authenticity.

This battle was over quickly, and when chimaycha artists spoke in 2013–14 of public insult they spoke with the security of the victorious. Surrendering to popular demand, the station's staff had come to support younger artists

148 CHAPTER FIVE

and their music. In the same interview where he spoke of chimaycha's dwindling "originality," Graciano conceded that the station "doesn't exclude," and elsewhere he affirmed that times change and that chimaycha artists needed to change as well in order to reach "a bigger stage." Still, Graciano asked younger DJs to "prioritize the [music of] peasant communities," and in his own broadcasts he seized repeatedly on passing opportunities to promote traditionalism.

Extended treatment of musical traditionalism remained rare, but when it happened it was often placed prominently in the schedule. Quispillaccta's 2013 anniversary celebration provided a particularly apt opportunity. It featured a song competition, to be run by the UNSCH's quispillacctino student organization, and Radio Quispillaccta's staff seized the moment. Discussing the event days beforehand, Graciano emphasized that lyrics were required to echo those of the town's past, not those of Andean huayno artists like "Sonia Morales, Chinito del Ande, Amor Amor: our own [*kikinchikpa*]."[17] Around the same time, on October 15, 2013, he interrupted the broadcast of a recording he was contractually obliged to play, by young artist Ilde Luz Pomasoncco, grumbling on air about the song's excessive reliance on Spanish. A more extensive foray into aesthetic moralism came on the same morning as he returned to the microphone after playing an old field recording from the station's library:

> Brothers and sisters, such songs come from *our* town, *our* community, *our* sentiments. Not like these recent songs, all about wandering eyes, drinking, chasing after women. Our real songs, sung by people from our town, are about our trees, the names of our mountain deities, everything that makes up our lives. Our ancestors gave them to us. Lately there's too much requinto coming into them, there's a distortion—where will that end? Our songs, our customs, hopefully we can help them come back, so that we can show where we are from, where we are, and revive our ways.

This effort culminated with a "special" that aired from 8:00 to 9:00 a.m. the day before the festival itself, hosted by regular DJ Melecio Llalli. His guests included UNSCH students Tony, Luz, and Pablo, representatives of the student organization responsible for the competition. Llalli spun track after track featuring traditionalist groups like Waylla Ichu de Llacctahurán and Los Auténticos de Patario, and one song that thematized chimaycha itself, by a group called Los Kusikusichas de Quispillaccta (The happy little guys of Quispillaccta). After naming the Pampas Valley towns where chimaycha is considered to be the defining genre, it ended with a fuga asking "quispillacctino brothers and sisters" and "fellow quispillacctino peasants" not to forget "our chimaycha, our custom, our beautiful song." Following its conclusion

BROADCASTING AND BUILDING PUBLICS

Llalli handed the mic to his guests, who deployed the same languages that Graciano had used some days earlier:

LUZ: Yes, that's it, brother Melecio, that's good for us to hear. Like all quispillacctinos, we too are traditionalists [*típicasuninchik*], fans of chimaycha, no? This chimaycha we've just heard, with its message comes from the famous Patario, and we too cultivate this chimaycha, we too recognize it for what it is. "Quispillacctina, look to your name, quispillacctino, you too," it tells us. Wear your decorated hat, your decorated skirt, your brown poncho. Isn't that right, brother Tony?

TONY: Exactly, sister Luz, you've said it. Decorated hat, decorated skirt, black pants with a *chumpi* belt, rubber sandals on our feet, like quispillacctinos, like peasants—that's how we should dress. Brother Melecio, why don't you come along tomorrow afternoon and dance with us?

MELECIO: Sure, sure. Tony, tomorrow afternoon or the next day. Let's sing and dance chimaycha, purely chimaycha, right? Our custom, our knowledge, it will be there in the chimaycha competition, Tony. Let's see, tell about before when it was only [played on] number 2, 4, 6, 8, 10, and 12 vigoylas. Right?

TONY: You said it, brother . . . I only play the 4, just the 4. But they also speak of the 2, the *takra* [chinlili], the *sapo* [chinlili], 6, 12, etc. In the vida michiy the quispillacctinos and quispillacctinos played sweetly, whatever was in their hearts. Today we young people are waking up and recovering our traditional knowledge. Sometimes today, brother Melecio, we're leaving aside chimaycha, that which is autochthonous, maybe with requinto, maybe twisting things, but not always, no? Even amid all that we always maintain our cultural identity as Quispillaccta. No matter where you've gone, where you are, we live with our values, no matter what town we walk in we don't forget to speak Quechua, listen to chimaycha, wear our clothes, brother Melecio.

Blending colloquial banter, languages of kinship and community, and figures of tradition and autochthony, this exchange captures in an unusually brief space the chain of signifiers that dedicated listeners gleaned from Radio Quispillaccta over a longer period of engagement and in a less concentrated form. Subtler techniques for building a sense of indigenous corporate identity included, for instance, the mere act of broadcasting in highly idiomatic Quechua, impenetrable to anybody but a native and habitual speaker. Graciano took pains to ensure that the station remained committed to this principle, ejecting hosts who broke too often into Spanish conversation. The injunction

150   CHAPTER FIVE

to speak in Quechua even led to the coining of neologisms like *wayra wasi* (air house), a pervasive in-house term for "radio station," as if to prove the language's ductile aptness for modern life.

More subtle and yet perhaps more effective was the staff's use of Quechua's grammatical affordances to create a sense of intersubjectivity among listeners. In broadcasts they pervasively used the first-person plural inclusive pronoun, *ñuqanchik*, that marks speaker and listeners as members of a shared community. They also attached the optional possessive ending associated with that pronoun, *-nchik*, to nouns that thereby became marked as the shared property of this Quechua-speaking public. Sometimes the possessive was used in a way that implicated quispillacctinos alone, as during a discussion with community elder Félix Calderón about healing practices. Describing how town elders and teachers promoted "Andean medicine" over Western pills, the two interlocutors repeatedly invoked the *hatun yachay wasinchik* (all-of-our school) and the *yachachiqninchikkuna* (all-of-our teachers). Elsewhere, though, he appended the suffix to indigenous towns, festivals, and cultural expressions unrelated to Quispillaccta, leading to on-air formulations like *pumpin costumbrinchik* (all-of-our pumpin custom), a phrase designed to assert a sort of shared ownership of the pumpin genre cultivated in communities downriver from Quispillaccta. Such a phrase makes grammatical sense only when spoken from a subject position that includes both residents of pumpin's home communities, *and* Graciano's own Quispillaccta. It is, in other words, a calculated linguistic enactment of the indigenous corporate identity that the station's staff and allies hoped to broker—a means to reify the otherwise theoretical notion of an indigenous public.

Tentative Environmentalism

By 2012 Radio Quispillaccta's strategies had evolved in tandem with those of ABA, and increasingly politicized languages of indigeneity began to merge with notions of environmental stewardship. In that year, for example, Graciano explained to me that "we do things in our own way, and following our cosmovisión," citing an eco-religious term that had appeared nowhere in our conversations ten years before. Several posters in the broadcast booth advertised indigenous political meetings such as the Fourth Congress of the Indigenous Nations of Peru. Others promoted workshops on traditional knowledge sponsored by NGOs that promoted indigenous cultural vitalization, including ABA, Chirapaq, CEDAP, and Asociación Kanas. Run by former ABA employee Oseas Núñez, Kanas bore the name of the pre-Columbian ethnic group from which quispillacctinos claim descent, and although its activities in that year revolved around water management, it also ran at least one program on Radio Quispillaccta in 2013 that enumerated the principles of the Rio Declaration.

Over 2013–14 the station's airwaves hosted ample coverage of environmental themes, much of it centered on water and climate change, topics at the center of projects that both Asociación Kanas and ABA ran with foreign support. Related content was featured on Asociación Kanas's regular Wednesday-morning program, and much more prominently on *Kawsayninchikmanta* (About our lives), a series of short informational segments sponsored by ABA in partnership with Weltungerhilfe, which ran regularly throughout Radio Quispillaccta's broadcast day. One such spot, which was in heavy rotation over late 2013 and 2014, tied agricultural and ritual practices together via the words of a community elder. Against a background of chimaycha performed by Ninay Urucha, a stentorian voice intoned the spot's standard opening: "Let's speak of our lives, of how to live." What followed was an interview excerpt in which a man can be heard stating, "If you want a body of water to run, you have to make it an offering," before moving on to describe the offering's material elements (wine and other foodstuffs), as well as the proper time of day for burying it (midnight). Finally, such spots were regularly followed by one of Radio Quispillaccta's prerecorded station identifications: "Radio Quispillaccta, coming to your town and your home, every day." A coincidence of timing, perhaps, but still a powerful index of the close relationship the station had with the indigenist ecological mission of its parent organization.

Radio Quispillaccta's broadcasts designated Quechua speakers as members of a corporate community, linked that community to traditional expressive culture, and brought the environmental discourse of contemporary indigenous politics into their mediated space. However, connections among this chain of signifiers were rarely drawn overtly, and the different projects of agronomic, cosmological, and expressive vitalization that animated their work were integrated in halting and tentative fashion. Especially given Marcela Machaca's easy references to its agronomic value, chimaycha's ecocentric elements were referenced rarely in station activities, and DJs only episodically highlighted the knowledge that song lyrics encoded. In 2013–14 the only outstanding occasion involved water, and it was the very event that encouraged me to ask after the links between ABA's activities and the content of Radio Quispillaccta, for it clearly showed how the two agencies worked together in the cause of indigenous empowerment.

The cycle of events began when Graciano announced on air a colloquium at the UNSCH to promote the results of an ABA-sponsored study concerning water management. He interspersed his comments with chimaycha songs about rivers and lakes, including groups that he was otherwise loath to program, such as Alberto Infanzón's Aires Chuschinos. This rather tenuous link between environmentalism, indigeneity, and music was only somewhat strengthened at the event itself, which was framed as a project report for funding agencies. Held before scholars, community leaders in full traditional attire, staff from ABA and Radio Quispillaccta, and representatives from the sponsoring NGO Welthungerhilfe, it offered the Machacas an opportunity to lay out their vision. An introductory video narrated ABA's history before telling of its research into ancestral techniques of water management, illustrated by the use of *putaqa* plants and clay dams to "call" and then retain springs. Puzzlingly, the video's music consisted of the "internationalized" pan-Andean fusion music that the organization ostensibly opposed, using the sound of the Middle Eastern *qanun* to add a mystical quality to scenes of yachaqs performing ceremonies. Afterward, however, the crowd was entertained by Los Ichu Tullmas, a chimaycha band that had recently been organized by DJ and promoter Tío Miki Espinoza.

Following these opening presentations, each of the Machacas delivered a statement. Magdalena, underlining the opposition between Andean and Occidental approaches to resource management, spoke about the importance of treating water as a living being rather than a resource, especially in an era when the climate "has gone crazy." Marcela followed up by speaking of the "cosmovisión" of the "originary communities," characterizing climate change as the product of a "crisis of care" (*crisis de cariño*), a breakdown in the maintenance of proper relationships between human and nonhuman beings. Both attacked the Peruvian school system's aversion to non-Occidental knowledge, asking instead for a "vigorization" of the cosmovisión via the education system. Their respondents, drawn from the ranks of UNSCH professors, adopted the sisters' rhetorical style, with one mestizo professor joking that he had prayed to the *apus* (indigenous deities) for help, and contrasting the "mechanical" conception of Western water management with an Andean ethic of care.

Ideological seams, however, showed that some participants were not quite full-fledged interlocutors in Quispillaccta's indigenous politics. One participating community organization was headquartered in faraway Huánuco, and its representatives repeatedly spoke of "campesino" communities, even as they stood before slides characterizing them as "indigenous-campesino." The moderator stumbled when introducing Quispillaccta's community president, quickly adjusting course to emit the phrase "comunidad cam—er, indígena de Quispillaccta." Worse, the agronomist respondent began his remarks by pointing to the featured musicians as evidence for quispillacctinos' receptivity to "new methodologies, [for] the community has accepted electronic instruments into its heart." The music group represented, instead, precisely the sort

BROADCASTING AND BUILDING PUBLICS   153

of "modern" chimaycha that the ABA resisted. Tío Miki, director of Los Ichu Tullmas, was often the subject of remonstrance at Radio Quispillaccta due to his overreliance on the Spanish language, and Lorenzo Núñez later told me that ABA had fruitlessly tried to hire the decidedly more palatable Marcela Flores for the occasion instead.

Conclusion

As of 2014, rhetorical links between nature, culture, and indigeneity hovered around the edges of ABA and Radio Quispillaccta's public activities, but they were major resources in their expansive plans for Quispillaccta. A magazine profile of Magdalena Machaca published that year noted that "ABA accompanies the initiative of Quispillaccta's comuneros to establish a new indigenous district and promotes the creation of a 'Natural Reserve of Hydric Resources and Agrobiodiversity'" (Orjeda 2014:2). This extraordinary proposal was subject to intense community suspicion, but by December 2017 even resistant quispillacctinos deemed it likely to pass (see epilogue). Whether or not the project develops excactly as proposed, the apparent effectiveness of such discursive tactics has consolidated a greater sense of identification with the global indigenous ideologies that ABA and Radio Quispillaccta brokered in the local context. This crucial sense of identification remained lacking in other efforts, such as those of the allied NGO Chirapaq. In 2014 Chirapaq employee Edwin Qunislla told me that the organization's activities began in the 1990s with "cultural affirmation workshops." Its staff moved on to teach peasants about ILO 169 and encourage the use of the term *indigenous*, but the task was difficult given the term's "contemptuous" ring. More successful, he said, were workshops that brought comuneros to reflect on their distinctiveness and their commonalities—for yes, he said, they did respect the earth, and yes, they did make ritual offerings to it and perform collective labor. In the end the organization set aside the project of explicit ethnic mobilization, focusing on introducing local knowledge into grade-school lesson plans in the Quechua language, alongside the principles of ILO 169.

The element of ethnic self-consciousness that remained latent in Chirapaq's efforts moved to the center of activities associated with ABA over the 2000s and 2010s. As in the Combapata Valley region studied by Hogue and Rau, ABA's "rhetorical juxtaposition of the campesino way of life with the 'foreign' approach to the natural world both results from and dialectically reinforces a consciousness of their ethnic difference, and it has served as a moral and cultural stance" (2008:302) from which to demand greater respect and autonomy. However, in contradistinction to Combapata, in Ayacucho Quechua cultural distinctiveness stood above ecocentric discourse as a useful tool for rallying an indigenous public that understands itself as such. In this sense it is worth noting the statement that greeted visitors to Radio Quispillaccta's website as of 2016: "Radio Quispillaccta, valorizing and strengthening our Andean lifeways, music, and song. Listen mornings from 5:00 a.m. to 11:00 a.m. and afternoons from 3:30 p.m. to 8:30 p.m., and enjoy our autochthonous music: chimaycha, harp and violin, pumpin, and *llaqtamaqta* among other melodies from Deep Peru."[18] By encouraging listeners to valorize "our" "autochthonous" music, Radio Quispillaccta became instrumental in building an indigenous public, composed of Quechua-speaking people with common investments,but also cognizant of their membership in an ethnic group with distinctive rights.

Of course the most effective kind of public is characterized by its capacity to act as self-organizing system for debate and introspection about its concerns, and not merely a self-aware community of taste or ethnic identity. The public that ABA and Radio Quispillaccta gathered quickly showed this capacity by engaging in actions and forms of communication that seemed to disavow the station's own cultural politics. More specifically, they patronized decidedly hybrid types of chimaycha performance, demonstrating the cultural heterogeneity that exists *within* Ayacucho's indigenous public and the fallibility of an indigenous politics that relies upon a univocal understanding of indigenous idenity. From a traditionalist point of view this must be evaluated as a disappointment. However, from another perspective, the creation of a public defined by its commitment to a dynamic Quechua-language popular culture might be treated as a raging success.

6

Success and Sentiment

Radio Quispillacctaʼs success laid the groundwork for a shift in chimaychaʼs sound and meaning. Many of the genreʼs newfound fans held no reservations about stylistic change, and despite the stationʼs resistance, chimaycha recordings began to feature instruments and idioms copied from the recordings of national huayno stars. When radio staff yielded to audience pressure and began to broadcast them, their sanction redrew the sonorous parameters of indigeneity, rendering legible a public for which the urban culture industry was a venue for elaborating indigenous sensibilities, and not a threat to indigenous difference.

This chapter explores the business that grew up around chimaycha in the late 2000s and early 2010s, foregrounding qualities of aesthetic eclecticism, hustling self-promotion, and emotional identification that animated it. None of these elements was new. Andean musicians had adapted novel sounds for centuries, and their music was always designed to elicit feelingful response. However, the particular sounds, themes, and practices of consumption that transformed the chimaycha scene at this time are important, because they exemplified all the principles that are typically associated with contemporary cholo culture—even as performers, promoters, and consumers continued to experience the genre as a symbol of indigenous heritage. Insofar as it manifests a staunchly metropolitan variety of indigeneity, the chimaycha scene challenges the assimilationist ideology that often underpins conversations about Peruvian social identity. Those discussions imply that cholo mores and aesthetics demonstrate the willing sacrifice of commitments to indigenous difference, in favor of a heterogeneous, shared, and therefore more virtuous culture. By contrast, diacritics of lo cholo accrued around chimaycha music without displacing its ties to indigeneity: indeed, the entrepreneurial attitude that is often called a central facet of lo cholo remained suspect to chimaycha listeners and proved difficult to reconcile with local expectations about the continuing development of the style. Changes in chimaycha music demonstrated, in short, that commitments to urban indigeneity and cholo culture can coexist without dissolving into one another and that popular culture acts as a medium for resisting the hegemony of cholo nationalism as easily as for acceding to it.

Hustle, Struggle, and Suffer: The Musical Discourse of Lo Cholo

Chimaycha broadcasts of the 2010s clearly registered a shift in the genre's social position by adopting the hectoring style of mainstream pop shows. One example was the daily special that aired throughout October 2013, promoting an "anniversary concert" by quispillacctina artist Ninay Urucha (Glowworm). It opened with DJ Víctor Pauza promising to "move your molecules" with danceable tunes by acts from the "caravan" of a concert promoter called Altamirano Producciones. The ensuing hour featured tracks by Ninay Urucha and colleagues like Bertita Corazón, "the Beer Sweetie," all packed with the drum machines, synthesizers, and shouted "animation" that typify the work of Peru's national huayno stars. Above them Pauza deployed raucous sound effects including laughter, cheering crowds, and a series of rapid pops meant to represent beer bottles cracking open. This manufactured energy suggested the atmosphere that listeners could expect at the advertised show, featuring—in the words of a spot that ran repeatedly over the hour—"the beer-drinking barfly, the only one that fills all the best venues, Ninay Urucha!"

The program's hard sell and the music that it featured were modeled on the work of Lima's Andean music stars. Since the 1980s such stars had combined highland tunes with electric instruments and "tropical" percussion, singing about romantic deception and the social challenges of the poor. However, cultural gatekeepers largely demeaned their music as artless bricolage until the years around the millennium. At that time Andean migrants finally attained leading positions in the social and commercial hierarchy of Lima.[1] Their ascent forced a public reckoning with dominant criollo ideas of national identity, which came instead to center on the experiences and mores of migrants. New conversations about the state of the nation highlighted on one hand a work ethic and business savvy that had allowed cholo migrants to succeed in a hostile city, and on the other a recombinant cultural creativity that had allowed them to forge a sense of collective self. Huayno was claimed as a pillar of a new national culture in formation, and its icons cannily brought elements of Peru's emergent national narrative to bear upon one another. They sang songs of struggle that they pitched as autobiographical tales, and presented their careers as striving stories of hard-won opportunity. Figures like the emblematic Dina Paucar converted their public selves into lucrative commodities, spinning off products like T-shirts, caps, doll figurines, and TV series. Far from crass commercialism, their entrepreneurial sensibility was presented as evidence of a managerial élan that had guaranteed the advancement of the entire migrant community and that was set to vitalize Peruvian society generally.[2]

Stated differently, Lima's huayno stars had become focal symbols of a go-getting sensibility that is central to lo cholo. *Cholo* was once a derogatory term for indigenous migrants who failed to master the metropolitan norms of white and mestizo elites. Today it is as often used as a term of admiration, indicating the migrant's unique capacity to cross boundaries and disrupt structures. On this reading, cholo practices and products are no longer viewed as faulty misinterpretations of others' customs. Rather, they are evidence of a sui generis sensibility, one premised on irreverent cultural mixture, radical self-invention, and freedom from the confines of any prior social category. The consumption of cholo music is, in turn, pitched as a way for listeners to celebrate the triumph of this distinctive habitus—a hymn to the combination of capitalist ingenuity and cultural creativity that define lo cholo.[3]

This is an expansive challenge to Peru's deleterious essentialisms of race, class, and culture, but it bears at least three limitations. First, accounts of lo cholo often take cholo beliefs, behaviors, and material culture as evidence for the waning of other social identities. Studies of situational variability in Peruvian ethnic and racial terminologies suggest otherwise. Of particular interest are Thorp and Paredes's findings from Ayacucho (2010), where the term *cholo* is associated with city residents who maintain an indigenous identity—urban Indians, a category that is invisible to Peru's dominant racial schemas. Second, as several scholars have argued, the lionization of hustling aligns with a dubious neoliberal philosophy that has guided recent Peruvian social policy. Neoliberalism's hypercapitalist program of social progress through privatization, deregulation, and social disinvestment finds a convincing emblem in the figure of the scrappy migrant fighting up from poverty without aid and against all odds. Narratives of cholo ingenuity that emphasize hustle may pander to the neoliberal state's reluctance to address Peru's real and persistent inequalities (Vich 2002), and everyday citizens may readily interpret hustling businesspeople as rapacious and self-interested threats to the things they hold dear, rather than symbols to be admired. Third, celebratory accounts of lo cholo poorly represent the lived experience of the label's carriers, which are often painful. They especially distort readings of contemporary Andean music, where the careers of workaday musicians and the songs of suffering testify amply to experiences of continuing marginality that define lo cholo for many who bear the identity.

Against this background it is worth returning to Ninay Urucha's anniversary special and taking note of its rhetorical emphasis on alcohol. Beer is central to scenes of chimaycha consumption, where it helps attune listeners to the qualities of emotional angst that make the genre meaningful for fans. Concerts are characterized by grief-charged recognition of shared pain, channeled via "hyperemotional" displays of stylized feeling (Yano 2013:147) and facilitated by voluminous alcohol consumption. Beer sales are, in fact, used as a benchmark for artistic skill, because they index a performer's ability to give audiences the experience that they seek: ecstatic sadness, motivated by songs that present relatable experiences of moral injury, moving hearers to dance and weep under the disinhibiting effects of alcohol. Such displays elicit responses of recognition and care from fellow attendees, thereby ratifying the shared nature of the experiences that lie behind them. Chimaycha concerts, in other words, provide one apparatus for Quechua-speaking Ayacuchanos to socialize common histories of struggle.

By following the trends of Lima's huayno industry, chimaycha artists and promoters showed their conversancy with emergent conventions of cholo nationalism and the place of Andean migrants within that discursive formation. However, by adopting a mode of consumption premised on recognizing their community's hardships, they testified to a persistent, aggrieved sense of race-based marginality that lingers behind lo cholo's facade of reconciliatory hybridity. This is one more variety of indigenous experience, but understanding it means describing the dynamics of the live performances where it is actualized and inhabited. Concerts unfold via a series of techniques for regulating emotional response, which in turn depend upon alcoholic commensality and intoxication.

The Social Politics of Emotion and Alcohol

It is routine to describe Andean song as sad—excessively so, since actual Andean songs present a range of emotional experiences. It is also common for Andeanist ethnographers to describe ritual drinking and drunkenness as devices for building community, and studies are filled with analyses of alcoholic commensality.[4] Here I argue that ethylic emotionalism enacts a communal mode of critique, a way to register and cope with shared injustice, echoing Saignes's argument that ever since colonial times, alcohol has opened "a space for discussion or criticism of established forms of power and authority. . . . a space of liberty, of 'useless' expenditure and ambiguous affirmations of self that lies beyond the reach of any power" (1993:17–18). Traditionalists are predictably dismayed at the conjoined elements of alcohol abuse and lyrical anomie that have come to characterize the chimaycha scene. However, "'rules to feel music by' are political" (Qureshi 1997:5), and situations of social change often yield new, contentious notions of emotional propriety. With this in mind I think it better to approach drunken emotion as socially productive, a way to cultivate a "morally configured sensory attunement" (Throop 2010:42) through which individuals identify, recognize, and commiserate with the emotional needs of fellows.

Attentive ethnographers have long located emotions "not only in the person, but in the social situation and interaction which, indeed, they help construct" (Schiefflin 1983:190–91).[5] On this view emotions are learned, conventionalized means whereby people gauge and express their relationship with the world around them. Culture conditions the bodily habits and forms of self-perception that individuals perform and construe as emotional states, furnishing them with the means to convert affective experiences "into semantically and semiotically formed progressions . . . into function and meaning" (Massumi 2002:28). Precisely for this reason it might be expected for emotional habitus to evolve in tandem with societal change. In one sense, the chimaycha scene merely sustained assumptions already characteristic of Quechua-speaking communities, where "actions speak louder than emotions [and the] display of crying is a precondition for feeling sorrow" (Mannheim 1998:256). However, by weaving performative grief together with the tropes of aspiration and frustration that drive the contemporary huayno scene, chimaycha and alcohol consumption also provided a means for listeners to articulate "internal" feelings with new kinds of "external" narratives, thereby aligning self and community at a most intimate level.

Chimaycha listeners rely on the aid of beer to "produce themselves as social agents with attendant styles of feeling" (DeNora 2010:167–68), and alcohol plays such a constitutive role in its affective system that it demands discussion, despite the danger of condescending sensationalism.[6] In fact chimaycha's associated drinking practices resemble those featured in much ethnographic work on Andean life, where drinking behavior is characterized by extreme inebriation, leading to impairment and often unconsciousness.[7] Such apparent excess lends itself easily to caricature or condemnation, but it is guided by a distinctive ethics. In Quechua-speaking communities, for instance, people have traditionally imbibed copiously at festivals but otherwise rarely used alcohol. Public, celebratory drinking lubricates interaction, but more important, it amounts to a demonstration of fellowship, and "the refusal to accept a drink can be interpreted as a lack of confidence and a denial of respect and affection"

(Harvey 1993:119–20). Especially in urban contexts, drinkers typically arrange themselves in a circle, passing around a single bottle and cup. This arrangement underlines alcohol's social intimacy, not only because everyone imbibes from the same vessel but also because each is aware of surveillance by the group, which remains vigilant before slowdowns or surreptitious dumping. Finally, intimacy is further secured through the intensified sentimentality and physical expansiveness that develop in the course of intoxication, allowing for increasingly frank expressions of friendship and respect.

At the same time the alcoholic frame permits people to break Andean taboos against expressing negative feelings, and "festering hostilities, submerged under layers of praise and endearment, break out while [Quechua speakers] are drunk" (C. Allen 2002 [1988]: 124). In an exceptional account Harvey has noted that drinking occasions often follow a bipartite sequence. Early moments involve rituals of solidarity while the second involves increasingly troubled rhetoric, which may include aggression but is sure to include open angst. In an Andean context characterized by severe ethnic inequality, the verbal performances of this second moment segue easily into plaintive laments about the costs and benefits of indigenous identity. Linguistic competence breaks down, and people may cycle between anger, tears, and bravado, delivering extended monologues about

> how hard life is and how much one has to suffer. . . . People cry about being alone . . . people are no longer concerned with any kind of linear communication and instead repeat their preoccupation of that moment. . . . They assert that their power or authority lies in the assumption of a positive Indian identity while simultaneously acknowledging that the moral values of kinship and hard work leave them in a degraded state of poverty. (Harvey 1991:18)

Elsewhere Harvey has noted that "even if the inebriated have no power to undermine such norms and conventions, by confronting them they reveal the artificality of social life and allow themselves to imagine an alternative social order" (Harvey 1993:138). Spurred by songs of sadness, chimaycha listeners often fall into just such a discourse of "despair and defiance" (Harvey 1991:15), but when their statements are met with recognition, they secure the kind of empathy that underpins a functioning sense of solidarity and identity. Drinking occasions, then, provide an accepted framework for acknowledging debasement and also a means to assuage that state, as fellows who share their plight ratify their sense of moral injury. This is where studies linking cholo cultural production to individual subjectivation tend to fall short, for they rely on the analysis of recordings and other "texts" rather than observation of consumption. When songs are put to use and images of striving and success get rerouted through listeners' emotional responses, people may come to inhabit a different relationship with the role of urban indigenous migrant than celebratory nationalist accounts typically imply.

More particularly, the observation of such emotional peformances undermines the notion that the Andean music scene, with its ardent lionization of hustling artists who struggle and succeed, has become a vehicle for naturalizing neoliberal values.[8] Commercial Andean music may be one technology of neoliberal governmentality "whereby subjectivities are formed or refashioned in alignment with values of individualism, entrepreneurialism, and market competition" (Ganti 2014:94), but those values appear more properly in the business of promoting concerts and careers than in the lyrics of songs themselves or in their mode of reception.[9] It is not even clear that the hard-sell business tactics of the huayno scene are met with the kind of naiveté that would facilitate such neoliberal subjectification. Below I turn to one account of failed musical entrepreneurialism in order to show how the will to incarnate the hustling values of lo cholo can fail, defeated by everyday consumers' investments in communal control over locale and practices. First, though, this discussion requires an overview of the way that chimaycha has indeed been influenced by the national huayno industry.

Drum Machines and Tales of Woe: The Andean Culture Industry

María Ccallocunto was one of many aspiring singers negotiating Ayacucho's chimaycha scene in the early 2010s. A student of social work at the UNSCH and a DJ at Radio Quispillaccta, she spent her childhood in the barrio of Llacta Urán, watching her father rehearse with José Tomaylla's group Waylla Ichu de Llacctahurán. She only began to sing, however, as a young woman in the early 2010s, long after moving to Ayacucho for secondary schooling. She had never attended the vida michiy, but most of her compositions were based on melodies recorded there by her uncle Pachi, director of another influential group called Los Amaynis de Llacctahurán. She was not fully satisfied with the conditions she faced. Chatting about aesthetics during a broadcast one March day in 2014, she illustrated the problem by rotating songs into her playlist, beginning with a popular track that delayed the chinlili entrance, foregrounding instead synthesized melodies borrowed from cumbia dance music. By way of contrast she played tracks by Waylla Ichu and Los Qarwaypiñichas, a group sponsored by ABA and featuring children from Quispillaccta's orphanage. Each recording demonstrated quispillacctino bona fides by using the spare, three-chinlili format I associated with Los Auténticos de Patario. She herself would prefer to record with that format, she said, but she faced listeners with ears that had been aestheticized by Lima's huayno industry, ears that could only hear a recording without percussion and synthesizer as "dead."

For María, the "imposition" of those instruments was a practical problem: it drove local artists to waste money on players from outside their community. For others, including workers at ABA and Radio Quispillaccta, it represented a deeper problem of social philosophy. It seemed to mark a concession to the pernicious idea that indigenous traditions required "modernization." This musical teleology lay behind the words of artists like chinlili player William Pacotaype, who suggested that chimaycha's musical "modernization" was a natural consequence of infrastructural change. "Before, in the countryside," he said, "there wasn't any electricity, but there is in the city, so now we play modern instruments." However, musicians often expressed bemusement when I contrasted metropolitan instruments with indigenous tradition. María's uncle Pachi Ccallocunto spoke for many when he described drum machines and synthesizers as simple cognates of the clapping and whistling that had always enlivened the vida michiy—a significant claim from a traditionalist who also told me that his group was created to "preserve and carry forward" his ancestors' customs.

Stylistic change, in other words, was not necessarily experienced as a threat to indigenous cultural integrity. After all, the all-important chinlili itself originated within living memory as a distinctive version of an earlier instrument. And chinlili aside, chimaycha musicians are more concerned with proper musical functions than with any particular sonority. It is therefore more profitable to attend to the element that artists and listeners foreground when discussing their art: lyrics, especially lyrical qualities of emotional force and sincerity. Here too María Ccallocunto's response was especially pithy when I asked about the qualities that listeners valued in chimaycha songs and the reasons they drank while hearing them. The genre's "characteristic" theme, she said, was "love and lost love," and people drank because "they recognize themselves in those songs," for in the end "everybody has had a bad experience." Of course by the time we spoke romantic deception was but one of chimaycha's core themes, along with drinking, lived hardship, and nostalgia for an abandoned home—all themes that center, in Óscar Conde's terse gloss, on "disillusionment."

The unanimity among aficionados concerning chimaycha's connection to painful experience and affective response reveals an underlying music ideology: a set of expectations about what music is for and what it should do. Like most such ideologies, it is a partial mystification, for it overlooks the picaresque, jocular, and celebratory qualities that actually animate many chimaycha songs. Furthermore, despite the routine assertion that artists drew upon personal experience in their songwriting, it is less accurate to describe songs as literally autobiographical than to say that they allow performers to adopt a stance that listeners find meaningful. Much like American country artists, they succeed by portraying the lived predicaments of their fans through styles of figuration and characterization that are understood as both contrived and real—as flattening stereotypes and as meaningful sites of identification.[10]

Here chimaycha owes a debt to Lima's huayno industry. There is no better source on this subject than Dina Paucar, Peru's most prominent twenty-first-century huayno star. In a 2008 interview, Paucar told me that huayno songs move people when they recognize themselves in them and recognize the speaker's personal authority to deal with the material. Outlining the themes that guided her work and that of her peers, she spoke first of the toil and hope that inform her public biography and then of the content that dominates songs: lovelorn tales, poverty, and its associated perils, including alcohol abuse, gendered violence, and libertinism. Treated as condemnable pathologies, these hazards are nevertheless approached with an air of sympathy for those who fall afoul of them. Paucar and her colleagues, in other words, are beloved not only because they embody the promise that Peru's popular classes can rise above their condition, but more properly for modeling an attitude of empathy toward those who fail to transcend difficulties.

By the middle of the 2000s Mario Carhuapoma, a Lima-based performer who hails from Chuschi's neighboring district of Sarhua, began to copy elements of this huayno style. Reinforcing his chinlili with an electric bass, he moved on to add drum machines, synthesizers, and eventually the electrified chinlili that he required to match the power of those forces. His lyrics, too, converged with huayno aesthetics, as his plainspoken songs came to explore romantic tribulation, alcohol's dangerous attractions, or both at once. Crucially, unlike commercial huayno artists, he continued to sing them in Quechua, thereby committing himself to an indigenous public. Still, in their sheer bluntness they contrasted starkly with the lyrical figuration of older songs, dismaying traditionalist connoisseurs like Óscar Conde: "Before there was also disappointment but it wasn't treated so frankly, they made a comparison. For instance, you might know a song that alludes to the poppy, a poppy that's wilting, more or less like that. That's the big difference with the chimaycha that has copied contemporary lyrics. Modern chimaycha."

Carhuapoma's song "Alcoholchay" (My little alcohol) might be taken as illustrative of the trend, insofar as it is designed to evoke, in the most prosaic manner imaginable, the mental state of a man torn between two different kinds of commitment:

Alocholchay, tragoschay, tomayki manaschu imaynaram	My little alcohol, my little liquor, let's see if I can still get a drink
Cervezay, cerveza, tomayki manaschu imaynaram	My little beer, my little beer, let's see if I can still get a drink
Tomay, tomaykusqaypurallamantam,	Ever since I started drinking you,
kuyasqay yanallay rabiachillawachkan	my beloved has been making me mad
Tomay, tomaykusqaypurallamantam,	Ever since I started drinking you,
kuyasqay yanallay piñachillawachkan	my beloved has been annoying me
kuyasqay yanallay rabiachillawachkan	my beloved has been making me mad

Sung in a rueful, humorous tone, "Alcoholchay" nevertheless depicts a real anxiety about the consequences of dissolution, and especially its effects on the institution of marriage (or at least romantic commitment). At the same time, by inviting alcoholic commensality along with emotional response, it addresses the twin concerns of chimaycha concertgoers and is ingeniously designed for success in that context.[11]

In Quispillaccta, Carhuapoma's first follower was David Galindo, who went on to collaborate with so many Ayacucho-based artists that he can be called a nodal point in the city's chimaycha scene. Galindo honed his chinlili skills at the vida michiy as a teen in the 1980s and later at ABA-sponsored contests in town. He followed Los Chikitukus and other folkloric chimaycha artists of the 1990s, but his high barrio of Cuchoquesera also captured radio signals carrying Spanish-language stations from faraway Cusco. Blending the instrumental hooks of the huayno and cumbia heard there with chinlili technique (see figure 15), Galindo had already defined an audibly hybrid idiom by the mid-2000s, when he took up the bass reinforcement that he heard on Carhuapoma's recordings. He then brought that sound to his brother's group upon moving to Ayacucho in 2009 and also encouraged further experimentation, incorporating a friend's 2.5-octave keyboard and then a drum machine. Finally, in 2010, newly renamed Los Legales de Cuchoquesera, the band made what is widely recognized as Quispillaccta's first "modern" chimaycha recording. Combined with his renowned humility and reliability, it made him into a prized accompanist for emerging vocalists, and his personal style became a fixture of concerts and recordings.

Meanwhile, many of the singers seeking Galindo's aid owed their own careers to the mediation of Pachi Ccallocunto, director of Los Amaynis de Llacctahurán. Pachi moved to Ayacucho in 2002, years before the experiments of Carhuapoma and Galindo, and joined a band backing the young vocalist Corina Barrios. By 2006, when the group produced a VCD, its traditionalism had made it a resounding success. Based largely on melodies that Pachi had

FIGURE 15. "Modern" introductory passage, typically used by Los Reales del Perú. Transcribed by author.

gleaned during his youth, its songs rotated heavily on Radio Quispillaccta, and the group was regularly tapped for festival performance. This success in turn drew hobbyists eager to sing with them with a regularity that was fortunate, since such singers typically formed their own bands after a short apprenticeship. As a result most of Ayacucho's chimaycha singers maintained a strong, high vocal delivery that closely tracked the vida michiys of Pachi's youth, though they also tolerated the electrified instruments that Pachi had, in the 2010s, followed Galindo in bringing to chimaycha performance. The chimaycha style that dominated Ayacucho in the 2010s, in other words, featured vocal performances and sung pentatonic melodies that were virtually indistinguishable from those described in chapter 2, while most innovation was reserved for the realm of instrumentation and instrumental melody.

The chimaycha scene of the early 2010s, then, was a patchwork of established and aspiring artists with different kinds of investments in a musical career. They included freelance performers like Galindo who gigged as accompanists for new or casual vocalists without steady bands, as well as steady projects like Los Amaynis. Each actor provided a stylistic anchor in a still-inchoate music scene, but neither worked solely as a professional musician. Galindo worked as a bricklayer and Pachi as a weaver. Rather than making stars, the chimaycha scene mostly allowed local singers to act like stars: to adopt, on weekends and in a limited sphere of their lives, the stage mannerisms and habits of self-promotion that made up the apparatus of Andean stardom. It was a rare performer who, like Pachi, still framed their work in terms of cultural safeguarding, or his niece Maria, who simply hoped to inspire her peers to take up the chinlili and sing. Most were motivated by a combination of sheer fun, self-actualization, and especially in the case of freelance instrumentalists, the chance to earn some pocket money. Still others, well aware that the huayno industry demanded a new regional artist to market as a revelation every few years, hoped to leverage chimaycha's rising local prominence into a star turn on the national stage.

Marcelina Flores and Julia Barrios, vocalists with devoted followings in the early 2010s, nicely illustrate the scene's dynamics. A cosmetologist by trade, Flores continued to cut hair at a market near Ayacucho's city center some years after the success of her fortuitous breakout recording, and I spoke with her there in 2014. She had no plans to pursue an exclusive singing career. Raised in an evangelical chuschino family and prohibited from singing, she nevertheless had an older brother who defied family strictures to bring her songs from the vida michiy, as well as recordings like Carhuapoma's "Vecinopa warmi" (The neighbor's wife). Thus when she returned from cosmetology studies in Lima in the early 2010s, having abandoned her evangelical faith, she was able to sing for fun with people like Edgar Vilca, a relative who played chinlili with Los Amaynis.[12] Invited to his house one day, she was surprised to find him rehearsing with Pachi Ccallocunto, and even more surprised when Pachi enjoined her to sing along. Having tested her voice, Pachi asked her to attend a recording session they had scheduled the next day and to bring an original song. Rising to the challenge, she thought of a personal experience and prepared a song of sad love, framing it with the stock trope of an evil weed amid valued crops and setting the words to a familiar melody. After that song and a second appeared on Los Amaynis' third VCD, she received such a quantity of performing solicitations that she produced one of her own. It was packed with similar songs, always—she insisted—autobiographical, and although she specifically resisted the sound of cumbia, it relied on the electronic instruments that her mentors had made de rigueur, for she believed that a recording without them lacked all "flavor."

At the end of our interview, and in response to my question, Flores expressed certainty that chimaycha was more than a passing fad, but she had no desire to perform in more than casual fashion. The younger Julia Barrios, by contrast, responded to the same question days later by saying, "I know that chimaycha is going to grow. It's already reached the national and even the international level. I want to be part of that, to carry our custom far and wide."[13] Although she worked as a juice seller in Ayacucho's central market, she had already made a credible, if ultimately unfortunate, stab at nationwide success by moving into the orbit of Huayhua Producciones, a national record label known for launching the career of Chinito del Ande, Peru's dominant huayno star in the early 2010s.

Barrios had aimed to perform alongside her huayno idols ever since girlhood in the late 1990s, when she sang songs gleaned from older women at Mother's Day observances and school concerts in her hometown of Chacolla. She moved to Ayacucho in 2007, and like Flores's, her career was launched when a guest spot on a cousin's recording led to performing invitations. That

SUCCESS AND SENTIMENT

led to a VCD backed by Galindo's chinlili, which achieved such unprecedented success that Galindo described her followers as "a little fanatical." They made songs like "Coca kintucha" and "Tuquito" into hits despite the overt animosity of Radio Quispillaccta, and brought her to the attention of Huayhua's scouts, who promised to "make her famous" via a recording session in Lima. The considerable expense involved in traveling to the capital alongside a local chinlili player and hiring studio players for the other parts was all wasted, for the recording was a debacle. In her words, Huayhua's studio players had "no feel" for chimaycha. Left with a dud, she was seeking to finance a recovery at the time of our interview.[14]

Other artists regarded Barrios's experience as a cautionary tale about the possible effects of chimaycha's success and especially the effects of interest from community outsiders. Investment and advertising by business interests unconnected to Chuschi or Quispillaccta were, for example, often blamed for a growing association between chimaycha and thuggery.[15] Looking down on central Ayacucho one afternoon from Acuchimay Hill, I asked Jorge Núñez, husband of Ninay Urucha, about the genre's negative reputation, and he made a face before saying that such things came of involvement by outsiders concerned more with making money than with the interests of chimaycha's community. By way of example he pointed out two venues that had hosted concerts until the recent stabbing of a security guard, each managed by a man from faraway Huancayo. Good promoters, he insisted, took care to hire artists and advertise in venues that were not associated with *marginales*, a word that glosses various kinds of threatening individuals.

By the early 2010s musical performance in Ayacucho was dominated by such commercial promoters. Expert at managing relationships with the advertisers, licensing agencies, venues, and suppliers that guaranteed a successful show, they had already created the infrastructure for a successful scene when chimaycha became a viable musical commodity in the 2010s. Inevitably, chimaycha's rising artists sought a comparable infrastructure, a project that demanded the kind of hustling managerial facility stereotypically incarnated in the cholo businessman—because the scene had grown beyond a level where it could be navigated in easy and informal fashion.

How Concerts Happen

By the mid-2000s Radio Quispillaccta's annual Easter Sunday concert had come to feature as many as eighty groups, and performers began to differentiate themselves with a unique, ear-catching style and a distinctive stage presence. Meanwhile the rise of cheap local recording studios allowed them to finance decent VCDs, sold at concerts and stands near interprovincial bus stops and advertising their services via phone numbers that scrolled across the screen during music videos. Together, these developments encouraged the growth of a scene that quickly encompassed several venues in peripheral southern neighborhoods like Arenales and Carmen Alto, where migrants from Chuschi District tended to reside.

In fact, the growth of the scene was part of a wider explosion in performance over the late 2000s and the 2010s. Formerly occasional, largely local affairs, concerts became regular events, and many featured expensive national stars. The change was so notable that in 2012 William Pacotaype summarized recent musical developments simply by running down the list of expenses incurred in organizing a major show.[16] He estimated a total outlay of some 60,000–80,000 soles, an amount well beyond the means of most individual Ayacuchanos. The high end of the business was in fact dominated by Corporación Daxi, a longtime promoter tied to Ayacucho's powerful Palomino family. Daxi had the kind of stage, sound, and lighting equipment demanded by Peru's grandest artists, but as of the 2010s its real strength lay in its control of wholesale beer distribution. Over the 1990s and 2000s, Peru's major beer companies came under the control of a shifting series of foreign enterprises, with the transnational SABMiller conglomerate in charge by the 2010s. In tandem with changes in governmental regulation, the process forced most local wholesalers out of the business, leaving Daxi as Ayacucho's lone major-label concessionaire. This meant the promoter might acquire beer at a bargain price and sell it high at concerts, increasing its profit margins and allowing for the hire of expensive national stars. However, its monopoly also allowed the company to dictate terms to other promoters, who grumbled about the way Daxi leveraged that advantage to control the city's live music scene. Some promoters involved in smaller shows, below the financial threshold that Daxi deemed to be worthwhile, told me that they felt well advised to source beer from the company and name it as a cosponsor, because they had heard rumors of strong-arm tactics that were visited upon malingerers—a belief that must be regarded as folkloric in the absence of concrete evidence, but that testifies eloquently to the perceived power of the organization.[17] On a less sinister note, the promoter recruited local artists into exclusive contracts, binding them to perform only at Daxi events. The arrangement allowed the company to recruit opening acts at a moment's notice, but it barred performers from playing at the inexpensive concerts where chimaycha flourished. Finally, the most important result of the relationship was to make any concert's success into a function of beer sales—a factor that directly affected the music heard, the pacing and tenor of performances, and popular understandings of the concert experience.

By contrast with Daxi shows, chimaycha concerts unfolded mainly in unfinished venues, using far less sophisticated equipment. The smallest took place on a near-monthly basis at clubs like Hatuchay (My little hut) in the Carmen Alto neighborhood. Hatuchay held a permanent municipal entertainment license, allowing artists to organize a show without securing a temporary performing permit, but it was small and peripheral. Up-and-coming artists typically began here by putting together a show with five to ten colleagues from different towns, thereby ensuring a larger and more diverse audience.[18] Larger chimaycha shows took place at locations nearer the city center. They were organized either by one of Ayacucho's small promoters, who might maintain a subcontracting arrangement with Daxi, or on an occasional basis by artists themselves, perhaps with affiliated investors. Unlike events at Hatuchay, these might turn a handsome profit. Marco Tucno, for instance, had put together a 2012 Mother's Day show, using his musical reputation to persuade the municipality to grant him all relevant licenses. It featured local artists and Lima-based performers like Zenaida Paredes, Élida Núñez, and Los Aires Chuschinos, and it was a major investment even at the steeply discounted rates that such old friends offered, ranging from 500 to 1200 soles. Held in the Complejo San Luis, a venue of sufficient prestige to host national rock stars Líbido in 2013, it required an outlay of about 8000 soles, but it also made him a net profit of some 7000–8000 soles, mostly from the six hundred cases of beer that were consumed by its twenty-five hundred attendees.

Such success demonstrated the heights that chimaycha might scale, if it attracted the right kind of promotional flair. However, few could afford regular investments of money and labor, and fewer still wanted to devolve the task onto a promoter like Daxi, thereby placing control over the chimaycha scene in the hands of mercenary outsiders. What was required, I heard from actors ranging from Marco Tucno to Graciano Machaca to Jorge Núñez, was a community insider who might organize chimaycha artists and care for their interests. My arrival in Ayacucho coincided more or less with the arrival of just such a figure, a gregarious quispillacctino named Miguel Espinoza who went by the nickname Tío Miki (Uncle Mickey). He had but recently moved to Ayacucho from Lima, after a stint as president of Lima's quispillacctino migrants' association. Brash and personable, he was versed in the kind of informal dealmaking that such a position entails—negotiations that often attract charges of financial chicanery and imply a presumed talent for shady business—and thus he brought with him just the right kind of entrepreneurial reputation. He made a push into the burgeoning chimaycha scene, and his actions over the 2013–14 cycle of performances demonstrated vividly the promise and peril that everyday citizens see in the buccaneering disposition that is stereotypically associated with lo cholo. For while many musicians conceded their need for an assertive manager who might take their careers to greater heights, others felt that reckless promotion, conducted with an eye to profit and prominence, threatened the sustainability and the core values of the nascent scene. Stated otherwise, not everyone relished the image of chimaycha's assimilation to the machine of cultural production that guided commercial huayno music, and they did not trust such a figure to safeguard the style's distinctive qualities.

Hustling on the Chimaycha Scene: Tío Miki's Business

Born in the late 1940s, Tío Miki left for Lima at the age of fifteen, later climbing into relative prosperity as an employee of a Spanish power company. He had dabbled in broadcasting at Lima's Radio San Isidro but made no serious attempts at musical work before returning to Ayacucho in 2011, in need of a salutary climate for his ailing wife. He took an apartment and opened a restaurant just below Radio Quispillaccta's offices in the city center, a perch from which he insinuated himself into the orbit of the artists and DJs who frequented the station. Those people included Jorge Núñez and his wife Ninay Urucha—stage name of María Pacotaype Dueñas. Possessor of an extraordinarily high, strong voice, she had recorded a much-appreciated cassette for *Allpanchik* in 1994, at the age of eighteen, only to marry and give up her singing career. The chimaycha boom had led her to resume singing in 2011, and she attracted enough avid followers to suggest the realistic possibility of becoming a full-fledged recording and performing artist. Lacking the time and the disposition to carry off the venture, the couple approached Tío Miki at a funeral, asking him to turn his entrepreneurial skills in the direction of artist management.

Tío Miki took up the task, using every possible opportunity to advance her career. Upon first meeting me at Radio Quispillaccta one day in September 2013, for instance, he invited me to his nearby restaurant. There, alongside Núñez and over a large bottle of orange Fanta, he secured my commitment to act as a godfather for Ninay Urucha's October "anniversary" concert. Such unorthodox "godparenting" relationships are common in Peru, where people customarily seek the support of wealthy or respected acquaintances for Catholic observances well beyond baptism, all of which involve onetime expenses that can be secured from a convenient patron. They usually entail a casual commitment, so I was surprised when Tío Miki produced a photocopied contract and informed me that I was to make a speech and present a gift at the concert itself. Insisting that the gift's size was at my discretion, he pressured me to specify mine on a dotted line, promising me a carbon copy of the signed contract.[19] We settled on a pollera skirt worth 200 soles, featuring the beautiful needlework of Sarhua. This gift would help diversify the artist's performing wardrobe, following a trend that had been established by national huayno artists, whose extravagant polleras priced at thousands of soles had set new standards in stage outfits over the 2000s. Female performers now felt the need to maintain a variegated set of outfits, and while they were of humbler stock, the relative expense and complexity of sarhuino designs served nicely as a stand-in for the eye-popping attire of Lima's stars.

Insofar as they signified status, such skirts served a similar function to the artistic godparenting relationship itself. This was not a custom of terribly long standing: it had originated in the 1990s, when artists used it to raise money from patrons. In the age of cholo entrepreneurialism it had acquired new valences, for it also made a public claim about business savvy and hence success. Only the most naive of concertgoers interpret godparenting commitments as fully sincere evidence of artistic appreciation. Most understand that the majority of these relationships are minimal, fleeting, and secured from reluctant patrons through wheedling pressure. In this sense they testified more properly to performers' skills in working systems of patronage—that is to say, they demonstrated the business hustle that is lauded in Peru's national huayno scene.

The very notion of anniversary concerts was a similar sort of marketing ploy. Live concerts in Ayacucho had always been associated with major festive holidays, when listeners were sure to have time off and perhaps some pocket money to spend on a show. As the chimaycha scene boomed, its growing number of groups found themselves competing for audiences as they scheduled concerts in those limited slots. Increasing audience wealth made it feasible to spread concert dates throughout the calendar, but concerts tied to no special purpose seemed strange. A reasonable solution was to fabricate one, giving rise to the notion of an "artistic anniversary." The chosen dates rarely had any relationship with an artist's actual debut but instead bore another personal significance or an auspicious place in the calendar. Above all, they were selected so as to avoid coincidence with a fellow artist's date.[20] Finally, this cycle also guided the production of recordings, which were typically released in tandem with concerts. Sales of recordings at concerts might be considerable: Ninay Urucha's first VCD, for instance, sold some 2000 copies at the standard price of 5 soles, while Los Amaynis continued to sell copies of their three VCDs at rural concerts years after their initial release.

Navigating the promotional tactics of this system took some managerial brio, and it was widely agreed that whatever Tío Miki lacked in local expertise he made up in verve. It was obvious when attending his daily program at Radio Quispillaccta in late October 2013. At that time he used the hour to promote three concerts he had arranged over the long weekend of All Saints, in partnership with Isaac Guillén, a small chicha promoter who had recruited Tío Miki to help him capitalize on chimaycha. As engineer Melecio Llalli spun songs by the featured singers, Tío Miki conferred with a constant stream of instrumentalists seeking work in house bands, voiceover artists seeking payment for the creation of advertising spots, and gofers reporting back on quoted prices for publicity at other stations. He sounded out all his visitors about attendance at recent shows, the reliability of various musicians, and the evolving relationships, often amorous, that linked people throughout the chimaycha scene. This gossip was in fact a crucial facet of the promoter's business, alerting Tío Miki to the sensitivities that he would need in approaching and scheduling potential musicians. Certainly all this socializing frustrated Llalli, who regularly beat on the glass of the DJ booth, calling the distracted host's attention to the dead air left hanging between songs. These reminders were essential, for Tío Miki held a written list of listeners to hail in those pauses, cosponsors and invitees who might raise the tone of his shows, including elected officials and respected community leaders. Most of his on-air performance was designed to hype the concerts as season-making events, persuading listeners that their attendance would represent money well spent.

Such a figure could be a significant ally for an artist like Ninay Urucha. However, his activities also demonstrated the challenges that enterprising promoters faced and the hazards that aspiring artists ran in aligning themselves with someone who, after all, had grown up in Lima with few connections to chimaycha or to Ayacucho's bureaucracy. Ninay Urucha's anniversary event was, in point of fact, a limited success. Despite low attendance, a power failure that Núñez described as weather related, and modest beer sales of only 80 cases, they recouped their investment, largely due to the large number of godparents that Tío Miki had recruited—some nineteen, whose total contributions almost certainly covered its expenses. Still, Tío Miki's other efforts confirmed the skeptical opinion of artists who viewed him as a threat. Three developments in particular raised the community's ire.

The first was an alarming overture he made to Corporación Daxi on behalf of Ninay Urucha, whom he had presented to the company as a candidate for their exclusive roster of opening acts. Núñez viewed the development favorably, explaining that as the company's lone chimaycha artist, she was sure to be called once Daxi found it desirable to place the genre in its shows. However, Tío Miki also told me that he offered to act as a subcontracting agent for the corporation, organizing midsized chimaycha shows of his own. Such an arrangement would have allowed him to take advantage of its resources and protections and possibly to become the chimaycha scene's Maecenas.

SUCCESS AND SENTIMENT

Any such efforts became impossible—at last temporarily—after a series of miscalculations, which began to present themselves on the first day of the All Saints festival as Tío Miki hosted his regular daily program. With shows scheduled that night and the next, he sat in uncharacteristic silence, irritably awaiting the arrival of headliners Élida Núñez and Los Aires Chuschinos, who were on the road from Lima. Scheduled to speak live on the air, they were running late, and the matter was critical, for rumors had been circulating that the show was a sham. It was here that reputation truly mattered, for Ayacuchano audiences were wearily accustomed to artistic no-shows.[21] As a relatively untested promoter with a wheeling and dealing reputation that some found unsavory, Tío Miki had generated some distrust, so he sat with phone in hand, insistently calling to gauge the artists' progress. The sudden news that singer Alicia Conde had incurred funeral obligations and canceled her appearance worsened matters, so Tío Miki was visibly encouraged when Élida, Alberto, and Aires Chuschinos vocalist Wilma Flores arrived with ten minutes to spare. Bustling them upstairs and immediately placing them before the microphones, he had each vocalist speak on air, and they promised listeners a lively show, recommending that attendees bring extra shoes for dancing. Returning to the microphone invigorated, Tío Miki railed about false rumors of malfeasance and ended with a triumphal reminder that his events would feature only chimaycha of the highest quality, the "takiycha de los campesinos" ("beloved song of the peasants," in mixed Quechua and Spanish).

Tío Miki's worries were not misplaced, for both events were disastrous. One of them, dubiously scheduled at a tony venue called El Palmero, was shut down by the municipality, and it was later suggested to me that Tío Miki had probably failed to secure permission to keep the venue open past 10:00. The other, held at a more typical venue called El Lucero, was simply unattended. I arrived at 10:30 to find a mere ninety-five people listening to Élida Núñez's performance, a shockingly sparse number at such a prime hour. The already meager door fee of 5 soles had been canceled in an effort to lure passersby who might make up the difference in beer sales, but as I stood conversing with acquaintances, curious faces peeked time and again around the doorway only to move on, perhaps to a less disheartening event. Tío Miki, meanwhile, rushed from acquaintance to acquaintance, sharing drinks and chatting volubly in an attempt to inject some energy into was what clearly a flop.

These events demonstrated the challenges Tío Miki faced as a promoter of chimaycha. His parallel effort to become a singer himself presented observers with another avenue of skepticism. Tío Miki had spoken to me of the idea when we met, insisting that young performers required a kind of artistic guidance he could offer. When he eventually did form a group called Los Ichu

Tullmas, it was a bitter turn for Jorge Núñez and Ninay Urucha, who had been planning a new VCD with Tío Miki's help, only to see him leave for Lima without them in early 2014 and record with the instrumentalists they had retained. More broadly, the recording was viewed askance by much of the established chimaycha community, for whom good performance remained rooted in youthful experience in the community itself. Jorge Núñez had already told me that true chimaycha artists had to have lived and suffered in the countryside to write proper lyrics, giving as examples a song by Ninay Urucha that figured the feeling of abandonment through words describing a rare and solitary puna flower. Others stated the matter more bluntly, asking, "When was Tío Miki ever in the vida michiy?" Many agreed that the man lacked the depth of local experience needed to perform well and that Los Ichu Tullmas represented the most mercenary aspects of chimaycha's ongoing transformation.

Tío Miki's foray into the chimaycha scene suggested that its creeping commercialism and its increasing debts to Lima's huayno industry were not necessarily portents of its seamless absorption into the broader cultural formation that I have been calling lo cholo. Novice promoters who failed to convince the community of their bona fides could expect suspicion from its core listenership, while artists who adopted its stylistic traits without paying the experiential dues that animated song lyrics could expect to be treated with cynicism. The power of the culture industry to interpellate consumers, making ready subjects for an assimilative cholo identity that revolved around entrepreneurialism and mestizo urbanity, met a match in desires to safeguard local control over urban indigenous expressive culture. Ayacucho's chimaycha scene would unfold according to a dialectic of accommodation and resistance, as Lima's imposed standards were cross-cut by the preservation of treasured localisms.

Finally, however, it remains impossible to understand chimaycha's significance without an account of all-important live performances.

Regulating Emotion: Chimaycha in Performance

Whenever I tried to evaluate chimaycha's impact by asking listeners about the basis of their fandom, I was told that people responded to the stories: that everyone had had, in the words used by María Ccallocunto, Marcelina Flores, and Julia Barrios, "a bad experience" and that the songs were successful because they tracked listeners' lives so faithfully. Such statements are not meant literally, for few listeners find an exact representation of their life in song lyrics. Rather, like other proletarian genres that blend strong emotion with dancing and playfulness with tales of abjection, ranging from Delta blues to American country music to tango to bachata, song texts are best regarded as

SUCCESS AND SENTIMENT

archetypal rather than truthful in any simple sense. Their tendency to paint a state of mind, and gesture but vaguely toward its cause, helps listeners find in them a personal resonance and summon the appropriate emotional response.

In this sense there is considerable continuity between chimaycha and other Andean genres. Quechua-language song has always been a helpmeet to disruptive emotions that are otherwise carefully controlled in everyday life, and although Andean songs cover many affective states, grief and angst are prominent among them, for they are among the most disruptive. What is new in the current moment is the genre's saturation by the tropes of woe, anomie, and self-celebration that animate mass-popular huayno music and are tantamount to lo cholo's structure of feeling. Through this act of appropriation chimaycha artists align their wares with a hegemonic national culture industry, but it is also a light repurposing of an older aesthetics. It facilitates, using new contextual referents, an experience that indigenous listeners have always expected from Andean music: a shock of recognition, the sense that others can corroborate one's own struggles, and hence a palliative for feelings of loneliness.

It is, above all, in the collective effervescence of live shows that these emotional sonorities take effect, for that is where affected listeners body forth signs of distress and find the catharsis of community recognition. Here beer sales become integrally related to the notion of music as an emotional aid, for alcohol surpasses even sound in its tie to emotional performance. The state of disinhibition that comes from alcoholic consumption, quite simply, frees listeners from the behavioral strictures of mundane life. Songs that invite affective identification therefore drive liquor sales as listeners prepare themselves to give the emotional performances that align with the songs they have come to hear. Promoters seeking beer sales and artists seeking gigs focus in turn on perennial themes of sadness: above all, romantic tribulation, personal dissolution, and nostalgia for home.

This dynamic is so transparent to promoters that they strategize the internal scheduling of their events to maximize beer consumption and hence financial rewards. Marco Tucno explained the strategy to me in granular detail, upon my request. The basic trick, he said, lay in monitoring the mood of the crowd, yanking acts if they appeared to slow beer sales and extending sets that promoted it. Timing was key, however, and smart promoters began slowly. If people got enthusiastic too early, in response to truly outstanding acts, they were likely to reach their ethylic capacity or even pass out, thus spending fewer soles over the course of the evening. Alternatively, if they were too bored, they might simply leave. Savvy promoters, then, encouraged early drinking with music that was fun but only moderately popular. Once people had attained a light buzz, the stage was given over to increasingly admired performers. This led listeners to scramble for the alcoholic euphoria that would facilitate full enjoyment, but there would also come a point when many or most were past the point of caring about what they heard: once people are really drunk, Marco said, "they'll dance to anything." For this reason a promoter might program untested or undistinguished acts toward the wee hours. In all cases, this system might involve a great deal of on-the-fly reprogramming.

The texture of these performances can be conveyed by describing the Corina and Julia Barrios concert where I first met Tío Miki and Jorge Núñez. I approached it in a state of heightened attention because it was my first, but later attendance at dozens of chimaycha shows proved it to be typical in most respects. Here I portray its unfolding dynamics as I observed them, while enriching that description with post hoc insights gleaned from later experiences and from the observations of various friends who accompanied me to the show. I have taken the liberty of anonymizing these events due to their sensitive, possibly embarrassing nature.[22]

Held on a Saturday night at El Lucero (The star), a venue consisting of an enclosed dirt lot amid automotive businesses in Ayacucho's Arenales neighborhood, the program promised chimaycha and huayno acts. Arriving at the very early hour of 9:00, I stood with two Ayacuchano friends amid a crowd outside El Lucero's corrugated metal gate, all gauging the likelihood that enough people had entered to provide a lively atmosphere. Deciding to risk it, we made our way past a security pat-down from a truncheon-bearing guard, entering a large, uneven space open to the sky, with a stage at one end and a booth selling Brazilian Brahma beer at the other.

We had chosen poorly, for it was nearly empty. Onstage a singer delivered huayno tunes to the accompaniment of a house band, but only a few dozen people listened stiffly, standing around the edges of a space that was perhaps 100 by 150 feet in size. Three women in polleras made an exception, dancing near the stage with a middle-aged man. All four showed signs of advanced inebriation, advertising their mood via the semiotics of movement, beer, and song. They danced demonstratively, stomping their feet in an energetic version of huayno's two-step pattern, and stopping only to drink from a bottle of beer that moved among them. When the performer sang a popular tune about the joys of liquor, they raised hands and bottle toward the stage. At one point the man danced his endorsement of a different song's text, using a physical routine that I had already learned to spot as a sign of euphoric abandonment: head downcast, eyes closed but eyebrows raised, with a grin on his face and hands in the air, he swayed his body in time while whistling the melody through his teeth.

Against the backdrop of the other concertgoers, who watched with sober

SUCCESS AND SENTIMENT 177

detachment, the dancers seemed clearly aberrant, and as we spoke of the atmosphere one of my companions ratified this observation: "Yes, that lady's really got ahead of herself." His comment, however, was aimed at criticizing not their drunkenness but their timing. From this point on the night unfolded so as to ensure that we too would achieve much the same state, on a more appropriate schedule. The process began immediately, when we fetched up at the back of the venue with a circle of acquaintances, all clustered around Tío Miki. We stood in an irregular circle, passing beer and conversing about community events, the music scene, and especially the crowd around us. People called attention to passersby, ranging from elegant ladies in nightclub attire, to rural politicians gladhanding ahead of upcoming municipal elections, to three young women in the distinctive polleras of Huarcaya. People mainly watched, however, for friends and notables. The growing mood of commensal solidarity was amplified by regular announcements from the stage, as performer and emcee read salutations from the backs of peeled beer labels. Bottles ran dry at an increasing rate as the venue filled, but companions fetched more by turns, and there was never a moment in which our circle lacked a beer in motion.

Amid such sociable talking and drinking, the mood began visibly and audibly to shift. One friend told me that "people are already demanding chimaycha" and pointed out that the crowd had been drinking at a restrained pace. The promoter indeed limited remaining huayno artists to a mere fifteen minutes or so onstage, long enough to fulfill contractual obligations without damping beer sales too badly. As they ceded to the chimaycha of singer Alicia Conde, the sound of the chinlili replaced the requinto, familiar melodies from youthful times replaced more contemporary huaynos, reserved bodily comportment melted away, and people spoke in terms of confidence that they might avoid in everyday life. One young man leaned close, bringing his body deep into my corporeal space, and shouted, "I've got a gun," into my ear, claiming that Tío Miki had asked him to watch out for me. Another, attired in a flashy Nautica jacket and sunglasses, placed an entire case of beer at the circle's center and shepherded its quick consumption while performing some vigorous, high-stepping footwork, trying to force a quick rise in the mood. Around us the crowd grew to some three hundred attendees, and people began to sing along demonstratively, while performers and emcees elicited crowd investment by shouting "Todos los cheleros!" (All the beer-lovers!) and "Todas las solteras!" (All the single ladies!), inciting bottles to be raised in salute.

The mood built to a peak at roughly 1:00 a.m., when the emcee invited to the stage some ten to fifteen godparents. Mainly they were successful figures from Chuschi District, including politicians representing two different rural constituencies. Speaking in turn, they delivered speeches touching upon

Barrios's talents, the need to safeguard chimaycha's vitality, and the strength of their home communities. In each case they ended with the bestowal of a token, and some took the opportunity to promote their own interests—resulting in my acquisition of a baseball cap bearing a gas station logo, hurled into the crowd among other giveaways.

After this interlude Barrios herself took the microphone, and as the crowd danced to chimaycha songs about liquor, love, and hometown life, the mood began to turn once more. Signs of severe intoxication appeared everywhere, and I dodged men who wheeled toward the bathroom or the beer stand as if careening down the deck of a listing ship. Solicitous care broke out in equal measure, with people half-carrying those who could barely stand to the door, and one man trying to pull a motorcycle helmet onto the head of a prone, unconscious friend. Many dancers, meanwhile, began adopting postures that bespoke a loss of bodily control, unremitting sadness, or both at once. They hung their heads, swaying arhythmically to the music, and when they lifted their voices it was more often in the wail of the sufferer than in euphoria. It was in these wee hours that Harvey's "discourse of despair and defiance" began to inflect the tone of my own interpersonal interactions. I inquired about one politician who had shared a drink with our group, and a companion, well into his cups and weaving on his feet, drew my head down so that he could jam his face directly, uncomfortably, into my ear. "Garbage!" he hollered, underlining the word with a horizontal cutting motion of the hand. Then he pulled me to the nearby side of the venue, festooned with posters advertising past events. Placing one finger on his own name, he shoved his other thumb into his chest and, near tears, shouted a fragmentary jumble of statements contrasting his low state with the opportunistic bonhomie of politicians, human "trash" whose community values were evident only during election season.

We soon rejoined our other companions, who had gathered around a middle-aged man, seated on a bench and cradling the head of a severely inebriated woman. Well drunk himself, and eyeing my approach, he pointed and remonstrated "Look what he has done!" The blunt yet vague accusation took me aback, having never laid eyes on either person, and it puzzled my acquaintances, who waited expectantly for a follow-up that was not forthcoming. Still sober, Tío Miki took charge, hoping to mollify the man by redirecting conversation. "No," he said, describing me as an anthropologist newly arrived from the United States to study chimaycha. This gambit failed miserably, as this appeared to be precisely the problem, and the man launched into a rambling diatribe about imperialism and the domination of indigenous communities. The demeanor of the others changed conspicuously to accommodate the outburst: no longer socializing cheerily, they stood mostly in silence and continued to

SUCCESS AND SENTIMENT

pass beer while placing brief, noncommittal words of agreement or acknowl-edgment into the spaces between outbursts. Tío Miki, having abandoned his opening attempt at placation, led this effort at conspicuous comfort with a litany of soothing statements and the repeated proffer of a reassuring drink. Eventually, seeing that there was no solution in conversation, he turned to me and said, "Look, go buy some beer, because with two beers you can solve a lot." After I fetched two bottles, he essayed a final attempt to secure commensal harmony: grabbing one of them, he turned and called attention to the offering. When he was rebuffed with more invective, a friend finally intervened, taking my arm and leading me from the venue.

When I spoke later with Tío Miki, Marco Tucno, and others about this puzzling incident, it became clear that the emotional outburst was not odd in and of itself. Such rants are so formulaic that well-recognized mechanisms exist for addressing them. The usual mechanisms had, however, failed drasti-cally in this instance. Usually, Marco said, such drunken rants simply peter out after some conspicuous sympathy from nearby listeners. Tío Miki, in other words, had not spoken in error: usually it was possible to repair a drunken sense of injury with a commensal pair of beers aimed at underlining the sense of fellowship that unites drinkers over and above momentary conflict. In this sense the man had stepped beyond what was considered "normal," closing the circle of commensality before someone he placed outside its appropriate bounds—but of course my presence at the event was not precisely "normal," and local mores did not necessarily dictate his reconciliation with someone he took to emblematize his community's enemies.

Finally, these experiences suggest ties between music, alcohol, and emo-tion, but they do not precisely demonstrate links between the song content and listeners' experiences. Indeed, at this point I lacked the required familiar-ity with song lyrics to draw any such inferences. They were properly drawn out in conversation with other artists, and none so thoroughly as Dionisia Espinoza.[23]

Experiential Fidelity: Chimaycha as Personal Testimony

Long resident in Lima, where she and her husband Teodosio ran a clothing business in a major migrant neighborhood, Dionisia Espinoza was one of the most widely admired of chimaycha vocalists in the early 2010s. Careful not to oversaturate her market, she rarely appeared in Ayacucho, and friends encouraged me to seek her out in the capital. When I finally did, her narrative crystallized the relationships between lived experience, indigenous heritage, and personal challenge that others described but struggled to specify. Her

180   CHAPTER SIX

words indeed validated what I had obtusely failed to take at face value: that
songs were valued for their perceived truth to experience, experiences that
were familiar to singer and listeners alike, and that underneath their variegated topics and moods, the thread that unified them was personal struggle
and perseverance.

Dionisia began by telling me about her youth in Chuschi District. Her narrative revolved around "audacity," a quality that she credited with her success
as a performer and a businesswoman. She had demonstrated it early on, she
said, garnering a districtwide reputation as a fierce volleyball competitor and
as a powerful singer, via appearances at school events and the town's annual
patron saint festival, where she delivered songs that her older brother Alfredo
gleaned from the vida michiy. It showed most of all, however, in the stoic
persistence with which she had met the difficulties of life in the impoverished,
violence-wracked circumstances of her childhood. She spoke of atrocities she
witnessed during the Shining Path–era violence but mostly of leaving school
after the third grade to care for her younger siblings, made head of household
when her parents left for Ayacucho to seek care for her ailing mother. Her
voice broke, and she paused, before saying, "I have lived such a suffering life!"
I intervened to suggest that we stop the interview, but Dionisia steamrolled
more than once over my interjections, going on to describe the couple's move
to Lima in the 1990s. There a goodhearted brother-in-law helped her over-
come her husband's resistance to make a cassette recording with Libertadores-
Wari, a label that catered to homesick Ayacuchano migrants in the capital.

By the time Dionisia came to describe the music she sang and the songs
she wrote, the reasons for her emotion and for her insistence that I hear her
story seemed at least partially clear. Touching upon the themes of drinking,
abandonment, and struggle that appear in her hit songs, she noted that they
were rooted not in her experience alone but in "the lives of real people," and
"people appreciate and like them, because they are about suffering." Having
suffered, she sang of suffering, knowing that others would recognize themselves in that suffering. Moreover, she had been able to confirm her success
with a proud observation made in the late 2000s, when she returned to Ayacucho to perform for the first time. Singing "audaciously," she made the event
a smashing success, but it was neither the huge beer sales nor the ample tears
that she elicited that struck her most—people, she said, "always cried at her
songs." Instead, it was an odd behavioral disjuncture that she observed, for her
music was apparently so moving that people "danced *even when* they weren't
drinking" (emphasis added).

This experience, and others like it, made clear there was nothing more
profound than the explanation I was repeatedly offered for the success of

Dionisia and her peers, and for the physical manifestations of appreciation they received: people cry because they find it moving to have their experiences of suffering recognized and validated in song. The narratives they present are tropic constructions, but they are still sincere and deeply felt means through which people interpret an ongoing lifeworld and organize the selves they bring to that lifeworld. Perhaps only a blinkered Western observer for whom happiness, not sadness, is the "hypercognized" emotion (Levy 1973) would find this to be extraordinary in the first place. After all, Dionisia's tearful narrative may have been more discomfiting to me than to her: at the interview's end I apologized profusely, only to receive repeated assurances that there was no problem at all. Within a few minutes, as we ate chicken and rice, we were chatting amiably, and it was as if the previous conversation had never happened at all.

Conclusion

In speaking about the contemporary chimaycha scene, Óscar Conde lamented in our 2012 interview, "It's all changed because of modernization. Now it's all for business purposes, for the market. Today if you sing [like Los Auténticos de Patario], it's not salable." Such a sentiment is easily mistaken for the reactionary fear of change that Boym has glossed as "reflective nostalgia" (2010), but there is little doubt that it signals real and momentous transformations in sonorous indigeneity. If chimaycha was once a means to explore and sustain a hard-won sense of cultural distinctiveness within which Quechua speakers' lives were suspended, then its contemporary iteration centers instead on the challenges of urban life in a harsh neoliberal society. Being a chimaycha musician in this climate means managing self and sound as brands to be developed and catering to a sensibility that is organized more properly around loss and lament than around social production and reproduction. It is little wonder that key sectors of the chimaycha public show a lack of confidence in everything that is signified by promoters like Tío Miki. Their mediation promises a kind of success that is commensurate with that of the Andean stars who are so widely admired by everyday listeners and theorists alike; however, that success is conceptualized in terms of a commercial marketplace where concessions to indigenous difference, such as the continued use of the Quechua language, are liabilities that inhibit the recruitment of the widest listenership.

By the same token, however, the loss of one indigenous lifeworld does not mean the wane of indigeneity per se, only its reorganization. Chimaycha continues to act as a frame for organizing listeners' sense of what it means to sound and to be indigenous, and the emotional habitus it stabilizes is nothing more or less than the affective content of urban indigenous experience.

Radio Quispillaccta created some initial channels through which Ayacucho's indigenous public came to self-awareness as such, to the extent that listeners were interpellated by the station's discourse of indigeneity. The chimaycha scene, however, channeled further developments that were no less important for being conducted in the more labile, less self-conscious realm of emotional experience. Bringing listeners together around songs of contemporary ills and specifying how one should respond, chimaycha offered people a way to aurally coordinate and enact emotive ways of understanding indigenous identity. By insisting upon narratives of suffering and earmarks of persistent difference amid the triumphalism of cholo nationalism, chimaycha's public insists that this project will not overwrite their sense of distinctiveness. Even in the absence of an articulated political program, the style offers something like the thing that Stokes associates with Turkish arabesk: a "civic project, a way of imagining affable relations of dependence [amid] the shrunken public spaces of late twentieth- and early twenty-first-century urban life" (2010:193).

In the end, what this chapter has chronicled is the way that struggles over indigenous musical representation continue to be transacted in deference to local concerns, even as local actors engage an emergent national discourse of ethnic change. Indeed, by 2013 people across the chimaycha scene shared the conviction that the style was poised to make them a part of that national conversation. Increasing numbers of artists were willing to sing in Spanish, and a growing number of chimaycha performers toured to neighboring departments, playing with what Marco Tucno called "midlevel artists." Whether or not chimaycha achieves such resonance, its public's interest in "customizing" the style (Greene 2009)—in tailoring treasured customs past for survival in a world of changed circumstances—suggests that it will continue to serve as a vehicle for that indigenous public's future.

7

Wood and Work

Man and matter invent one another through the medium of the tool.
BRADLEY 2011:24

Marco Tucno's instrument workshop lies behind an adobe wall in Ayacucho's Carmen Alto neighborhood, across a steep, rutted courtyard from the home that he built for his family in the mid-1990s. At that time the property lay on the city's outskirts, amid rustic houses built by fellow migrants. By 2013, however, Ayacucho's booming cocaine economy had allowed neighbors to replace their dwellings with three-story concrete boxes and to park Toyota 4×4s outside. Marco himself had acquired a modest cement house a block away, but his shop retained a casual, bootstrapping aura. Tools lay scattered across the dirt floor and outside in the courtyard, amid shavings, sawdust, bits of fret wire, scraps of paper, and a half-buried electrical conduit that became more exposed with each rainstorm. Inside, light entered through a plastic square set in the corrugated metal roof, illuminating clusters of neck blanks, bent sides, guitar molds, and raw boards acquired in catch-as-catch-can fashion from clients, lumber stores, Lima-based importers, and the occasional police auction, where hardwood seized from illegal loggers sold at bargain prices (see figure 16). Unsheathed power cables hung unnervingly at the height of my head, connected to power tools that were indispensible in a shop where demand outstripped the meager personnel—Marco, his wife Zaida, and their two teenage sons. Indeed a visitor might easily mistake a typical workday for a hobby-centered family holiday, with Marco assembling parts inside the shop while chatting amiably with relatives who sat sanding, painting, or lacquering in the sunny courtyard.

In fact, the easy rhythms of independent work are one reason that Marco loves his career, and the humility of his workspace belies his importance as a mediator of Ayacucho's cultural life. The foremost maker of the instruments through which Quechua-speaking musicians stake aural claims to the city,

FIGURE 16. A corner of Marco Tucno's workshop, filled with ready instrument parts. Photograph by author.

and especially the chinlili that provides chimaycha's "instrumental identity" (Neuenfeldt 1998:255), Marco has a job that is dialectically linked to Ayacucho's demographic and ideological transformation. He builds instruments adapted to the material and technical conditions of the city and to the changing priorities of the indigenous youths who follow its political and cultural trends. At

WOOD AND WORK

the same time he calibrates his creations so as to preserve inherited timbral qualities that he and his peers deem constitutive of indigenous distinctiveness. To the extent that debates over sonorous change are debates over the very boundaries of the indigenous musical imaginary, his labor helps to shape Ayacucho's cultural politics of indigeneity.

In this chapter I explore Marco as a key actor in a network of sounds, ideas, and materials, all of which interact to shape what it means to be and to sound indigenous in Ayacucho today. I treat his hand skills, material knowledge, and ideological dispositions as elements of his musical agency, without losing sight of the cultural, material, and socioeconomic factors that constrain his choices.[1] I deal with points of contact between bodies and things, arguing that certain kinds of cultural sensibilities are efficiently created and transmitted through objects. Deposited into the very form of cherished tools, these sensibilities come to reside in users' habits of motion and perception, outside the realm of conscious ideology, in the realm of the true "body politic"—that is, the realm of socioculturally determined bodily hexis. In a sense, then, this chapter raises questions about indigeneity and ecological experience that appeared in chapters 2 and 3, albeit from a very different angle. For the labor of instrument making involves substantial natural and meteorological knowledge, and it has led Marco to a distinctive form of environmental awareness.[2] It is compatible with elements of indigenous political discourse but does not arise directly from it: considered in tandem with Marco's own ideological stance on Andean history and on indigenous aesthetics, it provides a striking example of an indigenous sensibility that lies outside the realm of social politics.

Instrumental Networks: Culture, Bodies, Sounds, and Materials

Describing how organic intellectuals have shaped Aguaruna cultural discourse, Greene (2009) has characterized their labor as "customizing" both Amazonian traditions and indigenized foreign practices, making elements from each register over into habits and objects that suit the evolving interests of their community. The chinlili should be regarded as a similarly customized object, for Jacinto's invention was already a blend of mandolin and guitar, calculated to satisfy Ranulfo Infanzón's demands for new timbral effects without taxing the established abilities of chuschino performers. In this sense the chinlili already bore at birth the "accumulated sensibilities" (Théberge 1997:159) of chimaycha performance. This did not preclude performers' developing new techniques that responded to the instrument's affordances. They created a tremolo technique, for example, partly to compensate for its severe lack of sustain. In this sense the chinlili is best viewed as a networked object that ties together, at minimum, the aesthetic, ideological, and technical context of its invention; the parts of the instrument and the materials from which they are fashioned; its players and makers; and the "motional picture" that they develop in playing it (Kubik 1979; see also Baily 1985), come to expect from it, and is therefore designed into individual models.

This network entails the creation, transmission, and transformation of particular kinds of bodies, as well as instruments and cultural habits. A body, after all, is not simply given: its boundaries, habits, capacities, and means of proprioception are all made in and through interactions with objects. Among other things, instrumental training is a means of inculcating physical habits into existing bodies, and while musicians may go to great lengths to find an instrument that "fits" their body (Alperson 2008), they usually find themselves wrestling instead with a recalcitrant tool that demands an idiosyncratic kind of bodily motion in exchange for desired sounds. This mutually constitutive "embodiment relation" (Ihde 1990) has been captured nicely by Mosely, who describes an instrumental interface as "a physical system of checks and balances that trains its players by establishing its affordances and mapping them onto a delimited range of sonic outcomes . . . imposing discipline on the generation of acoustic material as well as the body of the player and the sensibility of the listener" (2015:179; see also Miller 2011; Mrázek 2008; Perlman 2004).[3] Viewed from a slightly different, more comparative angle, these "checks and balances" might be regarded as the archive of a gestural repertoire, a means through which contemporary players saturate their own bodies with the "culturally honed bodily sensation" of performers past (Qureshi 1997:29).[4] The chinlili is, then, more than a mere symbol of indigenous difference. By eliciting techniques that indigenous performers past made native to the instrument itself, it motivates the construction of new bodies that host an intimate, uncognized variety of indigeneity. And the body of the performer is not the only relevant point of contact between flesh, sound, and indigenist discourse, for the instrument is produced by a maker, his body imbued with distinctive capacities developed in and for the task.

It is, in short, Marco who facilitates the embodied continuity of indigenous musical culture. In order to understand the materials, manual skills, and finished products through which he operationalizes his ideas about indigenous music, I read his experience through lenses provided by the music scholars cited above, and by the work of "thing theorists" who place objects on a footing comparable to that of biological agents in their accounts of the earth's systems. Following Serres (1995), I view the chinlili as an object that stabilizes social relations and slows the rate of cultural change (cf. Mosely 2015:158), preserving the shape of arrangements past in the present day. However, following

Adam Smith's rather different work on material culture (2015), I also treat it as part of the network type that he has dubbed a "machine": a dynamic network of human and nonhuman elements whose potentialities and capabilities are continually remade through interaction with each other.[5] Unlike other thing theorists (see especially Latour 1993; Bennett 2010), Smith refuses to level the human-nonhuman distinction. He calls instead for specification of the different roles that operators and nonoperative things play in a given assemblage. His approach demands an inventory and description of things that matter and also of their modes of entanglement with humans—the forms of need, constraint, and desire with which they are approached. It requires, too, that a synchronous assemblage be recast as a diachronic "machine," a dynamic system that sustains older social arrangements even as its new members facilitate the production of new ones. This means specifying not only its member elements but also the operations of those that operate on one another. This in turn means attending to the body, "itself a kind of material culture, shaped and reshaped by a lifetime of encounters with things" (A. T. Smith 2015:53; see also Latour 2004). Such constructed, sensitive bodies, filled with affordances that arise from interaction with other things, are the points of interface that allow objects to "grip" the human: they are the place where assemblages contact flesh, generating "the human-thing collaboration we . . . call 'the social'" (Smith 2015:54).

Smith's emphasis on the social determination of human-object relations echoes some of Bernard Stiegler's work on the role of technics in the making of the human—which, in a startling coincidence, has recently adopted organology as a guiding metaphor for philosophical inquiry (A. T. Smith 2015).[6] Stiegler's definition of humanity turns on the human ability to deposit habits, ideas, and behaviors learned by an individual into things external to the body, including "exosomatic organs" (Innis 2002) like texts and tools.[7] Systems of such things transmit knowledge across boundaries of space and mortality, ensuring that later users are shaped by experiences they have not personally lived. Of course not all experiences become preserved in this way. Instead things discretize, from reality's continuous flow, otherwise ephemeral moments, ideas, and gestures that have become significant to the makers of things, holding their form and rendering them perceptible to future users—in Stiegler's words, they "grammatize [the] flows and continuities which weave our existences" (2013:31). Moreover, when used systematically such objects naturalize the modes of attention that they demand from humans, influencing "the criteria that [users] use to select what to retain in every new perception" (Bradley 2011:133). In this way such exosomatic organs, through their formal inertia, carry and sustain the sociocultural arrangements that governed their

188 CHAPTER SEVEN

emergence. Attending to their creation and their mode of usage is therefore one way to understand the clusters of habits and dispositions that are typically glossed as "culture."

Naturally, the influence of objects is provisional, liable to repurposing by agents facing new conditions, and another task for analysts is to show how they are adapted by human agents with needs and ends that differ from those of the past.[8] Here different tools are needed, for Stiegler's account is not designed to specify agents or acts of grammatization. I find one useful framework in Sennett's brief discussion, in *The Craftsman* (2008:130–35), of the maker's mark. Sennett has in mind not the modern trademark but rather the bodily trace that a maker leaves in a crafted object and that testifies ever after to the presence of a body, a mind, and an individual at the moment of creation.[9] Most such marks carry no political message, testifying only that "'I made this,' 'I am here, in this work,' which is to say, 'I exist'" (Sennett 2008:130). However, when the maker hails from a subaltern group, those marks may come to count as highly political indeed. They may grammatize experiences left unrecorded in dominant systems of memory, such as textual media that favor the literate and the powerful.

Finally, the maker's mark need not be entirely a matter of the human will, for the resistance of materials—moments of breakage, limitations in malleability—can drive "adaptive irregularities" (Sennett 2008:134) into the form of the product itself. Such is the case of the figured Roman tiles that Sennett describes, which were mortared into walls to cover imperfect joints, only later contributing to the culturally distinctive character of Roman buildings. Objects like these testify more eloquently to provisional encounters between bodies and materials than to the triumph of human ingenuity. By emphasizing the contingent role that imaginative embodied identification plays in collective memory, Sennett opens a space for treating the connection between retention and cultural specificity that is absent from Stiegler's work. Of course such experiences always begin through work with objects themselves.

Wood, Weather, and Work: How Bodies and Things Build One Another

One morning, as I scalloped a strip of Douglas fir, I mentioned to Marco how much I enjoyed working with chisels. The comment indulged my sense of accomplishment at my growing ability to sense the wood's grain, adjust the tool's angle, and gradually bring forth the elegant profile of a properly shaped brace. However, Marco took the comment seriously, pausing to tell me that there was no better way to acquire the tacit knowledge that was crucial to the luthier's craft. Working with machines, he said, one might never learn how

WOOD AND WORK   189

perfectly my piece of fir balanced stiffness with lightness—essential qualities
in a reinforcement that glued directly to the soundboard's underside, where
heavier wood might dull the top's response and hence the instrument's sound.
Worse, one might be tempted to substitute a lighter piece of European spruce
if one had never carved it by hand, learning that it was far more porous than
fir and therefore liable to warp and crack during Ayacucho's rainy season, with
its intense daily fluctuations in humidity.[10]

Marco often spoke about the capacity-building process that Ingold has
called enskilment (2000; see also Marchand 2010), through which makers
come to know their materials and gain a kinesthetic sense of the way they
respond to tools. He contrasted his perceptual acuities and manual dexterities,
gained over thirty years of hand building, with that of luthiers based in Lima
or North America who use machines, electronic sensors, and elaborate jigs to
measure proportions, calibrate humidity, and assemble parts. These devices,
he said, robbed makers of a tactile sensitivity to wood and climate that was
crucial in his modest circumstances.[11]

Statements like these do not arise from a romantic belief in the dignity
of manual labor, nor from any interest in ensuring the individuality of each
creation—central elements of artisanal ideology in other times and places
(Morris 1888; Ruskin 1854), and not least among contemporary luthiers (see
Dudley 2014). Like most craftspeople who live from their work, Marco values
anything that allows him to produce quick and precise copies (Pye 1968), and
he uses templates, table saws, belt sanders, and spray guns without lamenting
the uniformity they impose. Technical aids and embodied sensitivities are
simply complementary means to stabilize the relationships between wood,
metal, and environment that support the sonorities he expects from his wares.
Such ecumenism has probably abetted his influence, for it has become an article of faith among scholars of technics that the adaptive, irregular methods
that flourish in conditions of "creative marginality" often lead to trend-setting
innovation (Bijsterveld and Schulp 2004:667). In Marco's case, some of his
faculties were acquired through informal childhood experience with the tools
and materials used by adult workers. However, most of them were gleaned
through a long, late process of apprenticeship, which carried him through
most of Ayacucho's guitar shops over the 1980s and 1990s.

Marco's peripatetic learning process is surprising, given his ancestors'
centrality to the guitar-making culture of the Pampas Valley. Family lore, as
reported by Marco and Jacinto as well as several musician colleagues, credits
a Tucno ancestor from Cusco with introducing the guitar to Chuschi District after settling there in some long-ago era. This is unlikely, but there is no
doubt that Marco represented a fifth generation of Tucno luthiers at the very

least. His great-great-grandfather Francisco is the honoree of an inscription acknowledging him as the town authority who commissioned Quispillaccta's church bells in 1918.[12] He was also a renowned luthier who continued to make instruments well into the twentieth century. His designs, Jacinto told me in 2014, were copied by rival carpenters all over the district, as were some of his material innovations, such as the use of a hard local wood called *chachas*, which Marco favored in the present day for linings (strips of reinforcement glued along the interior joins of acoustic guitars).[13] Francisco's instruments and those of his descendants traveled well beyond Chuschi District too, since the men regularly sold them at festival markets across the region, especially Ayacucho's massive Easter fair at Acuchimay hill. In settings like these, members of the Tucno family expanded their skills by studying or purchasing charangos from Pampa Cangallo, guitars from Quinua, and other instruments from famed centers of production. Marco's own grandfather Marcos had even traveled as far as Sicuani, in the Department of Cusco, to study their methods.

Despite this rich tradition Marco's own father was not a luthier, and he did not draw deeply from the familial well of expertise. "Really, I didn't learn much from my ancestors," he told me before going on to summarize the little that he had learned on visits to Jacinto's shop when, as a child, he had asked his great-uncle to make two chinlilis in exchange for some scrap wood from his father's house:

> I'd go with some Tucno cousins, and as he made them I watched, I watched, until one day I started to sand one [and think,] "Hey, I can do this." . . . But I never made anything with him, not a chinlili, nothing. Still, I got that panorama, you know? How he made things, what kinds of things he made, what kinds of things he did, what kinds of things he used. Because I went constantly, daily, to his house, and stood, sat for hours and hours. All that was left was for me to use [tools], but I was small and I couldn't just grab them or [say,] "Uncle teach me," because it was dangerous.

Marco did work with his grandfather Marcos as a teen in the 1980s, in the nearby town of Auquilla. Recruited to assist in making minor parts like wooden tuning pegs, he learned techniques of bulk production, developed a facility with tools, and observed the entire process of assembly. Still, he did not start to work seriously as a maker until the 1990s, after he began performing with Los Chikitukus in Ayacucho. Bandmates and colleagues began asking him to repair their instruments, due to his family name and his real but still scant woodworking knowledge. Avid for the jobs but lacking the proper skills, he approached established luthiers for help, moving from shop to shop and gaining ever greater levels of expertise and responsibility. Initial consultation with one Ramos led to a quasi-apprenticeship with a maker named Pillaca, where he progressed sufficiently to take over repair jobs, before moving on to the more renowned shops of Solano and Flores, who subcontracted him to build instruments for their customers. He even worked briefly with Luis Camasca, then viewed as the city's leading guitar maker, though the relationship was mostly fruitless due to Camasca's impatience with Marco's idiosyncratic habits.

Each of these shops focused on producing the nylon-string Spanish-style guitars favored among the city's mestizo middle classes. However, the procedures involved were not very different from those that guide the construction of other stringed instruments, and Marco soon applied them in producing a set of chinlilis for Los Chikitukus. The instruments marked but a slight departure from the models created in Chuschi District, featuring the sturdier bracing systems and more elegant tonewoods of elite guitars. Nevertheless, they were striking enough to invite further requests from other colleagues.

Despite this early success, Marco's skills remained somewhat rudimentary. They attained a professional level under the tutelage of Lima-based luthier Abrahám Falcón, Peru's foremost maker. Marco's relationship with a man he always refers to as "Maestro Falcón" began in 1992, when he visited Lima to study choral singing during a truncated period of conservatory music studies. Happening upon a workshop that the maestro was offering at the city's Peruvian–North American Cultural Institute, he showed him one of his own guitars and received an invitation to spend a week in Falcón's shop. The week led him to the disappointing conclusion that he still "knew nothing." Fortunately Falcón was already engaged to run a longer workshop at Ayacucho's seat of the National Institute of Culture, and it would secure Marco's reputation as one of Ayacucho's foremost luthiers. Spotting Marco on the opening day, the maestro not only invited him to participate but also made him and another young luthier named David Loayza into his assistants.[14] In the end, the maestro came to Ayacucho several times over the subsequent years, and though dozens began his workshops only four stayed through the end, receiving what Marco described as the accumulated wisdom of a lifetime—that and, in Marco's case, a treasured set of guitar molds that hung in his shop, signed "1-1-1996 Abrahám Falcón" (visible in figure 1).

Marco's studies with Falcón deeply influenced his approach to lutherie, but they were not the only source of his practice, for every maker has a unique repertoire of tricks and insights, adapted to his or her distinctive circumstances. Marco's own methods reflected his ongoing engagement with different musical constituencies, as well as the changing social, aesthetic, and technological conditions in which he was suspended. One set of methods had come from apprenticeship in Ayacucho's economically straitened guitar shops, where simple fixes with everyday materials stood at a premium. One example, requiring nothing more than the scraps at hand in any working shop, was Solano's method of gluing veneer onto a guitar headstock. It involved hammering a wedge under a cord wrapped around the assembly, generating downward force as the string tightened, while saving the thin, soft veneer from the damaging pressure of a clamp. Other techniques were inspired by visits to modern operations in Lima, such as a plywood-manufacturing plant where Marco watched a giant machine create even glue joints by turning the component sheets and sliding them across one another, a method that he adapted for himself. Still others he chalked up to the everyday work of solving emergent technical problems, especially while repairing old, often perplexing instruments. He felt, for instance, that he had bettered the methods of Cusco's bandurria makers after repairing several instruments from that region and finding that their curved tops were made using a saw cut on their under-side—a technique that badly weakened the wood and that Marco replaced with a curved bracing system.

These examples were readily available to consciousness, but other elements of Marco's working knowledge resided in the tacit realm that reveals itself in every apprenticeship, where visual observation and physical mimesis are as central to the learning process as verbal communication (Herzfeld 2004; Marchand 2010). My experience in apprenticing with Marco often involved fits of envy at his embodied facility with tools and wood, and my proxy attempts to inhabit the histories of material engagement that lay behind them as I imitated his motions and imagined their significance. This was usually impossible, and when he redrew my measured lines freehand, dragging a pencil around the sides of an unfinished chinlili from one end to the other to produce a uniform mark precisely 2 millimeters from the edge; or when he bent the mahogany sides of my chinlili, also freehand, using a simple aluminum sheet folded over a blowtorch flame, rather than the complex system of molds and cauls to which I am accustomed from American lutherie (see figure 17); or when he noticed on my own bandurria the incipient "bellying" effect that results when high-tension strings torque a bridge forward, warping the top before and behind, an effect so slight that I was able to detect it only against a straight edge—in these and other instances I was made frustratingly aware of the sensory histories of material engagement that cannot be slighted in the process of artisanal enskilment.[15]

Either too difficult to convey in words or so thoroughly ingrained as to have become indistinguishable from instinct, these habits of movement and perception were traces of the most important tool Marco used in sustain-

FIGURE 17. Marco bending chinlili sides over an open flame in his workshop. Photograph by author.

ing Ayacucho's indigenous sounds: the distinctive body that he had acquired through practice. Its capacities were displayed especially well on another occasion, when a client arrived from nearby Huanta bearing some slabs of wood, gift of a relative in the Amazonian lowlands. The client didn't know what it was, and Marco didn't recognize it, so he deployed all of his senses to investigate its possibilities. Holding the boards at an angle oblique to the sun, he gauged the surface for grain direction and spacing, evaluating its potential to generate the resonance that comes from tight, straight grain. He hefted it, feeling its mass, and smelled it, testing for signs of residual dampness or of lingering oils, resins, or alcohol. Only after these visual, proprioceptive, and olfactory tests did he turn to sound, knocking the pieces against a table and nodding in satisfaction at the well-defined, sustained tone they produced. Finally, he grabbed a nearby plane and, setting it for a thin shaving, ran it across the wood, grunting with satisfaction as narrow ribbons rolled from its mouth, promising a material resistant to chipping and easy to work.

Lutherie, as Kies has noted (2013:79), demands a multisensory engagement with materials, and it forces luthiers to grow a particular kind of body, one with a heightened perceptual apparatus and a bundle of kinesthetic instincts that are adapted to the profession. Many of the relevant habits are haptic, visual, or olfactory, but the resulting instruments are judged mainly through aural criteria, and Marco justified most decisions by reference to proper sound. With respect to the chinlili, whether we discussed material for top and sides, the instrument's proper scale length, or the placement of the bridge, the conclusion was determined by the need to make the instrument *chillar*. The word, which translates literally as "to scream," glosses the combination of shrillness and tonal complexity that distinguishes the instrument and allows it to function as an aural sign of chuschino tradition. Indeed, as far as the chinlili is concerned, it might be said that Marco's expertise was deployed primarily to ensure the preservation of that sound amid the changing conditions of chimaycha performance—a process that required adaptation as the genre moved from small-scale contexts to the electrified context of mass-popular urban concerts.

Moving the Indigenous Machine: The Chinlili's Transformation

The chinlilis that came to Ayacucho in the 1980s produced the pleasingly "chaotic" sound that characterizes many indigenous instruments worldwide, thanks to the mutually interfering harmonics that they are designed to produce (Hill and Chaumeil 2011; Ryan 2003:286; Turino 1993). Its brilliance was, as detailed in chapter 3, a recent and complex sort of historical accident, a local response to broader musical fashions. Nevertheless its accidental timbre had become sonorously constitutive of indigenous traditionalism, bound up as it was with a distinctive structure of feeling, one tied in turn to stories and memories of youthful prowess and community custom. As Ayacucho's performers began to alter the parameters of chimaycha music, Marco's shop became the place wherein this crucial signifier of indigeneity was transformed

WOOD AND WORK

so as to sound effectively amid the demands of urban life—the place where relationships between objects, sounds, and people were recast and concretized in new exosomatic organs of retention. Here the very idea of "the chinlili" was reconstituted around a new kind of electric instrument, an invention that helped to articulate a new network of agents, materials, and ideas.

THE TRANSFORMATION: MATERIALS AND MUSICALITY

Marco made the importance of the chinlili's shrill quality especially clear one afternoon as we examined the oldest example in his shop. Dating, he thought, from the 1970s, its back and sides were made from thin pieces of *huayao*, a type of willow that, along with the cedars and alders that grew along the region's meager waterways, was used in the days before Pampas Valley makers had easy access to nonlocal lumber. All of these soft, pliable woods yield unstable instruments, but they also "scream more," Marco said, compensating for their structural deficiencies. The instrument's maker had in fact used some unique design elements to try to augment this quality. It featured a pair of slots under the fretboard, running the length of the neck, and opening out at a pair of holes beneath the nut, where two triangles drawn on the headstock above pointed to their location. In keeping with the anatomical designations for guitar parts, the feature was called a "throat" (Q: *tunquchu*), and Marco swore that it granted the instrument a louder sound, a contention that was echoed by Óscar Conde when he later showed me another old instrument with a similar feature.[16]

If wood selection and experimental design were noteworthy elements of the chinlili's sound, then Marco's thoughts on its fretboard and stringing were even more pointed and specific. Responding, for instance, to my question in a 2003 interview about whether it might be acceptable to replace the chinlili with the trendy requinto in chimaycha performance, he said, "No, never in my life." He went on:

> The requinto has a very different swing. On the chinlili, because the fretboard only has a few frets, it has a different sound. The distance from one to the other, the tension that you press it with, gives it a different flavor. A requinto has all the [chromatic] notes; when you press it, the tension of the string itself, it will never produce the same sound [as a chinlili], never in your life. So sometimes I make a chinlili, and the action [i.e. the height of the strings above the fretboard] is a little high and the musicians say, "No, the notes are off." And I know the frets aren't off, it's that the strings are too high, and because of that when you press they produce a different note. Some artists press hard, and when they press hard the tension on the string can raise the note, something

like a quarter tone. So when you play with a requinto, or something else, it's out of tune.

The last part of this quote suggests how emergent material constraints and aesthetic pressures affected Marco's ability to maintain the chinlili's acoustic traits. The traditional instrument was, simply put, difficult to pair with the requinto, especially when that requinto played cumbia-style melodies. Speaking in 2012 about performer William Pacotaype, Marco explained that "in his last recording, has a cumbia lead-in in some songs . . . so that music, with the [traditional] chinlili frets, it won't work." To play such melodies, which often used tones outside the chinlili's pentatonic capabilities, or to play in tune with the requintos, synthesizers, and electric basses that chimaycha groups used routinely by the 2010s, meant developing a chinlili that was tuned to the equal-tempered standards of those instruments and that was fretted so as to articulate their full chromatic series, rather than the intonationally casual pentatonic gamut of the traditional chinlili.

The fretboard was not the only point of intervention. Designed for the quiet grasslands of the high Andes, the acoustic chinlili hardly sufficed against the background noise of Ayacucho's extraordinarily loud soundscape.[17] Simple microphonic amplification was only a partial solution: beyond the feedback problems that are endemic to microphonic amplification anywhere on earth, Marco had discovered as early as 1990 that the swaying chinlili players of Los Chikitukus had trouble keeping the instrument pointed at onstage microphones. Fortunately, he studied electrical engineering at Ayacucho's Joaquín López Antay Institute in the early 1990s with an eye to maintaining speakers and amplifiers. He was therefore prepared to experiment with the soundhole and under-saddle pickups that began arriving on imported guitars around that time, often retrofitting older instruments to accommodate them.

Finally, around the turn of the twenty-first century, players began to request solid-body electric instruments. This was nearly inevitable: less prone to damage and climate-related stress, cheaper to make, easier to customize, their electronics more reliable, and bearing a sleek modern look, electric instruments presented a host of advantages to working musicians. However, the cumulative cost of addressing these demands was considerable. Chromatic fretting eliminated the chinlili's precious intonational variability, while the switch to electric instruments obviated the contribution of tonewoods. This was a matter of no small concern since the chinlili's shimmering harmonic richness secured chimaycha's difference from other huayno variants, allowing performers to flag their affiliation with the identity and worldview it stood for. With the instrument's character attenuated by refretting and electrification, bringing its sound into this new technical and sociomusical context mandated an adaptation that amounted to a translation.

Here Marco's ideas and skills made him into a key operator, in Smith's sense of the term: an entity whose actions altered the indigenous assemblage of which he and the chinlili are key members. Nobody else had both the performer's ear and the intimate knowledge of wood, metal, bone, glue, lacquer, and tools required to shape this as yet unrealized target object, and this is where Marco's own sensitive body meets the materiality of the sonorous indigenous assemblage in which he is suspended. His past engagements with raw materials and with finished chinlilis allowed him to successfully mediate the conversion of one into the other—to predict the behavior of wood, of glue under strain and strings under tension, and the response of electronic components not designed to accommodate the chinlili's arrangement of pitches and forces. Deploying these skills to make an instrument that preserved the chinlili's small size and its unique arrangement of strings, he helped musicians to approximate in an electric context the sound of the acoustic instrument, and hence of the indigenous past.

His centrality to this assemblage, however, does not equate to the totalizing dominance of his human ingenuity over his materials, nor does it imply that human-object interactions are always predictable. Material resistance can trump human intentions, as it did in the physical shape of Marco's electric chinlilis—a relation that recalls Sennett's discussion of the maker's mark. While examining a solid-bodied electric chinlili one afternoon, Marco called attention to the instrument's high modern outline, which reminded me of electric guitars like the Gibson Firebird or Fender Jaguar (see figure 18). Much of this effect owes to a sort of cutaway space on the bottom of the lower bout, which interrupts the classic guitarlike shape of the older acoustic version. Marco told me that this had become something of a "trademark" for his shop and that young musicians had come demanding that shape after seeing and being taken with the futuristic look of the first model that he put into circulation.

If this constitutes Marco's trademark then it is also an adaptive irregularity in Sennett's sense, an element introduced to solve a technical and economic challenge. Instrument makers in Ayacucho have limited access to high-end electrical components and often make do with poorly made Chinese models. Such was the case with the input jack sockets—the mechanism into which a cable is inserted—that Marco had available while developing his instrument. The problem was not electrical: rather, the jack socket's housing was too bulky to easily install in a way that preserved the graceful but tight curves of the classic instrument. The solution, to cut away some space in an appropriate place

FIGURE 18. An unfinished electric chinlili in the courtyard of Marco's shop. Photograph by author.

and install the metal object there, was an accident forced upon Marco and his prototype by the cheap, materially recalcitrant but indispensable component. That it was understood as a fashionable modernist gesture, in a moment when young musicians were seeking just such trappings for their performances, was but a happy coincidence. Even so, it led Marco's instruments, with distinctive

WOOD AND WORK 199

sonorities rooted in his beliefs about the proper indigenous aesthetics, to take a central place in Ayacucho's changing soundscape.

By 2013 this design was so dominant that Marco had trouble finding his disused acoustic chinlili templates when I approached him with the idea of an apprenticeship. He had even passed on his innovations to a young luthier named Ramos, who sold five or six electric models per month at an instrument store in Ayacucho's central market at the low rate of 150 soles (ca. $40 US). Marco was ambivalent about this kind of success, but he accepted the acoustic chinlili's dwindling prominence as a compromise between aesthetic continuity and socioeconomic pressure, an adequate response to forces beyond his control or that of his fellow musicians. He had, in fact, raised the issue of balancing change and continuity as long ago as our 2002 interview, when his business still revolved around acoustic chinlilis. Referring to their natural wood-tone finish, which evoked the look of high-end nylon-stringed guitars rather then the reddish-orange hue of Jacinto's chinlilis, he ruefully noted: "Disrespecting the color it's supposed to have, I use other colors, I do it my own way. In the Western style [*al mundo occidental*]. That is to say, more or less the way that globalization affects the guitar, it affects the chinlili."

Marco was well aware of his status as a key actor in a processual web that wove materials, technical skills, aesthetic change, and economic demand together to foster musical transformation. However, hand skills are not the only quality that made him into such a pivotal node in Ayacucho's machine of musical indigeneity, for an instrument is more than a material object: it is also a bundle of associated ideologies (Pinch and Trocco 2002; Waksman 1999 and 2003) and bodily practices (Baily 1985; Jihad Racy 1994; Qureshi 1997). Over his decades of working with and thinking about the chinlili and its relation to his musical community, Marco had developed lines of thought and practice in each of these areas too. The success of his instruments owed at least as much to the way that he framed them for his customers as it did to their material excellence.

Material Indigeneity: Wood and Weather

By the time I apprenticed with him, Marco had aligned his work as a luthier with his thinking on indigenous identity and on natural resource extraction. His sui generis combination of material knowledge and Andean cultural affirmation was informed by ideas about colonialism gleaned originally in his student days. It also resonated with contemporaneous developments in indigenous politics, although Marco had little investment in those developments.

One way to approach this point of connection between practice and politics is to revisit the interaction described above, wherein a client piqued Marco's interest with an unknown wood from the jungle lowlands. Most local makers are not disposed to look beyond the small group of tonewoods considered to be global standards, and for a long time Marco was one of them. Falcón had taught him the lessons about wood selection that are absorbed by fledgling luthiers around the world: proper sound means using spruce for tops, rosewood or mahogany for back and sides, or, failing these options, a series of acceptable substitutes such as cedar tops and sides of walnut or koa. He brought these values to his own work, replacing the alder and willow used in Chuschi. And yet over time he came to reconsider those principles. Such tonewoods are not cheaply to be had in Peru. Rosewood has been listed in the CITES treaty that regulates global trade in threatened species, and it is extremely difficult to acquire. Mahogany is also highly regulated, and access depends on fluctuating levels of enforcement. North American Sitka spruce, by contrast, is always available in Lima—for now—but it is very costly, beyond the means of most Ayacuchano buyers.[18]

Marco's experimentation with local woods grew not only from financial imperatives, however. It grew more precisely from his evolving ideas about the intersection between aesthetics and ethnic inequity. He explained this during a discussion about alternate woods, after he told me about building a guitar entirely of eucalyptus, a notoriously difficult and unstable material.[19] In what seemed like a non sequitur, he told me to look at the city's old mansions next time I was in the center of town, where I would see beams and other structural elements made from European spruce. He said, "When the Spanish came they thought everything here was worthless, even the people, and so they brought everything from Europe." He went on to speak in detail about the lasting effects of such colonial disrespect and about the need to revalorize local resources, in line with the ongoing broader revalorization of Andean culture.

Some of Marco's thoughts on this matter involved impractical schemes, like the idea—proposed to a visiting legislator—of establishing a sustainable forestry initiative, one that would populate Ayacucho's denuded hillsides with conifers useful to local artisans. Other ideas were more feasible, such as the notion of making a research trip to the Peruvian jungle, seeking out underutilized woods that might serve. He knew that likely candidates existed, woods like the *yanamachu* (Q: "old black man") that a friend had brought him from the northern jungle city of Pucallpa, slabs with the coloring of ebony but that proved less prone to curling over time. Lacking the time and money for such a long trip, he was nevertheless experimenting with woods from the local Ayacuchano jungle, making fretboards of *chonta* palm (*Bactris gasipaes*) and *quebracho* (*Schinopses* spp.), woods even harder than the typical ebony or jacaranda. Many instruments already circulated in Ayacucho bearing these kinds of innovations, but other novelties met with more resistance, like his proposal to make sides and backs of chachas, which he claimed was equal in stability and superior in tone to rosewood. Even the chonta that he praised for its striking hardness—I was nearly unable to scratch it with a chisel when he invited me to test it—came from a log that a friend had given him free, eager to dispose of useless scrap lumber.

Marco means to make an overt ideological statement by using these native Peruvian woods. However, this kind of work also involves a more implicit labor of indigenization, for it requires an emplaced environmental awareness that has come to be conventionally associated with the very notion of indigeneity. Marco knew, for instance, that mahogany from the Ayacuchano jungle served for necks alone, given its inferior appearance, while the same species yielded attractive backs and sides when it came from faraway Ucayali. Jacaranda also varied depending on its sourcing, with markedly different kinds of wood appearing from Bolivia and Brazil. Above all, local trees in highland Ayacucho required special treatment, since climatic change and urban pollution had rendered most of them inferior for woodworking purposes. By treating all of these South American tonewoods as possible resources for an anti-imperialist, affirmatively local lutherie, Marco grew his frame of reference to encompass colonized spaces well beyond his native Andean highlands, a conceptual move echoing the translocal acts of articulation that have built the global indigenous movement itself.

The act of working those woods further grounded Marco's conceptual gesture in a radically local system of environmental knowledge, for it demanded an acute, predictive attunement to daily interactions between weather and wood. This especially affected work with glue. Glue dries differently depending on weather conditions and the type of glue in question, posing a challenge for a luthier who lacks an enclosed, climate-controlled building. Marco, however, maintained that Ayacucho's climate, with dry heat and strong sun available at some point in every day, provided superior conditions for someone who knew how to manage them, rendering superfluous the mechanized drying processes he had observed in Falcón's shop. He had used elements at his disposal to create different microclimates, inserting a plastic sheet into the corrugated iron roof so as to create a "Goldilocks" space in the shop corner: warm enough to promote drying on cool mornings, when lit by the sun, but always less torrid than the courtyard outside. Managing this simple tool required a thorough familiarity with local climatic cycles and signals and a corresponding care, when working on a particular instrument, to think about the prevailing humidity and cloud cover. Marco routinely moved instruments around his space and glued at different times of day, sometimes placing an instrument in the sunny courtyard for a few morning hours and sometimes performing glue-ups at night, according to prevailing conditions.

Marco's job, then, required the cultivation of a place-based environmental awareness and facilitated the exercise of an affirmatively indigenous imagination, making his chinlilis into material precipitates of different registers of indigenous knowledge. Finally, though, his very ability to sustain sounds of Ayacuchano indigeneity had come to depend upon a radically different form of local knowledge: a mastery of illicit commodity chains, which allowed him to acquire parts at prices low enough for his instruments to remain attractive to his clientele. Noticing at one point that certain parts sold more cheaply in Ayacucho than they should, given the markup that goods typically accrue when they travel from Lima to Peru's provinces, he had traced them to their source, discovering a group of Chinese Peruvian wholesalers in the capital who had easy access to suspiciously underpriced electronics. He had therefore contrived a means to source parts from them, thereby lowering the cost of instruments for his often insolvent customers.

It is, of course, now routine to note that discourses of local cultural affirmation depend heavily upon translocal frameworks for their success (Appadurai 1996; Turino 2000; Tsing 2005). Still, this case further underlines the specificity of Marco's entangled web of craft capacities, material knowledge, and indigenous politics, all of which intersect in the physical forms and the sonorities of the instruments he placed in the hands of chimaycha musicians. There is, moreover, one final element that makes Marco a central operator in chimaycha's network of musical indigeneity: his skill as a performer, and his consequent qualities as an instructor.

Embodied Musical Indigeneity: Making Music in the Workshop

Like other tools, musical instruments are "the human mind and body externalised and extended . . . the materials of the physical world shaped into 'human friendly' form [and] made to 'fit' our bodies" (Dawe 2005:59). However, as surely as instruments are made to fit bodies, bodies are made to fit instruments. Archives of physical gesture, their shapes solicit idiosyncratic movements and actions, as players seek to produce the sounds dear to their creators. If, per Gadamer, "all playing is a being-played" (cited in Mosely 2015:152), then instrumental competence demands the inducement of a musculature and a nervous system like the one inhabited by previous performers; instrumental performance revives the gestural culture of generations past;

and instruments themselves are deposits of kinesthetic memory, sites of what Stiegler has called "tertiary retention." A coach typically mediates the transmission of these tertiary retentions, a player for whom performance amounts to the deployment of muscle memories and cognitive schema stored in the body—types of recall that Stiegler classifies as "secondary retentions." With this distinction Stiegler's system usefully sets apart the rather different ways that trained and novice performers experience musical tools, a distinction that matters in situations of social or technical change, where new performers treat instruments as means to access otherwise lost forms of experience and identity. Especially when the instruments themselves evolve, effective instruction is required to attune bodies, sounds, and cultural continuity—for there is always the risk that a new variant will be defined as another instrument entirely (Tresch and Dolan 2013:288), thereby breaking an established chain of signification.

During my apprenticeship with Marco one experience, above all others, motivated me to think about the chinlili and the human body as material components within a network of cultural memory. A middle-aged man from Chuschi District came to the shop, desperately needing chinlili repairs ahead of an upcoming show. He didn't appear to be fazed by my unusual presence, and unlike other more curious clients, he took pains to show his indifference. He folded my hand in a crushing shake before launching into a routine of probing insult that often greets visitors to Quechua-speaking communities, where social norms and memories of white abuse can dictate the presentation of a tough demeanor to foreigners. Without letting go he performed a mush-mouthed parody of my speaking voice, before turning my hand over in his own hardened agriculturalist's hands and snorting derisively at my "office hands."

The client was, in short, an astute performer of truculence. Knowing full well that presence is pressure, he spent the entire day waiting in the dirt courtyard outside Marco's shop, impressing family members and other clients with his blunt observations and coarse jokes. By midafternoon the instrument was ready, and as we worked inside the shop, he strung it up and began to play through some chimaycha tunes. Leaning out to see, I was startled by the change in his demeanor. Feet planted wide in a stance suggesting bodily strength or force of will, he cradled the instrument against his chest, turning his farmer's hands to the production of the music-box tinkling that characterizes good chinlili playing. With eyes closed, lips parted, and head cocked in an attitude of concentrated audition, he was gauging the instrument's sound with what looked like rapture, and his body swayed back and forth in time to the music. It seemed hard to mistake the attitude of tenderness in which he

204 CHAPTER SEVEN

was enveloped, and I retreated into the shop, embarrassed by the sense that I had been spying on something intensely private.

In fact, the client's demeanor was fairly typical of chimaycha performance, and had I already been used to it I would not have felt so discomfited. Still, my impression of motivated tenderness was on the mark: as a courting tradition in which songs of love, loss, and longing are framed through delicate metaphors of natural beauty, traditional chimaycha is for its performers ineluctably tied to memories of tenderness and its embodied communication. This indeed is one way in which an instrument "grips" a sensitive body, developed through a lifetime of engagement with the object and with the performance context wherein it is designed to sound, bending that body into a shape that is appropriate to the instrument's intended ends.

Most of Marco's clients are not rural peasants but rather youthful migrants who play contemporary pop chimaycha for an urban audience. Such youths can never exactly access the lost realm of experience that motivated the older man's attitude of performance. They seek instead tools that bear the ghostly traces of those experiences, sonorous objects that induce them to move, act, and sound like him, bodying forth a variety of indigeneity that is native to a cultural milieu they have not lived. Here Marco's technical innovations present something of a challenge, for his electric chinlilis might, after all, be understood and treated as very small, unusually strung electric guitars. That they are not owes to choices that Marco made as he went about creating and then disseminating the variant. As Bijsterveld and Schulp have noted (2004), the very judgment that a new instrument is a cognate of other models relies as heavily upon makers' powers of persuasion as on the new instrument's fitness for the duties of the old, adding an ideological component to Jihad Racy's observation that instruments are best treated as "a physical and acoustical 'package' that incorporates construction and performance modes" (1994:37).

In the case of the electric chinlili, Marco took care to establish material, technical, and ideological continuity between old and new models. First, and most basically, his new design preserved the older instrument's unusual stringing and small size, traits that allowed it to retain its unique acoustic signature. Second, he took advantage of his regular contact with Ayacucho's indigenous musical community, and his standing as a performer, to shape the technique that players brought to the new instrument. This meant modeling for them the distinctive physical habits that he had accrued over a lifetime of making those sounds, but it also meant creating new kinds of gestural information, information required by the gaps between the new instrument's physical properties and the old repertoire it was being asked to produce.[20]

Marco mainly coached two kinds of customers in this fashion. One kind included rank beginners, whom he encouraged with gifts of inexpensive chinlilis, worth some 300 or 400 soles, complete with elementary instruction. Another, equally numerous kind of customer included experienced players transitioning to electric models, who required advice about adjusting their fingering habits to elicit the proper notes, for the instruments' full chromatic complement of frets and the significant difference in string tension and deflection entailed by the solid-body instrument produced a change in intonation. "Sometime I give them guidance," Marco said, "because look, modern chinlilis require a special kind of fingering, because we're including some [new] frets and some people aren't used to it, don't know it. [So you say,] 'You should put your fingers here, here, and here, and you can play those things.'" At one point he even contemplated producing an instructional booklet in collaboration with a student from the local conservatory, much like those sold at corner stands all over Peru featuring advice on playing guitar, charango, harp, and other Andean instruments.

Lacking the wherewithal to produce such a text, Marco instead relied upon personal communication, and the casual model by which he ran his business lent itself well to the task. Rarely did a customer come to the shop only to communicate details of an order. Instead they sat and conversed, sometimes for a full hour or more, and this allowed him to remain informed about ongoing events in Ayacucho's rural and urban migrant communities. Marco alerted me to this aspect of his work early on, describing himself as the "gossip [*chismoso*] who knows everything," a label that seemed increasingly apt as I watched him catch up with old friends and converse with new clients over the course of several months. Politics occupied much of the conversational space, but most of it revolved naturally around musical dynamics, featuring information about the changing membership of local groups and the fluctuations in their influence, or demonstrations of trends and techniques that circulated in Chuschi and Quispillaccta. This form of musical infrastructure development allowed him to exert a great deal of influence as he guided clients toward instruments that struck a balance between their needs and his own aesthetic preferences. Some of this labor was performed in the guise of gossip about other people and their instruments as he led visitors to speak of and lament the disastrous choices of other players: a flawed requinto, sitting in the shop and awaiting repairs, that the performer had acquired in Lima for no less than two thousand soles; or instruments with onboard distortion, delay, tone controls, and other effects rendered useless when they were amplified through the inferior sound systems that chimaycha performers encountered at rural festivals. More often it took the form of Marco's attempting to dissuade buyers from decisions that he thought were poor: an electric requinto performer who refused to understand that the expensive shape he wanted had no effect whatsoever on the instrument's sound; a client seeking an ebony fingerboard which, at some $45 US, would still be inferior to the local chonta wood that Marco suggested; a chinlili player demanding a 24-fret chinlili, unconcerned that the useless high frets were never to be used and merely for show.

It was in contexts like these that Marco aided visiting performers in the development of their chinlili performance skills, shaping new kinds of indigenous bodies as he directed the force they exerted on new electric chinlilis. I watched one short lesson on a November afternoon in 2013 as a father and son visited the shop together. Marco and the father had disappeared into the shop to consult about an order, leaving the teenager to wait outside, where he soon seized a chinlili from the group sitting on a bench. Hearing his halting attempts to pluck its strings, Marco reemerged to give him advice. Noting the young man's flailing hands, he showed him the single position that was needed to produce the proper tones, counseling him to hold the instrument still and in the same way every time so that his hands might learn where to find the strings and the frets needed to produce chimaycha music—advice that might have come from any knowledgeable guitar teacher anywhere on earth. He told the teenager to leave trailing fingers on the strings, below fretted notes, since melodies would inevitably descend by the same route and his fingers would be prepared. He covered fretting pressure and its effect on intonation, and the muting of bass strings with the back of the thumb, a technique required to produce chimaycha's punchy, staccato rhythms. None of this advice had an immediate effect on the young man's playing. However, it is likely that repeated visits, like those that many other young musicians made to Marco's shop, augmented by private practice, would mold him into a performer with the bodily capacities needed to preserve the sounds of indigeneity that Marco deemed essential. And of course, as Marco showed him the ropes of manual dexterity, his own body swayed in time.

Conclusion

Dawe has noted that musical instruments affect "states of mind as much as joints, tendons and synapses, ergonomics and social interaction" (2005:60). They are devices for the transmission of bodily hexis, for the preservation of sounds that would otherwise fade away (Kittler 1999), and symbols of cultural continuity—but this is not the entire story. For elsewhere Mosely has noted that the tertiary mnemonic capacity of instruments allows users "to *construe* musical recreation as reenactment" (2015:158; emphasis added), and the qualifying verb makes all the difference, for in truth nothing is ever repeated verbatim. If objects, per Serres, slow time and arrest cultural change, then it is also true that mores, aesthetics, and performing contexts still change. Instrumental morphology itself is altered over time, and all of these elements develop together as mutually constitutive elements of the dynamic system of the kind that Smith has called a "machine." This is why it is important to attend to the activities of operators like Marco: situated at the nexus of sound, society, and material objects, people like him mediate the evolving relationship between these domains. In his case, that changing relationship wheels around the changing terms of indigenous experience, and his actions show how thoroughly that experience comes to lie in realms that are well outside official political discourse—everyday, unmarked realms that may be all the more powerful for being unmarked, for perduring below the level of conscious insight and hence conscious manipulation. In this sense Dawe has elsewhere described the instrument workshop aptly indeed as "a place where craftwork, retailing, and social space are combined to create a particular type of world . . . a cultural space and a social world as much as a place of work" (2003:271).

As young performers bend their hands to the technical operations that the chinlili elicits, bodying forth the physical attitudes and aesthetic norms of previous performers, they conjure indigenous sensorial experiences of the past and project those distinctive sensorial traces in new spaces. If their unprecedented audibility in the urban soundscape testifies to a new politics of indigenous affirmation, then it also testifies to the power of sound to articulate such abstractions to bodies and minds in motion. It is Marco's material and manual skills that allow this to happen, and if his capacities to act are determined in part by the properties of his materials, then these materials are brought into alignment with bodies and ideas via the force of his embodied skills. Sonorous indigeneity is the always-emergent product of contingent alignments between all of these entities, alignments that shift constantly due to the ever-changing demands placed upon performers, luthiers, and consumers alike.

Epilogue

In December 2017 I brought this book manuscript to Peru to review it with the people represented in its pages. Perhaps inevitably as I was primed with thoughts about the changing relationship between Peru's indigenous peoples and the nation-state that houses them, I stumbled everywhere across potential signs of that relationship's status. This explains why a piece of graffiti I passed on Manco Capac Street in Lima's tony Miraflores District seemed to leap from the stucco wall where it was written in small black letters. It read "Don't pretend to tolerate me when the rest of you hate my origin." The directive admits of many interpretations, not least because it was written in English, raising questions about its intended audience. However, at the time I could hardly help but read it as a statement about the limits of indigenous validation in a country where indigenous peoples still gain cultural citizenship mainly by consenting to absorption within a proleptic, putatively shared "mestizo" identity. As if to underscore this line of thinking, I found its complement moments later on the shelves of Pulga, a shop that specialized in expensive clothing, especially shirts bearing stylized images of migrant Lima's cultural manifestations. Members of Lima's hipster elite wear such shirts in order to flag their devotion to the tenets of cholo nationalism, and the centerpiece of Pulga's seasonal display made things as explicit as possible: it was a black T-shirt with a Spanish-language message reading "The Future Is Mestizo."

It would be absurd to read very much into these particular artifacts. Such resonance as exists between them owes to their timely conjunction in the experience of a scholar with an overdetermined habit of reading Peruvian public culture for signs of ethnic ideology. And yet persistent limits to indigenous rights and the banalization of interculturalism are real and related qualities of Peruvian social discourse. Peru's intractable inequalities depend in part on the tendency to treat elite representations of indigenous culture as signs of tolerance rather than acts of surrogation. If nothing else, then, these items might help to remind observers that an assimilative vision of mestizaje persists beneath the inclusive rhetoric of cholo nationalism and that it remains difficult for indigenous voices to make themselves heard without passing through the aesthetic and ideological filters of mestizo society. If, in other words, I have argued in this book that indigenous Peruvians are making chimaycha music one site in which to debate and valorize their changing identities, then it would also be hasty to suggest that the space they are carving out is coextensive with Peru's public sphere or that their claims of indigeneity are audible to people who stand outside their community.

What, then, does indigeneity mean in contemporary Peru? Is there any reason to believe that real change is happening, or will happen soon, with respect to social relations between indigenous Andeans and their conationals? And what has music got to do with the social identity that these words name?

As I have shown over the course of this book, there are no pleasingly clear answers to questions like these. The term *indigenous* and its cognates are interpretive tools, attempts to pin a name on social roles, systems of thought and behavior, and feelings of community that are all malleable in practice. That which seems appropriately described as "indigenous" according to one frame of reference may manifest rather differently, and gain a different name, within another. Moreover, such interpretive tools vary in their application by differently situated actors. For many social scientists, and for contemporary political activists, words like *indigenous* and *Indian* have typically glossed a notion of persistent cultural difference. They imply a commitment to evolving customs, beliefs, and social systems that are continuous with practices that predate European colonization, and the sense of Otherness that arises from the observation that neighbors do not share those commitments. Per Starn's argument (1991), however, such an interpretation is partial at best and pernicious at worst if it elides the capacity for self-transformation, the sociohistorical agency, and the cultural heterogeneity of indigenous communities. For the denial of fully coeval status and the claim of unfitness for modernity are both tools through which the powerful have secured the denigration of things indigenous, and with it their own domination over indigenous actors. It is imperative, then, to remember that ascriptions of indigeneity depend as much on disempowerment as on sheer difference in the Peruvian Andes, where "Indians" have typically been those denied the social, economic, and cultural capital to claim a less stigmatized social identity, rather than those who manifest any fixed set of cultural diacritics. And in this light it is worth remembering, once more, that the people so named have not usually cherished

EPILOGUE

the label—that it is better regarded as a sociological heuristic in the hands of social scientists, or as a tool for securing rights and resources in the mouths of political activists, than as a popular means for describing the self.

In this sense, "indigenous" differs little from any other named social identity. "Identity," per the cogent critique of Brubaker and Cooper (2000), is a crude cover term that gestures toward many things, including ascriptive acts of naming, attributions of likeness (including self-attributions), shared experiences and the feelings of communitas that arise from them, and performative acts of identification with any of these. Such imprecision does not lessen the experiential reality of any given social identity, but it does mean that it is important to specify the agents and circumstances in and through which it is made intelligible. It is also urgent to keep present the distinctive effects that accrue to different acts and methods of identification, and to ask if the thing that they reify is the same thing. Here I have followed such a program, describing how the subject position that I am calling Andean indigeneity comes, per Clifford's formulation (2007), in many different versions. It has indeed sometimes manifested as a shared set of beliefs and behaviors that distinguish members of certain social communities from their neighbors and colonizers (chapters 2 and 3); sometimes as a performative framework through which diacritics of that village experience are staged by and for community members and outsiders alike, so as to specify forms of difference that are newly valorized in an era of social justice (chapter 4); sometimes as a mode of identitarian politics through which old claims to redress and dignity are mobilized through new languages, and particularly the language of a global movement for rights and redress (chapter 5); sometimes as a distinctive bricolage of aesthetic and emotional habits that intersect with a persistent sense of disempowerment and distinctive habits of consumption, generating an affective hexis that is particular to urban indigeneity (chapter 6); and finally, in the person of one extraordinary individual, as a complicated sense of emplacement, as well as an impulse toward aesthetic curation, strands of experience that when intertwined speak volumes about the direction of indigenous experience today (chapter 7).

None of these varieties of indigeneity are mutually exclusive, and few real individuals are equally involved with all of them. Still, where they intersect they form a blurred but recognizable space, one wherein Ayacucho's Quechua-speaking people manage the diverse, partially overlapping qualities that make them tangible to one another as members of a community. If symbols and ethnic labels are transacted with outsiders, including European colonizers, their descendants, and other indigenous peoples, then such constant negotiation is not a sign of the identity's contrived nature—a charge that is often leveled at the activists who take up languages of indigenous identity (see introduction).

Rather, those acts of self-definition are the very processes in which those who call themselves and those who get called indigenous determine which of their treasured cultural practices have been important in the past, which should remain so going forward, and which might be changed without threat to autonomy and dignity.

Of course it should be reiterated that much of the account I have presented here is a provisional construct—an interpretation of Andean indigeneity that departs from one generation's musical experience in one highly localized corner of a vast and diverse highland region. Its historical elements are furthermore highly structured by the reminiscences of two men, whose words may well be inflected by the intervening years, by contemporary sociopolitical pressures, and by their later residence in a regional capital, saturated by habits and ideologies unlike those that guided village life in their youth. Limitations like these accrue to any reasonable account of social identity, which can proceed only via the self-aware examination of its bearers' real lives, and which can only fail when attempts are made to abstract from concrete examples to some putatively purer, less ideologized set of experiences. Surely the interpretations of Marco and Óscar are in some ways particular to them, and they should not be read as a complete report on Andean indigeneity writ large. Highland societies are too diverse to support such a totalizing claim. Still, they match too closely with the reports of dozens of their peers to suggest that their reports are especially eccentric. Moreover, I do not think that their urban experience renders their accounts more contrived than those of village residents, for the notion of a radical difference between the two contexts is too often overstated—at least insofar as the decades since the 1980s are concerned. It seems clear that their lives unfolded in an era when towns like Chuschi and Quispillaccta were already thoroughly connected with the city of Ayacucho via commerce, schooling, legal business, and a host of other mechanisms. Such tight links have only developed even further over the last twenty years.

The view that this book affords of indigeneity is, then, partial. It nevertheless reveals remarkable developments in practice, discourse, and social structure over the last fifty years, traces of larger changes that transected the lives of musicians in and from the District of Chuschi, leaving marks on the practices that they cherished and making music into one privileged site for exploring the changes themselves. It is clear, for instance, that the 1970s and 1980s were a watershed moment in the life of the District of Chuschi, a period in which social norms and patterns that regulated life in an earlier moment were swept away. Isbell's ethnography, drawing largely on observations from the 1960s and 1970s, already bore witness to this process. It suggested that indigenous chuschinos in the community were adapting old strategies and

EPILOGUE

adopting new ones, especially links with fellows in the cities of Lima and Ayacucho, to defend themselves and their lifeways from unwelcome outside pressures. By the late 1980s the signs of change that she reported had gathered force and driven severe dislocations in older lifeways, not only because of the violence but also because the arrival of schooling, the building of transport and communications infrastructure, and the work of development agencies all altered patterns of interaction and systems of belief that governed life in an earlier era. Changes in the material base of community subsistence and the consequent decrease in youthful hours spent in the puna all conspired to weaken the vida michiy over time, meaning that young residents of the district no longer experienced the tight connections between courtship, sound, and ecology that once governed their young lives. However, these same changes brought teachers dedicated to sustaining indigenous customs, and institutions with a vested interest in supporting the indigenous performance. The vida michiy's aesthetics were therefore carried forward, becoming sonic symbols that bore traces of an earlier indigenous habitus even as the habitus of chimaycha performers evolved away from older customs. Careful curation of the style means that it was available as a symbol of indigenous authenticity when the languages of global indigenous activism arrived in the 1990s and 2000s, while their promotion in that moment meant in turn that they were available as resources for the development of a localized cognate to Lima's cholo huayno scene. The musicians that I have discussed over the course of this book were sometimes buffeted by these changes, but at other times they assumed leading roles in directing them. In every case, however, they found new opportunities for the musical performance of indigeneity, registering and naturalizing large-scale changes in such minute realms as performance style and instrument construction.

Indeed, by way of conclusion it is well worth considering the considerably expanded possibilities for indigenous self-representation that are signaled in the twenty-first-century rise of Ayacucho's chimaycha scene. Indigenous peoples there have greater media access, and a louder public voice, than at any moment since Peruvian independence. There is not universal agreement about how to use these powers, but such debates as circulate around the question are premised on indigenous control over indigenous resources including indigenous culture, and this marks a salutary change from prior eras. Here it is worth returning to a thread that I left hanging in chapter 4. There I noted a number of disagreements that have set much of the chimaycha community against Ranulfo Infanzón, founder of Los Aires Chuschinos. From an outside perspective, a certain ridiculousness may seem to lie in claiming an alternate name for a musical genre or an instrument, or seeking to define exactly who was responsible for inventing them. Surely uses, not origins, are what count. Such controversies of attribution are common in the Andes, however, and conversations about them extremely heated. Staking claims on the invention of the chinlili, or on terms like *qisarita*, *chimaycha*, *chinlili*, and *vigoyla*, is best viewed as a way of claiming protagonism, ownership, and superior knowledge. These may be especially urgent in a social context like the rural Andes, characterized by severe inequality, interethnic violence, and also intimate relationships between perpetrators and their victims. Forced by social circumstance to work for and with one's class enemies, enemies with whom one shares space and custom, it is more difficult to make the hard-and-fast distinctions along parallel lines of race, culture, and power that typify other situations of social conflict. It may be precisely the difficulty of laying clear claim to any one innovation, either on one's own behalf or on that of one's community, that makes such acts of claim-staking into the strident affairs that they are.

In this context it might be noted that in his younger days Infanzón developed a reputation as a devoted anti-imperialist, a position that was and remains very common among members of Peru's heavily Marxist teachers' union. His former student José Tomaylla spoke most specifically about this subject, recalling that Infanzón harangued his pupils about "resisting the empire," but his position was well known among the district's population. Especially during the 1970s, when Peruvians lived under a socialist dictatorship dedicated to indigenous justice and to resisting American influence, identification with and promotion of indigenous cultural difference was a mainstream proposition in the Andes. This was true even for mestizos like Infanzón and may explain, in part, his claims for a unique sort of expertise about indigenous chuschino culture, even against the counterclaims of the very people about whom he speaks—they may have become one means through which to sustain an anti-imperialist self-image.

This, indeed, has been a perennial barrier to the just conduct of ethnic relations in the Andes. The conviction that mestizos have the right to speak for and about indigenous peoples is, in a very real sense, responsible for the political failure of well-intentioned movements like indigenismo and the pan-Andean music that descends from it (see Ríos 2008; Tucker 2013b), which remains unpopular among indigenous Peruvians despite its liberal prestation of indigenous imageries. Long accustomed to looking on while their culture is described, diagnosed, and derided by the very people who claim to defend them, many Quechua speakers have longed for an opportunity to resist outsider characterization and to seize control of the apparatus of representation—to publicly define their own values and tell the world what they think of themselves unfiltered. This is what explains their avid pursuit of the education

EPILOGUE   215

that the UNSCH offered in the 1960s, and conventionally it is used to explain
the initial attraction of many to the Shining Path (Degregori 1997).

It is, then, not to be wondered at that contemporary indigenous peoples
are wielding new political and technological tools to speak about who they
are, to themselves and to others, without the mediation of mestizos or other
outsiders. Nor is it to be wondered at that this effort involves seizing control
of, renaming, or redefining terms of discourse that they have long shared with
their mestizo fellows: why not do so when those terms were never "shared"
on equal footing in the first place? When contemporary Quechua speakers
broadcast languages of politicized indigeneity or sing of their continuing marginality in urban spaces, or even when they reject those acts and seek instead
to hold fast to more "intimate" indigeneities (Canessa 2012), those forged in
the village rather than in the transnational mediasphere—in all of these cases,
what they are doing is nothing more nor less than what Isbell described them
as doing some forty years ago: they are defending themselves. And to the
extent that these efforts are directed toward the maintenance of sounds that
are deeply intertwined with a distinctive indigenous habitus, they also seek to
defend their sounds.

Of course the kind of cultural autonomy that chimaycha musicians have
achieved, as incarnated in the institution of Radio Quispillaccta and its parent NGO ABA, brings its own kinds of challenges. Like other communities,
indigenous communities are riven by philosophical differences and outright
factionalism. All new forms of social, economic, and cultural capital become
ready grist for the mill of intracommunity conflict, and control over the idea
of indigeneity is no exception. The station's attempt to shepherd chimaycha
musicians toward traditionalism, which was successfully resisted by the performers and audiences that the station had convoked, is one example of such
conflict, but not all conflicts are resolved so easily. As noted in chapter 5, many
of Quispillaccta's comuneros (to say nothing of neighboring chuschinos) mis-
trusted ABA's motives over the 2000s and 2010s. Some were Protestant funda-
mentalists who saw the organization's promotion of Andean religious custom
as backsliding toward damnation. Other observers, versed in Peru's repertoire
of financial malfeasance, interpreted the NGO's activities as a naked power
grab. According to this view, people associated with the powerful Machaca
family had manipulated indigenous identity politics, with all its potential to
attract international funding and state resources, only to secure their own
enrichment.

Charges like these are routinely attached to successful NGOs in the Peruvian Andes, and there is no reason to believe that they are accurate in the case
of ABA, but still they circulated among comuneros discontent with the direc-

tion of the community's politics. By the mid-2010s, observers grounded such claims by pointing at ABA's apparent influence in the community's proposal to create a new indigenous district (described above in chapter 5). Pitched as an advance for indigenous quispillacctinos, who would achieve cultural and economic autonomy from the mestizo district capital of Chuschi, the project certainly seemed to benefit the community's Cachi-side barrios at the severe expense of its Pampas-side barrios. For it proposed to divide the community in two, granting the Cachi-side barrios not only the title District of Quispillaccta but also control over the ample water resources that spring from Cachi-side puna lands. The tensions generated by this project were omnipresent over the 2013–14 year. They depressed attendance at chimaycha shows, since many partisans were loath to encounter rivals from the other side; the UNSCH's quispillacctino student organization split in two over the issue, at least temporarily; and, most memorably for me, they nearly led to a melee during one rainy-season community meeting in the courtyard outside Radio Quispillaccta's studios. Angry voices penetrated the broadcast booth, and the DJs on duty leaped up to try to get a glimpse at such unusually public community discord. As of December 2017, the situation had become markedly worse from the point of view of the Pampas-side communities. The project seemed close to fruition, despite their appeals to authorities at every level of government in the form of documents that specified the various kinds of cultural and material dispossession that their barrios would suffer in the process of the new district's creation. Discouraged residents expressed bafflement at the power that the Cachi-side barrios were poised to acquire—for their new district would control not only Quispillaccta's water sources but also those of Ayacucho City, which depends upon the Cachi River for some of its capacity. Few, however, had any doubt that ABA's funding sources and its conversancy with the mechanisms of Peruvian politics should be credited with the project's probable realization.

On another level, it might be noted that Radio Quispillaccta's success, and that of chimaycha more broadly, represented the establishment of a beachhead within Peru's public sphere but not the achievement of indigenous parity with Ayacucho's mestizo community. The city's circuits of communication continued to act with relative independence and to address different audiences, meaning that the internal effervescence of the chimaycha public might have little impact on those who were not directly included, and especially not on the local elite. As of 2017, businesses in Ayacucho's city center continued to program artists representative of the city's mestizo huayno style in restaurants aimed at tourists, local businessmen, and other elite or middle-class audiences. Here once again, chimaycha music's ongoing transformation provides

EPILOGUE

one way to evaluate the possibilities and limitations of indigenous popular culture as a vehicle for social transformation. The style's conversion into an urban-popular style, commensurate with the products of the national huayno industry, certainly provided a means to foster and audibilize communities that were otherwise intangible. But audibility is not readily translatable into power, and only time will tell whether chimaycha music moves, with its patrons, into a position of greater power and visibility.

Despite such caveats there was little doubt, as of late 2017, that the style had provided opportunities undreamed of by previous generations of chimaycha performers. The style had transcended many, if not all, limitations of geography and social community and seemed on the verge of becoming absorbed into the national huayno scene as a representative style of Quechua-speaking Ayacuchanos. Within the city, relative oldtimers like David Galindo continued to amass ever-greater performing opportunities, and newcomer Judith Ccollahuacho had become a stable artist on the roster of the Daxi Corporation, performing alongside major singers from other styles in a way that implied a new sort of parity between them. William Pacotaype organized caravans of artists who traveled to cities like Cusco and Ica, where the style was becoming unexpectedly popular among communities with no connection to the District of Chuschi. Inevitable challenges to chimaycha's popularity loomed, given the inevitable cycle of stylistic ascendancy and exhaustion that governs popular music the world over. In the case of Ayacucho, the llaqtamaqta style associated with the District of Chungui, a relatively unknown music from an even more remote and more indigenous province, was growing in popularity. According to Marco Tucno, no fewer than three separate groups had appeared at once, playing to growing audiences around Ayacucho City. They had even approached him to craft respectably high-quality instruments, a request that resulted in an innovation—Marco's design of a new instrument, halfway between the bandurria traditionally associated with the style and the sturdier mandolin, in a process of instrumental hybridization that echoes the development of the chinlili.

Of course alongside such outside business opportunities Marco maintained his commitment to chimaycha music and to his own ideas about balancing a respect for tradition with the promise of new aesthetics. With one ear planted firmly to the ground, he had become convinced that chimaycha was poised to become big business in Lima, and he was positioning himself for that eventuality. With Los Chikitukus on apparently permanent hiatus, he had organized a new group, drawn mainly from within his own extended family, to disseminate compositions, arrangements, and musical principles that he had long encouraged other groups to develop. These included tunes like "Rosalinaschay," a song he had learned as a boy and had never managed to get recorded by any of his associates, but also songs of his own authorship. Dubbed Dinastía Tucno (Tucno Dynasty), the band featured his sister Reny as lead vocalist, his son as guitarist, himself on chinlili, and it had traveled to Lima in November 2017 to make a recording. The CD was not slated for release until Mother's Day 2018, but two videos had been placed on YouTube by way of advance promotion, and Marco encouraged me to seek out the video for "Rosalinaschay." As expected, the song was an arrangement of traditional chuschino melodies and Marco's own verses, accompanied by a mix of electric instruments and traditional chinlili. Tellingly, however, the videos marked a notable departure from chimaycha videos past. Not only was it superior in terms of production values, with high-quality video and overhead drone shots; it featured the performers in the rural lands of Chuschi District but also dancing on the beaches of Lima as waves washed in over their ankles. When we spoke of this, Marco pitched the images as a mix of marketing savvy and social realism. Everyone, he said, films the same images, in the same locations, within Chuschi District, and it seemed imperative to provide something different and eye-catching. More important, however, it was also true that Chuschi, like most Andean communities, was as much a part of Lima as it was of Chuschi itself. More people of chuschino descent resided in the national capital than in the village. Why not, he asked, take a page from the videos of Lima-based huayno artists and fill the space of the capital with the traditions of those who actually lived there? What use was the videographic pretense that chimaycha resided in the highlands when it was just as fervently appreciated by highland settlers in the city?

Marco's position on the reception of chimaycha in Lima was not purely theoretical, for the style had become as popular among the national capital's chuschino migrant community as it was in the city of Ayacucho. It was impossible, he said, to attract the musicians who backed his recording to live in the city of Ayacucho, given the regular gig money they could make in Lima. Even during its brief visit to record, the group had found some half-dozen opportunities to perform at occasions ranging from religious festivals to marriage celebrations. These shows had given him an opportunity to gauge the fervent reception of the music his band was making, a judgment that continued to revolve around the conventions outlined in chapter 6. Chuckling fondly at their perdurability, he told me of a venue in which the band provoked an especially intense response from the attendees. The sung verse in question, repurposing age-old verses familiar to generations of chuschinos, addressed the sun and moon, asking whether they look upon the speaker's mother and father, and implying that the speaker herself is unable to do the same; they finish by

EPILOGUE

expressing the desire to become the wind so as to travel and reunite with the long-lost parents, however momentarily. The song caused many attendees to burst into tears, Marco said, people who had probably fled the highlands and their own parents, perhaps decades ago, never to see them again. One woman, however, expressed herself with particular clarity within the conventions of chimaycha performance. Beginning at the very back of the venue, Marco said, she gradually danced her way to the front until she stood before his sister Reny, tears streaming down her face—at which point she offered the singer a drink from her beer.

Acknowledgments

It would not have been possible to write this book without the aid of many people who facilitated fieldwork, critiqued ideas in development, and provided other, less definable kinds of support. It is not possible here to specify all the individuals upon whom its successful completion depends, but I would like to single out many whose contributions were especially critical.

In Peru, Marco Tucno, Óscar Conde, and Máxima Machaca spent more time than they needed to helping me to understand chimaycha music and the experiences of their generation. At Radio Quispillaccta, Graciano Machaca provided valuable commentary on the same issues as well as access to the station's activities, where I had ample opportunity to consult with DJs Joel Espinoza, Melecio Llalli, and Miguel Núñez about their activities. Employees of ABA, including Marcela Machaca and Lorenzo Núñez, helped me to understand that institution's activities in great detail. More generally, there are many artists and mediators who spent time speaking with me and accompanying me in various activities around Ayacucho, who merit my thanks, including Julia Barrios, Mario Carhuapoma, María Ccallocunto, Pachi Ccallocunto, Arturo Chiclla, Adrián Conde, Carlos Condori, Marcelina Flores, David Galindo, Miguel Espinoza, Mardonio Huaracc, Alberto Infanzón, Ranulfo Infanzón, Demetrio Leandro, Valeriano Mendoza, Alejandro Núñez, Edilberto Núñez, Jorge Núñez, María Pacotaype, William Pacotaype, Zenaida Paredes, Uriel Salcedo, José Tomaylla, don Marcelino Tomaylla, and Jacinto Tucno. I must also recognize the generosity of Zaida Jimenez and Yúber Cubas, who generously provided comfortable living arrangements in the city of Ayacucho.

More people than is easy to name helped to clarify the ideas that organized my work during the process of its development, but James Butterworth, Jonathan Ritter, Raúl Romero, and Henry Stobart deserve special thanks for their especially close and trenchant engagement. Kiri Miller and Jeff Titon have both provided valuable encouragement and commentary after public presentations, while faculty and students associated with Brown University's Andean Project provided cogent critiques of early chapter drafts—especially Violet Cavicchi, Lauren Deal, Kim Lewis, and Jeremy Mumford. Faculty and student fellows at Brown University's Cogut Center for the Humanities, including Amanda Anderson, Dana Graef, Iris Montero, Adi Ophir, and David Wills, provided especially helpful commentary on the material that later became chapter 7 of the manuscript, in the fall of 2015. So too did Abigail Wood, in her capacity as editor of *Ethnomusicology Forum*, where that chapter was initially published as an article, in 2017. Two anonymous reviewers for the University of Chicago Press also deserve credit for prodding me to clarify some of the content of the manuscript, which has made it much stronger than it would otherwise have been.

I am grateful to have received material support from the Wenner-Gren Foundation, which supported field research in both 2002–3 and 2013–14, and Brown University's Cogut Center for the Humanities, which provided fellowship support for writing in the fall of 2015. Shorter trips to Peru were supported by Brown University Humanities Research Funds, and by funds provided to me via the David Josephson Assistant Professorship in Music. An earlier version of chapter 7 was published in *Ethnomusicology Forum* in 2017 (vol. 25, no. 3), as "The Machine of Sonorous Indigeneity: Craftsmanship and Sound Ecology in an Andean Instrument Workshop," while some of the book's other ideas were initially developed in an article titled "Producing the Andean Voice: Popular Music, Folkloric Performance, and the Possessive Investment in Indigeneity," which appeared in *Latin American Music Review* (vol. 34, no. 1) in 2013. Permission to reprint is hereby gratefully acknowledged. At the University of Chicago Press, editor Elizabeth Branch Dyson and editorial associate Dylan J. Montanari have been unfailingly patient and helpful during the process of the manuscript's completion, and I acknowledge them gratefully. I would like to thank Lynn Carlson, whose superb mapmaking skills are responsible for the map that appears herein as figure 5.

Finally, it is not possible to enumerate the different ways that I have been supported in this endeavor by my wife, Jessaca Leinaweaver, and my son Leo, who provide not only invaluable observations, critiques, and editorial advisement (in one case) but also forms of extra-laboral relief and support that make possible everything else (in both cases).

Online Resources

Many of the things described in this book can be illustrated effectively via online archives and resources. As of January 2018, the following sites were current and provided many useful images, videos, or streaming content that might aid in such illustration.

Photographs

The photographic archive of anthropologist Billie Jean Isbell contains hundreds of images take in the District of Chuschi since 1960. Found at http://isbellandes.library.cornell.edu/, its content can be searched by the numbered identifier associated with each photograph. Especially useful are the following, listed by their content and identifier.

corrals with attached chuqllas (or "estancias") in the puna: ISB_01073, ISB_00218
perfomers playing vigoylas and chinlilis: ISB_00195, ISB_00008, ISB_00289
a Mother's Day performance in a local school, also featuring an early vigoyla: ISB_00281
Jacinto Tucno making a guitar: ISB_00159
the scale of verticality that Andean communities live within, as seen from Quispillaccta: ISB_00210

Videos

Most of the artists referenced in the text have uploaded videos, and sometimes old audio tracks, to YouTube. A list of artists and illustrative videos is provided here, for ease of reference.

Los Chikitukus de Chuschi
"Campesino," https://www.youtube.com/watch?v=cZB-DvcpVtE

Los Aires Chuschinos
"Chuschinita" and "Relojito de oro," https://www.youtube.com/watch?v=u9e-0IsOXos

Dina Paucar
"Madre," https://www.youtube.com/watch?v=6mll0I5-BfA

224 ONLINE RESOURCES

Mario Carhuapoma
"Alcoholchay," https://www.youtube.com/watch?v=FYd7pAIZr5o

Julia Barrios
"Chacollinito," https://www.youtube.com/watch?v=cdD0WzkZCHE

Marcelina Flores
"Chuschinito," https://www.youtube.com/watch?v=Fn7fNtSsF9A

Reny Tucno and Dinastía Tucno
"Rosalinascha," https://www.youtube.com/watch?v=HJwP0YXF-ek

Website

Radio Quispillaccta's broadcast can be streamed via the station's website during broadcast hours: http://www.radioquispillaccta.net/en-vivo.

Glossary

allin kawsay. Literally, good life / good living (Quechua). A term associated with Andean indigenous movements, especially in Bolivia and Ecuador. In general terms, it glosses the idea of human communities living in harmony with nature and with other beings.

Amayni. A place near the plain of *Patario* where residents of barrios within the Pampas River drainage camped with their animals after driving them down from the puna in June and July.

anexo. Barrio (see below); the term *anexo* is used more rarely than *barrio* within Chuschi District.

apu. In indigenous Andean communities, the powerful beings that either reside in or consist of mountain peaks. Often they are described as "gods."

barrio. A small settlement that is considered to "belong" to a different municipality and is politically subordinate to it. In effect, a neighborhood within a larger municipality, though *anexos* may lie very far from the municipality's central neighborhood.

bayeta. A cloth made from sheep's wool, widely used in indigenous communities.

burrier. A person who smuggles illicit drugs, especially cocaine.

centro poblado. Literally, populated center. In the District of Chuschi, the "main" *barrio* of each of the district's communities—its political center, and typically its largest settlement.

comunero. A person who is regarded by an indigenous community as one of its members. Typically someone who participates in the ritual obligations, respects the cultural norms, and maintains relations of reciprocity that govern indigenous life, including the performance of collective labor tasks.

comunidad campesina. Peasant community. The term that became current under the Velasco and Bermúdez governments (1968–80) to designate what had formerly been regarded as *comunidades indígenas.*

comunidad indígena. Indigenous community. An official term that became current under the second Leguía government (1919–30) to designate communities that traced their existence and that of their members to precolonial times, and that were supposed to be granted certain rights and protections on the basis of that status.

cosmovisión. A combination of cosmological beliefs and the customary behaviors or social pat-

226 GLOSSARY

terns that are related to them. The term is associated with indigenous movements throughout Latin America.

chimaycha. The variant of *huayno* music performed in the District of Chuschi and neighboring District of Sarhua, distinguished mainly by the use of the *chinlili* as its dominant accompanimental instrument.

chinlili. A small lute resembling a guitar, featuring eight steel strings in six courses, with the fourth doubled at the octave and the first at the unison.

cholo. Typically, an indigenous person who has moved the city and is held to be in the process of abandoning an indigenous identity, "in progress" toward a *mestizo* identity. Once derogatory, the term is used by many contemporary Peruvians to express a certain pride in or identification with the culture and mores that Lima's migrant community especially has forged over the last several decades.

chumpi. A woven belt worn in indigenous communities.

chuqlla. A small hut like the ones that were typically attached to corrals in the *puna* of Chuschi District and in which pastoralists lived temporarily while herding their animals in different sectors of the community.

chuschino. A person from Chuschi.

crianza. Care or husbandry (Spanish).

criollo. As used in everyday Peruvian parlance, the cultural formation that is associated with the Peruvian coast, and especially with its Eurodescendant elite (despite the fact that many of its manifestations derive partially from Andean, Asian, and especially African antecedents).

cumbia. A "tropical" musical style, relying heavily upon Afro-Caribbean instrumentation and rhythms, that is originally from Colombia but has become popular all over Latin America.

department. A political division in Peru, roughly equivalent to an American state. Each department is subdivided into provinces, and then into districts.

huayno. The most popular music genre in the Peruvian Andes, and the most popular Andean genre in Lima, where its production has been concentrated since the middle of the twentieth century.

indigenismo. An artistic and, to a lesser extent, sociopolitical movement of the late nineteenth and early twentieth centuries, in which nonindigenous Peruvians sought to valorize indigenous peoples and their customs in the hope of aiding their social uplift. It typically involved the creation of highly idealized artworks or elitist arrangements by *mestizo* intellectuals, usually lacking the direct participation of indigenous peoples themselves.

laza. A small cleared patch in the rural countryside that was associated with the performance of the *vida michiy.*

llaqtamaqta. Townboy (Quechua). An indigenous musical style associated with communities in Ayacucho's District of Chungui.

marginal. A person considered to be socially deviant, especially a criminal.

mestizaje. Mixture (Spanish). The process of cultural interaction that generated the "mixed" cultures of Latin American states.

mestizo. Mixed (Spanish). A person who is held to have mixed ancestry, especially indigenous and European ancestry. The term is also applied to the cultural manifestations typical of such people. Within the Andes the connotations of mixed ancestry are less important than the implication of nonindigeneity: the term is typically reserved for relatively powerful people who do not reside in indigenous communities or claim an indigenous identity.

misti. Quechua term for *mestizo.*

oca. An Andean tuber and dietary staple.

GLOSSARY

olluco. An Andean tuber and dietary staple.

paslla. A nighttime custom much like caroling, once associated with Chuschi's *yarqa aspiy*, in which musicians visited houses within the community to sing songs and be rewarded for their entertainments.

Patario. A plain near the *centro poblado* of Quispillaccta, where the community's animals were driven in late June, and which then served as the key site for the practice of the *vida michiy* until mid-July.

pollera. A skirt typically worn by women in the Andes.

Pukawasi. Used in Quispillaccta to denote a place near the plain of *Patario* where residents of *barrios* within the Cachi River drainage camped with their animals after driving them down from the *puna* in June and July.

puna. The cold high-altitude grasslands that are found throughout the Andean region.

qala. Naked or peeled (Quechua). Denotes *mestizos*, or indigenous peoples who have abandoned proper indigenous lifeways—for instance, by refusing to wear indigenous attire—and who therefore lie outside the social boundaries of an indigenous community.

qipakuna. Those from behind [the peak] (Quechua). Used in Quispillaccta to denote resident of communities in the Cachi River drainage, behind the peak that separates that drainage from the Pampas River drainage.

qisarita. An alternate name for *chimaycha*, used mainly by the family of Ranulfo Infanzón.

Quechua. The most widely spoken indigenous language in Andean Peru, especially in the south of the country. The term is sometimes used as an ethnonym, especially by people who do not speak Quechua, and especially in international contexts and forums where global indigenous politics are conducted. Its use as an ethnonym is, for now, severely limited within Peru itself (though not in neighboring Bolivia).

quispillacctino. A person from Quispillaccta.

requinto. A small guitar variant that became very popular in commercial *huayno* music between the 1990s and the 2010s, and that came to stand as the instrumental symbol of that style for many people in Ayacucho.

sapo. Toad (Spanish). A *chinlili* with two small decorative "horns" resembling guitar cutaways.

sinchi. A Peruvian counterterrorism officer. Sinchis were especially feared during the years of the Shining Path–related violence.

sirena. Literally, siren. A nonordinary being that inhabits springs and waterways, held to have the power to fill instruments with musical power.

tankar. A thorny flower that is commonly used as a symbol in Andean songs.

tinya. A small drum held in one hand and played with a stick. The only instrument that is typically played by women in the southern Andes.

varayuq. Staff bearer (Quechua). A holder of one of the political offices that traditionally rotated among members of indigenous communities, whose authority was symbolized by the staff that they bore during their tenure.

vecino. Neighbor (Spanish). Typically used in Andean communities to designate *mestizo* residents.

vida michiy. A nocturnal custom once practiced by indigenous youths in Chuschi District and neighboring areas, in which participants gathered in sites outside their towns to play music, dance, engage in physical and verbal contests, and court one another.

vigoyla. An older word for the *chinlili*, derived from the Spanish term *vihuela*, and still used by some quispillacctinos to refer to the instrument.

wamani. See *apu*, above.

228   GLOSSARY

yachaq. Literally, knower (Quechua), sometimes translated as "shaman." Someone who wields a body of esoteric knowledge.

yarqa aspiy. The canal-cleaning ceremony that happens in indigenous communities throughout the Andes before the beginning of the rainy season, in preparation for watering the fields.

Notes

Prologue

1. As of December 2017, the videos could be found gathered at https://www.youtube.com/channel/UClg41F_XgypsO-bwpLCVVbA.

2. In an article touching upon these same events (2013c) I described Arturo, a man who has been unfailingly generous to me in seventeen years of research on Peruvian music, as a *qala*. Discussed below, this term is generally reserved for people who are not indigenous, or for indigenous people who are deemed to have abandoned customary lifeways and hence their indigenous identities. My characterization was based on readings about the district and conversations that I had had with some chuschinos, filled with disdain for people who fit the bill. Arturo himself had told me ruefully about his upbringing at arm's length from Chuschi's distinctive customs. However, Arturo and his family had, in fact, remained respected members of the indigenous community. In 2013 Marco Tucno would tell me that "there [were] no qalas anymore," that social change had rendered older cultural diacritics less relevant as markers of ethnic identity. My initial characterization was incorrect, even if some chuschinos would agree with it. I deeply regret the error and retract that characterization.

Introduction

1. For more extensive treatments of Peruvian huayno music see Llorens Amico 1983; Ritter 2012; Romero 2001; Montoya et al. 1997 [1987]; Tucker 2013b; Turino 1984 and 1988.

2. Peruvianist scholars have long recognized this refusal of the label *indigenous* and its cognates in the Andes, and it has been powerfully argued that Quechua and Aymara speakers see more value in claiming full enfranchisement as Peruvian citizens than in the meliorist politics involved with adopting the role of ethnicized "cultural Other" (see especially Degregori 2002). Such a perspective, however, scants the pervasive prejudice that has always inhibited the easy adoption of a distinctive ethnic identity. It also ignores the sites and practices in and through which such identities are in fact persistently affirmed. Given this, other scholars have sought to parse the coded languages of ethnic distinction that are actually used in the everyday lives of the people they so name (see de la Cadena 2000; Orlove 1998; Thorp and Paredes 2010; Van den Berghe and Primov 1977), and sometimes to link these matters to music (see especially Romero 2001; Tucker 2013b).

3. Many years ago anthropologist Kay Warren (1998) described a parallel situation in Guatemala, where conservative commentators and postmodernist intellectuals alike undermined indigenous claims to rights and redress by wielding a constructivist understanding of social identity that called into question the very reality of a boundary between indigenous and *ladino* (nonindigenous) Guatemalans—two communities with an enormous store of common customs, yet separated by a gulf of privilege and prestige. This perennial threat to indigenous rights claims has been much discussed and decried among indigenous activists and allies: see Graham and Penney 2014 for an overview.

4. Salazar-Soler similarly describes how indigenous identities are "the object of a valorized appropriation on the part of indigenista and Indianist organizations that see in the figure of the Indian a representative of an ancient culture with a glorious past" (2014:82; see also Alfaro 2005; Azevedo 2009; Cavero Cornejo 2011; Salazar-Soler 2009). This is an accurate enough description of some indigenous activists and fellow-travelers, but such sweeping generalizations slight the very real investment in living culture and continuing marginalization that animates most of what might effectively be described as "indigenous movements."

5. Canessa has similarly maintained that even while we recognize "'strategic essentialisms,' a concern for academic rigor should not blind us to historic injustices. . . . A claim to indigenous identity is at its root quite simply a claim to historical injustice: it is a claim to rights and resources on the basis of long-standing exclusion" (2012:69). See also Lucero 2006 and 2010.

6. Settler elites in Andean cities often considered themselves criollos, but by the late twentieth century the word was overwhelmingly associated with the distinctive culture of Peru's wealthier coastal cities.

7. In de la Cadena's words, the situation is one wherein "being and not being indigenous interpenetrate each other [allowing] some [Andean mestizos] both to claim indigeneity (at least occasionally) and to distance their own condition from Indianness" (2015:21).

8. In addition to the above-cited literatures on race in Peru, especially effective reviews and critiques of mestizaje can be found in Stutzman 1981; Wade 1997 and 2007.

9. De la Cadena (2000), Tarica (2008), and Turino (1993) provide very good critiques of Peruvian indigenismo and its failures. For a considerably more positive counter-reading, see Mendoza 2008.

10. They emerged in neighboring Bolivia and Ecuador, overwhelmingly similar in their demographics and history (see Becker 2012; Colloredo-Mansfeld 2009; Fabricant 2012; Gustafson 2009; Pallares 2002; Postero 2007), and even the Peruvian Amazon, which is characterized by distinctive dynamics that cannot be addressed here (see Greene 2006 and 2009).

11. Salomon (2002) notes that that this program was impractical for many reasons, not the least of which were the essentialist notions of indigenous legitimacy that underlay the proposed norms. Leguía and his peers based their policies on what they "ahistorically assumed to be the twin native essences of traditional rural land tenure: immemorial possession and collective ownership" (Salomon 2002:476–77), overlooking the dynamic and diverse social realities of actual indigenous communities.

12. Naturally, the actual result of this move was to ethnicize the term *peasant*, which is universally associated with indigeneity in the southern Peruvian Andes. As González has noted, "The term comunidad campesina is a political and legal construct. . . . A public servant once told me, 'The government changed the name from indigenous to peasant, but at the end it's the same thing because they treat us like indios [Indians]—or have we stopped being Indians?'" (2011:26).

13. Yashar (2005) has attributed the dearth of indigenous activism over this period between

NOTES TO PAGES 7–18   231

the 1960s and the 1990s to an extraordinary deficit of transcommunity networks and political associational space—consequences of the events I have outlined here.

14. Referring to a 1996 survey taken among district mayors in the Department of Ayacucho, Degregori has provided a striking illustration of this phenomenon: "In countries like Bolivia local authorities identify themselves as Quechuas or Aymaras, in Guatemala as Mayas but here nobody defines themselves as Indians or Quechuas. . . . [When asked about their self-defined identity] they considered it an insult and preferred to identify in occupational terms . . . moreover, they didn't use the term 'peasant' but rather 'agriculturalist' [*agricultor*], because peasant is stigmatized as synonymous with poor, Indian, or servant" (1999:68).

15. The emblematic CONACAMI leader Mario Palacios stated that "nobody in Peru knew these [instruments] existed. Maybe legislators knew, I don't know, but in peasant communities nobody had told us that there was a treaty that could serve as a tool for us" (Poole 2010:30).

16. Especially at issue here was Peru's Law of Prior Consultation, which specified indigenous communities as beneficiaries without reversing the 1960s-era policy that had converted former "indigenous communities" into "peasant communities."

17. See Cánepa Koch 2002; Cánepa Koch and Ulfe 2006; Degregori, Blondet, and Lynch 1986; Gandolfo 2009; García 2013; Greene 2016; Matos Mar et al. 2004; Sánchez León 2014; Tucker 2013a.

18. For discussions of mestizaje or cholo identity, see Alfaro 2006; Portocarrero 2007; Quijano 2014.

19. Such resonance between different domains of reproduction is not confined to the Andes, of course. Mohawk scholar Audra Simpson has made a similar point in her lecture "The Chief's Two Bodies: Theresa Spence and the Gender of Settler Sovereignty" (2014).

20. Alfaro 2006; Cánepa Koch 2010; Llorens Amico 1983; Mendoza 2000 and 2008; Romero 2001 and 2002; Tucker 2011, 2013a, 2013b, and 2013c; Turino 1988, 1990a, and 1993.

21. Excellent reviews of these developments can be found in de la Cadena and Starn 2007; Merlan 2009; and Warren 2005.

22. The foundational work here is Viveiros de Castro 1992. For more recent work on the topic see especially Descola 2013; Kohn 2013.

23. Much of this literature focuses on Bolivia and Ecuador, which placed indigenous parties in national government in the years around the millennium. Peruvian literature on this topic was long dominated, in contrast, by the question of why indigenous movements had failed to emerge. See Lucero 2006 and 2010; Pajuelo Torres 2007; Van Cott 2005; Yashar 2005.

24. The Rio declaration affirmed, in the quincentenary of the Spanish invasion of the Americas, that "indigenous people . . . have a vital role in environmental management and development because of their knowledge and traditional practices. States should recognize and duly support their identity, culture and interests and enable their effective participation in the achievement of sustainable development" (UNCED 1992).

25. Writing of future research possibilities within Latin America, Warren and Jackson noted early on that indigenous politics "are contingent on wider political and economic pressures as well as on local history. Communities with indigenous roots find themselves in very different demographic situations. . . . We can expect that the peoples identifying themselves as indigenous will pursue a variety of struggles and accommodations in different parts of the Americas" (2002:11).

26. Manuel's 1993 work on cassette culture is perhaps the first completely fleshed-out statement of the ideas I gloss here.

232   NOTES TO PAGES 18–26

27. This is a literature that defies easy summary, but besides the works discussed in the text my primary points of reference include C. Allen 2002 [1988]; Brush 1977; Gose 1994; Mayer 2002; Sallnow 1987; Salomon 2004.

28. Canessa's position here resembles that of Gros, who describes the politicized form of identity that Morales represents as that of a culture "reduced to a few parameters selected or invented because of their performativity, as instruments appropriate insofar as they provide an antithesis to whatever is constructed, simultaneously, as the dominant culture, as the Other against whom one has to define oneself" (2000:15).

29. The two positions may not be incompatible, and Canessa recognizes that indigenous leaders are often politically "bilingual," willing and able to articulate and enact different sorts of indigeneity for different audiences.

30. One of the striking things that I have found in speaking with people in Ayacucho is that many do not think of the conflict as a distinctive historical era but rather as continuous with the previous state of affairs—an intensification of the mundane violence that has always surrounded indigenous communities and has flared into bloodshed from time to time. On the deep roots of violence in the Ayacucho region, see Méndez 2005; Stern 1993.

31. In their pioneering work on market women in the Andes, Babb (1989), Bourque and War-ren (1981), and Seligmann (1995) all presented such advancement as a real possibility for female migrants, but they also cautioned that opportunities are leavened by continuing structures of patriarchal control. Women, for instance, have historically tended to move toward lower-paying jobs than men, due to their lack of education and Spanish-language skills, or to work in markets, where it is easier to combine labor in the cash economy with childcare and other household tasks that still fall disproportionately to women. On the notion of patriarchy in the Andes, see note 3, p. 238.

32. Scholars have always observed that gendered differentiation by labor task in Andean com-munities remains more flexible in practice than elicited norms would lead outside interlocutors to believe (see, for instance, Harris 1978). Men may perform household tasks that are ostensibly women's work, while women sometimes perform heavy farm labor, especially when husbands are away (Collins 1986; Paulson 2003). Such flexibility does not, however, change the gendered cod-ing of the tasks themselves. Exceptions to gendered musical practices, including those by which men play instruments and women do not, are virtually unheard of. Such possible exceptions as do exist ratify rather than challenge norms of gender expression. Men, for instance, sometimes cross-dress in festive performance and adopt female characters, but these are understood as temporary liberties permitted by the festive framework. Moreover, in requiring men to act and dress in stereotypically female fashion—affecting girlish voices, wearing skirts and braids, flirt-ing with male audience members or insulting their manhood—they underline the binary gender norms that regulate daily life outside that frame. Nor does the often-observed fact that gender is performative—that it is what an individual *does* that establishes their gender—challenge the firm gender binaries of Andean life (see Canessa 2005). Not only do individual performances proceed according to a rather rigid set of prior expectations that are near-impossible to shed, but they overwhelmingly follow the expectations associated with the sex that individuals are assigned at birth. Exceptions are rarely reported in the literature on Andean life, and where they appear they mostly remain ambiguous, hedged round with vague language that seems to suggest clearly how universally underdiscussed the matter remains (see Van Vleet 2003; Stobart 2006)—indeed, it seems clear that in most of the Andes there are no indigenous words for homosexuality, in-tersexuality, or other nonbinary forms of gender expression (Canesssa 2005), besides strained neologisms that seem to respond to the insistent queries of outside parties. One outstanding

NOTES TO PAGES 26–34   233

exception is provided by Isbell and Barrios Micuylla (2016), who describe a transgender individual who was well-known within the community of Chuschi as a market vendor during the time of Isbell's research there, and who also report *wari* as a term for an individual with both male and female sexual organs. It is nonetheless noteworthy that Isbell provides this description as a means to comment upon the firm assertion, essayed by the Machaca sisters, that there are *no* transgender or homosexual individuals in indigenous communities—aseertions that are indeed, per Isbell and Barrios Micuylla's assertion, "revealing" to the extent that they reveal an everyday approach to the issue in Andean life.

33. It seemed clear to me that the era had passed when a foreign ethnographer might expect to be asked about connections to the CIA, that agency having yielded in importance to the United States Drug Enforcement Agency. More than once I was asked with implied menace about my possible employment by the DEA.

34. It was suggested to me that given a lack of serious oversight in the concert industry, businesses wishing to launder money can simply hold an event and then greatly inflate the number of attendees, thereby providing a ready explanation for cash on hand that is otherwise inexplicable. I cannot comment on the likelihood that this is a real method for laundering money, but I can confirm that the attendance at concerts by major artists in Ayacucho frequently does not seem large enough to cover the costs incurred in hiring them.

35. This is typical of the ethnographic method, and in fact speaking from the point of view of an erstwhile anthropology student, Marco actually advised me continually against interviewing, convinced that everyday conversation was a far more productive route to insight.

36. There are, of course, other examples of ethnomusicological studies that proceed through a comparably intense focus on a small handful of individuals. See, for example, Danielson 1997; Rice 1994; Titon 1988; Levin and Süzükei 2006.

Chapter One

1. Residents of Chuschi District have even consulted the Spanish-language translation of her book *To Defend Ourselves* (1985; trans. 2005), as part of their efforts to revive abandoned customs.

2. Such is the substance of a well-known article critiquing the era's ethnographies, penned by anthropologist Orin Starn (1991), which sparked a lengthy debate in the field of Andean studies about cultural theory and anthropological methods. Arguing that Andeanist anthropologists had ignored ongoing political and cultural change in the region in order to better present a static portrait that fit then-popular structuralist frames of analysis, Starn stridently denounced Isbell's work in particular for missing the imminent rise of Shining Path in the very towns under study. Starn's critique has great merit as a critique of the era's culturalist biases, correctly diagnosing an overemphasis on cultural continuity and isolation rather than interaction and change in the era's Andeanist texts. However, it has been called into question for its highly selective misreading of Isbell's text, which was politically trenchant in its defense of Andean cultural practices that outsiders often dismissed as laughable primitivism, and which hardly presented as static a portrait as Starn's article claimed. For an excellent review that balances the merits of Starn's critique against those of the work that he targeted, see Mayer 1992.

3. Some of these terms may have different meanings in their proper administrative context, and some are archaisms, holdovers from past eras that have lost their technical meanings. However, they are the terms used by locals in everyday parlance, and they are used in the manner indicated here.

4. The binary may be centuries old: in an important study, ethnohistorian Pierre Duviols

234   NOTES TO PAGES 34–37

(1973) draws out its operation in the colonial-era Huarochirí manuscript, a Quechua-language text that appears to detail the uneasy pre-Columbian alliance between two formerly distinct societies, one composed of settled agriculturalists and one of nomadic pastoralists.

5. Seeger's study of Suyá performance (2004) describes a similar process in which formal indigenous moieties become tangible through musical performance. Andean communities have typically been divided similarly, into formal moieties called *ayllus*, usually counterpoising an "upper" to a "lower" ayllu. Chuschi and Quispillaccta were so organized, but their ayllu organization does not appear to map neatly onto the geophysical and musical opposition I describe here.

6. The division between residents of the two river basins may also be traced to more concrete historical matters, for many of Quispillaccta's high barrios were formerly separate vassal communities, located on the territory of a neighboring hacienda. According to the interpretation of some quispillacctinos, they had forged a separate identity by the time of their acquisition by the community of Quispillaccta, with which they never came to feel fully identified (Flórez Salcedo 2012). With respect to terminology for residents of the district's lower reaches, the only term I have heard is *qichwas*, a word that Marco used to refer to chuschinos who came to the high grazing lands to care for the community's communal herds. This is a sort of ethnonym modeled on the Quechua term *qichwa*, which typically indicates the climactic zone that predominates in the low, warm valley bottoms of the Andes and is opposed to the term *puna*.

7. Spanish settlers extracted labor from those communities in exchange for the ostensible gifts of European civilization. In point of fact, processes of political domination and accommodation began earlier, as culturally and linguistically heterogeneous Andean communities came under the rule of pre-Columbian Inca rulers, and before that various predecessors of the Inca themselves.

8. The varayuq system of Chuschi and Quispillaccta was, in fact, abandoned and then revived later, in a diminished form that lacked formerly important offices.

9. As late as the 1970s, only 13 percent of Ayacucho's territory was under cultivation (Isbell 1985:43).

10. They might, for example, help to resist outside intrusions on Chuschi's lands or act as intermediaries in dealings between Quechua speakers and the lettered state. See de la Serna 2012.

11. The disdainful word *qala* could also apply to indigenous people who abandoned the clothing that Chuschi's comuneros customarily wore (Isbell 1985:70–71).

12. In Canessa's gloss, qalas were regarded as "a different kind of people, living in cities and towns and [who] don't have 'proper' relationships with each other or with the spirits of the earth and mountains" (2012:85).

13. Especially to the extent that they created a local patronage system that brought certain indigenous chuschinos into their social circle, Chuschi's mestizos encouraged some comuneros to consider themselves more "Spanish" and cosmopolitan, more allied with the social universe of European and later national authorities, than other indigenous subjects. To this day, even indigenous chuschinos may describe themselves as "more Spanish" in habits and their worldview than quispillacctinos, more apt to speak proper Spanish, to have cultivated equestrian skills, and to get along with urban-mestizo citizens, than their neighbors. Even the term *uqi* (gray or dark in Quechua), sometimes used to refer to quispillacctinos, is considered by some to be a racist idiom through which chuschinos express disdain for quispillacctinos. Meanwhile, quispillacctinos do not hesitate to draw upon age-old stereotypes about lazy and corrupt Europeans, favorably describing themselves as more solidary, hardworking, and continent than the dissolute, fractious residents of Chuschi.

NOTES TO PAGES 37–51

14. These assertions found sustenance in work by Zuidema (1966) and others, who identified in colonial documents firm evidence that the Chuschi River basin was inhabited by two rival ethnic groups at the time of the Spanish invasion. Many quispillactinos claim descent from the Kanas Indians, who are recorded as living in the contemporary territory of their community—an allied group that Inca rulers had resettled from faraway Cusco—with chuschinos claiming descent from the linguistically and culturally distinct Chanka. Given the massive changes in community composition, residence patterns, and other matters, these lines of descent cannot be verified as fact.

15. De la Serna's well-supported claim is that the guerrillas found strong support "in the villages where indigenous peasants perceived that a subversion of their cultural mores had taken place" (2012:12).

16. The Shining Path's official stance on indigenous ethnicity did not prevent its adherents from supporting indigenous cultural manifestations or even instrumentalizing them in the service of fostering revolutionary thought and deed. See Ritter 2002.

17. The discussion in this paragraph is largely synthesized from Isbell and Barrios Micuylla 2016; de la Serna 2012; and Sánchez Villagómez 2007 and 2009.

18. Infanzón was also affiliated with a rival leftist party, and his punishment may have been meted out for that reason.

19. A history penned by quispillacctinos from the Cachi side of the community notes that there had been efforts to cultivate such prosperity as early as 1840 (Múñoz Ruiz and Núñez Espinoza 2006). In that year the community of Quispillaccta acquired the land of the neighboring mestizo hacienda of Santa Catalina (later the barrio of Catalinayocc) and created communal herds to take advantage of the new pasture. These herds later were appropriated for use by the church and were not recuperated until 1973, as the Velasco regime sought to diminish the power of clergy and landlords, returning lands and goods to indigenous communities from which they had been appropriated in the past. It is also possible, per the same text, that the arrival of evangelical Christianity in the 1960s aided in these efforts, as Protestant sects worked to recover community wealth and agency from a Catholic church whose power they sought to undermine.

20. Typically in such a case, the urban dweller pays a community resident to perform the duties in his absence, returning only for protocolar events and important ceremonies.

Chapter Two

1. There was one exception: the village cemetery often hosted the vida michiy as well. Isbell (1985) interprets this curious fact in structuralist fashion, as a topological transformation of the morality that regulates the vida michiy more generally. According to this interpretation, both the puna and the cemetery are spaces "outside" everyday social mores and therefore suitable for the pursuit of the custom, with all its potential for social disorder.

2. Parents in rural Ayacucho, as in many parts of the world, were long reluctant to send daughters to school, since they were expected to manage their households after maturity in any case and presumably did not require the tools thay came with metropolitan education. This meant that they often assumed primary responsibility for herding animals. See Dionisia Espinoza's story below, in chapter 6.

3. In fact, as in many pastoral societies, herd animals were not crucial as sources of meat, dairy products, or even (in the case of alpacas and sheep) wool. These products were sold and provided welcome profits, but animals functioned primary as investments, hard assets that could

be traded in a sudden financial pinch. Families that owned many animals were therefore regarded as "rich" in the terms of the indigenous community, even if they were materially poor in other ways. Marco came from such a family and commented more than once on the impressive size of his father's camelid herds, as well as the enormous high-altitude corrals they had inherited to hold them. His father, he said, owned around 600–800 alpacas, 250–300 sheep, 80–100 horses, and 30 cows.

4. In her work on memory and violence in Sarhua, a town across the Pampas River from Chuschi, González describes connections between landscape, memory, and narrative that echo with remarkable fidelity my experience in eliciting musical histories: "Strolls were a source of inspiration for the storyteller in Sarhua. A path, a rock, a mountain, or a cave could evoke incredible stories. Some involved personal experiences, and others were stories that had been told and retold by everybody's parents and grandparents, an endless chain of storytellers" (2011:18). The stories I heard typically arose in the course of "strolls" that took place purely in the realm of imaginative recall, but the principle is the same.

5. I understand "landscape" here in the sense that has long been used in cultural geography and the social analysis of place: as the cultural process through which a given portion of the earth becomes framed and reified, designated as a meaningful unit, and demarcated from adjacent spaces (see Grimley 2006; Schafer 1977; Tuan 1974; Von Glahn 2003).

6. Impey has developed this point eloquently in her work on ecology and sound in the Maputaland region of South Africa: "Land, nature and kinship are . . . mutually implicated, and it is through this insinuation that notions of physical space and culturally constructed place emerge" (2002:70; see also Norton 2013). That is, the very things and places that count are mediated through social practices, including kinship, political structure, and sound. On the Andes, see Abercrombie 1998; Bigenho 2002; Solomon 2000; Stobart 2006; Turino 1993. An ample literature on Andean pilgrimage also treats such physical pathways as socially significant, while rarely exploring the ecological distinctions that interest me here; see Poole 1988; Sallnow 1987.

7. See also C. Allen 2002 [1988]; Mannheim and Salas 2015. Both studies are focused on the ways that indigenous Andeans cultivate relationships with the nonhuman beings that interanimate their view of the world around them, and both emphasize the continuities of practice that link contemporary with pre-Columbian peoples of the region.

8. Of course Latour's point is that the modern constitution has never fully governed the lives of those at the heart of Western modernity either. The use I make here of his work should not be construed as an endorsement of the perspectivist idea that "Westerners" and indigenous peoples inhabit mutually unintelligible ontological systems.

9. Glossing Anderson's work, Ingold describes the development of an orientation like the one I describe here, asserting that "it is by engaging with these manifold [i.e., human and nonhuman] constituents that the world comes to be known by its inhabitants" (2011:10). See also Ingold 2000.

10. A number of scholars have also begun to investigate such links between music and ecological practice in recent years. Work that I have found particularly useful includes A. Allen 2011; Allen and Dawe 2015; Post 2007; Simonett 2014.

11. Besides the pieces mentioned, outstanding accounts of such "mapping" processes include Basso 1996; Feld 2012 [1982]; Gordillo 2004. Levin and Süzükei (2006) provide a thorough study that is in many ways parallel to what I provide here—however, the processes of natural mimesis that they locate at the heart of Tuvan performance are extremely rare in Andean performance.

12. Meanwhile, music scholars have described practices elsewhere in the Quechua-speaking Andes that are direct parallels to the vida michiy, including the *kashwa* from Peru's Cusco region

NOTES TO PAGES 54–68

(Bolin 2006; Turino 1983) and various cognate practices in highland Bolivia (Arnold 1997; Harris 1978; Stobart 2006).

13. Relevant passages indicating the tone of Isbell's treatment include the following: "Young single people arrange group rendezvous in the [puna], which begin with marathon dancing and drinking and terminate in indiscriminate sexual intercourse" (1985:59). Further: "During the 1970s, competitive group sexual relations, accompanied by intellectual riddling and sung 'duels,' characterized adolescence in the Quechua-speaking communities. . . . These sexual marathons gave young women an elevated status, due to the superior sexual prowess they demonstrated via their capacity to outlast young men during the nighttime rigors of group sex. Young men compensated by forming quasi-military organizations. The boys, who did not yet take part in the 'games,' accompanied and served older boys who had gained the title of 'captain.' . . . The duties of the boys, the 'soldiers,' included bringing alcohol, grabbing hats, and generally supporting the captains during sexual and verbal battle" (Isbell 1997:280).

14. Speaking of comparable practices in Andean Bolivia, Stobart notes similarly that "initial amorous interest during feasts or markets often leads to sexual rendezvous between couples on the hillsides" (2008:85), suggesting that perhaps the vida michiy and its cognate practices elsewhere are not the debauched free-for-alls they have sometimes been made out to be.

15. There are, in turn, two possible ways to construe this interpretation of historical contingency. One is to say that Isbell's report represents the extravagant acts of rebellious youths whose sexual mores were part of a more general challenge aimed at contesting elders' standards of "normal" behavior. La Serna's work suggests a broader climate in the community that is congruent with this reading. A second possibility is the opposite interpretation: that Isbell's report represents a norm that was in force until the 1960s and 1970s, after which things changed. In this scenario, the generational experiences of Marco, Óscar, and their peers, with the far lower rates of sexual promiscuity they observed, would represent the very sort of turn away from traditional values and pactices that La Serna's interlocutors lamented.

16. It is a truism in Andean ethnography that full adult status comes with the establishment of a married household. See, for example, Collins 1986; de la Cadena 1995; Harris 1978.

17. This tie between male instrumental performance and romance has been reported in indigenous communities across the entire southern Andes. See Harris 1978 and Stobart 2008 for similar accounts from Andean Bolivia, and Turino 1983 for the Peruvian region of Cusco.

18. According to patrilocal kinship practice in the Quechua-speaking communities of the Andes, women moved to the home of their partner's family once the determination to marry had been made, initiating a period of cohabitation that typically anticipated legal marriage by some years (see Van Vleet 2008).

19. In their study of Quechua-language song in rural Ayacucho, the Montoyas note that the same trick may be played in the opposite direction, such that a single girl "leaves a ring, shawl, or handkerchief for the man she's chosen, taking care that it won't be found by others. The pledge is simple: he who finds the article will be HER partner" (1997 [1987]: 49).

20. Both trends described here—increased alcohol consumption due to easier access, and changes in the use of floral emblems—were also observed in the same era by anthropologist Denise Arnold (1992) among young indigenous performers of huayno in Bolivia.

238   NOTES TO PAGES 73–77

Chapter Three

1. Don Marcelino gave no titles for these songs, and in fact most chimaycha songs are known by their first line. I have followed this format here and given them titles for ease of reference. It might be noted, further, that Quechua song is extremely difficult to translate well, and the rather prosaic, literal translations I've provided here do not capture the elliptical elegance of the originals. Indeed, though I speak Quechua well enough to understand these songs, elementary conversation, and radio broadcasts, I have relied here and elsewhere on the Spanish-language glosses that Óscar provided for me, which filled out implications that I would never have appreciated otherwise. The translations to English, here and throughout, are my own.

2. Seeger (2004) makes a remarkably similar speculation about old field recordings he had made with the Suyá and later published, recordings that were marred by a mistaken recording speed and a corresponding pitch shift. When he later played the deep, ponderous version for the community, they nevertheless claimed that the recording represented a lost mode of proper virile performance.

3. Some scholars have made the compatible argument that precolonial structures of Andean egalitarianism were partially disrupted by the Spanish expectations of male leadership, such that state-oriented demonstrations of male dominance are elsewhere inflected by older and deeper patterns of balance inside indigenous communities (see Seligmann 2004:5). In related fashion, still others seek to qualify the notion of thoroughgoing masculine dominance by documenting how women exert agency behind the scenes, as it were, through rumor, gossip, and household persuasion aimed at convincing men to transmit their concerns in public (see C. Allen 2002 [1988]; Van Vleet 2008). My own position is that a situation in which women's range of opportunities is structured so as be narrower than that available to men, and in which female political or economic activity requires male consent, shows precisely the kind of gendered hierarchy that is commonly denoted by the term *patriarchy*. Further, I do not accept the proposal that a woman's power within other domains is an effective egalitarian counterweight to the univocal power that men wield in public meetings, where community business is discussed and priorities determined. It may be true that "'Western' criteria have incentivized feminist scholars to privilege political meetings over other occasions for public discourse, valorized by women themselves" (Arnold 1997:47). However, the power to intervene within the realm of public politics, and thereby define what counts as a matter of collective importance as opposed to a private crisis, is power indeed (Fraser 1990; Lukes 1974). Andean scholars have not overlooked this fact, with Harris insisting early on that "representing the whole Laymi society in terms of the relationship between husband and wife in a single household . . . leaves out of consideration the significance of men and women as social groups. For example it is when men act as a group that the asymmetry of the gender relationship is revealed" (Harris 1978:38). Finally, however Western the public-private distinction may be, it is a norm that indigenous communities under colonial rule, and in neocolonial circumstances within modern states, have been required to confront and incorporate.

4. Scholars of gender in the Andes have sometimes explored in more subtle detail the possible range of gender expression in indigenous communities (see especially Canessa 2005), but their portraits do not really change the underlying binary system, nor do they suggest that alternative gender expressions might effectively challenge its terms. For instance, de la Cadena's admonition (1995) that age, gender, and race all intersect to inflect individuals' identities and their access to power—such that younger men are "feminized" before their more powerful elders, and indigenous women are "racialized" before male peers who can more easily achieve recognition

NOTES TO PAGES 77–87

as mestizos—is well taken but only shows how forcefully gender distinctions are lived by Andean women and men.

5. Individual gender performances overwhelmingly follow the expectations associated with the sex that those individuals are assigned at birth, and reference in Andeanist literature to non-normative adoption of gender roles is parsimonious at best. Such exceptions as do exist remain ambiguous, hedged round with vague language that seems to suggest how underdiscussed the matter remains (see Van Vleet 2003; Stobart 2008). It is not even clear that there is a firm boundary between "constructivist" and "essentialized" notions of gender in Andean communities. Several authors have discussed local practices and beliefs that, taken together, suggest a widespread belief that male and female identities are cultivated in children before and after birth, thereafter becoming a core facet of their identities. Arnold and Yapita (1996), for example, describe the creation of proper male "heads" and female "hearts" through the feeding of different foods to growing children, while Valderrama and Escalante (1997) talk about swaddling newborn babies in the clothing of ancestors whose gender matches the genital sex of the babies.

6. Scholars have always observed that gendered differentiation by labor task in Andean communities remains more flexible in practice than elicited norms would lead outside interlocutors to believe. Men may perform household tasks, like weaving, that are ostensibly women's work, while women perform agricultural labor, such as placing seeds in plowed ground, and even heavy farm labor on occasion (Collins 1986; Harris 1978; Paulson 2003). However, these exceptions tend to be driven by circumstances, such as male migration or the death or sickness of a spouse, and other emergent demands. Given this, the gendered coding of the tasks themselves does not really change.

7. Many of the tasks that make for a successful life in an indigenous community, including required participation in communal labor, are premised on the participation of a household, not an individual. A single man clearly cannot mobilize the requisite forces as easily as a married man.

8. Isbell has essayed the idea that androgyny, and not marked maleness or femaleness, is the default category of an Andean gender system (1997). In this reading a male-female binary develops as an important distinction upon adolescence and then persists throughout adult married life, until the onset of old age and a return to androgyny. This interpretation has not featured in my conversations with people from the same communities: however, this might be explained by the fact that those conversations centered on a practice that has been associated precisely with adolescence and the onrushing urgency of establishing gendered identity.

9. None of this is to deny the gendered violence that does indeed dog Andean communities (see Van Vleet 2008), as it does most communities on earth. It is, however, to say that those are not necessarily reflected in this particular tradition of competitive sexual wordplay.

10. There is an exception at the end of each verse and in the instrumental runs that fall between verses, where an E minor tonality is produced by stopping the fourth string to produce an E, thereby outlining an inverted E minor chord (GBE) in the three bass strings.

11. In performance this eight-and-two-sixteenths pattern is delivered with remarkable rhythmic variation, sometimes approaching a triplet instead. Stobart (2006) claims that in Bolivian communities the rhythmic values more typically approximate a ratio of 3:2:2, and anecdotally (i.e., in the absence of sustained analysis) this feels correct to me for rural Peru as well.

12. It is possible, for instance, that older performers were already used to harmonizing, or to making do with instruments that produced clashing pitches, when they found themselves performing with peers bearing differently sized guitars (cf. Turino 1990b).

13. In 2017 Marco told me that some ensembles played in parallel 4ths and others in parallel 5ths.

14. See Turino on the indigenous charango in Cusco (1983, 1984), Romero on the *huaylas* of the Central Peruvian Andes (2001), and Stobart on the concepts of *tara* and *q'iwa* in highland Bolivia (1994, 2006).

15. Pachi Ccallocunto (see chapter 6 below), speaking from the point of view of his group's musical director, told me that the relevant aesthetic revolved not so much around sheer volume as around the ability to deliver words at volume, with precision. This is as much as to say, however, that performers tend to evaluate singers by asking whether she can manage to produce a lot of sound while retaining clear diction.

16. I heard nearly the same words from other chuschinos and quispillacctinos, including Oseas Núñez, Ranulfo Infanzón, Graciano Machaca, and Valeriano Mendoza.

17. Turino described this belief many decades ago (1983), but Stobart has provided the most complete recent account: "Men magically tune their instruments at remote springs, waterfalls or rocks inhabited by water spirits. Players visit these dangerous, but powerful, enchanted musical beings known as sirinu (or sirina) late at night, leaving offerings alongside their instruments, whose sound will then become enchantingly beautiful and irresistibly attractive to girls. These various traditions highlight the ferocious competition between young men to acquire the intimate and privileged role of accompanist to desired female singers" (2008:85).

18. Recordings are not the only means through which such a consciousness may be developed: song competitions, which were already a feature of life in Chuschi District before the composition of "Yutuchay," may have the same effect on compositional craft.

19. Lott's reading of Howlin' Wolf's performances in fact raises the notion that his boasts may not be bluffs and suggests that the power of the performance rests on the ambiguity. Chimaycha songs seem more transparently to have resided in the realm of bluff, not least because they unfolded in live contexts where such bluffs were traded between actors who competed to outdo one another.

20. See Harvey 1993:130–33 for a strongly discrepant portrait of drunken youthful sexual activity and its relation to gender equity. Harvey reports complaints from women in Cusco that such practices are often not consensual, despite masculine ideologies about the meaning of female drunkenness; nor are they necessarily free from sanction, since some men may take to punishing wives later in life for what they describe as wayward youthful practices—premarital unfaithfulness, as it were.

21. It is worth considering the proposal, made eloquently by Arnold (1992) and echoed by many other scholars of Andean life, that weaving and song are modes of feminine discourse whose weight is equal to the public political discourse of men—a fact that would escape Western scholars conditioned to approach political activity in the public sphere as the only form of power worth the name. It is indeed possible, per Femenías (following James Scott), that such modes of discourse may matter more within indigenous communities, precisely because they are opaque to outside observers with suspect motives (2005:14–15).

Chapter Four

1. My use of the term *register* relates to the rather technical way in which sociolinguists use the term, but here I mean only to suggest a musical cognate of its everyday meaning, as (per Merriam-Webster) "any of the varieties of a language that a speaker uses in a particular social context."

NOTES TO PAGES 103–118 241

2. This is a literature almost too voluminous to cite. However, I have been guided in my thinking by the excellent reviews or theoretical musings by Askew 2002; Bendix 1997; Filene 2000; García Canclini 1995; Harker 1985; Hobsbawm and Ranger 1992 [1983]; Rowe and Schelling 1991; A. Smith 1986; Turino 2000; Whisnant 1983.

3. For full reviews of Andean migration and its social consequences, see Cánepa Koch 2010; Degregori, Blondet, and Lynch 1986; Gandolfo 2009; Matos Mar et al. 2004; Tucker 2013a.

4. For fuller background on the rise of the social sciences in Ayacucho, see Millones, Ochatoma, and Gamarra 2007; Degregori 1997.

5. "You will never make colonialism blush for shame by spreading out little-known cultural treasures under its eyes" (Fanon 2001 [1959]: 265).

6. In fact scholars of the Andes have been perennially attentive to such negotiations. They have shown how indigenous performers adopt a contrived traditionalism in the pursuit of concert fees and contest prizes (Solomon 2015), how deference to outsiders' stereotypes can be a self-aware move to gain leverage in debates over political inclusion (Mendoza 2008), and how musical changes advocated by elite intellectuals become incorporated as treasured markers of indigenous distinction (Turino 1993).

7. Degregori and Sandoval (2008) provide a general review of Peruvian anthropology that traces such an arc from "speaking for" to "speaking with."

8. For accounts of the UNSCH's reopening, see also Cavero Carrasco 2012; Degregori 1997.

9. In 2017, after reading Isbell's 1997 account of the vida michiy and rejecting it as an inadequate account of his own experiences, Marco Tucno speculated aloud about whether the qalas of Chuschi might have had their own vida michiy, one that was conducted without the presence of indigenous neighbors. It is possible that some attributions of Infanzón's practices by other people relate to such a thing.

10. Alberto Infanzón, who participated in the recording at the age of thirteen or fourteen, told me that it was not actually *recorded* in Lima; rather, a transfer was made from a cassette that Infanzón sent to the company from Ayacucho.

11. These considerations are a part of Turino's framework for understanding different modes of musical performance, as described above. For more specific considerations of recording consciousness, see H. S. Bennett 1980; Middleton 1990.

12. The term *vigoyla* is a Quechua-language rendering of the Spanish *vihuela*, a term first applied to Iberian lutes of the Renaissance and which survives as the name for some Latin American descendants, most notably the small strummed guitar used in mariachi performance.

13. Such photos can be found in the archive of Billie Jean Isbell, available at the Cornell website: http://isbellandes.library.cornell.edu/.

14. It is possible that the smaller chinlili was influenced by other small guitar variants that were played throughout the region. Marco, for instance, remembered the charangos brought to Chuschi by students from nearby Pampa Cangallo, where that instrument is favored in performance. However, nobody spoke to me specifically about such influences on the instrument's design.

15. These sorts of events are also documented in Isbell's archived photos from the era.

16. "Sociodrama" refers to didactic dramatic programs, much like educational soap operas.

17. Gavilán left to take up a fellowship in Holland and later gained tragic renown as a victim in the Uchuraccay Massacre—a turning point in the violence era. See Mayer 1992.

18. In their history of the UNSCH, Castillo Melgar and Cueto Cárdenas (2010) provide some valuable statistics related to enrollment. Such statistics should be treated with care, since they list students by province and region of origin rather than ethnicity. However, given the minuscule

numbers of mestizos who resided in many rural provinces, some of the numbers can be taken as strong indicators of a rising student population of indigenous origin—especially in tandem with the oral testimonies of people like Tucno and his peers. For instance the sparsely populated province of Cangallo, which contained (and still does) both an overwhelming indigenous majority and the District of Chuschi, sent 58 students in 1968 and 485 in 1978, respectively representing 4.5 percent and 6.7 percent of all students at the university—which itself had grown from an initial class of 228 nonindigenous students in 1959, to host 6,095 students overall in 1980. There was a significant drop in students from Cangallo by 1988, when the university enrolled 152 people from that province, representing but 2 percent of the overall population—a drop that can surely be traced in part to the effects of the violence in the region.

19. The name owes, according to Marco, to the euphony between the Quechua word *tuku* (owl) and the family name borne by Emilia, Marco, and later other members as well.

20. The Montoyas exaggerated only slightly when they claimed in their contemporaneous collection of Quechua-language music that "political songs, by which we mean pamphleteering songs, or musical flyers by university students, do not exist. So-called 'protest' or 'popular' song,' made 'for the people' from outside and above makes no sense to the . . . women and men of the Andes" (Montoya at al. 1997 [1987]: 77).

21. This parallels the process of regional differentiation that had organized production in the mass-commercial huayno industry for decades: see Tucker 2013b, Turino 1988.

Chapter Five

1. In Quechua, the first-person inclusive plural pronoun *ñuqanchik* is used to indicate that a statement's subject includes "I the speaker, you the listener(s), and perhaps others of the same group." By contrast, the first-person exclusive plural pronoun *ñuqayku* indicates that the statement's subject includes "I the speaker, others of the same group, but *not* you the listener."

2. See García 2005 for a somewhat similar claim, centered on bilingual education rather than music.

3. Unless otherwise noted, all subsequent references to the words of Marcela Machaca are drawn from this 2014 interview.

4. A good introduction to the thinking of Marcela Machaca, and to the tenor of ABA's activities in general, can be found in Machaca 2007.

5. The yarqa aspiy, or canal-cleaning festival, is a prime example of the water's sociopolitical centrality. Despite the brevity of my mention of the practice in chapters 2 and 3 above, the festival is a major event in the life of indigenous Andean communities, a centerpiece of the agricultural year as well as a prime occasion for ratifying the social and cultural ties that bind.

6. Insofar as the Quechua-speaking public stands in opposition to a putative Peruvian "mainstream" that is entirely organized around the Spanish language, it might be better regarded as a counterpublic (Fraser 1990): however, processually there is little distinction between these two formulations, and I use *public* for the sake of clarity.

7. Note that the participatory aspects of this need not be significant, or even real, for a public to be effective as such: what matters is the feeling of being addressed as a part of a community.

8. This is in many respects the same thing that Raymond Williams had in mind when he coined the notion of an emergent "structure of feeling" (1977).

9. After the arrival of FM radio in the 1980s, with its clearer signal and its cachet of technological and cultural superiority, most stations in Ayacucho moved to that band and left the AM

NOTES TO PAGES 134–156

airwaves virtually unoccupied (see Tucker 2013b). The rural region was, after all, not regarded as a significant target for the urban advertisers whose revenue supported the stations. Those stations that did remain on the AM band, then, were stations with a different kind of interest in rural Peru—La Voz de Huamanga, which maintained a political mandate to serve peasant communities, and various evangelical stations, which targeted Ayacucho's countryside aggressively during and after the violence (see Scarritt 2013).

10. The term *cosmovisión* is not very familiar to English speakers, but it is so widely used in indigenous circles, and especially in Spanish-language circles, that it is not easy to specify its origins or point to key sources. With respect to the way that it is used by Quispillaccta's activists, see Rengifo Vásquez 2010; Valladolid and Apffel-Marglin 2001.

11. It is noteworthy that many indigenous scholars within North America, or North American colonies, have also challenged this schema of identitarian purification, charging that it fits poorly with everyday practices of kin- and community-making among their own peoples. See especially Sturm 2002; Kauani 2008; Tallbear 2013.

12. See, for example, Conklin 1997; Ginsburg 1991; Himpele 2008; Rekedal 2014; Scales 2012; Turner 1991; Wortham 2013; Zamorano Villareal 2017.

13. Fascinating work has documented the use of indigenous radio in lowland South America (Bessire 2012), Australia (Forde, Foxwell, and Meadows 2009; Fisher 2016), and even neighboring Andean countries (Hornberger and Swinehart 2012; A. O'Connor 2006), but not in Peru. Furthermore, except for Swinehart, who touches upon Aymara-language hip-hop, all of this research scants music in favor of other communicative modes. For work on indigenous media within the Andes, see Stobart (2008, 2010, and 2011).

14. According to her, the very rules of the indigenous community, the *ley comunal*, had been altered so as to demand that returnees to the community dress in traditional attire—if not a full complement of traditional clothing, then at least the highly recognizable embroidered hats. I was not able to verify this claim, but it is one that I heard from a great number of quispillacctinos and chuschinos, suggesting that it has the force of social pressure, if not law.

15. The station actually won a 2001 prize from UNESCO's International Programme for the Development of Communication, recognizing its work to support rural development and Quechua language vitalization.

16. Peru's 1993 constitution and a later land law passed in 1995 abolished rights that communities had enjoyed over their natural resources, as well as the inalienability of collective lands. Much later, in 2006 and 2008, the García administration passed more effective legislative decrees to facilitate these controversial measures. Though those laws were repealed in 2008, efforts to implement such laws have continued, and have continued to be the subject of indigenous protest. See Hogue and Rau 2008:289–90.

17. "Amor amor (Mi propuesta)" is actually a song, not an artist—one of the most successful Ayacuchano mestizo huaynos of all time.

18. Llaqtamaqta is a related genre from the Ayacuchano province of La Mar—not coincidentally, another region with a reputation for indigenous traditionalism.

Chapter Six

1. Given the instability of racial and ethnic identification in Peru, Lima's demographics are difficult to characterize in precise terms. However, the city's official population grew from 533,600 in 1940, on the cusp of the migrant boom, to almost 6.3 million by the year 2000 and reached

9,752,000 in 2017. It is safe to say that nearly all of the growth owes to migration from the Andes, to a lesser extent from the rural provinces of the coast, and to an even lesser extent from those of the lowland rainforest. Simply stated, an overwhelming percentage of Lima's population claims descent from ancestors born and raised in the Andes, and most of those people can trace their Andean roots to people who arrived to the capital within the last three or four generations.

2. On Dina Paucar, her colleagues, and their links to Peru's emergent neoliberal nationalist narrative, see Butterworth 2014 and 2017; Tucker 2013a, 2013b, and 2013c; Vich 2009.

3. For some accounts that consider the elite uptake of lo cholo and its symbols, see Clayton 2010; Montero Díaz 2016.

4. For a slightly different interpretation see Harvey 1993, which explores better than any other account how the precise behaviors that attend Andean intoxication relate to indigenous identity, especially when they are deployed during community-level fiestas. She focuses on rhetorical performances of pain and frustration, arguing that they reveal cracks in the community identity that comuneros presented so solidly while sober and that they therefore testify to the conflictive work of maintenance involved in sustaining that fractious sense of identity. My reading builds on hers, by emphasizing the fact that people not only lament their Indian status and their social precarity but also care for people who lament those things—a matter observed but not developed in Harvey's account (see p. 123). I argue that these quasi-ritualized techniques of care repair solidarity and foster the kind of fellow-feeling that amounts to a sense of shared identity, inasmuch as they are also performances of empathy.

5. My assumptions about emotion here are largely informed by now-classic anthropological work on the topic, including Lutz 1996; Lutz and Abu-Lughod 1990; Lutz and White 1986; Myers 1988. However, it also resonates strongly with the more recent work of Sarah Ahmed (2004), whose account likewise focuses on the relation between the cultural construction of emotion, the embodied enactment of emotive states, and the alignment between emoting individuals—an alignment that helps to reify communities of emotional practice as communities, while establishing distinctions between them and other communities.

6. There is, in fact, ample precedent for serious study of the beverages that the Western temperance movement stigmatized as "alcohol," and the role of ethylic commensality in chimaycha consumption is familiar from many other contexts (Gefou-Madianou 1992). So too is its distinctive "technique du corps" (Mauss 1950 [1936]), encompassing serving order and quantity, proxemics, and bodily carriage, all of which can be manipulated to communicate feelings and intentions (Dietler 2006:236; see also Manning 2012). Speaking of the Andean context, Saignes has argued eloquently that the pathologization of indigenous alcohol use has, ever since the early days of European colonization, served the cause of ethnic domination more than that of public health. Church authorities, for instance, used condemnatory language about "drunkenness" in an attempt to control indigenous festivals that escaped their power. Elsewhere authorities and everyday mestizo citizens made styles of alcohol consumption into one more shibboleth separating decent Europeans and criollos with properly private drinking habits from their subjects, who had inherited customs of public, communitarian drinking and the expectation that shared intoxication was key to the sustenance of community bonds (see also Harvey 1993:118). In this situation the person who "abuses" rather than simply uses alcohol "is always the neighbor, the 'other' who doesn't know 'how to drink' [and] the use of the term 'drunkenness' to describe autochthonous practices of inebriation reveals the level of incomprehension and disgust the Conquistador bore toward the 'Other'" (Saignes 1993:12). Nor was this situation improved in the nineteenth century, when alcohol became "a victim of its monopolization by medical discourse"

NOTES TO PAGES 159–167

(Saignes 1993:18), which read certain forms of drinking as evidence of continued savagery and others as reasonable entertainment, without establishing clear and culturally sensitive criteria for distinguishing between the two.

7. Long ago Heath noted that "practically every [Andean] ethnography alludes to drinking and drunkenness" (1987:25), and the trend has hardly abated (Castillo Guzmán 2002). It has also been widely noted that drinking occasions are plentiful as well as intensive, especially in past years, with Harris estimating that Aymara men in highland Bolivia "may spend at least thirty days per year in full-time ritual drinking" (1978:33)—a situation that can foster domestic conflict, as women are seldom entitled to such a large number of festive evenings and instead often find themselves dealing with the consequences (see also Bourque and Warren 1981; de la Cadena 1995).

8. See especially Vich 2009. Entrepreneurial narratives and praise for hustle are, of course, a real and pervasive facet of the contemporary huayno scene—see Butterworth 2014 and 2017; Tucker 2013b—but their actual uptake has been little studied in the way that I propose here.

9. My understanding of neoliberalism's cultural effects in Peru is the same as that proposed for neoliberalist societies in general, where state policies not only create new kinds of business structures but also encourage citiens to develop a notion of the self as "a flexible bundle of skills that reflexively manages oneself as though the self was a business" (Gershon 2011:537; see also Wacquant 2012). Vich (2009) has adeptly traced the way that such conceptions of self have wormed their way into Peruvian popular cultural products, an analysis that I echo in Tucker 2013a.

10. For especially good explorations of this quality of country music see Ching 2001; Fox 2004.

11. It should also be noted that Carhuapoma's song plays upon a common stereotype about gendered attitudes toward alcohol in the Andes. As noted throughout this book, both men and women are expected to drink on festive occasions. However, as the family representative most responsible for curating the household's good relations with other in the public sphere, men in indigenous communities have typically been required to drink much more frequently, and to greater excess, than women. Studies of Andean gender, such as those touched upon in the introduction and chapter 2, frequently describe female frustrations about men who drink away family incomes as a key driver of gendered inequality and even spousal abuse. See especially Bourque and Warren 1981; de la Cadena 1995; Harris 1978; Harvey 1993.

12. In fact Vilca was her father's godson.

13. Barrios's reference to chimaycha's "international" stature here refers to the chinlili player Mario Carhuapoma, who was invited to play on one track by prominent mestiza artist Saywa and who in that capacity had the opportunity to travel to Chile's Viña del Mar International Song Festival.

14. This was an especially daunting challenge because Barrios worked independently, contracting freelance players for shows and recordings. A local recording with a reputable Ayacuchano producer, where she might work with qualified personnel, was no meager undertaking: 500 soles for the studio alone, with a further 200 each for chinlili, requinto, bass, and synthesizer, plus refreshments for all during the recording process, amounting to some 1500 soles (ca. $500 US).

15. My own friends and godchildren sternly cautioned me away from chimaycha concerts, concerned about the violence that supposedly reigned there. Others dismissed the chimaycha scene as at best a put-on designed to capture the money that filled the pockets of the drug trade's low-level employees and at worst as a means for their bosses to launder their income. None of

these positions was entirely unjustified. Chimaycha musicians knew that concert attendance fluctuated in accordance with governmental drug enforcement, and I had heard chinlili players entreat Marco Tucno to extend credit as they awaited a cyclical downturn in policing.

16. To begin with, Radio Quispillaccta charged 250 soles for a month's rental of a daily, hour-long promotional slot. The local television station charged 400 soles for a similar service, as did Uriel Salcedo's fledgling station La Primera. All would air spots during general programming too, but those ads themselves cost several hundred soles. Fliers and posters had to be distributed around town, amounting to several hundred soles more. The rental of a stage and a venue cost 1000 and 2000 soles, respectively, while security guards were hired at 80 soles each, the number to be determined by the expected size of crowd and venue. Artist fees varied widely, but huayno stars like Anita Santiváñez, Sonia Morales, and Chinito del Ande charged 15,000 for one two-hour set, and this was not to speak of the lesser acts that preceded and followed the headliner. Pacotaype did not enumerate the cost of licensing municipal permission, nor of beer, an all-important item that represented promoters' major source of profit, with hundreds of cases sold at a good show. It was acquired from the distributor at 40 soles per case of twelve, with the expectation of selling each 750 ml bottle at roughly 8 soles, representing a markup of over 100%.

17. Small promoters who failed to make such arrangements, I was told, might find the power cut to concert venues midshow or face nuisance visits from governmental officials, checking for permits and documentation that were normally overlooked.

18. Hatuchay cost a mere 500 soles to rent. Invited performers for shows there typically asked event organizers for a nominal fee of some 50 soles, knowing that their efforts would be reciprocated later on. All artists played with a house band assembled for the evening, instrumentalists who typically made between 20 and 40 soles for a night's work.

19. Typically such gifts ranged from cakes to envelopes containing up to hundreds of soles in cash.

20. Los Amaynis, for instance, had originally celebrated on June 24, the day that livestock were traditionally driven into Patario. However, this was also Peru's official "Peasant Day" (Día del Campesino), designated as such in 1969 by the leftist dictator Juan Velasco Alvarado (replacing the older "Day of the Indian" instituted in 1930 by indigenista president Augusto B. Leguía). Rather than compete against major artists brought in for the day by large promoters, Pachi moved the anniversary to Father's Day. Other artists placed their anniversaries similarly, creating an annual chimaycha cycle that tracked holidays and festivals: Rosas Huayta on New Year's Eve, Alicia Conde on the night before Mother's Day, María Ccallocunto in August, Ninay Urucha on October 19, Edwin Barrios on All Saints' Day, and Los Auténticos de Patario on Quispillaccta's November 29 municipal holiday, among many others.

21. Indeed, a chicha concert scheduled for the same weekend was abruptly canceled in a frenzy of bottle-throwing after headliner Lobo sent his son Lobito onstage as an opener, leading audience members to believe that they were the victims of a bait and switch.

22. Harvey's 1993 description of a festive evening in Cusco details a series of events and ethylic states that are startlingly similar to the account I present here, suggesting the widespread, durable, and quasi-ritualistic nature of drunken behavior and alcohol use across the Andean region. See especially pp. 114, 121, and 123 for descriptions of early light drinking to "animate" attendees, a later switch to more serious drinking, the eventual loss of consciousness, and across the entire evening the speaking of frank truths and the attempt to calm upset speakers with soothing gestures.

23. I have chosen to give this performer and her family members pseudonyms due to the potentially sensitive turn taken by our interview.

NOTES TO PAGES 185–189   247

Chapter Seven

1. For similar proposals about the study of musical instruments see Dawe 2001 and 2013; Libin 2000; Waksman 2003.

2. Musicologist Aaron Allen (2011 and 2012) has similarly called attention to links between instrument making and natural resource management. See also J. Anderson 2012 and Martinez-Reyes 2015 for excellent accounts of the relationship between wood and making.

3. More briefly, an "embodiment relation" can be described as a mutually constitutive dynamic between a body and a technology that shapes it (and that was shaped by one or more bodies in the first place).

4. Qureshi has usefully elaborated on this point in discussing Terdiman's formulation of "materials memory" (1985), a phrase that designates "the conservatism of 'things' that literally embody the past in the present. . . . A musical instrument offers a special kind of materials memory, in its dual capacity of a physical body and its embodied acoustic identity" (1997:3–4). Dawe has captured something of the same dynamic too in noting that "instruments in the lyra-laouto ensemble might be said to help transform individuals into a community, Cretan boys into Cretan men . . . masculine ideals into a powerful discourse, and musical ideas into affecting sounds" (2005:63; see also Dawe 2001 and 2013).

5. Smith's machine metaphor is not meant to cue high technology but rather to suggest an element of diachrony that remains muted in the now-familiar but structurally static metaphor of the "assemblage."

6. Stiegler's first major statement is volume 1 of *Technics and Time*, titled *The Fault of Epimetheus* (1998), but he has developed it over many subsequent works. Especially in that text, his interest lies in the temporal cycles of technical development and the way that the epochal gaps between innovations and their embodied or cultural accommodation relate to biological and social evolution—matters beyond the scope of my immediate interests.

7. I understand "exosomatic organs" in Innis's sense, as technical objects that are "extensions of our 'bodies' [that] have their own tacit and material logics. . . . We become so fused with them that we cannot avoid being subjected to their operational conditions" (2002:9).

8. Indeed, Serres's vision of object-human relations relies precisely on such differences: it draws insights from information theory to describe how nonidentity between the moment of articulation and the moment of reception produces the very sense of individuation that is required for successful communication.

9. Sennett's central example is the brick, sized and weighted to fit the adult male hand, and therefore distinct in its perceptual effects from something like concrete, designed to miraculously hide its manner of constitution, and fashioned into finished work at a scale well beyond the individual body.

10. "Douglas fir" and "European spruce" or "Englemann spruce" are the usual English-language translations of *pino Oregón* and *pino báltico* respectively, and Marco used these Spanish terms to name the woods. However, their application varies according to world region, supplier, and individual maker, among other factors. In Ayacucho they seem to be used flexibly to refer to woods that have similar properties, so I cannot be sure that the woods Marco was using were in fact these woods. It might also be noted here that his preference for fir bracing is shared by few luthiers located elsewhere, precisely because it is heavier than spruce.

11. It should be noted here that few independent guitar makers, in either Lima or North America, actually work so infrequently with their hands as to justify Marco's contrast. His understanding of international practice probably derived from the factory-built instruments

248 NOTES TO PAGES 189–204

that dominate Peru's import guitar marketplace, though his characterization of Lima's makers arises from direct experience in the shop of Abraham Falcón, who did indeed use the electronic tools to which Marco referred. Whatever the validity of the contrast, his sense of the discipline and sensitivity that arise from handwork stands as a serious point, and one that resonates with the claims of peers elsewhere. See, for example, Somogyi 2012.

12. The bells bear two inscriptions, one reading "efforts of Municipal Agent Francisco Tucno and *teniente* Félix Tucno" ("Esfuerzos del agente municipal Francisco Tucno y teniente Félix Tucno"), and another reading "Bell of the Virgin of Mount Carmel of Quispillaccta year 1918" ("Campana de la Vírgen del Carmen de Quispillaccta año 1918").

13. I have been unable to glean other terms for the tree that is locally called chachas, and cannot currently provide its proper taxonomical name.

14. Marco and David Loayza developed a healthy mutual respect and later became Ayacucho's two leading luthiers, in part by dividing its trade. Loayza specialized in the nylon-stringed guitars favored by the urban-mestizo market, and Marco served the indigenous countryside and the migrant community of the city with the distinctive guitar variants favored in those communities.

15. Erin O'Connor (2005) and Sonja Petersen (2013) have written similarly about the acquisition of embodied knowledge in craft labor.

16. Current thinking among American luthiers does not support this contention, though there is an ongoing debate about the possible value of hollow necks. They are thought by some to provide players with a faster attack and are reported to transmit a stronger vibration to the fretting hand, thereby fostering a feeling of tactile connection to the instrument's sound. Neither factor, however, translates into louder sound per se.

17. This was not the case when Marco initially moved to the city, nor when I first lived there between 2000 and 2003. However by the time we had the conversations cited here, between 2012 and 2014, Ayacucho's downtown had become clogged with traffic. Poorly muffled engines, very liberal use of car horns, loud music pouring out of public transport, hollering of bus conductors who hawk rides to waiting passengers, and increasing use of loudspeakers by other businesses in an attempt to be heard over all of this sound, all refracted by the concrete walls that increasingly lined the streets, yielded a level of ambient noise that challenged aficionados of unamplified music.

18. Sitka spruce, ebony, and other key tonewoods are increasingly controlled by international treaty and are likely to become difficult to obtain for luthiers the world over—at least through legal means. See Dudley 2015; Trump 2012.

19. Eucalyptus was planted throughout the Peruvian Andes after the mid-twentieth century as part of a reforestation scheme.

20. See Stokes 1992 for a similar account of musicians who reconcile the competing pressures of "modernization" and "traditionalism" (among others) by threading the needle between instrumental adaptation, versatility of technique, and the retention of audible links to past practices. Of course the notion that a technology is defined as much by its mode of use as by its components, and that such technologies typically derive their modes of use from prior technologies, has been widely addressed in science and technology studies, especially in relation to the "cell phone" or "smartphone," neither of which relies upon the wired systems of the older land-line system.

References

Abercrombie, Thomas Alan. 1998. *Pathways of Memory and Power: Ethnography and History among an Andean People*. Madison: University of Wisconsin Press.

Ahmed, Sara. 2004. *The Cultural Politics of Emotion*. London: Routledge.

Alberti, Giorgio, and Enrique Mayer, eds. 1974. *Reciprocidad e intercambio en los Andes peruanos*. Lima: IEP.

Albro, Robert. 2010. "Neoliberal Cultural Heritage and Bolivia's New Indigenous Public." In *Ethnographies of Neoliberalism*, edited by Carol J. Greenhouse, 146–61. Philadelphia: University of Pennsylvania Press.

Alfaro Rotondo, Santiago. 2005. *Nacion, política e identidad en el movimiento indígena peruano*. Lima: Ridei.

Alfaro Rotondo, Santiago. 2006. "El lugar de las industrias culturales en las políticas públicas." In *Políticas culturales: Ensayos críticos*, edited by Víctor Vich and Guilermo Cortes, 137–76. Lima: IEP.

Allen, Aaron. 2011. "Prospects and Problems for Ecomusicology in Confronting a Crisis of Culture." *Journal of the American Musicological Society* 64(2): 414–24.

Allen, Aaron. 2012. "'Fatto di Fiemme': Stradivari's Violins and the Musical Trees of the Paneveggio." In *Invaluable Trees: Cultures of Nature, 1660–1830*, edited by Laura Auricchio, Elizabeth Heckendorn, and Giulia Pacini, 301–15. Oxford: Voltaie Foundation.

Allen, Aaron S., and Kevin Dawe, eds. 2015. *Current Directions in Ecomusicology: Music, Culture, Nature*. London: Routledge.

Allen, Catherine. 2002 [1988]. *The Hold Life Has: Coca and Culural Identity in an Andean Community*. Washington, DC: Smithsonian Institution Press.

Alperson, Philip. 2008. "The Instrumentality of Music." *Journal of Aesthetics and Art Criticism* 66(1): 37–51.

Anderson, David G. 2000. *Identity and Ecology in Arctic Siberia: The Number One Reindeer Brigade*. Oxford: Oxford University Press.

Anderson, Jennifer L. 2012. *Mahogany: The Costs of Luxury in Early America*. Cambridge, MA: Harvard University Press.

REFERENCES

Apfel-Marglin, Frédérique, ed. 1998. *The Spirit of Regeneration: Andean Cultures Confronting Western Notions of Development*. London: Zed.

Appadurai, Arjun. 1996. *Modernity at Large: Cultural Dimensions of Globalization*. Minneapolis: University of Minnesota Press.

Arce Sotelo, Manuel, and César Vivanco. 2015. *La danza de Tijeras y el violín de Lucanas*. Lima: Institut français d'études andines.

Arguedas, José María. 1966. "La cultura: Un patrimonio difícil de colonizar." In *Notas sobre la cultura latinoamericana y su destino*, edited by Francisco Miró Quesada, Fernando de Syslso, and José María Arguedas, 21–26. Lima: Industrial Gráfica.

Arguedas, José María. 1985 [1941]. *Yawar Fiesta*. Translated by Frances Horning Barraclough. Austin: University of Texas Press.

Arnold, Denise Y. 1992. "En el corazón de la plaza tejida: El wayñu en Qaqachaka." *Anales de la Reunión Anual de Etnología*, 17–70.

Arnold, Denise Y. 1997. "Introducción." In *Más allá del silencio: Las fronteras de género en los Andes*, edited by Denise Y. Arnold, 1–47. La Paz: CIASE/ILCA.

Arnold, Denise Y., and Juan de Dios Yapita. 1996. "Qipa Mama wawampi: Analogías de la producción de la papa en los textiles de Chukiñapi, Bolivia." In *Madre Melliza y sus crías (Ispall Mama Wawampi): Antología de la papa*, edited by Denise Y. Arnold and Juan de Dios Yapita, 373–411. La Paz: Hisbol / Ediciones ILCA.

Askew, Kelly. 2002. *Performing the Nation: Swahili Music and Cultural Politics in Tanzania*. Chicago: University of Chicago Press.

Azevedo, Valerie Robin. 2009. "Linchamientos y legislación penal sobre la diferencia cultural: Reflexiones a partir de un juicio por homicidio contra unos comuneros del Cuzco." In *El regreso de lo indígena: Retos, problemas y perspectivas*, edited by Valérie Robin and Carmen Salazar-Soler Azevedo, 71–101. Lima: Instituto Francés de Estudios Andinos.

Babb, Florence. 1989. *Between Field and Cooking Pot: The Political Economy of Market Women in Peru*. Austin: University of Texas Press.

Babb, Florence. 2012. "Theorizing Gender, Race, and Cultural Tourism in Latin America: A View from Peru and Mexico." *Latin American Perspectives* 39(6): 36–50.

Baily, John. 1985. "Music Structure and Human Movement." In *Musical Structure and Cognition*, edited by Peter Howell, Ian Cross, and R. West, 236–58. London: Academic Press.

Bant, Astrid, and Françoise Girard. 2008. "Sexuality, Health, and Human Rights: Self-Identified Priorities of Indigenous Women in Peru." *Gender and Development* 16(2): 247–56.

Barad, Karen. 2007. *Meeting the Universe Halfway: Quantum Physics and the Entanglement of Matter and Meaning*. Durham, NC: Duke University Press.

Barth, Fredrik, ed. 1970. *Ethnic Groups and Boundaries: The Social Organization of Culture Difference*. Boston: Little, Brown.

Basso, Keith H. 1996. "Wisdom Sits in Places: Notes on a Western Apache Landscape." In *Senses of Place*, edited by Steven and Keith H. Basso Feld, 53–90. Santa Fe, NM: School of American Research Press.

Bates, Eliot. 2012. "The Social Life of Musical Instruments." *Ethnomusicology* 56(3): 363–95.

Becker, Marc. 2012. *Pachakutik: Indigenous Movements and Electoral Politics in Ecuador*. Lanham, MD: Rowman & Littlefield.

Bellenger, Xavier. 2007. *El espacio musical andino: Modo ritualizado de producción musical en la isla de Taquile y la región del lago Titicaca*. Lima: IFEA, Pontificia Universidad Católica del Perú.

REFERENCES

Bendix, Regina. 1997. *In Search of Authenticity: The Formation of Folklore Studies*. Madison: University of Wisconsin Press.

Bennett, H. Stith. 1980. *On Becoming a Rock Musician*. Amherst: University of Massachusetts Press.

Bennett, Jane. 2010. *Vibrant Matter: A Political Ecology of Things*. Durham, NC: Duke University Press.

Berglund, Jeff, Jan Johnson, and Kimberli Lee, eds. 2016. *Indigenous Pop: Native American Music from Jazz to Hip Hop*. Tucson: University of Arizona Press.

Bessire, Lucas. 2012. "'We Go Above': Media Metaphysics and Making Moral Life on Ayoreo Two-Way Radio." In *Radio Fields: Anthropology and Wireless Sound in the 21st Century*, edited by Lucas Bessire and Daniel Fisher, 197–214. New York: New York University Press.

Bessire, Lucas. 2014. *Behold the Black Caiman: A Chronicle of Ayoreo Life*. Chicago: University of Chicago Press.

Bigenho, Michelle. 2002. *Sounding Indigenous: Authenticity in Bolivian Music Performance*. New York: Palgrave.

Bigenho, Michelle. 2007. "Bolivian Indigeneity in Japan: Folklorized Musical Performance." In *Indigenous Experience Today*, edited by Marisol de la Cadena and Orin Starn, 247–272. Oxford: Berg.

Bigenho, Michelle. 2012. *Intimate Distance: Andean Music in Japan*. Durham, NC: Duke University Press.

Bijsterveld, Karin, and Marten Schulp. 2004. "Breaking into a World of Perfection: Innovation in Today's Classical Musical Instruments." *Social Studies of Science* 34(5): 649–74.

Blaser, Mario. 2010. *Storytelling Globalization from the Chaco and Beyond*. Durham, NC: Duke University Press.

Bolin, Inge. 2006. *Growing Up in a Culture of Respect: Child Rearing in Highland Peru*. Austin: University of Texas Press.

Bourque, Susan, and Scott Palmer. 1975. "Transforming the Rural Sector: Government Policy and Peasant Response." In *The Peruvian Experiment Reconsidered*, edited by Cynthia McClintock and Abraham F. Lowenthal, 179–219. Princeton, NJ: Princeton University Press.

Bourque, Susan C., and Kay Barbara Warren. 1981. *Women of the Andes: Patriarchy and Social Change in Two Peruvian Towns*. Ann Arbor: University of Michigan Press.

Boym, Svetlana. 2001. *The Future of Nostalgia*. New York: Basic Books.

Brabec de Mori, Bernd. 2013. "Shipibo Laughing Songs and the Transformative Faculty: Performing or Becoming the Other." *Ethnomusicology Forum* 22(3): 343–61.

Bradley, Arthur. 2011. *Originary Technicity: The Theory of Technology from Marx to Derrida*. New York: Palgrave Macmillan.

Brown, Michael. 2003. *Who Owns Native Culture?* Cambridge, MA: Harvard University Press.

Browner, Tara. 2009. *Music of the First Nations: Tradition and Innovation in Native North America*. Urbana: University of Illinois Press.

Brubaker, Rogers, and Frederick Cooper. 2000. "Beyond 'Identity.'" *Theory and Society* 29(1): 1–47.

Brush, Stephen B. 1977. *Mountain, Field, and Family: The Economy and Human Ecology of an Andean Valley*. Philadelphia: University of Pennsylvania Press.

Bueno-Hansen, Pascha. 2015. *Feminist and Human Rights Struggles in Peru: Decolonizing Transitional Justice*. Urbana: University of Illinois Press.

Butterworth, James. 2014. "Rethinking Spectacle and Indigenous Consumption: Commercial Huayno Music in Peru." In *Recasting Commodity and Spectacle in the Indigenous Americas*, edited by Helen Gilbert and Charlotte Gleghorn, 131–50. London: Institute of Latin American Studies, School of Advanced Study, University of London.

Butterworth, James. 2017. "The Animador as Ethical Mediator: Stage Talk and Subject Formation at Peruvian Huayno Music Spectacles." In *Collaborative Intimacies in Music and Dance: Anthropologies of Sound and Movement*, edited by Evangelos Chrysagis and Panas Karampampas, 121–38. New York: Berghahn.

Caballero Martín, Víctor. 1995. *Ayacucho: Las migraciones y el problema laboral*. Lima: Chirapaq / Centro de Culturas Indias.

Calhoun, Craig J. 1992. "Introduction: Habermas and the Public Sphere." In *Habermas and the Public Sphere*, edited by Craig J. Calhoun, 1–48. Cambridge, MA: MIT Press.

Cánepa Koch, Gisela, ed. 2002. *Identidades representadas: Performance, experiencia y memoria en los Andes*. Lima: Pontificia Universidad Católica del Perú.

Cánepa Koch, Gisela. 2010. "Performing Citizenship: Migration, Andean Festivals, and Public Spaces in Lima." In *Cultures of the City: Mediating Identities in Urban Latin/o America*, edited by Richard Young and Amanda Holmes, 135–50. Pittsburgh: University of Pittsburgh Press.

Cánepa Koch, Gisela, and María Eugenia Ulfe, eds. 2006. *Mirando la esfera pública desde la cultura en el Perú*. Lima: CONCYTEC, 2006.

Canessa, Andrew. 2005. "The Indian Within, the Indian Without: Citizenship, Race, and Sex in a Bolivian Hamlet." In *Natives Making Nation: Gender, Indigeneity, and the State in the Andes*, edited by Andrew Canessa, 3–31. Tucson: University of Arizona Press.

Canessa, Andrew. 2012. *Intimate Indigeneities: Race, Sex, and History in the Small Spaces of Andean Life*. Durham, NC: Duke University Press.

CAOI (Coordinación Andina de Organizaciones Indígenas). n.d. *Impulsando la integración de los pueblos*. Lima: n.p.

Castillo Guzmán, Gerardo. 2002. "Fiesta y embriaguez en comunidades andinas del sur del Perú." In *Identidades representadas: Performance, experiencias y memoria en los Andes*, edited by Gisela Cánea Koch, 437–56. Lima: Pontificia Universidad Católica del Perú.

Castillo Melgar, Severino, and Mario T. Cueto Cárdenas. 2010. *Remembranzas Cristobalinas*. Ayacucho: n.p.

Cavero Carrasco, Ranulfo. 2012. *Los senderos de la destrucción: Ayacucho y su universidad*. Ayacucho: Praktico L&C.

Cavero Cornejo, Omar. 2011. "Movimiento indígena en el Perú: Transnacional antes que local?" In *Nuevas miradas al Perú contemporáneo: Movimientos sociales, identidades y memoria*, edited by Diana Carolina Flores Rojas, 175–211. Lima: Programa Democracia y Transformación Global.

Cepek, Michael L. 2016. "There Might Be Blood: Oil, Humility, and the Cosmopolitics of a Cofán Petro-Being." *American Ethnologist* 43(4): 623–35.

Ching, Barbara. 2001. *Wrong's What I Do Best: Hard Country Music and Contemporary Culture*. New York: Oxford University Press.

Clayton, Jace. 2010. "Vampires of Lima." In *What Was the Hipster? A Sociological Investigation*, edited by Mark Greif, Kathleen Ross, and Dayna Tortorici, 24–30. New York: n+1 Foundation.

Clifford, James. 1986. "Introduction: Partial Truths." In *Writing Culture: The Poetics and Politics of Ethnography*, edited by James Clifford and George E. Marcus, 1–26. Berkeley: University of California Press.

Clifford, James. 2007. "Varieties of Indigenous Experience: Diasporas, Homelands, Sovereignties." In *Indigenous Experience Today*, edited by Marisol de la Cadena and Orin Starn, 197–223. Oxford: Berg.

REFERENCES 253

Collins, Jane L. 1986. "The Household and Relations of Production in Southern Peru." *Comparative Studies in Society and History* 28(4): 651–71.

Colloredo-Mansfeld, Rudolf Josef. 2009. *Fighting like a Community: Andean Civil Society in an Era of Indian Uprisings*. Chicago: University of Chicago Press.

Comaroff, John L., and Jean Comaroff. 2009. *Ethnicity, Inc.* Chicago: University of Chicago Press.

Conklin, Beth A. 1997. "Body Paint, Feathers, and VCRs: Aesthetics and Authenticity in Amazonian Activism." *American Ethnologist* 24(4): 711–37.

Conklin, Beth A. 2006. "Environmentalism, Global Community, and the New Indigenism." In *Inclusion and Exclusion in the Global Arena*, edited by Max Kirsch, 161–76. New York: Routledge.

Conklin, Beth A., and Laura R. Graham. 1995. "The Shifting Middle Ground: Amazonian Indians and Eco-Politics." *American Anthropologist* 97(4): 695–710.

Crisóstomo Meza, Mercedes A. 2012. *Legítimos y radicales: Una aproximación al estudio del frente de defensa del pueblo de Ayacucho*. Lima: Pontificia Universidad Católica del Perú.

CVR (Comisión de la Verdad y Reconciliación). 2003. *Informe final*. Lima.

Danielson, Virginia. 1997. *The Voice of Egypt: Umm Kulthum, Arabic Song, and Egyptian Society in the Twentieth Century*. Chicago: University of Chicago Press.

Dawe, Kevin. 2001. "People, Objects, Meaning: Recent Work on the Study and Collection of Musical Instruments." *Galpin Society Journal* 54:219–32.

Dawe, Kevin. 2003. "Lyres and the Body Politic: Studying Musical Instruments in the Cretan Musical Landscape." *Popular Music and Society* 26(3): 263–83.

Dawe, Kevin. 2005. "Symbolic and Social Transformation in the Lute Cultures of Crete: Music, Technology and the Body in a Mediterranean Society." *Yearbook for Traditional Music* 37:58–68.

Dawe, Kevin. 2013. "Guitar Ethnographies: Performance, Technology and Material Culture." *Ethnomusicology Forum* 22(1): 1–25.

Dean, Carolyn. 2010. *A Culture of Stone: Inka Perspectives on Rock*. Durham, NC: Duke University Press.

Degregori, Carlos Iván. 1997. "The Maturation of a Cosmocrat and the Building of a Discourse Community: The Case of Shining Path." In *The Legitimization of Violence*, edited by D. E. Apter, 33–82. New York: New York University Press.

Degregori, Carlos Iván. 1999. "Multiculturalidad e interculturalidad." In *Educación y diversidad rural* (conference proceedings), 63–69. Lima: Ministerio de Educación.

Degregori, Carlos Iván. 2002. "Identidad étnica, movimientos sociales y participación en el Perú." In *Estados nacionales, etnicidad, y democracia en América Latina*, edited by Mutsuo Yamada and Carlos Iván Degregori, 161–78. Osaka: Japan Center for Area Studies, National Museum of Ethnology.

Degregori, Carlos Iván, Cecilia Blondet, and Nicolás Lynch. 1986. *Conquistadores de un nuevo mundo: De invasores a ciudadanos en San Martín de Porres*. Lima: IEP.

Degregori, Carlos Iván, and Pablo Sandoval. 2008. "Dilemas y tendencias en la antropología peruana: Del paradigma indigenista al paradigma intercultural." In *Saberes periféricos: Ensayos sobre la antropología en América Latina*, edited by Carlos Iván Degregori and Pablo Sandoval, 19–72. Lima: IEP.

de la Cadena, Marisol. 1995. "'Women Are More Indian': Ethnicity and Gender in a Community near Cuzco." In *Ethnicity, Markets, and Migration in the Andes: At the Crossroads of History and Anthropology*, edited by Brooke Larson, Olivia Harris, and E. Tandeter, 329–48. Durham, NC: Duke University Press.

de la Cadena, Marisol. 2000. *Indigenous Mestizos: The Politics of Race and Culture in Cuzco, Peru, 1919–1991.* Durham, NC: Duke University Press.

de la Cadena, Marisol. 2015. *Earth Beings: Ecologies of Practice across Andean Worlds.* Durham, NC: Duke University Press.

de la Cadena, Marisol, and Orin Starn, eds. 2007. *Indigenous Experience Today.* Oxford: Berg.

DeNora, Tia. 2010. "Emotion as Social Emergence: Perspectives from Music Sociology." In *Handbook of Music and Emotions: Theory, Research, Applications*, edited by Patrick N. Juslin and John A. Sloboda, 159–85. London: Oxford University Press.

Descola, Philippe. 2013. *Beyond Nature and Culture.* Chicago: University of Chicago Press.

Dewey, John. 1946. *The Public and Its Problems: An Essay in Political Inquiry.* Chicago: Gateway Books.

Diamond, Beverley. 2012. "'Re' Thinking: Revitalization, Return and Reconciliation in Contemporary Indigenous Expressive Culture." In *Trudeau Lectures, 2010–11*, 118–40. Montreal: Trudeau Foundation of Canada.

Diamond, Beverley. 2017. "Mixing It Up: A Comparative Approach to Sámi Audio Production." In *Music, Indigeneity, Digital Media*, edited by Thomas R. Hilder, Henry Stobart, and Shzr Ee Tan, 106–26. Rochester: University of Rochester Press.

Díaz Martínez, Antonio. 1969. *Ayacucho: Hambre y esperanza.* Ayacucho: Ediciones Waman Puma.

Dietler, Michael. 2006. "Alcohol: Anthropological/Archaeological Perspectives." *Annual Review of Anthropology* 35:229–49.

Dudley, Kathryn Marie. 2014. *Guitar Makers: The Endurance of Artisanal Values in North America.* Chicago: University of Chicago Press.

Dueck, Byron. 2013. *Musical Intimacies and Indigenous Imaginaries: Aboriginal Music and Dance in Public Performance.* New York: Oxford University Press.

Duviols, Pierre. 1973. "Huari y llacuaz, agricultores y pastores: Un dualismo prehispánico de oposición y complementariedad." *Revista del Museo Nacional* (Lima) 39:153–91.

Ellis, Clyde, Luke Eric Lassiter, and Gary H. Dunham, eds. 2005. *Powwow.* Lincoln: University of Nebraska Press.

Fabricant, Nicole. 2012. *Mobilizing Bolivia's Displaced: Indigenous Politics and the Struggle over Land.* Chapel Hill: University of North Carolina Press.

Fanon, Frantz. 2001 [1959]. "On National Culture." In *Nations and Identities: Classic Readings*, edited by Vincent P. Pecora, 264–75. Malden, MA: Blackwell.

Faudree, Paja. 2013. *Singing for the Dead: The Politics of Indigenous Revival in Mexico.* Durham, NC: Duke University Press.

Favre, Henri. 2009. "El movimiento indianista: Un fenómeno 'glocal.'" In *El regreso de lo indígena: Retos, problemas y perspectivas*, edited by Valérie Robin and Carmen Salazar-Soler, 29–37. Lima: Instituto Francés de Estudios Andinos.

Feld, Steven. 2012 [1982]. *Sound and Sentiment: Birds, Weeping, Poetics, and Song in Kaluli Expression.* Durham, NC: Duke University Press.

Femenías, Blenda. 2005. *Gender and the Boundaries of Dress in Contemporary Peru.* Austin: University of Texas Press.

Filene, Benjamin. 2000. *Romancing the Folk: Public Memory and American Roots Music.* Chapel Hill: University of North Carolina Press.

Fisher, Daniel. 2016. *The Voice and Its Doubles: Media and Music in Northern Australia.* Durham, NC: Duke University Press.

Flores Ochoa, Jorge A. 1988. "Mitos y canciones ceremoniales en comunidades de puna." In *Lla-*

REFERENCES

michos y paqocheroes, pastores de llamas y alpacas, edited by Jorge A. Flores Ochoa, 237–51. Cusco: Centro de Estudios Andinos.

Flórez Salcedo, Gustavo. 2012. "Rivalidades comunales y contiendas electorales: Micropolítica en las elecciones distritales de Chuschi; El caso de las comunidades campesinas de Chuschi y Quispillaccta." In *Tensiones y transformaciones en comunidades campesinas*, edited by Alejandro Diez Hurtado, 225–61. Lima: CISEPA-PUCP.

Forde, Susan, Kerrie Foxwell, and Michael Meadows, eds. 2009. *Developing Dialogues: Indigenous and Ethnic Community Broadcasting in Australia.* Chicago: University of Chicago Press.

Fox, Aaron. 2004. *Real Country: Music and Language in Working-Class Culture.* Durham, NC: Duke University Press.

Fraser, Nancy. 1990. "Rethinking the Public Sphere: A Contribution to the Critique of Actually Existing Democracy." *Social Text* 2:56–80.

Frith, Simon. 1996. *Performing Rites: On the Value of Popular Music.* Oxford: Oxford University Press.

Gandolfo, Daniella. 2009. *The City at Its Limits: Taboo, Transgression, and Urban Renewal in Lima.* Chicago: University of Chicago Press.

Ganti, Tejaswanti. 2014. "Neoliberalism." *Annual Review of Anthropology* 43:89–104.

García, María Elena. 2005. *Making Indigenous Citizens: Identities, Education, and Multicultural Development in Peru.* Stanford, CA: Stanford University Press.

García, María Elena. 2013. "The Taste of Conquest: Colonialism, Cosmopolitics, and the Dark Side of Peru's Gastronomic Boom." *Journal of Latin American and Caribbean Anthropology* 18(3): 505–24.

García Canclini, Néstor. 1995. *Hybrid Cultures: Strategies for Entering and Leaving Modernity.* Minneapolis: University of Minnesota Press.

Gefou-Madianou, Dimitra. 1992. "Introduction: Alcohol Commensality, Identity Transformations and Transcendence." In *Alcohol, Gender and Culture*, edited by Dimitra Gefou-Madianou, 1–35. London: Routledge.

Gelles, Paul. 2000. *Water and Power in Highland Peru: The Cultural Politics of Irrigation and Development.* New Brunswick, NJ: Rutgers University Press.

Gershon, Ilana. 2011. "Neoliberal Agency." *Current Anthropology* 52(4): 537–48.

Ginsburg, Faye. 1991. "Indigenous Media: Faustian Contract or Global Village?" *Cultural Anthropology* 6(1): 92–112.

Gioia, Ted. 2008. *Delta Blues: The Life and Times of the Mississippi Masters Who Revolutionized American Music.* New York: W. W. Norton.

Goertzen, Chris. 2001. "Powwows and Identity on the Piedmont and Coastal Plains of North Carolina." *Ethnomusicology* 45(1): 58–88.

González, Olga M. 2011. *Unveiling Secrets of War in the Peruvian Andes.* Chicago: University of Chicago Press.

Gordillo, Gastón R. 2004. *Landscapes of Devils: Tensions of Place and Memory in the Argentinean Chaco.* Durham, NC: Duke University Press.

Gorriti Ellenbogen, Gustavo. 1999. *The Shining Path: A History of the Millenarian War in Peru.* Chapel Hill: University of North Carolina Press.

Gose, Peter. 1994. *Deathly Waters and Hungry Mountains: Agrarian Ritual and Class Formation in an Andean Town.* Toronto: University of Toronto Press.

Graham, Laura R., and H. Glenn Penney. 2014. "Performing Indigeneity: Emergent Identity, Self-Determination, and Sovereignty." In *Performing Indigeneity: Global Histories and Con-*

temporary Experiences, edited by Laura R. Graham and H. Glenn Penney, 1–30. Lincoln: University of Nebraska Press.

Greene, Shane. 2006. "Getting over the Andes: The Geo-Eco-Politics of Indigenous Movements in Peru's Twenty-First Century Inca Empire." *Journal of Latin American Studies* 38(2): 327–354.

Greene, Shane. 2009. *Customizing Indigeneity: Paths to a Visionary Politics in Peru*. Stanford, CA: Stanford University Press.

Greene, Shane. 2016. *Punk and Revolution: 7 More Interpretations of Peruvian Reality*. Durham, NC: Duke University Press.

Grimley, Daniel. 2006. *Grieg: Music, Landscape and Norwegian Identity*. Rochester, NY: Boydell Press.

Gros, Christian. 2000. "Ser diferente para ser modern, o Las paradojas de la identidad: Algunas reflexiones sobre la construcción de una nueva frontera étnica en America Latina." *Analisis Politico* 36:3–19.

Gustafson, Bret. 2009. *New Languages of the State: Indigenous Resurgence and the Politics of Knowledge in Bolivia*. Durham, NC: Duke University Press.

Habermas, Jürgen. 1989. *The Structural Transformation of the Public Sphere: An Inquiry into a Category of Bourgeois Society*. Cambridge, MA: MIT Press.

Hale, Charles R. 2002. "Does Multiculturalism Menace? Governance, Cultural Rights and the Politics of Identity in Guatemala." *Journal of Latin American Studies* 34: 485–524.

Hale, Charles R. 2006. *Más que un Indio = More Than an Indian: Racial Ambivalence and Neoliberal Multiculturalism in Guatemala*. Santa Fe, NM: School of American Research Press.

Hale, Charles R., and Rosamel Millamán. 2006. "Cultural Agency and Political Struggle in the Era of the Indio Permitido." In *Cultural Agency in the Americas*, edited by Doris Sommer, 281–304. Durham, NC: Duke University Press.

Harker, Dave. 1985. *Fakesong: The Manufacture of British "Folksong" 1700 to the Present Day*. Milton Keynes, UK: Open University Press.

Harris, Olivia. 1978. "Complementarity and Conflict: An Andean View of Women and Men." In *Sex and Age as Principles of Social Differentiation*, edited by J. S. La Fontaine, 21–40. London: Academic Press.

Harris, Olivia. 1980. "The Power of Signs: Gender, Culture, and the Wild in the Bolivian Andes." In *Nature, Culture, and Gender,* edited by Carol MacCormack and Marilyn Strathern, 70–94. Cambridge: Cambridge University Press.

Harvey, Penelope M. 1991. "Drunken Speech and the Construction of Meaning: Bilingual Competence in the Southern Peruvian Andes." *Language in Society* 20(1): 1–36.

Harvey, Penelope M. 1993. "Género, comunidad y confrontacion: Relaciones de poder en la embriaguez en Ocongate, Perú." In *Borrachera y memoria: La experiencia de lo sagrado en los Andes*, edited by Thierry Saignes, 113–38. Lima: IFEA.

Heath, Dwight. 1987. "A Decade in the Development of the Anthropological Study of Alcohol Use." In *Constructive Drinking: Perspectives on Drink from Anthropology*, edited by Mary Douglas, 16–69. Cambridge: Cambridge University Press.

Heilman, Jaymie Patricia. 2010. *Before the Shining Path: Politics in Rural Ayacucho, 1895–1980*. Stanford, CA: Stanford University Press.

Hernández Castillo, Aída. 2005. "Between Complementarity and Inequality: Indigenous Cosmovision as an Element of Resistance in the Struggle of Indigenous Women." Paper presented

REFERENCES

at the conference Indigenous Struggles in the Americas and around the World: Land, Autonomy and Recognition, York University, Toronto, February 10–11.

Herzfeld, Michael. 2004. *The Body Impolitic: Artisans and Artifice in the Global Hierarchy of Value.* Chicago: University of Chicago Press.

Hilder, Thomas R. 2015. *Sámi Musical Performance and the Politics of Indigeneity in Northern Europe.* Lanham, MD: Rowman & Littlefield.

Hill, Jonathan David. 2009. *Made-from-one: Trickster Myths, Music, and History from the Amazon.* Urbana: University of Illinois Press.

Hill, Jonathan David. 2013. "Instruments of Power: Musicalising the Other in Lowland South America." *Ethnomusicology Forum* 22(3): 323–42.

Hill, Jonathan David, and Jean-Pierre Chaumeil, eds. 2011. *Burst of Breath: Indigenous Ritual Wind Instruments in Lowland South America.* Lincoln: University of Nebraska Press.

Himpele, Jeff. 2008. *Circuits of Culture: Media, Politics, and Indigenous Identity in the Andes.* Minneapolis: University of Minnesota Press.

Hobsbawm, Eric, and Terence Ranger. 1992 [1983]. *The Invention of Tradition.* Cambridge: Cambridge University Press.

Hogue, Emily J., and Pilar Rau. 2008. "Troubled Water: Ethnodevelopment, Natural Resource Commodification, and Neoliberalism in Andean Peru." *Urban Anthropology and Studies of Cultural Systems and World Economic Development* 37 (3/4): 283–327.

Holzmann, Rodolfo. 1986. *Qero, pueblo y música: Un estudio etnomusicológico basado en 33 piezas del repertorio vocal e instrumental de los Qeros.* Lima: Patronato Popular y Porvenir, Pro Música Clásica.

Hornberger, Nancy H., and Karl Swinehart. 2012. "Bilingual Intercultural Education and Andean Hip Hop: Transnational Sites for Indigenous Language and Identity." *Language in Society* 41(4): 499–525.

Huber, Ludwig. 2008. "La representación indígena en municipalidades peruanas: Tres estudios de caso." In *Ejercicio de gobierno local en las ámbitos rurales: Presupuesto, desarrollo e identidad*, edited by Romeo Grompone, Raúl Hernandez Asensio, and Ludwig Huber, 175–272. Lima: IEP.

Ihde, Don. 1990. *Technology and the Lifeworld: From Garden to Earth.* Bloomington: Indiana University Press.

Impey, Angela. 2002. "Culture, Conservation and Community Reconstruction: Explorations in Advocacy Ethnomusicology and Participatory Action Research in Northern Kwazulu Natal." *Yearbook for Traditional Music* 34:9–24.

Impey, Angela. 2006. "Sounding Place in the Western Maputaland Borderlands." *Journal of the Musical Arts in Africa* 3(1): 55–79.

Ingold, Tim. 2000. *The Perception of the Environment: Essays on Livelihood, Dwelling and Skill.* London: Routledge.

Ingold, Tim, ed. 2011. *Redrawing Anthropology: Materials, Movements, Lines.* Burlington, VT: Ashgate.

Innis, Robert E. 2002. *Pragmatism and the Forms of Sense: Language, Perception, Technics.* University Park: Pennsylvania State University Press.

Isbell, Billie Jean. 1985. *To Defend Ourselves: Ecology and Ritual in an Andean Village.* Prospect Heights, IL: Waveland.

Isbell, Billie Jean. 1997. "De inmaduro a duro: Lo simbólico femenino y los esquemas andinas de género." In *Más allá del silencio: Las fronteras de género en los Andes*, edited by Denise Y. Arnold, 253–301. La Paz: Biblioteca Andina.

Isbell, Billie Jean. 1998. "Violence in Peru: Performances and Dialogues." *American Anthropologist* 100(2): 282–92.

Isbell, Billie Jean. 2005. *Para defendernos*. Cusco: Centro Bartolomé de Las Casas.

Isbell, Billie Jean. 2009. *Finding Cholita*. Urbana: University of Illinois Press.

Isbell, Billie Jean, with Marino Barrios Micuylla. 2016. "Reflections on Fieldwork in Chuschi." In *A Return to the Village: Community Ethnographies and the Study of Andean Culture in Retrospective*, edited by Francisco Ferreira and Bille Jean Isbell, 45–68. London: Institute of Latin American Studies.

Jacobsen, Kristina M. 2017. *The Sound of Navajo Country: Music, Language, and Diné Belonging*. Chapel Hill: University of North Carolina Press.

Jihad Racy, Ali. 1994. "A Dialectical Perspective on Musical Instruments: The East-Mediterranean Mijwiz." *Ethnomusicology* 38(1): 37–57.

Kauanui, J. Kehaulani. 2008. *Hawaiian Blood: Colonialism and the Politics of Sovereignty and Indigeneity*. Durham, NC: Duke University Press.

Kies, Thomas J. 2013. "Artisans of Sound: Persisting Competitiveness of the Handcrafting Luthiers of Central Mexico." *Ethnomusicology Forum* 22(1): 71–88.

Kittler, Friedrich A. 1999. *Gramophone, Film, Typewriter*. Stanford, CA: Stanford University Press.

Kohn, Eduardo. 2013. *How Forests Think: Toward an Anthropology beyond the Human*. Berkeley: University of California Press.

Krech, Shepard. 1999. *The Ecological Indian: Myth and History*. New York: W. W. Norton.

Kubik, Gerhard. 1979. "Pattern Perception and Recognition in African Music." In *The Performing Arts*, edited by John Blacking and J. W. Kealiinohomoku, 221–49. The Hague: Mouton.

La Serna, Miguel. 2012a. *The Corner of the Living: Ayacucho on the Eve of the Shining Path Insurgency*. Chapel Hill: University of North Carolina Press.

La Serna, Miguel. 2012b. "Murió comiendo rata: Power Relations in Pre-Sendero Ayacucho, Peru, 1940–1983." *A Contracorriente* 9(2): 1–34.

Lassiter, Luke E. 1998. *The Power of Kiowa Song: A Collaborative Ethnography*. Tucson: University of Arizona Press.

Latour, Bruno. 1993. *We Have Never Been Modern*. New York: Harvester Wheatsheaf.

Latour, Bruno. 2004. *Politics of Nature: How to Bring the Sciences into Democracy*. Cambridge, MA: Harvard University Press.

Lawrence, Tim. 2003. *Love Saves the Day: A History of American Dance Music Culture, 1970–1979*. Durham, NC: Duke University Press.

Levin, Theodore, and Valentina Süzükei. 2006. *Where Rivers and Mountains Sing: Sound, Music, and Nomadism in Tuva and Beyond*. Bloomington: Indian University Press.

Levy, Robert I. 1973. *Tahitians*. Chicago: University of Chicago Press.

Li, Fabiana. 2015. *Unearthing Conflict: Corporate Mining, Activism, and Expertise in Peru*. Durham, NC: Duke University Press.

Libin, Laurence. 2000. "Progress, Adaptation, and the Evolution of Musical Instruments." *Journal of the American Musical Instrument Society* 26:187–213.

Lima, Tânia Stolze. 1999. "The Two and Its Many: Reflections on Perspectivism in a Tupi Cosmology." *Ethnos: Journal of Anthropology* 64(1): 107–31.

Llorens Amico, José Antonio. 1983. *Música popular en Lima: Criollos y andinos*. Lima: IEP.

REFERENCES

Lott, Eric. 2011. "Back Door Man: Howlin' Wolf and the Sound of Jim Crow." *American Quarterly* 63(3): 697–710.

Lucero, José Antonio. 2006. "Representing 'Real Indians': The Challenges of Indigenous Authenticity and Strategic Constructivism in Ecuador and Bolivia." *Latin American Research Review* 41(2): 31–56.

Lucero, José Antonio. 2010. "Peoples of the Earth: Ethnonationalism, Democracy, and the Indigenous Challenge in 'Latin' America." *A Contracorriente: Revista de Historia Social y Literatura en América Latina* 8(1): 540–50.

Lukes, Steven. 1974. *Power: A Radical View*. London: Macmillan.

Lutz, Catherine. 1996. "Engendered Emotion: Gender, Power, and the Rhetoric of Emotional Control in American Discourse." In *The Emotions*, edited by R. Harre and W. G. Parrot, 152–70. Thousand Oaks, CA: Sage.

Lutz, Catherine, and Lila Abu-Lughod. 1990. "Introduction: Emotion, Discourse, and the Politics of Everyday Life." In *Language and the Politics of Emotion*, edited by Catherine Lutz and Lila Abu-Lughod, 1–23. Cambridge: Cambridge University Press.

Lutz, Catherine, and Geoffrey M. White. 1986. "The Anthropology of Emotions." *Annual Review of Anthropology* 15:405–36.

Machaca Mendieta, Magdalena 2007. *Los ánimos de la enfermadad, plantas medicinales, manos, y sitios sanadoras: La cosmovisión quechua sobre la salud, en los Andes centrales del Perú; Caso de las comunidades de Quispillaccta, Chuschi, Chacolla, Ayuta, Chuymay, y Huaripercca, Ayacucho*. Ayacucho: Asociación Bartolomé Aripaylla—ABA Ayacucho.

MacLennan, Hugh. 1945. *Two Solitudes*. New York: Duell.

Magowan, Fiona. 2007. *Melodies of Mourning: Music and Emotion in Northern Australia*. Santa Fe, NM: School for Advanced Research Press.

Mannheim, Bruce. 1998. "Time, Not the Syllables, Must Be Counted: Quechua Parallelism, Word Meaning, and Cultural Analysis." *Michigan Discussions in Anthropology* 13(1): 238–81.

Mannheim, Bruce, and Guillermo Salas Carreño. 2015. "Wak'as: Entifications of the Andean Sacred." In *The Archaeology of Wak'as: Explorations of the Sacred in the Pre-Columbian Andes*, edited by Tamara L. Bray, 47–74. Boulder: University Press of Colorado.

Manning, Paul. 2012. *The Semiotics of Drink and Drinking*. London: Continuum.

Manuel, Peter. 1993. *Cassette Culture: Popular Music and Technology in North India*. Chicago: University of Chicago Press.

Marchand, Thomas. 2010. "Embodied Cognition, Communication and the Making of Place and Identity: Reflections on Fieldwork with Masons." In *Human Nature as Capacity: Transcending Discourse and Classification*, edited by Nigel Rapport, 182–206. Oxford: Berghahn.

Marre, Jeremy, dir. 1990 [1983]. *Shotguns and Accordions: Music of the Marijuana Growing Regions of Colombia*. DVD, 60 min. Shanachie.

Martinez-Reyes, Jose. 2015. "Mahogany Intertwined: Enviromateriality between Mexico, Fiji, and the Gibson Les Paul." *Journal of Material Culture* 20(3): 313–29.

Massumi, Brian. 2002. *Parables for the Virtual: Movement, Affect, Sensation*. Durham, NC: Duke University Press.

Matos Mar, José, et al. 2004. *Desborde popular y crisis del estado: Veinte años después*. Lima: Fondo Editorial del Congreso del Perú.

Mauss, Marcel. 1950 [1934]. *Sociologie et anthropologie*. Paris: Presses universitaires de France.

Mayer, Enrique. 1992. "Peru in Deep Trouble: Mario Vargas Llosa's 'Inquest in the Andes' Re-examined." In *Rereading Cultural Anthropology*, edited by George E. Marcus, 181–219. Durham, NC: Duke University Press.

Mayer, Enrique. 2002. *The Articulated Peasant: Household Economies in the Andes*. Boulder: Westview.

Mayer, Enrique. 2009. *Ugly Stories of the Peruvian Agrarian Reform*. Durham, NC: Duke University Press.

McNally, Michael D. 2000. *Ojibwe Singers: Hymns, Grief, and a Native Culture in Motion*. New York: Oxford University Press.

Méndez G., Cecilia. 2005. *The Plebeian Republic: The Huanta Rebellion and the Making of the Peruvian State, 1820–1850*. Durham, NC: Duke University Press.

Mendívil, Julio. 2002. "La construcción de la historia: El charango en la memoria colectiva mestiza ayacuchana." *Revista Musical Chilena* 56:63–78.

Mendoza, Zoila S. 2000. *Shaping Society through Dance: Mestizo Ritual Performance in the Peruvian Andes*. Chicago: University of Chicago Press.

Mendoza, Zoila S. 2008. *Creating Our Own: Folklore, Performance, and Identity in Cuzco, Peru*. Durham, NC: Duke University Press.

Menezes Bastos, Rafael José de. 2013. "Apùap World Hearing Revisited: Talking with 'Animals,' 'Spirits' and Other Beings, and Listening to the Apparently Inaudible." *Ethnomusicology Forum* 22(3): 287–305.

Merlan, Francesca. 2009. "Indigeneity: Global and Local." *Current Anthropology* 50(3): 303–33.

Middleton, Richard. 1990. *Studying Popular Music*. Milton Keynes, UK: Open University Press.

Miller, Derek. 2011. "On Piano Performance—Technology and Technique." *Contemporary Theatre Review* 21(3): 261–75.

Millones, Luis, Jose Ochatoma, and Jefrey Gamarra, eds. 2007. *El desarrollo de las ciencias sociales en Ayacucho*. Lima: Universidad Nacional Mayor de San Marcos.

Minks, Amanda. 2013. *Voices of Play: Miskitu Children's Speech and Song on the Atlantic Coast of Nicaragua*. Tucson: University of Arizona Press.

Montero Díaz, Fiorella. 2016. "Singing the War: Reconfiguring White Upperclass Identity through Fusion Music in Post-war Lima." *Ethnomusicology Forum* 25(2): 191–209.

Montoya Rojas, Rodrigo, Luis Montoya Rojas, and Edwin Montoya Rojas. 1997 [1987]. *Urqukunapa yawarnin—La sangre de los cerros: Antología de la poesía quechua que se canta en el Perú*. Lima: Universidad Nacional Federico Villarreal.

Morris, William. 1888. *Signs of Change: Seven Lectures Delivered on Various Occasions by William Morris*. London: Reeves and Turner.

Mosely, Roger. 2015. "Digital Analogies: The Keyboard as Field of Musical Play." *Journal of the American Musicological Society* 68(1): 151–227.

Mrázek, Jan. 2008. "Xylophones in Thailand and Java: A Comparative Phenomenology of Musical Instruments." *Asian Music* 39(2): 59–107.

Mumford, Lewis. 1966. *The Myth of the Machine: Technics and Human Development*. New York: Harcourt Brace Jovanovich.

Muñoz Ruiz, Urbano, and Oseas Núñez Espinoza. 2006. *Los Kanas de Quispillaccta: Historia de un pueblo quechua*. Ayacucho: Comunidad de Quispillaccta, Acción Andina, Oxfam America.

Murra, John. 1972. "El 'control vertical' de un máximo de pisos ecológicos en la economía de las sociedades andinas." In *Visita de la Provincia de León de Huanuco en 1562*, edited by John Murra, 427–476. Huánuco, Peru: Universidad Nacional Hermilio Valdizán.

REFERENCES

Myers, Fred. 1988. "The Logic and Meaning of Anger among Pintupi Aborigines." *Man* 23(4): 589–610.

Nadasdy, Paul. 2007. "The Gift in the Animal: The Ontology of Hunting and Human–Animal Sociality." *American Ethnologist* 34(1): 25–43.

Neuenfeldt, Karl, ed. 1997. *The Didjeridu: From Arnhem Land to Internet.* Sydney: J. Libbey / Perfect Beat.

Neuenfeldt, Karl. 1998. "Notes on Old Instruments in New Contexts." *World of Music* 40(2): 5–8.

Niezen, Ronald. 2003. *The Origins of Indigenism: Human Rights and the Politics of Identity.* Berkeley: University of California Press.

Norton, Barley. 2013. "Engendering Emotion and the Environment in Vietnamese Music and Ritual." In *Performing Gender, Place, and Emotion in Music: Global Perspectives*, edited by Fiona Magowan and Louise Wrazen, 19–37. Rochester, NY: University of Rochester Press.

O'Connor, Alan. 2006. *"The Voice of the Mountains": Radio and Anthropology.* Lanham, MD: University Press of America.

O'Connor, Erin. 2005. "Embodied Knowledge: The Experience of Meaning and the Struggle towards Proficiency in Glassblowing." *Ethnography* 6(2): 183–204.

Ochoa Gautier, Ana María. 2014. *Aurality: Listening and Knowledge in Nineteenth-Century Colombia.* Durham, NC: Duke University Press.

Oliart, Patricia. 2008. "Indigenous Women's Organizations and the Political Discourses of Indigenous Rights and Gender Equity in Peru." *Latin American and Caribbean Ethnic Studies* 3(3): 291–308.

Orjeda, Antonio. 2014. "La tecnología occidental es para los desesperados." *Mujeres Batalla,* November 22, 1–8.

Orlove, Benjamin S. 1998. "Down to Earth: Race and Substance in the Andes." *Bulletin of Latin American Research* 17(2): 207–22.

Pajuelo Torres, Ramón. 2007. *Reinventando comunidades imaginados: Movimientos indígenas, nación y procesos sociopolíticos en los países centroandinos.* Lima: IEP.

Pallares, Amalia. 2002. *From Peasant Struggles to Indian Resistance: The Ecuadorian Andes in the Late Twentieth Century.* Norman: University of Oklahoma Press.

Palomino Flores, Salvador. 1971. "Duality in the Socio-cultural Organization of Several Andean Populations." *Folk* 13:65–88.

Palomino Flores, Salvador. 1984. *El sistema de oposiciones en la comunidad de Sarhua.* Lima: Editorial Pueblo Indio.

Paredes, Maritza Victoria. 2016. *Representación política indígena: Un análisis comparativo subnacional.* Lima: IEP.

Partridge, William, and Jorge Uquillas. 1996. "Including the Excluded: Ethnodevelopment in Latin America." Paper presented at the Annual World Bank Conference on Development in Latin America and the Caribbean. Bogotá, June 30–July 2.

Paulson, Susan. 2003. "Gendered Practices and Landscapes in the Andes: The Shape of Asymmetrical Exchanges." *Human Organization* 62(3): 242–54.

Perlman, Marc. 2004. *Unplayed Melodies: Javanese Gamelan and the Genesis of Music Theory.* Berkeley: University of California Press.

Petersen, Sonja. 2013. "Craftsmen-Turned-Scientists? The Circulation of Explicit and Working Knowledge in Musical-Instrument Making, 1880–1960." *Osiris* 28(1): 212–31.

Peterson, Richard A. 1997. *Creating Country Music: Fabricating Authenticity.* Chicago: University of Chicago Press.

Piedade, Acácio Tadeu de Camargo. 2013. "Flutes, Songs and Dreams: Cycles of Creation and Musical Performance among the Wauja of the Upper Xingu (Brazil)." *Ethnomusicology Forum* 22(3): 306–22.

Pinch, Trevor, and Frank Trocco. 2002. *Analog Days: The Invention and Impact of the Moog Synthesizer.* Cambridge, MA: Harvard University Press.

Platt, Tristan. 1986 [1978]. "Mirrors and Maize: The Concept of Yanantin among the Macha of Bolivia." In *Anthropological History of Andean Polities*, edited by John Murra, Nathan Wachtel, and Jean Reve, 228–59. London: Cambridge University Press.

Polanyi, Michael. 1966. *The Tacit Dimension.* Garden City, NY: Doubleday.

Poole, Deborah. 1988. "Entre el milagro y la mercancía: Qoyllur Rit'i." *Revista Márgenes: Encuentro y Debate* 6:101–9.

Poole, Deborah. 2010. "El buen vivir: Peruvian Indigenous Leader Mario Palacios." *NACLA Report on the Americas* 43(5): 30–40.

Portocarrero. Gonzalo. 2007. *Racismo y mestizaje y otros ensayos.* Lima: Fondo Editorial del Congreso del Peru.

Post, Jennifer C. 2007. "'I Take My Dombra and Sing to Remember My Homeland': Identity, Landscape and Music in Kazakh Communities of Western Mongolia." *Ethnomusicology Forum* 16(1): 45–69.

Postero, Nancy Grey. 2005. "Indigenous Responses to Neoliberalism: A Look at the Bolivian Uprising of 2003." *PoLAR: Political and Legal Anthropology Review* 28(1): 73–92.

Postero, Nancy Grey. 2007. *Now We Are Citizens: Indigenous Politics in Postmulticultural Bolivia.* Stanford, CA: Stanford University Press.

Povinelli, Elizabeth. 2002. *The Cunning of Recognition: Indigenous Alterities and the Making of Australian Multiculturalism.* Durham, NC: Duke University Press.

Pye, David. 1968. *The Nature and Art of Workmanship.* Cambridge: Cambridge University Press.

Quijano, Aníbal, ed. 2014. *Des/colonialidad y bien vivir: Un nuevo debate en América Latina.* Lima: Universidad Ricardo Palma.

Quispe Mejía, Ulpiano. 1969. *La herranza en Choque Huarcaya y Huancasancos, Ayacucho.* Lima: Instituto Indigenista Peruano.

Qureshi, Regula Burckhart. 1997. "The Indian Sarangi: Sound of Affect, Site of Contest." *Yearbook for Traditional Music* 29:1–38.

Ráez Retamozo, Manuel. 2002. *En los dominios del cóndor: Fiestas y música tradicional del valle del Colca.* Lima: Pontificia Universidad Católica del Perú.

Ráez Retamozo, Manuel. 2005. *Dioses de las quebradas: Fiestas y rituales en la sierra alta de Lima.* Lima: Pontificia Universidad Católica del Perú.

Ramos, Alcida. 2012. "The Politics of Perspectivism." *Annual Review of Anthropology* 41:481–94.

Rancière, Jacques. 1999. *Dis-agreement: Politics and Philosophy.* Translated by Julie Rose. Minneapolis: University of Minnesota Press.

Rancière, Jacques. 2006. *The Politics of Aesthetics: The Distribution of the Sensible.* London: Continuum.

Rancière, Jacques. 2010. *Dissensus: On Politics and Aesthetics.* London: Continuum.

Reily, Suzel Ana. 2001. "To Remember Captivity: The 'Congados' of Southern Minas Gerais." *Latin American Music Review* 22(1): 4–30.

Rekedal, Jacob. 2014. "Hip-Hop Mapuche on the Araucanian Frontera." *Alter/nativas* 2:1–35.

Rengifo Vásquez, Grimaldo. 2010. *Crisis climática y saber comunero en los Andes del sur peruano.* Lima: PRATEC.

REFERENCES 263

Rice, Timothy. 1994. *May It Fill Your Soul: Experiencing Bulgarian Music*. Chicago: University of Chicago Press.

Ríos, Fernando. 2008. "La Flûte Indienne: The Early History of Andean Folkloric-Popular Music in France and Its Impact on Nueva Canción." *Latin American Music Review* 29(2): 145–89.

Ritter, Jonathan. 2002. "Siren Songs: Ritual and Revolution in the Peruvian Andes." *British Journal of Ethnomusicology* 11(1): 9–42.

Ritter, Jonathan. 2006. "A River of Blood: Music, Memory, and Violence in Ayacucho, Peru." PhD diss., University of California, Los Angeles.

Ritter, Jonathan. 2012. "Peru and the Andes." In *Musics of Latin America*, edited by Robin Moore and Walter Aaron Clark, 324–70. New York: W. W. Norton.

Rivadeneyra Olcese, Carlos. 2009. "Las otras radios: El complejo escenario de la radio en el Perú." *Contratexto* 6(7): 6–15.

Rockhill, Gabriel. 2009. "The Politics of Aesthetics: Political History and the Hermeneutics of Art." In *Jacques Rancière: History, Politics, Aesthetics*, edited by Gabriel Rockhill and Philip Watts, 195–215. Durham, NC: Duke University Press.

Rockhill, Gabriel, and Philip Watts, eds. 2009. *Jacques Rancière: History, Politics, Aesthetics*. Durham, NC: Duke University Press.

Roda, P. Allen. 2015. "Ecology of the Global Tabla Industry." *Ethnomusicology* 59(2): 315–36.

Romero, Raúl R., ed. 1988. *Música, danzas, y mascaras en los Andes*. Lima: Pontificia Universidad Católica del Perú.

Romero, Raúl R. 2001. *Debating the Past: Music, Memory, and Identity in the Andes*. New York: Oxford University Press.

Romero, Raúl R. 2002. "Popular Music and the Global City: Huayno, Chicha and Techno-Cumbia in Lima." In *From Tejano to Tango: Latin American Popular Music*, edited by Walter Aaron Clark, 217–39. New York: Routledge.

Roseman, Marina. 1998. "Singers of the Landscape: Song, History, and Property Rights in the Malaysian Rain Forest." *American Anthropologist* 100(1): 106–21.

Rothenbuhler, Eric W. 2007. "For-the-Record Aesthetics and Robert Johnson's Blues Style as a Product of Recorded Culture." *Popular Music* 26(1): 65–81.

Rousseau, Stephanie. 2011. "Indigenous and Feminist Movements at the Constituent Assembly in Bolivia: Locating the Representation of Indigenous Women." *Latin American Research Review* 46(2): 5–28.

Rowe, William, and Vivian Schelling. 1991. *Memory and Modernity: Popular Culture in Latin America*. London: Verso.

Ruskin, John. 1854. *The Stones of Venice*. New York: Merrill and Baker.

Ryan, Robin. 2003. "Jamming on the Gumleaves in the Bush 'Down Under': Black Tradition, White Novelty?" *Popular Music and Society* 26(3): 285–304.

Saignes, Thierry. 1993. "'Estar en otra cabeza': Tomar en los Andes." In *Borrachera y memoria: La experiencia de lo sagrado en los Andes*, edited by Thierry Saignes, 11–22. Lima: IFEA.

Salas Carreño, Guillermo. 2008. *Dinámica social y minería: Familias pastoras de puna y la presencia del proyecto Antamina (1997–2002)*. Lima: IEP.

Salazar-Soler, Carmen. 2009. "Los tesoros del Inca y la madre naturaleza: Etnoecología y lucha contra las compañías mineras en el norte del Peru." In *El regreso de lo indígena: Retos, problemas y perspectivas*, edited by Valérie Robin and Carmen Salazar-Soler Azevero, 187–216. Lima: Instituto Francés de Estudios Andinos.

Salazar-Soler, Carmen. 2014. "El despertar del Perú andino?" In *De la política indígena, Peru y Bolivia*, edited by Georges Lomné, 71–126. Lima: IFEA and IEP.

Sallnow, Michael J. 1987. *Pilgrims of the Andes: Regional Cults in Cusco*. Washington, DC: Smithsonian Institution Press.

Salomon, Frank. 2002. "Unethnic Ethnohistory: On Peruvian Peasant Historiography and Ideas of Autochthony." *Ethnohistory* 49(3): 475–506.

Salomon, Frank. 2004. *The Cord Keepers: Khipus and Cultural Life in a Peruvian Village*. Durham, NC: Duke University Press.

Samuels, David William. 2004. *Putting a Song on Top of It: Expression and Identity on the San Carlos Apache Reservation*. Tucson: University of Arizona Press.

Sánchez León, Abelardo, ed. 2014. *Sensibilidad de frontera: Comunicación y voces populares*. Lima: PUCP.

Sánchez Villagómez, Marté. 2007. *Pensar los senderos olvidados de historia y memoria: La violencia política en las comunidades de Chu y Quispillaccta, 1980–1991*. Lima: Asociación Servicios Educativos Rurales, SER, Fondo Editorial de la Facultad de Ciencias Sociales UNMSM.

Sánchez Villagómez, Marté. 2009. "Memoria y olvido de la violencia política en el distrito de Chuschi." In *Ensayos en ciencias sociales 3*, edited by Enrique Jaramillo García, 59–108. Lima: Universidad Nacional Mayor de San Marcos, Instituto de Investigaciones Histórico Sociales, Fondo Editorial de la Facultad de Ciencias Sociales.

Sawyer, Suzana. 2004. *Crude Chronicles: Indigenous Politics, Multinational Oil, and Neoliberalism in Ecuador*. Durham, NC: Duke University Press.

Scales, Christopher A. 2012. *Recording Culture: Powwow Music and the Aboriginal Recording Industry on the Northern Plains*. Durham, NC: Duke University Press.

Scarritt, Arthur. 2013. "First the Revolutionary Culture: Innovations in Empowered Citizenship from Evangelical Highland Peru." *Latin American Perspectives* 40(4): 101–20.

Schafer, R. Murray. 1977. *The Soundscape: Our Sonic Environment and the Tuning of the World*. Rochester, VT: Destiny Books.

Schieffelin, Edward L. 1983. "Anger and Shame in the Tropical Forest: On Affect as a Cultural System in Papua New Guinea." *Ethos* 11(3): 181–91.

Seeger, Anthony. 2004. *Why Suyá Sing: A Musical Anthropology of an Amazonian People*. Urbana: University of Illinois Press.

Seeger, Anthony. 2013. "Focusing Perspectives and Establishing Boundaries and Power: Why the Suyá/Kĩsêdjê Sing for the Whites in the Twenty-First Century." *Ethnomusicology Forum* 22(3): 362–76.

Seligmann, Linda. 1995. *Between Reform and Revolution: Political Struggles in the Peruvian Andes, 1969–1991*. Stanford, CA: Stanford University Press.

Seligmann, Linda. 2004. *Peruvian Street Lives: Culture, Power, and Economy among Market Women of Cuzco*. Urbana: University of Illinois Press.

Sennett, Richard. 2008. *The Craftsman*. London: Allen Lane.

Serres, Michel. 1995. *Genesis*. Translated from French by Geneviève James and James Nielson. Ann Arbor: University of Michigan Press.

Sikkink, Lynn. 1997. "El poder mediador del cambio de aguas: Género y el cuerpo político condeño." In *Más allá del silencio: Las fronteras de género en los Andes*, edited by Denise Y. Arnold, 94–122. La Paz: CIASE/ILCA.

Simonett, Helena. 2001. "Narcocorridos: An Emerging Micromusic of Nuevo L.A." *Ethnomusicology* 45(2): 315–37.

REFERENCES

Simonett, Helena. 2014. "Envisioned, Ensounded, Enacted: Sacred Ecology and Indigenous Musical Experience in Yoreme Ceremonies of Northwest Mexico." *Ethnomusicology* 58(1): 110–32.

Simpson, Audra. 2014. "The Chief's Two Bodies: Theresa Spence and the Gender of Settler Sovereignty." Paper presented at Unsettling Conversations, Unmaking Racisms and Colonialisms: R.A.C.E. Network's 14th Annual Critical Race and Anticolonial Studies Conference, University of Alberta, Edmonton. Available as video at https://vimeo.com/110948627.

Smith, Adam T. 2015. *The Political Machine: Assembling Sovereignty in the Bronze Age Caucasus.* Princeton, NJ: Princeton University Press.

Smith, Anthony D. 1986. *The Ethnic Origins of Nations.* Oxford: Basil Blackwell.

Smith, Paul Chaat. 2009. *Everything You Know about Indians Is Wrong.* Minneapolis: University of Minnesota Press.

Sneed, Paul. 2007. "Bandidos de Cristo: Representations of the Power of Criminal Factions in Rio's Proibidão Funk." *Latin American Music Review* 28(2): 220–41.

Solomon, Thomas. 1994. "Coplas de Todos Santos in Cochabamba: Language, Music, and Performance in Bolivian Quechua Song Dueling." *Journal of American Folklore* 107: 378–414.

Solomon, Thomas. 2000. "Dueling Landscapes: Singing Places and Identities in Highland Bolivia." *Ethnomusicology* 44(2): 257–80.

Solomon, Thomas. 2015. "Performing Indigeneity: Poetics and Politics of Music Festivals in Highland Bolivia." In *Soundscapes from the Americas: Ethnomusicological Essays on the Power, Poetics, and Ontology of Performance,* edited by Donna A. Buchanan, 143–64. Aldershot, UK: Ashgate.

Sommer, Doris. 2006. "Introduction: Wiggle Room." In *Cultural Agency in the Americas,* edited by Doris Sommer, 1–28. Durham, NC: Duke University Press.

Somogyi, Ervin. 2012. *The Responsive Guitar.* Oakland, CA: Luthiers Press.

Starn, Orin. 1991. "Missing the Revolution: Anthropologists and the War in Peru." *Cultural Anthropology* 6(1): 63–91.

Steingo, Gavin. 2016. *Kwaito's Promise: Music and the Aesthetics of Freedom in South Africa.* Chicago: University of Chicago Press.

Stern, Steve. 1993. *Peru's Indian Peoples and the Challenge of Spanish Conquest: Huamanga to 1640.* Madison: University of Wisconsin Press.

Stiegler, Bernard. 1998. *Technics and Time,* vol. 1, *The Fault of Epimetheus.* Translated from French by Richard Beardsworth and George Collins. Stanford, CA: Stanford University Press.

Stiegler, Bernard. 2013. *For a New Critique of Political Economy.* Translated from French by Daniel Ross. Cambridge: Polity.

Stobart, Henry. 1994. "Flourishing Horns and Enchanted Tubers: Music and Potatoes in Highland Bolivia." *British Journal of Ethnomusicology* 3:35–48.

Stobart, Henry. 2006. *Music and the Poetics of Production in the Bolivian Andes.* Aldershot, UK: Ashgate.

Stobart, Henry. 2008. "In Touch with the Earth? Musical Instruments, Gender and Fertility in the Bolivian Andes." *Ethnomusicology Forum* 17(1): 67–94.

Stobart, Henry. 2010. "Rampant Reproduction and Digital Democracy: Shifting Landscapes of Music Production and 'Piracy' in Bolivia." *Ethnomusicology Forum* 19(1): 27–56.

Stobart, Henry. 2011. "Constructing Community in the Digital Home Studio: Carnival, Creativity and Indigenous Music Video Production in the Bolivian Andes." *Popular Music* 30(2): 209–26.

Stock, Jonathan. 2001. "Toward an Ethnomusicology of the Individual, or Biographical Writing in Ethnomusicology." *World of Music* 43(1): 5–19.

Stokes, Martin. 1992. "The Media and Reform: The Saz and Elektrosaz in Urban Turkish Folk Music." *British Journal of Ethnomusicology* 1:89–102.

Stokes, Martin. 2010. *The Republic of Love: Cultural Intimacy in Turkish Popular Music.* Chicago: University of Chicago Press.

Sturm, Circe. 2002. *Blood Politics: Race, Culture, and Identity in the Cherokee Nation of Oklahoma.* Berkeley: University of California Press.

Stutzman, Ronald. 1981. "El Mestizaje: An All-Inclusive Ideology of Exclusion." In *Cultural Transformation and Ethnicity in Modern Ecuador*, edited by Norman Whitten, 45–94. Urbana: University of Illinois Press.

Swinehart, Karl. 2012. "Tupac in Their Veins: Hip-Hop Alteño and the Semiotics of Urban Indigeneity." *Arizona Journal of Hispanic Cultural Studies* 16:79–96.

TallBear, Kimberly. 2013. *Native American DNA: Tribal Belonging and the False Promise of Genetic Science.* Minneapolis: University of Minnesota Press.

Tarica, Estelle. 2008. *The Inner Life of Mestizo Nationalism.* Minneapolis: University of Minnesota Press.

Taylor, Diana. 2003. *The Archive and the Repertoire: Performing Cultural Memory in the Americas.* Durham, NC: Duke University Press.

Terdiman, Richard. 1985. "Deconstructing Memory: On Representing the Past and Theorizing Culture in France since the Revolution." *Diacritics* 15(4): 13–36.

Théberge, Paul. 1997. *Any Sound You Can Imagine: Making Music / Consuming Technology.* Hanover, NH: University Press of New England.

Theidon, Kimberly Susan. 2013. *Intimate Enemies: Violence and Reconciliation in Peru.* Philadelphia: University of Pennsylvania Press.

Thorp, Rosemary, and Maritza Paredes. 2010. *Ethnicity and the Persistence of Inequality: The Case of Peru.* Houndmills, Basingstoke, UK: Palgrave Macmillan.

Throop, Jason. 2010. *Suffering and Sentiment: Exploring the Vicissitudes of Experience and Pain in Yap.* Berkeley: University of California Press.

Titon, Jeff Todd. 1988. *Powerhouse for God: Speech, Chant, and Song in an Appalachian Baptist Church.* Austin: University of Texas Press.

Titon, Jeff Todd. 2015. "Sustainability, Resilience, and Adaptive Management for Applied Ethnomusicology." In *The Oxford Handbook of Applied Ethnomusicology*, edited by Svanibor Pettan and Jeff Todd Titon, 157–98. New York: Oxford University Press.

Toner, P. G. 2005. "Tropes of Longing and Belonging: Nostalgia and Musical Instruments in Northeast Arnhem Land." *Yearbook for Traditional Music* 37:1–24.

Tresch, John, and Emily I. Dolan. 2013. "Toward a New Organology: Instruments of Music and Science." *Osiris* 28(1): 278–98.

Trump, Maxine. 2012. *Musicwood.* DVD. Cinema Guild, 80 min.

Tsing, Anna Lowenhaupt. 2005. *Friction: An Ethnography of Global Connection.* Princeton, NJ: Princeton University Press.

Tuan, Yi-Fu. 1974. *Topophilia: A Study of Environmental Perception, Attitudes, and Values.* Englewood Cliffs, NJ: Prentice-Hall.

Tucker, Joshua. 2011. "Permitted Indians and Popular Music in Contemporary Peru: The Politics and Poetics of Indigenous Performativity." *Ethnomusicology* 55(3): 387–413.

Tucker, Joshua. 2013a. "From *The World of the Poor* to the Beaches of 'Eisha': Chicha, Cumbia,

REFERENCES 267

and the Search for a Popular Subject in Peru. In *Cumbia! Scenes of a Migrant Latin American Music Genre*, edited by Héctor Fernández L'Hoeste and Pablo Vila, 138–67. Durham, NC: Duke University Press.

Tucker, Joshua. 2013b. *Gentleman Troubadours and Andean Pop Stars: Huayno Music, Media Work, and Ethnic Imaginaries in Urban Peru*. Chicago: University of Chicago Press.

Tucker, Joshua. 2013c. "Producing the Andean Voice: Popular Music, Folkloric Performance, and the Possessive Investment in Indigeneity." *Latin American Music Review* 34(1): 31–70.

Turino, Thomas. 1983. "The Charango and the 'Sirena': Music, Magic, and the Power of Love." *Latin American Music Review* 4(1): 81–119.

Turino, Thomas. 1984. "The Urban-Mestizo Charango Tradition in Southern Peru: A Statement of Shifting Identity." *Ethnomusicology* 28(2): 253–70.

Turino, Thomas. 1988. "Music of Andean Migrants in Lima, Peru: Demographics, Social Power, and Style." *Latin American Music Review* 9(2): 127–50.

Turino, Thomas. 1990a. "'Somos el Perú' (We Are Peru): Cumbia Andina and the Children of the Andean Migrants in Lima." *Studies in Latin American Popular Culture* 9:18–25.

Turino, Thomas. 1990b. "Structure, Context, and Strategy in Musical Ethnography." *Ethnomusicology* 34(3): 399–412.

Turino, Thomas. 1993. *Moving Away from Silence: Music of the Peruvian Altiplano and the Experience of Urban Migration*. Chicago: University of Chicago Press.

Turino, Thomas. 2000. *Nationalists, Cosmopolitans, and Popular Music in Zimbabwe*. Chicago: University of Chicago Press.

Turino, Thomas. 2008. *Music as Social Life: The Politics of Participation*. Chicago: University of Chicago Press.

Turner, Terence. 1991. "Representing, Resisting, Rethinking: Historical Transformations of Kayapo Culture and Anthropological Consciousness." In *Colonial Situations: Essays on the Contextualization of Anthropological Knowledge*, edited by George Stocking Jr., 285–313. Madison: University of Wisconsin Press.

Turner, Terence. 1993. "The Role of Indigenous Peoples in the Environmental Crisis: The Example of the Kayapo of the Brazilian Amazon." *Perspectives in Biology and Medicine* 36(3): 526–45.

Turner, Terence. 2009. "The Crisis of Late Structuralism: Perspectivism and Animism; Rethinking Culture, Nature, Spirit, and Bodiliness." *Tipití: Journal of the Society for the Anthropology of Lowland South America* 7(1): 3–42.

Ulfe, María Eugenia. 2004. *Danzando en Ayacucho: Música y ritual del Rincón de los Muertos*. Lima: Pontificia Universidad Católica del Perú.

UNCED. 1992. *Report of the United Nations Confrence on Environment and Development*. UN Doc. A/CONF.151/26 (vol. 1). http://www.un.org/documents/ga/confl51/aconfl5126-1annex1.htm.

Valderrama, Ricardo, and Carmen Escalante. 1997. "Ser mujer: Warmi kay, la mujer en la cultura Andina." In *Más allá del silencio: Las fronteras de género en los Andes*, edited by Denise Y. Arnold, 153–69. La Paz: CIASE/ILCA.

Valladolid, Julio, and Frédérique Apffel-Marglin. 2001. "Andean Cosmovision and the Nurturing of Biodiversity." In *Indigenous Traditions and Ecology: The Interbeing of Cosmology and Community*, edited by John A. Grim, 639–70. Cambridge, MA: Harvard Divinity School.

Van Cott, Donna Lee. 2005. *From Movements to Parties in Latin America: The Evolution of Ethnic Politics*. Cambridge: Cambridge University Press.

Van den Berghe, Pierre L., and George Primov. 1977. *Inequality in the Peruvian Andes: Class and Ethnicity in Cuzco*. Columbia: University of Missouri Press.

Van Vleet, Krista E. 2003. "Adolescent Ambiguities and the Negotiation of Belonging in the Andes." *Ethnology* 42(4): 349–63.

Van Vleet, Krista E. 2008. *Performing Kinship: Narrative, Gender, and the Intimacies of Power in the Andes*. Austin: University of Texas Press.

Vich, Víctor. 2002. "Mesa redonda y el incendio de las ciencias sociales." *Revista Quehacer* 134:104–6.

Vich, Víctor. 2009. "Dina y Chacalón del Perú: El secuestro de la experiencia." *La Mirada del Telemo* 2, http://revistas.pucp.edu.pe/index.php/lamiradadetelemo/article/view/3541/3421.

Viveiros de Castro, Eduardo Batalha. 1992. *From the Enemy's Point of View: Humanity and Divinity in an Amazonian Society*. Chicago: University of Chicago Press.

Von Glahn, Denise. 2003. *The Sounds of Place: Music and the American Cultural Landscape*. Boston: Northeastern University Press.

Wacquant, Loïc. 2012. "Three Steps to a Historical Anthropology of Actually Existing Neoliberalism." *Social Anthropology* 20(1): 66–79.

Wade, Peter. 1997. *Race and Ethnicity in Latin America*. London: Pluto.

Wade, Peter. 2007. *Race, Ethnicity and Nation: Perspectives from Kinship and Genetics*. Oxford: Berghahn Books.

Waksman, Steve. 1999. *Instruments of Desire: The Electric Guitar and the Shaping of Musical Experience*. Cambridge, MA: Harvard University Press.

Waksman, Steve. 2003. "Reading the Instrument: An Introduction." *Popular Music and Society* 26(3): 251–61.

Wald, Elijah. 2001. *Narcocorrido: A Journey Into the Music of Drugs, Guns, and Guerrillas*. New York: Rayo.

Warner, Michael. 2002. "Publics and Counterpublics." *Public Culture* 14(1): 49–90.

Warren, Kay B. 1998. *Indigenous Movements and Their Critics: Pan-Maya Activism in Guatemala*. Princeton, NJ: Princeton University Press.

Warren, Kay B. 2005. "Indigenous Movements in Latin America, 1992–2004: Controversies, Ironies, New Directions." *Annual Review of Anthropology* 34:549–73.

Warren, Kay B., and Jean E. Jackson. 2002. *Indigenous Movements, Self-Representation, and the State in Latin America*. Austin: University of Texas Press.

Weismantel, Mary. 2001. *Cholas and Pishtacos: Stories of Race and Sex in the Andes*. Chicago: University of Chicago Press.

Whisnant, David E. 1983. *All That Is Native & Fine: The Politics of Culture in an American Region*. Chapel Hill: University of North Carolina Press.

Williams, Raymond. 1977. *Marxism and Literature*. Oxford: Oxford University Press.

Wong, Ketty. 2012. *Whose National Music? Identity, Mestizaje, and Migration in Ecuador*. Philadelphia: Temple University Press.

Wortham, Erica Cusi. 2013. *Indigenous Media in Mexico: Culture, Community, and the State*. Durham, NC: Duke University Press.

Wrazen, Louise. 2013. "A Place of Her Own: Gendered Singing in Poland's Tatras." In *Performing Gender, Place, and Emotion in Music: Global Perspectives*, edited by Fiona Magowan and Louise Wrazen, 127–45. Rochester, NY: University of Rochester Press.

Yano, Christine R. 2013. "Singing the Contentions of Place: Korean Singers of the Heart and Soul of Japan." In *Performing Gender, Place, and Emotion in Music: Global Perspectives*, edited

REFERENCES

by Fiona Magowan and Louise Wrazen Magowan, 147–61. Rochester, NY: University of Rochester Press.

Yashar, Deborah J. 2005. *Contesting Citizenship in Latin America: The Rise of Indigenous Movements and the Postliberal Challenge*. Cambridge: Cambridge University Press.

Ypiej, Annelou. 2012. "The Intersection of Gender and Ethnic Identities in the Cuzco–Machu Picchu Tourism Industry: Sácamefotos, Tour Guides, and Women Weavers." *Latin American Perspectives* 39(6): 17–35.

Zamorano Villarreal, Gabriela. 2017. *Indigenous Media and Political Imaginaries in Contemporary Bolivia*. Lincoln: University of Nebraska Press.

Zorn, Elayne. 2005. "From Political Prison to Tourist Village: Tourism, Gender, Indigeneity, and the State on Taquile Island, Peru." In *Natives Making Nation: Gender, Indigeneity, and the State in the Andes*, edited by Andrew Canessa, 156–80. Tucson: University of Arizona Press.

Zuidema, R. T. 1966. "Algunos problemas etnohistóricos del Departamento de Ayacucho." *Wamani* 1:68–75.

Zuidema, R. T., and Ulpiano Quispe. 1968. "A Visit to God: The Account and Interpretation of a Religious Experience in the Peruvian Community of Choque-Huarcaya." *Volkenkunde* 1(124): 22–39.

Index

Page numbers in *italics* refer to images.

Achallma, Teófilo, 42
advertising, 144–45, 167, 246n16
agriculture: association with indigeneity, 4; in *chimaycha*, 11, 51; cultivated land, 234n9; development projects, 38, 131, 136, 137, 138–39; difficulty of, 36; ethnodevelopment, 131; tensions between herders and farmers, 34–35; vertical ecology, 32–34
alcohol: and community identity, 158–61; drinking stages, 160, 175–77, 178, 246n22; and emotionality at concerts, 155, 158–61, 174–79; gender norms, 78, 245n11; huayno music, 237n20; in lyrics, 163–64; pathologization of indigenous use, 244–45nn6–7; and sex, 240n20; at *vida michiy*, 68, 69
"Alcoholchay," 163–64
Allcca, Guillermo, 120–22
Allcca Tucno, Juana, 120, *121*
allin kawsay (term), 9
Allpanchik (radio program), 114–17, 119, 126
Amayni site, 65
Andean culture industry, 161–67
Andean Union of Indigenous Organizations (CAOI), 9
androgyny, 239n8
anexos (settlement), 32
Antaqaqa site, 61
APRODEH, 143
arabesk, 182
Ascarza, Walter, 126
Asociación Bartolomé Aripaylla (ABA): agricultural programs, 136, 137, 138–39; criticism of, 139, 215–16; cultural programs and effects, 42, 43, 140; development of, 131, 135–41;

environmentalism, 150, 151–53; founding, 42, 131, 137–38; indigeneity, 141, 153–54; influence of, 132, 140–41; and migrant associations, 44; political effects, 42, 43, 129, 141, 153. *See also* Radio Quispillaccta
Asociación Kanas, 150–51
assimilation, 5–6, 9–10, 210
Asurza Paucar, Bernardo, 113
autobiographical themes, 25, 81, 157, 163, 166, 179–81
Ayacucho: *cholo* culture dominance, 10; colonial rule, 4; cultivated land, 234n9; early indigenous politics, 45–46; economy, 26–27, 45, 46–47; founding, 45; literacy levels, 43; *mestizo* focus, 45, 46; migration to, 37, 41, 44, 45–46; noise of, 196; population, 37, 46; poverty levels, 43; Shining Path, 22–23
"Ay destino," 109, 110, 111
ayllus, 234n5
"Aymara lliqllacha," 120
Aymara speakers, 4, 229n2
Azcarza family, 107

bandurria, 192
Barrios, Corina, 164, 176–79
Barrios, Edwin, 246n20
Barrios, Julia, 147, 166–67, 176–79
barrios and relationships, 32, 34–35
bass: electric, ix, 163, 196; figures by Los Aires Chuschinos, 111, 124, 125; Galindo, 164; strings on *chinlili*, 58, 85, 206
Bautista, Luisa, 120, *121*
beer sales, 158, 168, 172, 175–76, 246n16. *See also* alcohol
binary oppositions, prevalence of, 34
bird imagery, 96–97

272 INDEX

blues, 81, 98
boasting, 97–99
body. *See* embodiment
Bolivia: alcohol use, 237n20; indigenous politics, 9, 20, 230n10, 231n23; rhythms, 239n11; use of indigenous term, 231n14; *vida michiy* cognate practice, 237n12, 237n14
bonsés, 57
brushing stroke, 86

Calderón, Félix, 150
Camasca, Luis, 191
"Campesino," 122–23
canal cleaning festival (*yarqa aspiy*), 48, 58, 242n5
Cancha Cancha and *vida michiy*, 61
Cánepa Koch, Gisela, 18, 19
Canessa, Andrew, 20
Cangallo district college enrollments, 242n18
CAOI (Andean Union of Indigenous Organizations), 9
Carhuapoma (first name unknown), *121*
Carhuapoma, Eusebio, 120
Carhuapoma, Mario, 163–64
Carhuapoma, Teodulfo, 117–18, 124. *See also* Los Chikitukus de Chuschi
Ccallocunto, Lucio "Pachi": anniversary date, 246n20; on enunciation, 240n15; on modern *chimaycha*, 145, 147, 162; recordings, 161, 164–65, 166; on *vida michiy*, 69–70
Ccallocunto, María, 161–62, 246n20
Ccallocunto, Saturnino, 65–66
Ccollahuacho, Judith, 217
CCC. *See* Centro de Capacitación Campesina (CCC)
CEDAP, 150
cemetery as *vida michiy* site, 60, 235n1
"Centro Andino," 99
Centro de Capacitación Campesina (CCC): agriculture projects, 38, 138; *Allpanchik*, 114–17, 119, 127; cultural support, 38, 114–17, 126–27; influence on ABA and Radio Quispillaccta, 136; music competitions, 116; recordings, 126–27, 143
Centro Progreso, 44
chachas (wood), 190, 201
Chanka Indians, 235n14
charangos, 241n14
Chiclla, Arturo, viii–ix, 119, 125
Chiclla, Rosa, 119
Chiclla, Salvador, 119
"Chikllarasu mayu," 94–96
chimaycha: as affirmation of indigeneity, 46, 146–47, 213–14, 216–17; agricultural associations, 11, 51; boom, 146–50, 218–19; as courtship ritual, 11; decline of, 70; disapproval of, 56; and ecocentric world view, 11, 51, 53–54, 129–30;

emotionality and alcohol, 155, 158–61, 174–79; enunciation, 91, 117; folklorization, 105–6; gender roles and norms, 25–26, 57, 68, 76–77, 79–83, 100–101; at *pasllas*, 57–58; relation to huayno, ix, 2, 83, 85, 161–67, 217; rhythms, 85, 86; rivalries between communities, 62–63, 65, 66, 67, 91; rivalries between musicians, 66, 75, 76, 89–90, 91; role in creating a public, 132–36; seasonal associations, 11, 51, 52; song titles, 238n1; sound and timbre, 82–83, 85–90, 185, 194; structure and style, 2, 83–85; as term, 107, 214; translations, 238n1; voice, 57, 79, 82–83, 90–91. *See also chimaycha* development and evolution; *chimaycha* lyrics; Radio Quispillaccta; recordings; *vida michiy*
chimaycha development and evolution: CCC, 113–17, 119; and *cholo* culture, 13, 155–58; Conde on modern, 68, 99, 145, 163–64, 181; drum machines and synthesizers, ix, 156, 161, 162, 163, 164, 165; funding, 26–27, 46–47, 165, 167, 170–71, 172; Ranulfo Infanzón, 106–12; promotion, vii–viii, ix, 155, 167–74, 181; relation to huayno, 161–67; by Marco Tucno and Los Chikitukus de Chuschi, 11–13, 110–11, 117–26; Marco Tucno on modern, ix, 99, 102, 146; urbanity, 181–82. *See also chimaycha; chimaycha* lyrics
chimaycha lyrics: alcohol, 163–64; autobiographical, 81, 163, 166, 179–81; emotionality in, 179–81, 218–19; humor, 79–80, 97–99; landscapes, 11, 48, 51, 71, 74, 75, 80–81, 94–97, 122–24; modern themes, 12–13, 99–100, 102, 110–11, 160–61, 162, 175; nature, 48, 73–74, 76, 80–81, 92–97; nonhuman beings, 11, 75–76, 93–94; rivalries, 74, 92, 98–99; romance, 2, 92–97, 162; sex, 74, 81–82, 97–99; Spanish use, 110–11, 148, 182; violence, 82, 97; wordplay, 79–80
"Chinkaqkuna," 122
chinlili, 84, 87, 198; amplification, 196, 197–98; consorts, 86–87, 87, 88, 90; development, 28–29, 106, 111–12, 124, 163, 183–84, 185–86, 191–202; electrified, 163, 196–99, 198, 204–5; embodiment, 186, 192–94, 202–7; frets, 88, 89, 195, 196, 200–201, 205; learning, 57, 58, 60; materials memory, 247n4; men's role, 57, 68, 79, 100; as networked object, 185–86, 187–88; rituals, 93; rivalries between musicians, 66, 75, 76, 89–90, 91; style and development of playing, 68, 75–76, 85–86, 117, 124, 125, 204–5; as term, 214; timbre and sound, 83, 85–90, 185, 194; tuning, 85, 85. *See also* instrument making
Chipana, Bernardo, 40
Chirapaq, 8, 131, 143, 150, 153
chivear (term), 88
cholo culture: assimilation, 9–10, 210; and *chimaycha*, 13, 155–58; *cholo* term, 6, 157; clothing, 209; dominance and rise of, 9–10, 44, 156–58;

INDEX

as hustle, 155–56, 157, 160–61; as unrecognized indigeneity, 10–11, 157
chonta palm, 200, 201
Chupas, 128
Chuschi, 33; as community seat, 32; designation as indigenous community, 44, 216; educational attainment, 37; geography, 32, 36; Indian descent, 235n14; population, 37, 41; resettlement projects, 41; rhythms, 85, 86, 111, 125; rivalry with Quispillaccta, 37, 51–52; and Shining Path, 39–41; Spanish speakers, 37
Chuschi District: ecology, 32–34; geography, 31–32, 36, 50; literacy rates, 43; map, 50; population, 41; precolonial Indians, 235n14; settlement patterns, 32–34. *See also* Chuschi; Quispillaccta
chuschino (term), viii
citizen-reporters, 115
climate change, 138, 141, 151, 152
clothing: as expression of indigeneity, 64, 140, 209, 243n14; gender expression, 78; of performers, vii, viii, 170–71; at *vida michiy*, 68
cocaine trade, 24, 26–27, 46–47, 167, 245n15
Colca, 19
colonialism: gender roles and norms, 238n3; governance, 35; land acquisition, 35–36; role in indigeneity, 3–9; settlement of Andes, 4
competitions: ABA, 140; CCC, 116; district anniversary, 113–14; effect on songcraft, 240n18; Los Chikitukus de Chuschi, 118–19, 120, 127; Quispillaccta anniversary, 147; tensions between *puna* and valley dwellers, 35
complementarity, 131–32
comuncha tuning, 85, 85
comuneros: perceptions of non-comuneros, 36–37; Shining Path recruitment, 39–40; term, 36. *See also* indigeneity; indigenous politics
comunidades campesinas, 6
CONACAMI (National Confederation of Communities Affected by Mining), 8–9
CONAPA (National Commission of Indigenous, Amazonian, and Afro-Peruvian Peoples), 7
concerts: advertising, 167, 246n16; anniversaries, 70, 146, 156, 167, 168, 170–71, 172; description, 176–79; emotionality and alcohol, 155, 158–61, 174–79; no-shows, 173; promotion, 167–70, 181; and recording schedules, 171; sites, 169
Conde, Alicia, 173, 177, 246n20
Conde, Óscar, 13, 33; on CCC, 116–17; courtship, 66–67; education, 11, 64; as key figure, 11–14, 28, 29, 212; on lyrics, 79, 93, 96–97, 163–64; on modern *chimaycha*, 68, 99, 145, 163–64, 181; research on *chimaycha*, 83; as traditionalist, ix, 147; on tremolo, 86, 117; use of consorts, 87; on *vida michiy*, 55, 59, 63–69. *See also* Los Auténticos de Patario
Condori, Carlos, 119, 124

consorts, 86–87, 87, 88, 90
constitution, modern, 53
contracts, artist, 168, 246n16, 246n18
COPPIP (Coordinadora Permanente de Pueblos Indígenas del Perú), 8–9
Corazón, Bertita, 156
Corporación Daxi, 168, 169, 172, 217
cosmovisión, 134, 137
COTESU, 38, 114
courtship: *chimaycha* as courtship ritual, 11; of Conde, 66–67; geographic obstacles, 34; *vida michiy*, 48, 54, 56, 58, 62, 63, 64, 66
criollo culture, 4
Cuerdas Andinas, 70
culture: ABA support, 42, 43, 140; Andean culture industry, 161–67; CCC support, 38, 114–17, 126–27; *criollo* culture, 4; erudite culture, 16; expressive culture, 16–20; folklorization, 103–6; huayno as central to, 156–57; object creation, 188. *See also cholo* culture
cumbia, 147, 161, 164, 196
Cusco: alcohol use, 240n20; *vida michiy* cognate practice, 236n12

dancing: at concerts, 158, 176–77, 178, 180, 219; at *vida michiy*, 48, 59, 82, 89
Dandanchayuq site, 61
de la Cadena, Marisol, 19
"Democraciaña libertadllaña," 122
development projects: agriculture, 38, 131, 136, 137, 138–39; education, 11–12; effect on economy, 38; effect on lifeways, 213; ethnodevelopment, 131
Dhalwangu, 81
Día del Campesino, 246n20
Dinastía Tucno, 217–18
DIRECTUR, 120
disappeared people, 40–41
dissensus, 133
Dolby JR./Dolly JR., viii, 119, 124–25
Douglas fir, 188–89
drinking. *See* alcohol; beer sales
drugs. *See* cocaine trade
drum machines, ix, 156, 162, 163, 164
Dueñas, Segundino, 120, 121

earth beings, 19, 73
Easter performances, 69, 70, 146, 167, 168
ebony, 248n18
ecology: Chuschi District, 32–34; *cosmovisión*, 134, 137; ecocentric world view, 11, 51, 52–54; 129–30; sentient, 53–54; vertical, 32–34. *See also* environmental awareness
economy: and cocaine trade, 26–27, 46–47; effect of development projects, 38; and evangelical Christianity, 235n19; Quispillaccta, 41; and UNSCH, 45

274 INDEX

Ecuador, indigenous politics of, 230n10, 231n23
education: attainment, 37, 38, 41–42, 213; of Conde, 11, 64; development projects, 11–12; respect for, 106; of Marco Tucno, 11, 60, 124, 188–91, 200; women, 38, 49. *See also* Universidad Nacional San Cristóbal de Huamanga (UNSCH)
elopements, 54, 63
embodiment: instrument making, 186, 192–94, 202–7; musicians, 186, 203–4, 206–7; of things, 186–88, 206–7
embodiment relations, 186
E minor tonality, 239n10
emotionality: and alcohol at concerts, 155, 158–61, 174–79; as learned, 159; in lyrics, 179–81, 218–19
entrepreneurship. *See* hustle
enunciation, 91, 117
environmental awareness: ABA, 150, 151–53; in *chimaycha*, 11, 48, 75–76; as cliché of indigenous culture, 53, 71; climate change, 138, 141, 151, 152; and indigenous rights, 7–9; and instrument making, 185, 199–202; NGO interests, 3, 8–9; Radio Quispillaccta, 150–53. *See also* ecology; landscape
erudite culture, 16
Espinoza, Dionisia, 179–81
Espinoza, Miguel "Tío Miki," 56, 152, 153, 169–74, 179
Espinoza, Teodosio, 179
ethnodevelopment, 131
eucalyptus, 200
evangelical Christianity: decline of *vida michiy*, 55–56, 70; effect on economy, 235n19; radio, 243n9; resistance to ABA, 139, 215; and Shining Path, 138
exosomatic organs, 187–88
expressive culture, 16–20

Falcón, Abrahám, 191, 200, 248n11
farming. *See* agriculture; livestock
fees, artist, 246n16, 246n18
Fernández, Julián, 119, 120
fertility: *chinlili* rituals, 93; *vida michiy*, 54, 55, 99
festivals: canal cleaning, 48, 58, 242n5; folklore, 140; Radio Quispillaccta anniversary, 70, 146, 167, 168; rivalries, 69–70
field recordings: *chimaycha*, 52, 143; Suyá, 238n2
fights at *vida michiy*, 59, 66, 75, 76, 79, 89, 91
First Summit of Indigenous Peoples, 9
Flores (luthier), 191
Flores, Domingo, 66
Flores, Marcela, 153
Flores, Marcelina, 166
Flores, Wilma, 173
folklore: folklorization, 103–6; music competitions, 116; as term, 103

food: and gender, 78, 239n5; security, 141
free trade, 9
frets, 88, 89, 195, 196, 200–201, 205
Fuentes, Ranulfo, 118
fuga, 96
Fujimori regime, 7

Galindo, David: on Graciano Machaca, 147; on music in youth, 69, 125; on respect, 146; success, 164, 165, 217; work with Barrios, 167
Gavilán, Félix, 116
gay and lesbian terms, 232n32
gender roles and norms: alcohol use, 78, 245n11; alternative expressions, 26, 77–78, 238n4; Andean, 77–80; androgyny, 239n8; in *chimaycha*, 25–26, 57, 68, 76–77, 79–83, 100–101; colonialism, 238n3; complementarity, 131–32; equity/parity, 25, 77, 100, 245n11; food, 78, 239n5; generational shift, 25; labor, 78, 232n32; research effects, 24–25; terms, 77; *vida michiy*, 54, 76–77, 79; violence, 239n9
genre communities, 133
geography: Chuschi District, 31–32, 36, 50; social relationships, 34–35; vertical ecology, 32–34; *vida michiy*, 48–49, 50. *See also* landscape
gifts, 170–71
G major tuning, 85
"godparenting," 27, 170–71, 172, 177–78
Górale, 81
Guatemala, indigeneity in, 230n3, 231n14
Guillén, Isaac, 172
guitar. *See* *bonsés*; *chinlili*; instrument making; *requinto*

Harvey, Penelope M., 160
hats, vii, 64, 68, 243n14
Hatuchay (club), 169
homosexuality, 232n32
Huaman, Marcelina, *121*
Huamanga, 45. *See also* Ayacucho
Huarochirí manuscript, 234n4
huayao (wood), 195
Huaycha, Haydé, *121*
Huaycha, Mauro, 113
Huaycha, Rosa María, *121*
Huaycha Rocha, Juan, 120, *121*, 124
Huayhua Producciones, 166, 167
huayno: alcohol use, 237n20; as central to culture, 156–57; concert promotion, 167–70; gender roles and norms, 25; relation to *chimaycha*, ix, 2, 83, 85, 161–67, 217; structure and style, 2, 83; as term, 109
humor, 79–80, 97–99
hustle, 155–56, 157, 160–61, 170–74

INDEX

identity: alcohol and community, 158–61; as performative, 211; research limitations, 212; role of social groups, 3; as term, 211

ILO 169, 16, 129, 141

indigeneity: ABA, 141, 153–54; *chimaycha* as affirmation of, 46, 146–47, 213–14, 216–17; clothing, 64, 140, 209, 243n14; colonialism's role in, 3–9; disdain for, 5–6; disinterest in discussing, 23–24; and folklorization, 103–6; indigenous as term, 2–3, 7, 23–24, 141, 210–11; indigenous perspectivism, 53; limits of validation/parity, 209–10, 216–17; modern changes in lifeways, 212–13; pureness of, 3, 20, 135; on Radio Quispillaccta, 134–36; scholarship and theory, 14–20, 31–32; as socionatural orientation, 52–53; as staged performance, 103; stereotypes, 4; transnational issues, 16; as varied, 1–2, 10, 211–12. *See also cholo* culture; indigenous politics; indigenous rights

indigenismo movement, 2–3, 5–6, 103, 214–15

Indigenous and Tribal Peoples Convention of the International Labour Organization (ILO 169), 16, 129, 141

indigenous politics: and ABA, 42, 43, 129, 141, 153; adoption of indigenous terms, 2–3; Bolivia, 9, 20, 230n10, 231n23; in *chimaycha*, 12–13, 122; early efforts in Ayacucho, 45–46; Ecuador, 230n10, 231n23; interest in Andean Peru, 6–7, 130–32; mechanisms for, 15–16; Radio Quispillaccta, 128–29, 132–36, 142; *varayuqs*, 35, 37, 42, 136; women, 25, 131–32. *See also* indigeneity; indigenous rights

indigenous rights: challenges to, 141; disagreements over, 212–14; Guatemala, 230n3; land dispossession, 35–36; protections for designated indigenous communities, 128; rise of interest in, 7–9, 42–43; water rights and management, 9, 130–31, 138–39, 151–53, 216. *See also* indigeneity; indigenous politics

Infanzón, Alberto: on background, 108; on *chimaycha* voice, 91; as musician, 91, 109, 110, *121*, 173; support for Los Chikitukus de Chuschi, 120

Infanzón, Erli, 109

Infanzón, Ranulfo: arrest and show trial, 40, 112; background, 106, 107–8; community tensions, 213–14; recordings by, 106, 108, 109–10; role in developing *chimaycha*, 106–12, 185; on *vida michiy*, 60. *See also* Los Aires Chuschinos

Infanzón, Wilber, 109

input jacks, 197–98

instrument making: commodity chains, 202; embodiment, 186, 192–94, 202–7; enskilment, 189, 192; environmental awareness, 185, 199–202; guitar molds, 12, 191, 192; materials memory,

247n4; tools, 188–89; by Jacinto Tucno, 60, 61, 111–12, 185; by Marco Tucno, 112, 183–84, *184*, 191–202; weather, 201–2; woods, 188–89, 190, 192–93, 195, 196, 200–202; workshop, 28–29, 183–84, *184*. *See also chinlili*

International Programme for the Development of Communication, 243n15

intersexuality, 232n32

Intiwatana site, 61

Isbell, Billie Jean: on changes in indigenous lifeways, 212–13; on gender, 78–79; on humor, 79, 98; on landscape and nature imagery, 80; on perception of *mestizos* and *qalas*, 36–37; on political lyrics, 122; as resource, 32; on sex, 81–82, 98–99; on *vida michiy*, 54, 55, 60

jacaranda, 201

Jorahua Dueñas, Julio, 120, *121*

Kanas Indians, 235n14

kashwa ritual, 236n12

Kawsayninchikmanta (radio program), 137, 151

labor: and gender, 78, 232n32; instrument making, 188–89

landscape: in *chimaycha*, 11, 48, 51, 71, 74, 75, 80–81, 94–97, 122–24; relation to memory and narrative, 54, 236n4; and sentient ecology, 53–54; as term, 236n5; *vida michiy*, 48–49, *50*, 52, 71; in videos, vii–viii. *See also* geography

La Primera radio station, 246n16

lapyay, 59, 66, 76, 89, 91

La Serna, Miguel, 55, 105

Las Once Estrellas de Quispillaccta, 116

La Voz de Huamanga, 114, 243n9

Law of Prior Consultation, 231n16

Leguía, Augusto B., 6

Lima: *chimaycha* reception, 218–19; *cholo* culture development, 9–10, 44; as *criollo* culture, 4; as dominant city, 45; gender roles in huayno, 25; migration to, 5, 37, 41, 44, 156; population, 243n1

literacy levels, 43

livestock: as asset, 235n3; at Patario, 65; tensions between herders and farmers, 34–35; Marco Tucno family, 60, 61, 236n3; vertical ecology, 32–34; and *vida michiy*, 49, 50, 51, 52, 58, 61, 64, 69

Llacta Urán: Mauro Huaycha's music group, 113; *vida michiy*, 69

Llalli, Melecio, 148–49, 172

llaqtamaqta, 217, 243n18

Loayza, David, 191

Lobito (artist), 246n21

Lobo (artist), 246n21

INDEX

Los Aires Chuschinos, 91, 108–12, 124–25, 152, 173
Los Amaynis de Llacctuahurán, 69, 161, 164–65, 166, 171, 246n20
Los Auténticos de Patario, ix, 72, 87, 147, 246n20
Los Chikitukus de Chuschi, *121*; development of *chimaycha*, 11–13, 110–11, 117–26; finances, 118, 120, 126; founding, 102, 117–19; instrument making, 191; lyrics, 12–13, 102–3, 122–24; name, 242n19; recordings, ix, 109, 119–21, 122, 126; videos, vii–viii, ix
Los Ichu Tullmas, 152, 173–74
Los Kulikulichas de Tomanga, 116
Los Kusikusichas de Quispillaccta, 148
Los Legales de Cuchoquesera, 69, 164
Los Qarwaypiñichas, 161
lutes, 241n12
luthiers. *See* instrument making
Luz (student), 148–49
lyrics. See *chimaycha* lyrics

Machaca, Graciano: on *chimaycha*, 143, 145, 146, 147, 148; on environmentalism, 150; on politics, 128, 129, 142; as Radio Quispillaccta administrator, 142–45, 149–50
Machaca, Magdalena, 137, 138–39, 140–41, 153, 233n32. *See also* Asociación Bartolomé Aripaylla (ABA)
Machaca, Marcela: on cultural effects of ABA, 140; on gender roles and norms, 233n32; on importance of music, 129; as indigenous scientist, 137; on Radio Quispillaccta, 145; on use of indigenous term, 141; on water management, 152. *See also* Asociación Bartolomé Aripaylla (ABA)
Machaca Ccallocunto, Máxima, 66–67
Machaca family rivalries, 66, 75
"machines," 187, 207
mahogany, 200, 201
maker's mark, 188, 197
maps, *vida michiy* sites, 49, *50*
Maputaland and landscape, 236n6
marriage: and adulthood, 56, 78; cohabitation before, 237n18; elopements, 54, 63. *See also* courtship
Marxism: effect on indigenous politics, 6–7; use of folklore, 105. *See also* Shining Path
MAS party, 20
materials memory, 247n4
"Maypitaq warma puñun," 74
Medina, Ernesto, 119
memory: materials memory, 247n4; relation to landscape and narrative, 54, 236n4; tertiary and secondary retentions, 203, 206
men: alcohol use, 245n11; *chinlili* role in *chimaycha*, 57, 68, 79, 100; *vida michiy*, 54, 76–77, 79. *See also* gender roles and norms

mestizo/mestizaje: as assimilation, 9–10, 210; clothing, 209; dominance of, 5, 45, 46, 107; *indigenismo* as, 5–6, 214–15; indigenous perceptions of, 36–37; land acquisition, 5, 36; relationship to indigeneity, 4–9, 214–15, 216; term, 4, 5
methodology, 22, 24, 27–30, 212
migration: associations, 44; to Ayacucho, 37, 41, 44, 45–46; to Lima, 5, 37, 41, 44, 156; and neoliberalism, 13; from Shining Path, 41, 115; ties to home community, 43–47
Milluyaku site, 62
Minas Quispe, Carmen Rosa, vii, 122
mining, 8, 9
minor chords, 85
misti (term), 4
modern constitution, 53
Morales, Evo, 20
Morales Bermúdez regime, 6

National Commission of Indigenous, Amazonian, and Afro-Peruvian Peoples (CONAPA), 7
National Confederation of Communities Affected by Mining (CONACAMI), 8–9
National Institute of Culture, 120
nature imagery in *chimaycha*, 48, 73–74, 80–81, 92–97. *See also* environmental awareness; landscape
-*nchik* ending, 150
neoliberalism, 13, 130, 157, 161
NGOs: agriculture, 38, 131, 136, 137, 138–39; complementarity, 131–32; distrust of, 215–16; environmentalism, 3, 8–9; food security, 141; gender roles and norms, 25, 132; indigenous rights, 8–9, 42–43; musical competitions, 120, 140. *See also* Asociación Bartolomé Aripaylla (ABA)
Ninay Urucha, 91, 156, 170, 171, 172, 174
nonhuman beings: ABA approach, 137, 139; in *chimaycha*, 11, 75–76, 93–94; as concept, 14–15, 53, 129; scholarship on, 19; in videos, vii–viii
no-shows, 173
Núñez, Alejandro, 69, 90
Núñez, Élida, 125, 173
Núñez, Jorge, 70, 91, 167, 170, 173
Núñez, Lorenzo, 137, 140, 153
Núñez, Miguel, 145
Núñez, Oseas, 150
Núñez Mejía, Edilberto, 142, 143, 144
ñuqanchik pronoun, 150

Ollanta Records, 119

Pablo (student), 148–49
Pacotaype (instrument maker), 111
Pacotaype, Teodulfo, *121*
Pacotaype, William, 162, 168, 196, 217

INDEX

Pacotaype Dueñas, María. *See* Ninay Urucha

pagos (settlement), 32

Palacios, Mario, 8

Pampas Valley and strength of Quechua traditions, 31–32. *See also* Ayacucho; Chuschi; Chuschi District; Quispillaccta

parades, 116

Paredes, Zenaida, 91

participation: participation format vs. presentation format, 104–5; and public, 133

pasllas, 57–58

"Patario pampachallapisi," 73

Patario site, 62, 63, 65, 67–70

Paucar, Dina, 157, 163

Pauza, Víctor, 156

peasant (term), 6, 231n14

Peasant Day, 246n20

performance: emotionality of *chimaycha*, 158, 159, 160–61, 174–75; identity as performative, 211; indigeneity as staged performance, 103. *See also* concerts

periodical readership, 133

perspectivism, indigenous, 53

Pichinkucha (musician), 109

pilgrimages, 236n6

politics. *See* indigenous politics

Pomasoncco, Ilde Luz, 147

pop culture, 16

poverty, 4, 7, 37, 43

PRATEC (Proyecto Andino de Tecnologias Campesinas), 131

presentation vs. participation format, 104–5

Progressive Society of Santa Rosa of Lima, 44

promotion: concert, 167–70, 181; and hustle, 155, 170–74; with music videos, vii–viii, ix

protest songs, 122

Proyecto Andino de Tecnologias Campesinas (PRATEC), 131

public: evolution theory, 133; formation, 17–18; Radio Quispillaccta's role in creating, 38–39, 132–36, 153–54, 182; as term, 132–33

"public secrets," 23

Pukawasi site, 65

pumpin, 117, 150

puna: defined, 32; vertical ecology, 32–34; and *vida michiy*, 49, 58

Putunku site, 61

qalas: indigenous perceptions of, 36–37; as term, 234nn11–12; *vida michiy* for, 241n9

qichwas (term), 234n6

qipakuna (term), 35

qisarita, 107, 214. See also *chimaycha*

Qonopa (cemetery), 60, 235n1

quebracho (wood), 201

Quechua: association with indigeneity, 4; lesson

plans, 153; monolingualism, 43; pronouns and grammar, 150, 242n1; strength of Pampas Valley traditions, 31–32. *See also* Radio Quispillaccta

Quispe, Modesta, *121*

Quispillaccta, *33*; anniversary celebration, 147; educational attainment, 37, 41–42; first indigenous mayor, 42; geography, 32, 36; Indian descent, 235n14; influence and power, 32, 41–43; population, 41; resettlement projects, 41, 139; rhythms, 85, 86, 111, 125; rivalry with Chuschi, 37, 51–52; secession discussion, 35; and Shining Path, 40–41; Spanish speakers, 37; tensions between *puna* and valley dwellers, 34–35

quispillacctino (term), ix

radio: *Allpanchik*, 114–17, 119, 127; evangelical Christian, 243n9; FM, 242n9; *Kawsayninchikmanta*, 137, 151; pop styles of 2010s, 156; *Takiyninchik*, 116, 120, 127. *See also* Radio Quispillaccta

Radio Quispillaccta: advertising, 144–45, 246n16; anniversary festival, 70, 146, 167, 168; author visits to, 28, 29, 144, 170; and development projects, 135–36; environmentalism, 150–53; founding, 38, 142; organization and structure, 142–45; recordings, ix; role in boom, 145–50; role in creating a public, ix, 38–39, 132–36, 153–54, 182; role in politics, 128–29, 132–36, 142; shift to modern music, 134–35, 151–53, 155, 161–62; and Tío Miki, 170, 171–72, 173; traditionalism, ix, 13, 147, 149–50, 215; UNESCO award, 243n15

Ramos (luthier), 199

Raymi Llaqta, 117

recording consciousness, 110

recordings: ABA-sponsored, 140; affordable, 167–68; *Allpanchik* (radio program), 115–16, 127; CCC, 126–27, 143; and concert calendar, 171; field, 52, 143; first commercial, 109; first modern, 164; musicians' use of, 109–10; neotraditional, 125; Radio Quispillaccta, ix. *See also* videos

"Relojito de oro," 109, 110, 111

requinto, ix, 195–96, 205–6

resettlement projects, 41, 139

revalorization, 135

rhythms: Bolivia, 239n11; Los Chikitukus de Chuschi, 124; Quispillaccta vs. Chuschi, 85, 86, 111, 125

Rio Declaration, 16, 129, 141, 151

Ritter, Jonathan, 18, 19

Rocha, Isabel, *121*

Rodríguez sisters, 120

romance in lyrics, 2, 92–97, 162

"Rosalinaschay," 218

278 INDEX

Rosas Huayta, 246n20
rosewood, 200

SABMiller, 168
Salcedo, Uriel: influence of, 114, 116; La Primera station, 246n16; support for Los Chikitukus de Chuschi, 118, 120, 124, 126
Saqsalqucha (lake), 61
Sarhua, 135, 236n4
seasons: in *chimaycha*, 11, 51, 52; vertical ecology, 32–34; *vida michiy*, 34, 51, 52, 58, 60, 61, 64, 71
secondary retention, 203
Sennett, Richard, 188
sentient ecology, 53–54
sex: and alcohol, 240n20; association with musical skills, 56; in *chimaycha*, 74, 81–82, 97–99; lack of stigma, 98, 99; and *vida michiy*, 54–55
Shining Path: avoidance of topic, 22–23; impact on area, 7, 39–41; as "indigenous," 39; in lyrics, 12–13; recruitment, 39–40, 105, 113, 215; and rise of ABA, 137, 138; scholarship on, 233n2; violence, 22–23, 40–41, 112, 115
sirenas, viii, 93
Sitka spruce, 200
Smith, Adam, 187
Solano (luthier), 191, 192
Spanish: percentage of speakers, 37; use by *mestizos*, 4; use in *chimaycha*, 110–11, 148, 182
specificity in lyrics, 95–96
Starn, Orin, 233n2
"statecraft, vernacular," 43
Stiegler, Bernard, 187, 203
strength in voice and playing, 59, 79, 90–91
strings: bass, 58, 85, 206; doubled, 85; electrified *chinlili*, 204; gut, 112; steel, 88, 112; Marco Tucno on, 195
structure of feeling, 242n8
Sullkaraypata site, 60, 62
Suyá: field recordings, 238n2; moieties, 234n5
synthesizers, 156, 161, 162, 163, 164, 165

tabla boards, 135
Takiyninchik (radio program), 116, 120, 126
technics, 187
tertiary retention, 203, 206
things: embodiment of, 186–88, 206–7; materials memory, 247n4; role of objects in humanity, 187–88
timbre: *chinlili*, 83, 85–90, 185, 194; female voice, 82–83
Tío Miki. *See* Espinoza, Miguel "Tío Miki"
Toledo, Alejandro, 7
Tomaylla, José, 33; on decline of *vida michiy*, 69; on festivals, 69–70; on Ranulfo Infanzón, 214; on lyrics, 93; on modern *chimaycha*, 145;

on social sanctions, 56; success as musician, 64, 65–66; tremolo development, 117; Waylla Ichu de Llacctahurán, 66, 127, 161. *See also* Los Auténticos de Patario
Tomaylla, Marcelino, 67, 68, 72–75, 87, 112
Tony (student), 148–49
tools, response to, 188–89
Totora site, 61, 62
Traditions for Tomorrow, 142
transgender people, 233n32
tremolo, 86, 117, 185
Truth and Reconciliation Committee, 23
Tucno, Celia, 120
Tucno, Emilia, 118, 120, *121*. *See also* Los Chikitukus de Chuschi
Tucno, Fernandina, *121*
Tucno, Francisco, 190
Tucno, Jacinto: on family history, 190; as instrument maker, 60, 61, 111–12, 185; on men's role in *chinlili*, 68; on rituals, 93; on *vida michiy*, 57
Tucno, Lucio, 120
Tucno, Marcos, 190
Tucno, Reny, *121*, 218
Tucno, Teodosio, 120, *121*
Tucno, Zaida, 183
Tucno Rocha, Marco, *12, 121, 193*; on alcohol, 175, 179; background, 188–90; on *charangos*, 241n14; *chimaycha* development and evolution, 11–13, 110–11, 117–26; *chinlili* making and development, 112, 183–84, 191–202; on *chinlili* rituals, 93; coaching by, 203–6; on concert promotion, 169; on consorts, 87, 90; Dinastía Tucno, 217–18; education, 11, 60, 124, 188–91, 200; on frets, 89; on huayno, 85; on interviews, 233n35; as key figure, 11–14, 28–29, 185, 212; on landscape, 94; livestock herding and holdings, 60, 61, 236n3; on *llaqtamaqta*, 217; on lyrics, 93; map by, 49, *50*; on modern *chimaycha*, ix, 99, 102, 146; on *pasllas*, 57–58; on permissions, 22; on *qalas*, 241n9; on recordings, 109–10; on support, 126; on tremolo, 86; on *vida michiy*, 49, 55, 60–63; on voice, 90, 91; workshop, 28–29, 183–84, *184*. *See also* Los Chikitukus de Chuschi
Tuco settlement, 69
Turino, Thomas, 18, 104–6

UNESCO, 243n15
Unión Potrero: CCC benefits, 38; *vida michiy* conflicts, 66
United Nations, 15–16, 129, 141, 151
Universidad Nacional San Cristóbal de Huamanga (UNSCH): enrollment statistics, 241n18; folklorization, 106; increase in indigenous students, 41–42; indigenous district proposal, 216; and Los Chikitukus de Chuschi, 103, 118, 122;

INDEX

reopening, 38, 45; respect for, 106; and Shining Path, 39. *See also* Centro de Capacitación Campesina (CCC)
uqi (term), 234n13
"Urqupim michiniy michiniy," 74
"Urqupi qasapi wayllacha ichucha," 73, 83

varayuqs, 35, 37, 42, 136
Velasco regime, 6
"vernacular statecraft," 43
vertical ecology, 32–34
vida michiy: alcohol use, 68, 69; attendance by nonindigenous people, 108; cognate practices, 236n12, 237n14; community rivalries, 35, 51–52, 59, 62–63, 65, 66, 67, 75, 76, 89–90, 91; as courtship ritual, 48, 54, 56, 58, 62, 63, 64, 66; dancing, 48, 59, 82, 89; decline of, 55–56, 68–70, 115, 213; defined, 48; description of, 55–60; disapproval of, 56–57; as fertility ritual, 54, 55, 99; fighting, 59, 66, 75, 76, 79, 89, 91; gender roles, 54, 76–77, 79; geography and landscape, 48–49, 50, 52, 71; scholarship on, 54, 55; seasons, 34, 51, 52, 58, 60, 61, 64, 71; and sex, 54–55; sites, 48–49, 50, 59, 60, 61, 62, 63, 65, 67–70; as term, 48; Marco Tucno on, 49, 55, 60–63; video references, viii. See also *chimaycha*
Vida michiy (album), ix, 120–21
videos, vii–ix, 134, 146, 218
vigoyla, 111–12, 214. See also *chinlili*
vihuela (term), 241n12
Vilca, Edgar, 166

Vilca, Francisco, 40
violence: in *chimaycha*, 82, 97; at concerts, 167; gendered, 239n9; for premarital unfaithfulness, 240n20; Shining Path, 22–23, 40–41, 115
vitalization (term), 17
voice, *chimaycha*, 57, 79, 82–83, 90–91

wari (term), 233n32
water rights and management, 9, 130–31, 138–39, 151–53, 216
Waylla Ichu de Llacctahurán, 66, 116, 127, 161
Wayunka site, 60
weather, 201–2
weaving, 240n21
Weltungerhilfe, 141, 151, 152
women: alcohol use, 245n11; education, 38, 49; fighting by, 79; indigenous politics, 25, 131–32; sexual dominance in adolescence, 81–82, 99; singing role in *chimaycha*, 57, 79, 82–83, 90–91, 100. *See also* gender roles and norms
wood: approach to unknown, 192–93; electric *chinlili*, 196; experiments with, 200–201; local, 190, 195, 200–201; terms, 247n10; and weather, 201–2; working by hand, 188–89

yanamachu (wood), 200
Yanaqaqa site, 61
yarqa aspiy (canal cleaning festival), 48, 58, 242n5
youth and *chimaycha* voice, 90–91
YouTube, 134, 146
"Yutuchay," 96–97